Comparative Politics

"*Comparative Politics* is a theory-centered introductory text that perfectly balances the substantive nature of our field with the level of accessibility necessary for an undergraduate class."—*Julie Mazzei, Kent State University*

"David Samuels provides a strong introduction to the themes, concepts, and current debates of comparative politics without burying the reader in a mound of empirical details. It encourages hypothesis testing, fosters students' critical thinking skills, and encourages students to place current political developments in context."—*John Scherpereel, James Madison University*

"I am impressed that Samuels does not shy away from introducing students to the major debates in comparative politics and having them evaluate competing arguments. In trying to get the students to think theoretically, he has definitely chosen an approach that will challenge the best students."—*Steve Barracca, Eastern Kentucky University*

"This is a readable and well-organized exploration of major topics in comparative politics that brings together basic as well as more advanced topics. It provides students with examples of how to actually do comparative politics and prompts them to think through the major arguments of the field."—*Wendy N. Whitman Cobb, Santa Fe College*

"David Samuels does a better job than any I have seen of discussing key themes in comparative politics in an intelligent and well-written way. He raises the big questions in a straightforward and engaged manner, and he does a good job of addressing them in comparative perspective with the American institutions that my students know well."—*Kevin Deegan-Krause, Wayne State University*

"Samuels offers students a theoretically robust yet highly accessible introduction to the study of comparative politics. He clearly introduces core concepts and theories, offering compelling examples that encourage students to think through different ways of answering fundamental questions that define the field. I'm thrilled to see the strong focus on political identity in an introductory textbook."—*James Ross, University of Northern Colorado*

"I have been teaching introductory comparative politics for over four years now, and I have examined some fifteen textbooks for this class. Samuels' textbook is one of the best, and I will strongly consider adopting it."
—*Anca Turcu, University of Central Florida*

Comparative Politics

DAVID J. SAMUELS

University of Minnesota, Minneapolis

Boston   Columbus   Indianapolis   New York   San Francisco   Upper Saddle River
Amsterdam   Cape Town   Dubai   London   Madrid   Milan   Munich   Paris   Montreal   Toronto
Delhi   Mexico City   São Paulo   Sydney   Hong Kong   Seoul   Singapore   Taipei   Tokyo

Senior Acquisitions Editor: Vikram Mukhija
Associate Editor: Corey Kahn
Editorial Assistants: Isabel Schwab, Beverly Fong
Executive Marketing Manager: Wendy Gordon
Senior Digital Media Editor: Paul DeLuca
Production Manager: Denise J. Phillip
Photo Researcher: Poyee Oster
Project Coordination, Editorial Services, Text
    Design, and Art Rendering: Electronic
    Publishing Services Inc., NYC

Art Rendering and Electronic Page Makeup:
    Jouve
Cover Design Manager: John Callahan
Cover Designer: Elina Frumerman
Senior Manufacturing Buyer: Roy Pickering
Printer/Binder: Quad/Graphics-Taunton
Cover Printer: Lehigh-Phoenix Color/
    Hagerstown

Credits and acknowledgments borrowed from other sources and reproduced, with permission, in this textbook appear on the appropriate page within text or on page 385.

Library of Congress Cataloging-in-Publication Data

Samuels, David, 1967-
  Comparative politics / David Samuels.
      p. cm.
  Includes index.
  ISBN 978-0-321-44974-0
  1. Comparative government. I. Title.

  JF51.S25 2013
  320.3--dc23

                              2011051475

Copyright © 2013 by Pearson Education, Inc.

10 9 8 7 6 5 4 3 2 1—QGT—15 14 13 12

ISBN 10: 0-321-44974-6
ISBN 13: 978-0-321-44974-0

BRIEF CONTENTS

DETAILED CONTENTS

PREFACE

S tudents who enroll in an introductory course on comparative politics should be prepared to encounter some tough but fascinating questions. Why are some states democracies while others are not? Why does ethnicity seem to be at the heart of so much conflict in the world today? Can religious extremism coexist with democracy? How and why do men and women participate in politics differently around the world? What prompts people to become politically active? And why are some countries increasingly rich while others remain desperately poor? These questions touch upon just a few of the themes that comparative politics explores today.

Students and scholars of comparative politics are trained to use these kinds of questions to delve into their own particular interests. I wrote this book—using a question-driven approach—to mirror the process of good political science research. I aimed to make this text different from other introductions to comparative politics, in that it focuses on asking the sorts of questions that engage *anyone* with an interest in politics—citizens, students, and scholars—and on *answering* those questions in ways that are meaningful to undergraduates.

What is the pedagogical payoff from a thematic, question-driven approach to comparative politics? I know from personal experience as well as from countless conversations with colleagues around the world that, in the classroom, we often struggle to teach students how to recognize a good argument in political science, not to mention the effort we put into teaching them to make their own arguments—that is, how to formulate a thesis, connect statements logically, determine whether evidence is confirmatory or contradictory, and bring everything together in a strong conclusion.

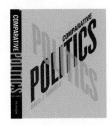

Comparative Politics not only introduces students to the main questions comparative politics explores; it introduces them to how scholars go about *doing* comparative politics. Our discipline is fundamentally about constructing arguments, and an introductory textbook should focus on developing not just informed and engaged citizens, but informed, engaged, and *analytical* citizens, the last being a core element in a liberal arts education. This may seem like a tall order, yet I have written this book with this goal as a central organizing principle. Students who use this text will learn to identify and discuss questions central to our subfield. They will also learn to recognize competing hypotheses, apply research to arguments by analyzing and critically assessing evidence, and relate different perspectives to each other analytically.

FEATURES

Approach

To support the question-driven approach described above, each chapter of *Comparative Politics* begins with a question that focuses on a core aspect of what politics is all about around the world. Framing the chapter's subject as a question provides a narrative thread for students to follow as they read the chapter; it also fosters classroom discussion, illustrates how scholars go about answering similar questions, and provides a clear reference point for students to articulate answers on their own that they can use for assignments and exams. To help students grasp the importance of the chapter-opening question, a real-world example is provided. For example, in Chapter 6, the opening image shows a French Muslim woman in a red, white, and blue headscarf and the example explores the French separation of church and state; both set up the question "when does identity become politicized?"

After the main question is introduced, each chapter is organized around the ways scholars have attempted to answer it. For example, Chapter 10 asks "what causes political violence?" It then guides students through the various facets of the topic and ways to critically assess and weigh sources of conflict. Every chapter in the book follows a similar approach, posing a question that introduces a theme and then exploring different ways to answer that question. Throughout every chapter, more real-world examples are employed to ground the question and clarify the discussion. Although the chapter topics are sometimes complex, they are all tightly organized and written in clear and accessible prose.

Furthermore, as the chapter progresses, each core chapter question is supported by subquestions that appear in the margins to encourage students to examine more than one facet of a political puzzle. For example, political economy can be an intimidating topic for many. Chapter 11's main question is "how do states promote economic development?" To answer that question, students must first understand how states and markets are intertwined. Therefore, the first section of the chapter asks and answers the question "what is the relationship between states and markets?" Every subquestion relates back to the chapter's core question and builds towards the next subquestion, and finally, each chapter concludes by returning the chapter question and summarizing what was learned. In short, each chapter shows students how political scientists engage a smaller piece of a larger puzzle and then explore, debate, and articulate plausible answers to key questions about politics in the world today.

Coverage

Comparative Politics introduces students to the full breadth of our subfield by exploring common themes like institutions and interests as well as topics that are often downplayed, particularly how political identities bridge institutions and interests. An understanding of political identity is vital today, because many of the most pressing and contentious political issues around the world—issues that students find personally compelling—touch on such questions as the tension between ethnicity and political instability, gender and political change, and religion and democracy.

Chapter 1 poses the question some undergraduates might ask their instructors—"why study comparative politics?"—and focuses on the methods we use to ask and answer these sorts of questions. At its simplest, the comparative method involves comparing and contrasting cases that share attributes but differ on outcomes, or that differ on attributes but share outcomes. The goal of such comparisons is to generate hypotheses that offer plausible answers to our questions about what politics is all about.

Chapter 2 asks the foundational question "where do 'states' come from?" and begins to answer it by unraveling Hobbes' collective action problem. Chapters 3 and 4 define and differentiate the different kinds of states: democratic and non-democratic political regimes. Chapter 5 focuses on the causes of transitions from democracy to non-democracy, or vice versa.

The next few chapters shift the focus toward political identities, keeping in mind that they cannot be fully separated from political institutions or interests. After all, institutions shape how identities gain representation in the formal realm of politics—and political identity is often the raw material from which individuals and groups construct their political interests. Chapter 6 asks "what is political identity?" and explores the conditions under which ethnicity and nationalism become politicized. Chapter 7 turns to another significant question—the compatibility between religious identity and democracy—while Chapter 8 explores the political consequences of changing conceptions of gender around the world.

The next two chapters turn to the question of how and why individuals' political interests and identities are mobilized collectively. Chapter 9 explores peaceful forms of collective action—interest groups, social movements, and political parties—while Chapter 10 asks why people sometimes take up arms against the established political order.

The last three chapters turn to pressing questions at the intersection of politics and economics. Chapter 11 asks, "why are some countries rich and others poor?" while Chapter 12 explores why some countries tax and spend more than others. Finally, Chapter 13 investigates the question of globalization and its impact.

Pedagogy

Extensive pedagogy is also included in every chapter to help students comprehend key concepts and to apply them.

- Hypothesis Testing boxes allow students to apply what they have learned in every chapter. As opposed to asking questions, each box opens with a statement that can be tested by exploring real-world country cases. Every box is consistently structured to walk students through the process of "Gathering Evidence" in order to "Assess the Hypothesis." Each exercise is meant to engage students actively with the process of comparative politics, providing them with opportunities to learn how to recognize and ultimately construct their own arguments.
- Every major section concludes with a summary table that reviews key concepts in an organized and easy-to-read format.

- Every chapter includes a marginal glossary to support students' understanding of new and important concepts at first encounter.
- For easy reference, key terms from the marginal glossary are repeated at the end of each chapter, along with review questions and an annotated list of suggested readings.
- Numerous color photos and figures are integrated into the text to enliven the narrative.

CASE STUDIES IN COMPARATIVE POLITICS

For instructors and students who want more specific country information to complement the questions raised here, an accompanying casebook is available that matches the pedagogical approach of this survey. Each chapter is written by a different country-expert, and the collection includes cases on the United Kingdom, Germany, France, Japan, India, Mexico, Russia, China, Nigeria, and Iran.

Just as each chapter in this book is organized around a core question, so are the country chapters in the casebook. Although every chapter takes on a different country and thus asks a different question, they all follow the same basic framework. First, an introductory section offers background information on the historical development of each country. The second section describes the country's political institutions and explains why each country has emerged as a democracy or remained a dictatorship. Each chapter's third section focuses on the main forms of political identity in each country, such as ethnicity, nationalism, economic class, language, religion, or gender. The fourth section focuses on the patterns of competition over the distribution of political power and wealth between the different organized interests and identities in each society—parties, interest groups, and social movements. Every chapter concludes by reviewing how the exploration of the country's institutions, identities and interests has helped answer the question posed at the start.

MYPOLISICLAB FOR *COMPARATIVE POLITICS*
The moment you know

Educators know it. Students know it. It's that inspired moment when something that was difficult to understand suddenly makes perfect sense. Our MyLab products have been designed and refined with a single purpose in mind—to help educators create that moment of understanding with their students.

MyPoliSciLab delivers *proven results* in helping individual students succeed. It provides *engaging experiences* that personalize, stimulate, and measure learning for each student. And it comes from a *trusted partner* with educational expertise and a deep commitment to helping students, instructors, and departments achieve their goals.

MyPoliSciLab can be used by itself or linked to any learning management system. To learn more about how MyPoliSciLab combines proven learning applications with powerful assessment, visit **http://www.mypoliscilab.com**.

MyPoliSciLab delivers *proven results* in helping individual students succeed

- Pearson MyLabs are currently in use by millions of students each year across a variety of disciplines.
- MyPoliSciLab works, but don't take our word for it. Visit **www.pearson-highered.com/elearning** to read white papers, case studies, and testimonials from instructors and students that consistently demonstrate the success of our MyLabs.

MyPoliSciLab provides *engaging experiences* that personalize, stimulate, and measure learning for each student

- *Assessment.* Track progress and get instant feedback on every chapter, video, and multimedia activity. With results feeding into a powerful gradebook, the assessment program identifies learning challenges early and suggests the best resources to help.
- *Personalized Study Plan.* Follow a flexible learning path created by the assessment program and tailored to each student's unique needs. Organized by learning objectives, the study plan offers follow-up reading, video, and multimedia activities for further learning and practice.
- *Pearson eText.* Just like the printed text, highlight and add notes to the eText online or download it to a tablet.
- *Flashcards.* Learn key terms by word or definition.
- *Video.* Analyze current events by watching streaming video from major news providers.
- *Mapping Exercises.* Explore interactive maps that test basic geography, examine key events in world history, and analyze the state of the world.
- *Comparative Exercises.* Think critically about how politics compare around the world.
- *PoliSci News Review.* Join the political conversation by following headlines in *Financial Times* newsfeeds, reading analysis in the blog, taking weekly current events quizzes and polls, and more.
- *ClassPrep.* Engage students with class presentation resources collected in one convenient online destination.

MyPoliSciLab comes from a *trusted partner* with educational expertise and an eye on the future

- Pearson supports instructors with workshops, training, and assistance from Pearson Faculty Advisors so you get the help you need to make MyPoliSciLab work for your course.
- Pearson gathers feedback from instructors and students during the development of content and the feature enhancement of each release to ensure that our products meet your needs.

To order MyPoliSciLab with the print text, use ISBN 0-205-24934-5.

SUPPLEMENTS

Pearson is pleased to offer several resources to qualified adopters of *Comparative Politics* and their students that will make teaching and learning from this book even more effective and enjoyable. Several of the supplements for this book are available at the Instructor Resource Center (IRC), an online hub that allows instructors to quickly download book-specific supplements. Please visit the IRC welcome page at **http://www.pearsonhighered.com/irc** to register for access.

Instructor's Manual/Test Bank

This resource includes learning objectives, lecture outlines, multiple-choice questions, true/false questions, and essay questions for each chapter. Available exclusively on the IRC.

Pearson MyTest

This powerful assessment generation program includes all of the items in the instructor's manual/test bank. Questions and tests can be easily created, customized, saved online, and then printed, allowing flexibility to manage assessments anytime and anywhere. Available exclusively on the IRC.

PowerPoint Presentation

Organized around a lecture outline, these multimedia presentations also include photos, figures, and tables from each chapter. Available exclusively on the IRC.

Sample Syllabus

This resource provides suggestions for assigning content from this book and My-PoliSciLab. Available exclusively on the IRC.

Longman Atlas of World Issues (0-205-78020-2)

From population and political systems to energy use and women's rights, the *Longman Atlas of World Issues* features full-color thematic maps that examine the forces shaping the world. Featuring maps from the latest edition of *The Penguin State of the World Atlas*, this excerpt includes critical-thinking exercises to promote a deeper understanding of how geography affects many global issues.

Goode's World Atlas (0-321-65200-2)

First published by Rand McNally in 1923, *Goode's World Atlas* has set the standard for college reference atlases. It features hundreds of physical, political, and thematic maps as well as graphs, tables, and a pronouncing index.

Passport

Choose the resources you want from MyPoliSciLab and put links to them into your course management system. If there is assessment associated with those resources, it also can be uploaded, allowing the results to feed directly into your course management system's gradebook. With MyPoliSciLab assets like videos, mapping exercises, current events quizzes, politics blog, and much more, Passport is available for any Pearson political science book. To order Passport with the print text, use ISBN 0-205-24933-7.

ACKNOWLEDGMENTS

My students at Minnesota initially inspired me to write this book. When I agreed to teach our Introduction to Comparative Politics class, I found that no existing text fit the way that I wanted to teach. So I developed and tinkered with lectures over a few years, "learning by doing" what worked well—and what didn't—from my students. Although he probably doesn't remember, I thank Jamie Druckman for nudging me to turn my lectures into textbook chapters. I also owe a debt to Phil Shively for inspiration, and for his hard-earned wisdom gained from decades of experience writing textbooks—and dealing with editors! For helpful comments on different chapters, I also thank Ethan Scheiner, Dara Strolovitch, Teri Caraway, Frances Rosenbluth, Edward Gibson, Druscilla Scribner, Kathleen Collins, Jeremy Weinstein, Wanjiru Kamau-Rautenberg, and my dear friend Donna Lee Van Cott, may she rest in peace.

The editorial team at Pearson provided tremendous support and encouragement at every stage of what turned out to be a lengthy and sometimes difficult writing process. Many years ago, Jude Hall came into my office to sell me on Pearson's texts—but perhaps for the first time in her career, I sold *her* on an idea, and she made the initial contact with Eric Stano. Vik Mukhija shepherded the project most of the way to publication, and I owe him thanks for his support and guidance. Susan Messer helped shape the chapters in their early stages, but I owe the biggest debt to Angela Kao, development editor extraordinaire. She patiently put up with my frustrations, always succeeding in winning me over with her "kinder and gentler" approach. I learned a great deal from her—mostly, but not exclusively, about textbook writing.

I would also like to thank the many reviewers who helped shape both *Comparative Politics* and *Case Studies in Comparative Politics*:

Dauda Abubakar, Ohio University

Janet Adamski, University of Mary Hardin-Baylor

Rebecca Aubrey, University of Connecticut

Steve Barracca, Eastern Kentucky University

Matthew Bradley, Indiana University at Kokomo

Cheryl L. Brown, University of North Carolina at Charlotte

Nic Cheeseman, Oxford University

Katy Crossley-Frolick, Denison University

Kevin Deegan-Krause, Wayne State University

Jason Enia, Sam Houston State University

Farideh Farhi, University of Hawaii at Manoa

Mark Frazier, University of Oklahoma

Lauretta Frederking, University of Portland

Daniel Fuerstman, State College of Florida

Wynford Grant, University of Warwick

Kenneth S. Hicks, Rogers State University

Jonathan Hollowell, SUNY Brockport

Debra Holzhauer, Southeast Missouri State University

Carrie Humphreys, University of Utah

Wade Jacoby, Brigham Young University

Ellis S. Krauss, University of California, San Diego

Eric Langenbacher, Georgetown University

F. David Levenbach, Arkansas State University Political Science

Yitan Li, Seattle University

Staffan Lindberg, University of Florida

Daniel Lynch, University of Southern California

Shannan Mattiace, Allegheny College

Julie Mazzei, Kent State University

Anthony O'Regan, Los Angeles Valley College

Angela Oberbauer, San Diego Mesa College

Rebecca K. Root, the State University of New York at Geneseo

James C. Ross, University of Northern Colorado

Amy Forster Rothbart, University of Wisconsin at Madison

John Scherpereel, James Madison University

Tracy H. Slagter, University of Wisconsin Oshkosh

Boyka Stefanova, University of Texas San Antonio

Tressa E. Tabares, American River College

Gunes Tezcur, Loyola University Chicago

Erica Townsend-Bell, University of Iowa

Anca Turcu, University of Central Florida

Wendy N. Whitman, Santa Fe College, Social and Behavioral Sciences

Mark Wolfgram, Oklahoma State University.

DAVID SAMUELS

MAPS

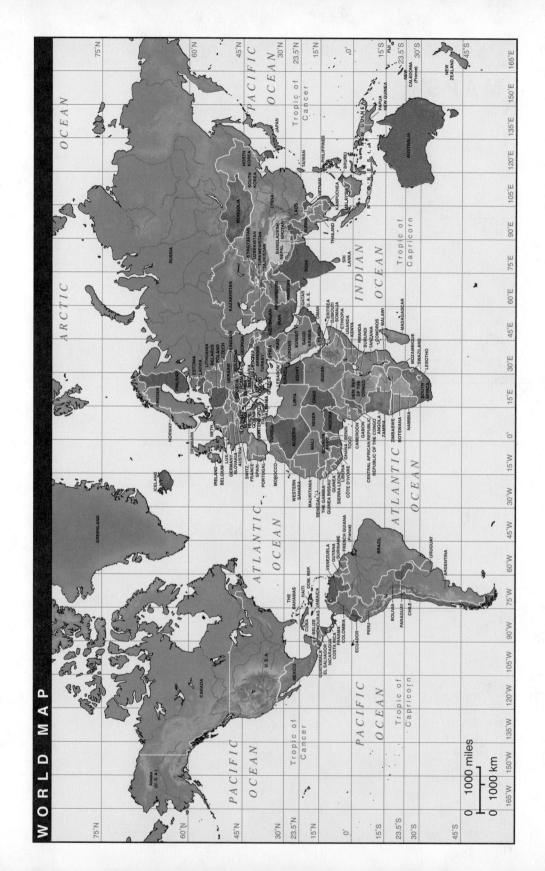

WORLD MAP

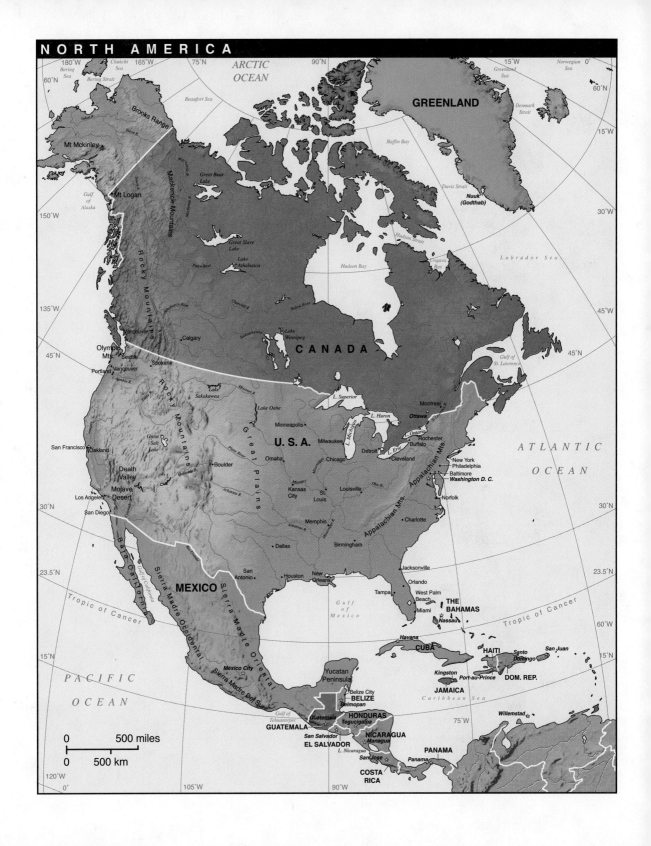

NORTH AMERICA

ARCTIC OCEAN

GREENLAND

Bering Sea
Chukchi Sea
Bering Strait
Beaufort Sea
Norwegian Sea
Greenland Sea
Denmark Strait

Mt Mckinley
Brooks Range
Yukon R.

Mt Logan
Gulf of Alaska

Mackenzie Mountains
Great Bear Lake
Mackenzie R.

Great Slave Lake
Lake Athabasca

Baffin Bay

Davis Strait
Nuuk (Godthab)

Peace River
Athabasca River

Hudson Strait

Labrador Sea
Ungava Bay

Rocky Mountains
Churchill R.
Nelson River
Hudson Bay

CANADA

Vancouver
Calgary
Saskatchewan R.
Lake Winnipeg

Gulf of St. Lawrence

Olympic Mts.
Seattle
Vancouver
Spokane
Portland
Columbia R.

Rocky Mountains
Snake R.
Lake Sakakawea
Missouri R.
Lake Oahe

Montreal
Ottawa
L. Superior
L. Huron
L. Ontario
Rochester
Buffalo

Minneapolis
Milwaukee
L. Michigan
Detroit
L. Erie
Cleveland

U.S.A.

San Francisco
Oakland
Great Salt Lake

Great Plains
Platte River
Omaha
Chicago

New York
Philadelphia
Appalachian Mts.

Death Valley
Boulder
Colorado R.

Missouri R.
Mississippi R.
Ohio R.
Baltimore
Washington D. C.

ATLANTIC OCEAN

Mojave Desert
Los Angeles
Kansas City
St. Louis
Louisville

Norfolk

San Diego
Arkansas R.

Memphis

Appalachian Mts.
Charlotte

Dallas
Birmingham

Baja California
Rio Grande
San Antonio
Houston
New Orleans

Jacksonville

Tropic of Cancer

Gulf of California

Sierra Madre Occidental

Sierra Madre Oriental

MEXICO

Orlando

Tampa
West Palm Beach
Miami

Gulf of Mexico

THE BAHAMAS
Nassau

Tropic of Cancer

PACIFIC OCEAN

Sierra Madre Del Sur

Mexico City

Havana
CUBA

HAITI
Santo Domingo
San Juan

Yucatan Peninsula

Kingston
Port-au-Prince
DOM. REP.

JAMAICA
Caribbean Sea

Willemstad

Belize City
BELIZE
Belmopan

Gulf of Tehuantepec

Guatemala
GUATEMALA
HONDURAS
Tegucigalpa

San Salvador
EL SALVADOR
L. Nicaragua
NICARAGUA
Managua

L. Nicaragua

PANAMA
Panama

San Jose
COSTA RICA

0   500 miles
0   500 km

60°N
60°N
75°N
45°N
30°N
23.5°N
15°N
45°N
30°N
23.5°N
15°N

180°W
165°W
150°W
135°W
120°W
105°W
90°W
75°W
60°W
45°W
30°W
15°W
0°
90°N

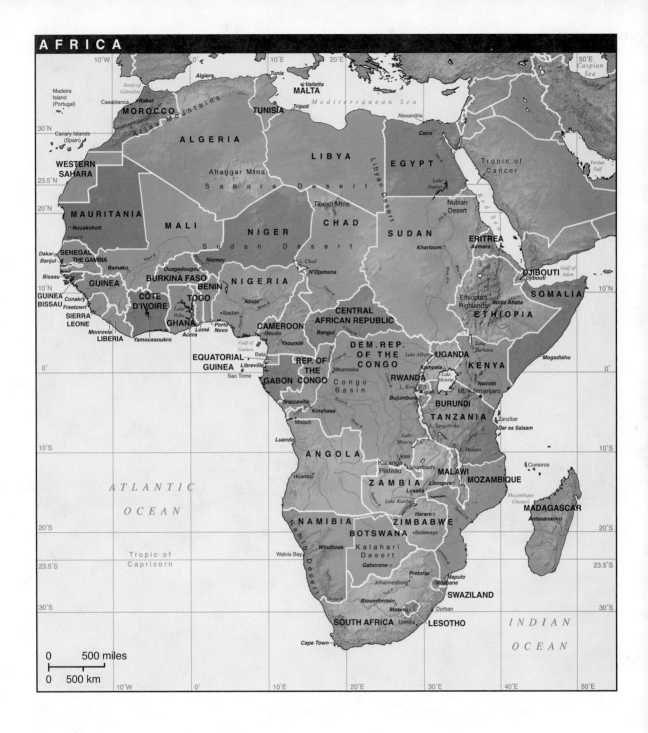

THE MIDDLE EAST

Black Sea

30°E   35°E

40°E

Caucasus Mountains

KAZAKHSTAN

50°E

60°E

Aral Sea

UZBEKISTAN

Caspian Sea

GEORGIA
Tbilisi

ARMENIA
Yerevan

AZERBAIJAN

Baku

Pontic Mountains

Istanbul

Bursa

Ankara

TURKEY

L. Tuz

TURKMENISTAN

Ashgabat

Izmir

Tigris R.

L. Van

Tabriz

Mashhad

Adana

Mosul

Elburz Mountains

Nicosia

Aleppo

Tehran

IRAN

CYPRUS

SYRIA

35°N

Mediterranean Sea

Beirut

Damascus

Baghdad

Zagros Mountains

Esfahan

AFGHANISTAN

LEBANON

ISRAEL

Tel Aviv

Jerusalem

West Bank

Amman

Dead Sea

IRAQ

Alexandria

JORDAN

Basra

Shiraz

Qattara
Depression

Cairo

Sinai
Pen.

Kuwait

KUWAIT

Persian Gulf

Str. of Hormuz

EGYPT

25°N

BAHRAIN

Manama

QATAR

Doha

Gulf of Oman

Abu Dhabi

U. A. E.

Muscat

Tropic of   23.5°N
Cancer

SAUDI
ARABIA

Riyadh

Red
Sea

Lake Nasser

Nubian
Desert

Arabian
Peninsula

OMAN

River Nile

20°N

Rub' Al Khali

20°N

Arabian Sea

SUDAN

Khartoum

YEMEN

15°N

15°N

Sanaa

Blue Nile

Gulf of Aden

50°E

Socotra
(Yemen)

0   500 miles

DJIBOUTI

Djibouti

45°E

55°E

0   500 km

500 km

60°E

SOMALIA

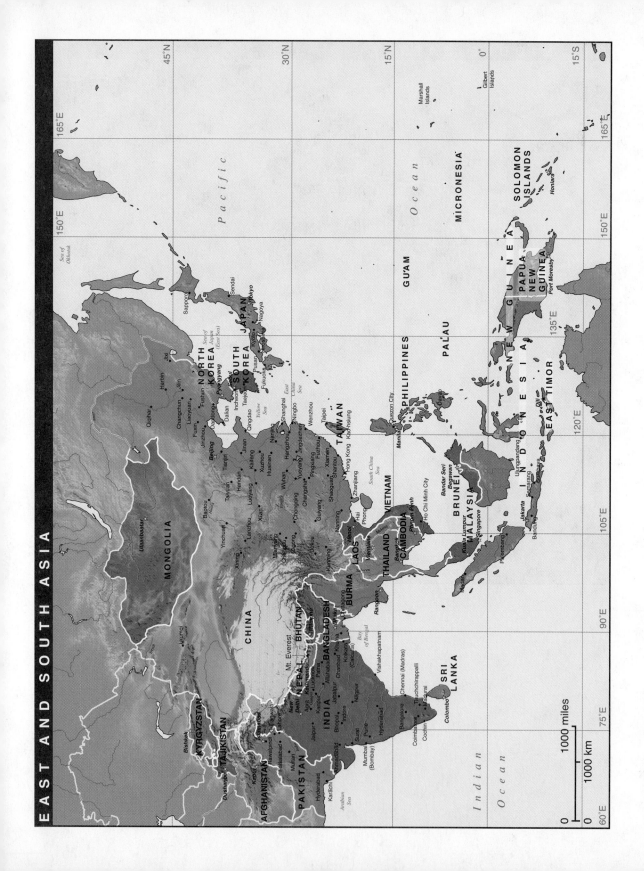

EAST AND SOUTH ASIA

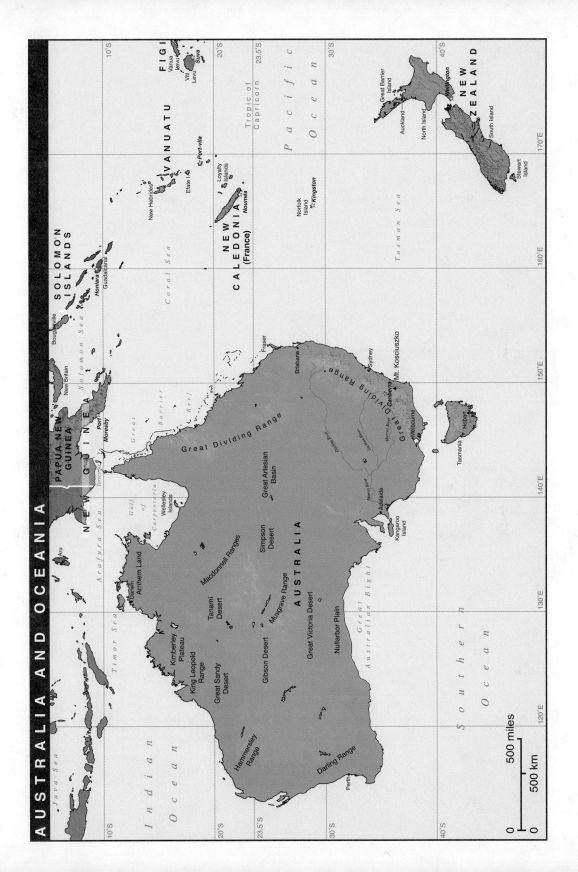

AUSTRALIA AND OCEANIA

Indian Ocean

Java Sea

Timor Sea

Arafura Sea

Aru

Darwin
Arnhem Land

NEW GUINEA

Gulf of Carpentaria

Wellesley Islands

Kimberley Plateau
King Leopold Range

Great Sandy Desert

Hammersley Range

Gibson Desert

Tanami Desert

Macdonnell Ranges

Musgrave Range

Great Victoria Desert

AUSTRALIA

Simpson Desert

Great Artesian Basin

Great Dividing Range

Nullarbor Plain

Darling Range

Perth

Great Australian Bight

Southern Ocean

Adelaide
Kangaroo Island

Murray River
Darling River

Melbourne

Tasmania
Hobart

Great Dividing Range

Canberra
Mt. Kosciuszko

Sydney

Brisbane

Fraser

PAPUA NEW GUINEA

Port Moresby

New Britain

Bougainville

SOLOMON ISLANDS

Honiara
Guadalcanal

Solomon Sea

Great Barrier Reef

Coral Sea

NEW CALEDONIA (France)

Nouméa
Loyalty Islands

VANUATU

Efate I.

New Hebrides

Port-vila

FIGI

Vanua Levu

Vanua

Viti Levu

Suva

Tropic of Capricorn

Pacific Ocean

Norfolk Island

Kingston

Tasman Sea

NEW ZEALAND

Great Barrier Island

Auckland
North Island

Wellington

South Island

Stewart Island

10°S
20°S
23.5°S
30°S
40°S

120°E
130°E
140°E
150°E
160°E
170°E

500 miles
500 km

0
0

Doing Comparative Politics

Taking to the street to protest allegations of widespread corruption, a young Brazilian calls for the

📖 Read and Listen
to Chapter 1
at mypoliscilab.com

✓ Study and Review
the Pre-Test & Flashcards
at mypoliscilab.com

After I graduated from college, I wanted to travel. In 1992 I ended up staying in Brazil for several months, living as the guest of a politician serving in Brazil's Congress. Brazil had recently emerged from a long military dictatorship, and its politicians had written an entirely new constitution—the country's seventh since independence in 1822. My friend and his colleagues in Congress were engaged in a high-stress and high-stakes effort to impeach Brazil's president, its first popularly elected leader since the military took power in 1964. Just a few years after the military had turned power over to civilians, things were not working out as millions of Brazilians had hoped.

One day, my friend turned to me in frustration and asked, "How did you *gringos* manage to write a constitution that has survived for 200 years, while we Latin Americans seem stuck with unstable governments and military takeovers? Your Founding Fathers must've been intellectual giants—but the people who've written our constitutions, not so much. Why? We're no different from you, really. But why are our politics so different?"

I had no answer—and political scientists still debate whether Latin America has put instability and military influence behind it—but my friend's query stuck with me. He had asked this question because he knew that I take for granted rights for which he had fought for years, such as freedom of speech. With 20/20 hindsight, I now know that he exaggerated the political challenges Brazil faced: despite successfully impeaching that president, it remains a democracy, and strong economic growth has ensured political stability. Moreover, militaries around the region for the most part no longer meddle in politics as they used to.

Even so, posing a contrast I'd never thought about before—why *was* political instability so pervasive in Latin America, but not in the United States?—and my own frustrating inability to offer an answer at that time—sparked a deeper interest not just in politics, but in political science, and over the years I have returned to my friend's question time and again in my teaching and research. What I've discovered is that the best way to think through any question about politics is by asking questions and posing comparisons.

Consider for a moment what's happened recently in the Middle East. Almost uniformly, dictators have long ruled the countries in the region. Yet in late 2010 and early 2011, massive popular protests exploded in several Arab countries. What made people so upset all of a sudden—and why would they risk going to jail just to complain about the government? Moreover, why did these protests quickly lead to the ouster of the long-term rulers of Egypt and Tunisia, but not rulers elsewhere in the region?

Now consider recent developments in China. Perhaps you watched some of the 2008 Olympics on TV—the games that were held in Beijing. I watched some with my dad, who reminded me that in the 1970s he would tell me to clean my plate of every last lima bean because "kids are starving in China." Seeing the gleaming sky-scrapers and traffic jams of Beijing today, one would hardly know that the country had been considered an impoverished global weakling just 30 years ago. Can poor countries just "become" rich, just like that? How did they do it?

Scholars will be grappling with these particular questions for some time—but at least we have some tools to use to develop useful answers. *Why study comparative politics?* We study comparative politics because we want answers to questions like those posed above. A comparative perspective on politics calls for analysis that pays close attention to the experiences of different countries. However, we don't study comparative politics just because we want to learn about this or that country—and, in any case, the world's political and cultural diversity presents a challenge to any comparative politics textbook: the danger is that we might become overwhelmed by the details of the world's nearly 200 countries, without learning how to answer any of the questions that grab our attention.

My friend's question certainly encouraged me to learn more about Brazilian politics—but it also forced me to rethink what I thought I knew about American politics, as well as to wonder what I could learn about the sources of political stability and chaos, in general. The only way to do that was to think about whether I could plausibly compare Brazil against the experience of other countries.

Scholars do not do comparative politics research simply by learning about a few countries. They approach their subject by asking interesting and important questions about our world. Although this is a textbook, it will become clear that the questions we ask in comparative politics are not merely "academic." Because comparative politics grapples with questions about the world in which we live, our inquiries are not mere intellectual flights of fancy or exercises in balancing angels on the head of a pin. The questions we ask have practical relevance for the lives of people all over the world.

The primary way this book differs from other introductory comparative politics texts is that it focuses on asking and answering questions. First, the book considers a set of key questions about politics around the world. Out of necessity, it cannot consider every question, or even every "important" question. However, the book's chapters cover the full range of important topics scholars and students explore today.

Second, this book helps you understand how we go about developing answers to the questions that we ask. Most people discuss and debate politics based on their opinions—but opinions can be fallible, particularly when confronted with uncomfortable facts or puzzling counterexamples. There is a difference between voicing an opinion and formulating an argument—and learning a comparative approach to the study of politics will help you learn how to build stronger arguments. To move from expressing an opinion based on intuition or feeling to articulating an argument based on facts and logic, political scientists put their curiosity to work—by asking questions in a particular way, and by employing particular methods that test the strength of their arguments. Studying politics this way helps us narrow down the range of plausible answers to questions like the one my friend posed.

This book is designed to give you the tools to learn how to critically engage key questions and build your own arguments about politics—to articulate strong answers to those questions we all have about how politics works. It is designed to help you learn how to gather evidence and articulate your own answers to important questions about poverty and wealth, democracy and dictatorship, and war and peace. Each chapter in this book explores a key question about politics around the world and considers the ways in which scholars have sought to answer that question. The payoff from this question-driven approach to comparative politics is that you will learn to recognize competing arguments, and learn the basics of how to begin to construct your own arguments—how to formulate a thesis, connect statements logically, and determine whether evidence confirms or contradicts an argument.

Political science is fundamentally about constructing arguments. This text will give you the tools to identify and discuss questions central to our subfield, recognize competing hypotheses, apply research to arguments by analyzing and critically assessing evidence, and relate different perspectives to each other analytically. In short, this book teaches you how to actually "do" comparative politics. This introductory chapter explains how we go about doing comparative politics, and considers several challenges to comparative politics research.

STUDYING COMPARATIVE POLITICS

1.1 What is comparative politics all about?

politics ■ the making of authoritative public choices from private preferences.

 Explore the Comparative "Civil Societies" at mypoliscilab.com

What is politics all about? Political scientist Harold Lasswell provided perhaps the best direct answer by defining politics as "who gets what, when, and how."[1] More specifically, politics is about the process of making and contesting authoritative public decisions about the distribution of rights, responsibilities, wealth, and power. How do groups of people come to make a choice that all members of the community agree to respect? And what kinds of decisions must these groups of people make? Political choices determine how order is imposed in societies, which political institutions will be created, and which policies are enacted. Others involve whether or when to contest the established order, and if so, what new institutions to construct or policies to reform. Interesting political science research focuses on these kinds of questions, which become increasingly focused and specific.

Political science is the study of politics. Political scientists search for explanations of political behavior and events by breaking down the "who get what, when, and how" into specific and targeted queries. The academic field of political science is divided into four subfields: American politics, which studies politics within the United States; political theory, which focuses on philosophical questions concerning the nature and purposes of politics; international relations, which studies politics between countries; and comparative politics.

Comparative politics is the systematic search for answers to political questions about how people around the world make and contest authoritative public choices. In essence, it compares and contrasts why people around the world make similar decisions under different political rules—or why they make different decisions under similar rules. Unlike international relations, comparative politics examines politics within different countries around the world—both in terms of how countries are similar, and how they differ—while international relations studies the interactions between countries.

We study comparative politics because we don't just want to describe "who gets what, when, and how" in different countries—we seek to explain how politics works around the world. Political scientists do not claim that their explanations will always be definitive, but they try to identify arguments that are more convincing than others. This is the process of moving from opinion to explanation. More often than not, widely held opinions—sometimes called the "conventional wisdom"—about politics frequently fall flat when confronted with comparative evidence.

Being the conventional wisdom doesn't mean an opinion is wrong. Political scientists use particular methods to show when the conventional wisdom is right, and when it is misleading. A comparative approach to understanding politics around the world seeks to ask questions, generate hypotheses that offer plausible potential answers to those questions, and test those hypotheses against evidence we gather from the real world to develop strong arguments, using what we call the *comparative method*. At its simplest, the comparative method involves comparing and contrasting cases (a set of countries, for example) that share attributes or characteristics but differ on the outcome you're exploring—or that have diverse attributes but experience the same outcome. The goal of such comparisons is to generate hypotheses that provide convincing answers to our questions about what politics is all about. Each chapter in this book thus poses a question and uses examples from around the world to compare and contrast different ways to address that question. Let us first consider how comparative political scientists go about posing interesting questions.

comparative politics ■ the systematic search for answers to political questions about how people around the world make and contest authoritative public choices.

THE FOUNDATIONS OF COMPARATIVE POLITICS

It's one thing to say that we study comparative politics because we want answers to questions about how politics works around the world—but it's another to recognize that comparative politics asks a set of "big" questions that in some cases we have been asking for centuries, but in other cases have emerged over time. It's also important to acknowledge that in attempting to offer answers that are more informative and convincing—better—than others, changes in world politics force us to continually re-examine both our questions and our answers.

The foundations of comparative politics were established in ancient times and evolved through history into the discipline we study today. Some of the questions

1.2 What sorts of questions do we ask in comparative politics?

that comparative politics research asks today are quite old, while others have become relevant only recently. Aristotle (384–322 BC) may very well have been the first comparative political scientist when he asked, "What sort of constitution best combines political stability and good government?" Aristotle then challenged his students to compare and contrast the constitutions of every country in the known world at the time. He was convinced that the only way to answer his question was to explore evidence from the real world—the same approach scholars and students employ today when considering the question of how to combine limited and effective government to sustain democracy in the Middle East or elsewhere around the world.

Prior to the 1700s, the study of politics was rooted in moral and religious principles. All this began to change during Europe's so-called age of Enlightenment, when new scientific discoveries justified a logical and empirical approach to studying the natural and social world, and chipped away at the influence of religious dogma. During the Enlightenment, scholars increasingly considered questions about politics to be secular matters, casting aside arguments based solely in religion. For example, the work of philosophers such as Montesquieu, Hobbes, John Locke, and Jean-Jacques Rousseau asked whether a rational and secular basis for government existed independently of arguments for monarchy rooted

Old neighborhoods being swallowed up by new construction in Shanghai, China. China's government has carefully managed the country's amazing economic growth—a fact that raises the question about the proper level of government intervention in the market.

in divine right, and whether there was room for individual rights and freedoms in such a secular political order. Their arguments provided the foundation for the U.S. Declaration of Independence and Constitution, and sparked questions we explore in upcoming chapters, such as, "What is the state, and where does it come from?" "How can limits be imposed on government authority to protect individual liberty?" and "What is the relationship between religious identity and democracy?"

In the 1800s, new questions arose as a result of the Industrial Revolution, which caused massive socioeconomic change, particularly in Western Europe. Scholars such as Karl Marx and Max Weber considered the political impact of the shift from rural, agrarian societies to urban, industrial societies. Their work finds echoes to this day, as scholars continue to explore questions about the relationship between political and economic power, such as, "How can governments promote economic development?" and "Why do some governments redistribute wealth more than others?"

New questions emerged in the late 1800s and early 1900s about the sources and consequences of nationalism and forms of political ideology such as fascism and communism. Nationalism was blamed for igniting the First World War; communism sparked revolutions in Russia (in 1917) and China (in 1949) and bloody rebellions elsewhere; and fascism inspired the regimes that started the Second World War. Scholars wondered why nationalism took a benign form in some countries but a virulent form in others, and puzzled over why some people found communism appealing, while others found inspiration in fascism. Because so many dictators ascended to power in the 1930s, political scientists even wondered whether democracy would survive. This fear proved unfounded, yet although fascism and communism have virtually disappeared as governing philosophies, non-democratic political ideologies continue to challenge the stability of democracy all over the world, pushing scholars to ask questions such as, "What differentiates democracy from non-democracy?"; "What causes peaceful political mobilization—and what causes political violence?" and "Why does democracy sometimes collapse into non-democracy?"

In the 1960s and 1970s, the emergence of so many new nations in the wake of European decolonization generated a host of new questions, particularly about what might foster economic development and political stability in Latin America, Asia, and Africa. Some scholars assumed that poor nations were doomed to perpetual exploitation by wealthier nations, but the rapid economic rise of "Asian Tigers" such as Taiwan, South Korea, and Singapore invalidated such ideas and pushed scholars to ask whether economic development was a function of political culture, non-democratic political institutions, or the ways in which governments intervened in and manipulated economic markets. The recent rise of the "BRICs"— Brazil, Russia, India, and China—has pushed scholars to reconsider questions such as, "What political factors can encourage economic development?" and "To what extent does globalization impact politics?"

By the 1980s and 1990s, dozens of formerly non-democratic countries had adopted democracy, forcing political scientists to take yet another look at the question, "Why do some non-democratic rulers relinquish their hold on power?" The Soviet Union collapsed, ending the Cold War and generating optimism that, for the first time, the whole world might become democratic. Indeed, many wondered whether the world was witnessing the twilight of the idea of dictatorship, and the end of non-democratic ideologies once and for all. Still, given democracy's roots in Western Europe, scholars also wondered, "Can democracy survive in so many different cultures?"

Most recently, political scientists have focused increased attention on questions related to the expanding role of women in politics, the growing influence of religion, and to the impact of globalization on domestic and international politics. More and more women are winning elections around the world, leading scholars to ask, "How do different attitudes about women's rights influence politics?" The impact of religion seems obvious, but many assume that religious faith is a recipe for irreconcilable conflict between groups—while others call that assumption into question. And globalization brings us back to the sorts of questions Hobbes and Locke were asking hundreds of years ago: with the rising importance of nontraditional actors in world politics such as terrorists and human rights activists, will the sovereign state wither away?

This is where we find comparative politics today—asking a series of important questions about how politics works, and offering a method to help you make sense of the often-confusing and rapid political change going on around the world. At its essence, comparative politics is an argument for the existence of patterns—whether similarities or differences—across countries, and for undertaking a systematic effort to understand why different outcomes occur in similar places, or similar outcomes occur in different places. These efforts help us make sense of and simplify these complex patterns, offering simpler yet convincing answers to the questions that concern real-world political events.

THE COMPARATIVE METHOD

1.3 How do we build arguments in comparative politics?

Explore the Comparative "Governments and Public Opinion" at mypoliscilab.com

The questions we ask in comparative politics are always inspired by real-world events; there are no easy answers. The worst sorts of arguments in comparative politics are based on opinions rooted in stereotypes, in the belief that the past predicts the future, or on generalizations drawn from specific facts. For example, someone might stereotypically claim that, "Democracy can never take root in Iraq because Iraqis are naturally anti-democratic," or, "Iraq will never be a democracy simply because it has never been a democracy." Such arguments are unconvincing because they fail to engage available evidence—for example, public-opinion polls consistently reveal that Iraqi citizens want a democracy; and obviously every democratic country today was not always so. Someone might also offer the opinion, "Kuwait is next door to Iraq and it's not a democracy, so obviously there's no way Iraq can become a democracy." This approach seems logical on the surface—but it too fails to consider the range of evidence. One cannot assume that if something happens in one place it is bound to happen in other places.

Asking Questions

So how does a comparative approach to politics move beyond merely stating an opinion? First, it takes a particular approach to asking and answering questions about political events that might seem inevitable or that might seem to have an "obvious" explanation: by exploring as wide a range of possible cases that have similar characteristics but that experience different outcomes—or vice versa, by looking at the set of cases with different characteristics that experience similar political outcomes. Both of these situations force us to dig deeper in such cases to find more viable explanations:

- Countries that share attributes but experience different political outcomes are puzzling because we expect countries with the same features to undergo similar experiences.
- Likewise, when a diverse set of countries experiences the same political outcomes, the reason cannot be mere coincidence.

To illustrate the kinds of questions comparativists ask, consider an example of a dictatorship turned into a democracy: South Korea in 1987. How has democracy prevailed in South Korea? To answer this question, a comparativist would not focus only or even largely on what transpired in South Korea in the 1970s or early 1980s. Instead, we would look to the broader world to find out if democratization in South Korea is part of a larger pattern of similar events that occurred in similar *and* dissimilar societies.

Think about the implications of focusing exclusively on South Korea. Perhaps, you reason, there is something about Korean culture that is inherently pro-democracy. Yet if that were true, then all countries that share Korean culture should have democratized—or at a minimum we would see popular demand for democracy in such countries. South Korea is most similar to North Korea, which was and remains a non-democratic regime. Both countries share centuries of language, culture, and history. If Korean people were inherently pro-democratic, and if political outcomes followed from similar characteristics, then North Korea should also be a democracy. Yet despite sharing many attributes, North and South Korea have taken different political paths.

Comparativists shy away from building arguments based exclusively on the particulars of a single case. A good comparativist would ask, "Is the emergence of democracy in South Korea just one example of a pattern?" and would explore not just whether democracy has emerged in other similar places at the same time, but also whether it has emerged in different places at the same time. Depending on what we observe from the real world, we can begin to discount some answers, and gain confidence in others.

It turns out that South Korea is an example of a common phenomenon—democratization—which becomes puzzling when we see that many other very different countries—such as Argentina, Turkey, the Philippines, and Poland—all experienced the same political outcome around the same time. To a comparativist, this pattern cannot be a coincidence, but calls into question the relative importance of factors unique to South Korea, and suggests that only by identifying the factors these diverse countries share will we be able to explain the pattern. South Korea's democratization raises interesting comparative politics questions both because similar countries (like North Korea) have not taken its path, and because different countries (like the above) have.

To nail down how comparativists ask questions about politics, consider how we might search for answers to the question of "What causes civil wars?" Let's apply the same logic as above. Suppose you had just read an article about recent bloodshed in the West African country of Côte d'Ivoire, and you wanted to understand why the conflict started. If you went online, it would take you just a few minutes to learn two key things about Côte d'Ivoire: it's very poor, and it's divided between Christians and Muslims. "Aha!" you might say. "They're fighting over scarce resources, inspired by religious dogma." These are both plausible answers—a decent start to an argument that explains the causes of conflict, both in Côte d'Ivoire and in general.

However, think about the implications of these two hypotheses: If they were true, we should see civil wars in similarly poor and religiously divided societies. And if you spent another few minutes on the Internet you would discover that civil war has also erupted in Nigeria, another poor and religiously divided country in West Africa—but you'd also probably find out that Ghana and Benin, next-door neighbors to Côte d'Ivoire and Nigeria, respectively, are also poor and religiously divided, but they have remained peaceful.

This again leaves us with a set of similar countries with divergent outcomes. And, of course, if you did just a bit more research, you'd find a number of very different countries that have also experienced civil war—countries that are neither so poor nor so religiously divided as Côte d'Ivoire. A comparativist will approach questions about specific political events or dynamics—such as democratization in South Korea and civil war in Côte d'Ivoire—by putting those events in perspective of what's happened (or not) elsewhere. The question a comparativist is interested in answering is why we see particular political outcomes in some similar places and times, but not in other comparable places and times—and why we see those same outcomes in very different places. We want to know why we don't see democratization, for example, in other countries that are similar to South Korea—and we want to know why we sometimes do see civil war in countries that are very different from Côte d'Ivoire. To come up with convincing answers to these sorts of comparative politics questions, we first have to formulate hypotheses, and then apply the comparative method.

Formulating Hypotheses

hypothesis ■ an argument linking cause to effect.

A hypothesis is an argument that links cause to effect. A reliable hypothesis has been tested across more than one case. Therefore, those who study comparative politics search for patterns of attributes and outcomes—their presence or absence—across cases. Scholars engaged in comparative research cannot always

> **TABLE 1.1**
>
> **Asking Questions in Comparative Politics**
>
> 1. Look for cases that have similar attributes, but different outcomes.
> 2. Look for cases that have different attributes, but similar outcomes.

gather information from all cases, but their research always involves more than one country. The goal of such comparisons is to generate hypotheses that seek to answer our questions. Hypotheses have two important characteristics: they are causal and they are testable.

First, implicitly or explicitly, hypotheses posit causal relationships between attributes and outcomes. For example, the hypothesis "Democracy will not survive over the long term in Iraq because Islam and democracy are incompatible" suggests a relationship between Islam (cause) and democracy (effect). In this hypothesis, some aspect of a country's dominant faith is said to influence a political outcome, democracy. In comparative politics—as in all social sciences—hypotheses should clearly articulate the relationship between cause and effect. In this case, a researcher must develop an argument that explains what it is about Islam that conflicts with democracy.

However, making a good argument that "X causes Y" is insufficient. Hypotheses must also be testable. It is not enough to simply seek out and find evidence that supports the hypothesized connection between cause and effect—comparativists must also account for discrepancies. For example, we would not just point to all of the non-democratic countries that are also predominantly Muslim. Instead, hypotheses in comparative politics must be falsifiable—they must be formulated to allow for the possibility that the hypothesized relationship can be shown to be incorrect, through observation.

falsifiable ■ the possibility that a hypothesized relationship can be shown to be incorrect.

Approaching hypotheses this way—by thinking about how evidence from the world might falsify them—helps us narrow down potential explanations for political outcomes. A falsifiable hypothesis can potentially be proven incorrect, because it logically generates predictions about what we would find if we explored available evidence. In this case, "Islam and democracy are incompatible" implies that we should never see evidence of democracy in Muslim countries. We can then go out and see which countries are Muslim and which are democracies. If we find just one Muslim democracy, the hypothesis is falsified.

This particular hypothesis is, in fact, easily falsified, because democracy has emerged in several Islamic countries, such as Indonesia and Turkey. When we find evidence that falsifies a hypothesis, we have to go back to the drawing board and come up with an alternative hypothesis. These new arguments cannot put an ad hoc twist on the original argument simply to explain away the anomalies. Instead, we must adopt one of two options: modify the original hypothesis in a way that can also be tested against the facts; or replace it with an entirely new hypothesis. For example, after finding examples where Islam and democracy appear to

Supporters of Turkey's ruling Justice and Development party stop for afternoon prayers before a campaign rally led by Prime Minister Recep Erdogan. The example of Turkey has pushed comparative political scientists to re-examine assumptions about the relationship between Islam and democracy.

be compatible, we might propose, "For reasons of geopolitics, the way that Islam has evolved in Middle Eastern Muslim countries has made it unlikely that democracy will survive in Iraq, but more likely to survive in countries outside the Middle East, such as Indonesia or Turkey." This hypothesis shifts the causal focus away from Islam itself. Or, we could shift the causal focus entirely and hypothesize that "Democracy is unlikely to survive in predominantly Islamic countries that depend economically on oil production."

Some kinds of hypotheses are not falsifiable, and these are to be avoided when building an argument in comparative politics: those for which no plausible evidence exists. For example, the hypothesis "This civil war was inspired by God's Will" cannot be refuted because there is no way to obtain direct and irrefutable evidence to falsify the proposition. In the social sciences, we are not satisfied with guessing—good arguments will offer hypotheses that are falsifiable against evidence from the real world.

Arguments in comparative politics proceed by asking questions that put world events in comparative perspective, and then by formulating causal hypotheses that can be falsified against the evidence. The degree to which a hypothesis stands up to attempts at falsification is a measure of its strength; the more explanations we can rule out, the stronger our arguments become. This approach to testing our arguments—by comparing and contrasting across cases, focusing on patterns rather than idiosyncrasies—pushes us to avoid generalizing from the specific, which is akin to stereotyping. To better understand this process of hypothesis-formation, let's explore how we "do" comparative politics in greater detail.

Using the Comparative Method

To assess the degree to which hypotheses can be falsified or stand up against the facts, we use the comparative method, a way of examining patterns of facts or events to narrow down what is important in terms of building a convincing comparative politics argument. There are two basic approaches to the comparative method:

comparative method ■ a way to examine patterns of facts or events to narrow down what is important in terms of building a convincing comparative politics argument.

1. The method of agreement compares and contrasts cases with different attributes but shared outcomes; or
2. The method of difference compares and contrasts cases with the same attributes but different outcomes.

Let's illustrate these two ways of answering questions in comparative politics by focusing on the question, "What causes civil war?"

The Method of Agreement We'll start with cases that differ on attributes but share outcomes. The outcome we're interested in is civil war. To start your research, you would first define civil war. Then, you'd look for cases of conflict that fit this definition. The logic of the method of agreement is the following: if two or more examples of a particular phenomenon have only one of several possible causal attributes in common, then the attribute that all the cases share ("agree") is the cause of the outcome.

method of agreement ■ compares and contrasts cases with different attributes but shared outcomes, seeking the one attribute these cases share in common to attribute causality.

To illustrate, suppose four countries all experience civil conflict. You posit that one of several characteristics might cause civil conflict: poverty, rough terrain, ethnic diversity, or religious diversity. When you assess the characteristics of each country, you find that all four countries share ("agree" on) only one attribute—ethnic diversity. The method of agreement leads you logically to infer that ethnic diversity causes civil war. This approach to figuring out causality pushes you to find the thing that is always associated with an outcome, or that when absent is never associated with the outcome. Suppose now that there is a fifth, ethnically homogenous, country—and that this country did not experience civil conflict. Such evidence lends further support to the hypothesis that ethnic diversity somehow causes civil war.

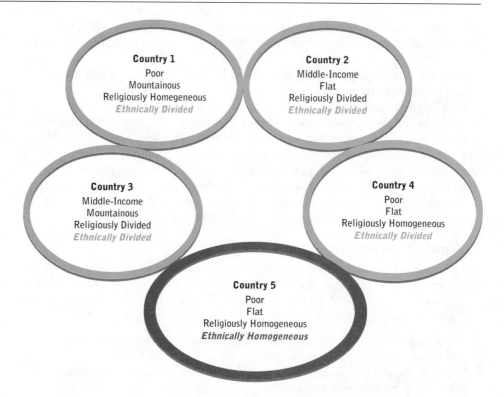

FIGURE 1.1

Using the Method of Agreement

Countries 1 through 4 all went to war, and by comparing them against each other you will note that they "agree" on only one attribute: ethnic diversity. The country that did not "agree" on this characteristic also did not go to war. The method of agreement finds the thing that all countries have in common—and in this example leads to the conclusion that ethnic diversity is a cause of civil war.

After consulting the evidence from real-world examples, we find that certain country attributes always match to certain outcomes, and that the method of agreement helps us generate strong causal hypotheses. However, the method of agreement is usually not the best way to build arguments. First, it is typically not the case that certain attributes always match up with certain outcomes. More often than not, countries "agree" on the key attribute but do not agree on the outcome. For example, although the example above implies that ethnic diversity is associated with civil conflict, many ethnically diverse societies have never experienced civil war. The more examples like this that we find, the weaker our original hypothesis.

Second, even though our original example points to the connection between ethnic diversity and civil war, it cannot rule out the possibility that other things may cause civil war, too. Some countries experience civil war for reasons having nothing to do with ethnic tensions. Although the method of agreement helps think through potential hypotheses and rule out some plausible explanations, the method of difference offers a stronger guide to causal inference.

The Method of Difference   The method of difference looks for some attribute that is present when an outcome occurs but that is absent in otherwise-similar cases when that outcome does not occur. Suppose you were doing lab research on plant growth, and you added the same quantities of plant food, water, and sunlight to five genetically identical seedlings. All five grow to exactly the same height. If you then did a second experiment in which you gave four seedlings identical amounts of food, water, and light, but gave the fifth seedling only water and light, you'd expect the fifth seedling to be scrawny. If four seedlings got three "inputs" and grew, and the fifth only got two "inputs" and did not grow, you could be pretty certain that decreasing the amount of food causes stunted growth.

method of difference ■ compares and contrasts cases with the same attributes but different outcomes, and determines causality by finding an attribute that is present when an outcome occurs but that is absent in similar cases when the outcome does not occur.

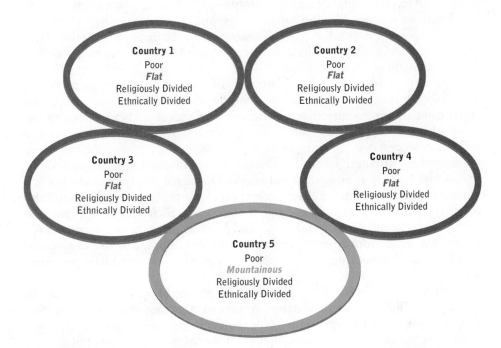

FIGURE 1.2

Using the Method of Difference

Countries 1 through 4 all remained at peace—and all share several characteristics. Country 5 went to war, and the only way it differs from the other countries is in its terrain. Using the method of difference in this example suggests a causal relationship between rough terrain and civil war.

> ## SUMMARY TABLE
>
> ### The Comparative Method
>
> | | |
> |---|---|
> | **Method of Agreement** | When several cases share an outcome but have only one attribute in common, that attribute is the cause of the outcome. |
> | **Method of Difference** | Determines the cause by finding an attribute that is present when an outcome occurs but that is absent in similar cases when the outcome does not occur. |

The method of difference works just like this, by comparing and contrasting the presence and absence of characteristics of our objects of study. For example, suppose you could only find one case of civil war that fits your definition, and you wanted to know what caused it. A truly weak approach would study only the case where we see civil war. If we did that, we would have several hypotheses (for example, "poverty causes war," "mountainous terrain causes war," "ethnic divisions cause war," and "religious divisions cause war"), but no way to assess their relative strength.

The way to assess the relative strength of each of these hypotheses would be to adopt a comparative approach, using the method of difference. To do so, you'd compare the country that experienced war against other countries to discover what it is that is "different" about Country 5. This approach helps isolate causal factors and develop stronger arguments. Suppose that four countries share the following attributes: poverty, flat terrain, ethnic diversity, and religious diversity. A fifth country is also poor, and ethnically and religiously diverse—but it is mountainous rather than flat. The terrain is the only thing that differentiates this country—and this is the only country that experienced war. This approach allows you to rule out poverty and ethnic and religious diversity as potential causes of civil war in the fifth country. Perhaps mountains offer rebels secure places to hide from government troops, while flat countries offer few such places to foment rebellion.

This approach is called the method of difference because it focuses on the country that "differed" on the outcome relative to other cases—it experienced war while the others remained peaceful—even though it "agreed" with other countries in terms of several of its attributes. Because it shared those attributes but differed on the outcome (war), those attributes cannot logically have caused the war. Only one attribute was present when war occurred and was absent when war did not occur. Therefore, only this attribute explains the different outcomes.

The two approaches to the comparative method, as summarized in the table above, make doing comparative research appear straightforward. Whether you choose to use the method of agreement or the method of difference, both approaches compare the relationships between cause and effect, and all comparative politics research employs these two approaches in some way. Unfortunately, most of the time when we're trying to answer a real-world question about politics, it is not a simple matter to match attributes and outcomes; comparative politics research involves several difficulties.

CHALLENGES OF COMPARATIVE RESEARCH

Why study comparative politics? We study comparative politics because we want to develop convincing arguments explaining how and why politics works around the world. Testing hypotheses confronts a series of challenges. Doing comparative research is hard work, because evidence from the world is often unclear or subject to multiple interpretations, and because—in contrast to studying microbiology, physics or chemistry, for example—the objects of study in comparative politics change every day. Peaceful countries erupt into civil war; a dictatorship becomes a democracy; poor countries grow rich within a generation or two. All arguments in comparative politics are necessarily provisional, because research confronts the challenges of separating causation from correlation; identifying causation; and assessing the reliability of "data" not obtained in a lab.

1.4 What challenges confront building arguments in comparative politics?

Separating Correlation from Causation

Suppose that after systematically gathering information we discover that civil war is more likely in ethnically diverse societies. What we've uncovered is a correlation—a measure of observed association between two variables. However, this is not a complete explanation—that is, a correlation between ethnic diversity and civil war does not allow us to say that the former causes the latter. We say that two variables "X and Y" are correlated when change in the value of X is accompanied by change in the value of Y. For example, "as ethnic diversity increases, so does the likelihood of civil war." Correlations can be positive—when one variable increases, so does the other—or negative, meaning that when one variable increases, the other decreases.

correlation ■ a measure of observed association between two variables.

The fact that attributes and outcomes appear to be associated with each other in a predictable way does not mean that one causes the other. Causation is defined as a process or event that produces an observable effect. Observing causation is often difficult. For example, the old riddle asks "Why did the chicken cross the road?" The riddle's humor lies in its ludicrousness, because we can't ask chickens about their intentions. We don't know what caused the chicken to cross the road, even though we certainly know how she did it—by putting one foot in front of the other. Without too much debate about poultry motivations we can say that "walking" (the cause) produced "crossing the road" (the effect).

causation ■ a process or event that produces an observable effect.

We can illustrate the difficulty of identifying causation with an example from comparative politics. Even though we do observe a correlation between ethnic diversity and war (the greater the diversity, the higher the likelihood of war), we cannot just conclude that ethnic diversity causes civil war. Constructing a causal argument requires a systematic search for and comparison of relevant examples by marshaling as much reliable evidence as possible, an effort to rule out potential alternative causes, and the development of an explanation for why we observe a relationship between ethic diversity and war. After all, more than one attribute could be correlated with a particular outcome. For example, suppose we find that both rough terrain and ethnic diversity are correlated with civil war. One attribute could be causally crucial, while the other could be irrelevant. It's entirely possible that ethnic diversity and war have absolutely nothing to do with each other, even though they occur together frequently. This leads to the second challenge facing comparative research.

Identifying Causation

To know whether ethnic diversity really does cause civil war or not, we'd have to develop a plausible argument linking diversity to bloodshed. The fact that a correlation exists raises a series of questions: How does diversity cause animosities? How do animosities cause group mobilization along ethnic lines? How does mobilization turn violent? The problem is that there is no necessary reason why diversity should always cause animosity, or why animosities should always cause mobilization, or why mobilization should always cause bloodshed. If we find a correlation between certain characteristics (such as ethnic diversity) and certain outcomes (such as war), we still need to explain how these things are causally connected—something that may ultimately rely more on logical argument than direct evidence.

Confirming a relationship between cause and effect in the social sciences is different from confirming such relationships in the natural sciences. In the natural sciences, researchers can conduct experiments in controlled, laboratory settings—meaning they can fully isolate the causal impact of different attributes. Controlling all the conditions of an experiment is the only true way to isolate causality. Political scientists do not have the luxury of experimenting on or with people or events—and in any case, trying to "control" the complexity of politics only makes the research less and less applicable to the real world. Because reasonable people interpret history differently, and because we cannot re-run history like scientists can redo experiments, it is often difficult to reliably compare across cases, much less control for all factors that might affect the outcome we seek to explain. And because political scientists cannot replicate the real world in a lab to test our theories, arguments about causality in the social sciences must rest on scholars' ability to accumulate evidence and construct a convincing argument that logically holds together.

Assessing Unreliable Information

Causal explanations in comparative politics are hard to pin down, partly because the information we gather as social scientists is fundamentally different from the data that natural scientists produce in a laboratory setting. Social scientists cannot "control" or "isolate" factors to determine causality as chemists might be able to in a lab, nor can they conduct additional experiments to obtain more data. Social scientists have to make do with the information that the world provides—we can-

SUMMARY TABLE	
Challenges to Comparative Politics Research	
Separating Correlation from Causation	The fact that attributes and outcomes are associated with each other does not mean that one causes the other.
Identifying Causation Is Hard	Social science evidence is not generated in a lab, meaning scholars cannot fully isolate causal attributes.
Assessing Potentially Unreliable Data	Social scientists must rely on information provided by the real world—information that may be ambiguous or even unavailable.

not turn back time, change some social or political attribute and "rewind" the world to see if the outcome would differ. Sometimes, the real world offers very few examples of either the attributes or the outcomes we're interested in exploring.

In addition, information can frequently be ambiguous or even downright confusing. For example, if scholars want to test the relationship between ethnic diversity and civil war, they have to agree on how to define "ethnicity," "diversity," and "civil war," which is not easy. Then, they have to agree on how to measure those concepts, which is even harder. And even if they agree on all of the above, they may find the historical record ambiguous in terms of membership in ethnic groups and the intensity of violence in particular countries.

Finally, even if scholars agree on definitions and the historical record is clear, the information needed to test a hypothesis might be difficult or even impossible to obtain. Information on such subjects as corruption, campaign finance, and lobbying activities are often unavailable to researchers. Interviewees are frequently unwilling to speak on sensitive issues such as religion, ethnic prejudice, or gender attitudes; and useful information is sometimes locked away in government archives. Some countries simply prohibit access to social scientists. And even if information is readily available, obtaining it may require months or years of work in the field, and years of preparation to learn a new language.

In comparative politics, articulating convincing answers to questions is always difficult and often contentious. The challenges noted in this section make comparing and contrasting across cases difficult—meaning that arguments in comparative politics are never perfect, and never final. The world is a very complicated and rapidly changing place, and sometimes our answers prove unsatisfying. Yet, this does not mean that we simply shrug our shoulders and give up. An unsatisfying answer sparks additional questions, giving scholars reason to go "back to the drawing board" and continue the search for a better answer. And in any case, as we will see in later chapters, in many cases the comparative method succeeds, providing useful answers to questions about our complicated and messy world. This chapter's feature box pushes you to think about how to formulate and subject a hypothesis to scrutiny.

HYPOTHESIS TESTING | Montesquieu's Theory of Climate

Canada and Saudi Arabia have very different climates. Based partly on the weather conditions, Montesquieu predicted whether these two places would have a democratic or non-democratic form of government.

Charles de Secondat, Baron de Montesquieu (1689–1755), was a French nobleman and political philosopher. In his most famous book, *The Spirit of the Laws*, published in 1748, Montesquieu hypothesized that a country's climate, terrain, and agricultural conditions affect the temperaments and customs of its inhabitants. In turn, these temperaments account for why some countries are democracies, monarchies, or dictatorships.

According to Montesquieu, cold climates constrict our body's fibers—tendons, muscles, and blood vessels—while hot climates expand them. Montesquieu believed these weather-induced body changes affect our characters and temperaments: people who live in cold climates tend to be "vigorous and bold, phlegmatic [calm and unemotional], frank, not given to suspicion or cunning," and relatively insensitive to pleasure and pain. In contrast, people who live in warm climates exhibit stronger but less durable sensations. They are "more fearful, more amorous, and more susceptible both to the temptations of pleasure and to real or imagined pain; they are also less resolute, and less capable of sustained or decisive action."

These climactic factors, Montesquieu hypothesized, directly impact the nature of

government that arises: excessive heat "enervates the body, and renders men so slothful and dispirited that nothing but the fear of chastisement can oblige them to perform any laborious duty." In contrast, "the bravery of those in cold climates has enabled them to maintain their liberties." In short, non-democratic governments would be found near the equator, while democracies were to be found closer to the poles.[2]

How far-fetched is Montesquieu's theory? How would you go about proving or disproving a similar hypothesis today? Let's hypothesize that *cooler climates tend to foster democracies while hotter regions tend to have non-democratic governments*. What sorts of empirical evidence would you need to gather to make your argument convincing?

GATHER EVIDENCE

Is there a relationship between climate and form of government? And if so, why is there a relationship between climate and form of government? To answer the first question, consider two countries with dramatically different climates: Canada and Saudi Arabia. These cases fit Montesquieu's hypothesis well: Canada has been a democracy since its independence in the 1800s, while Saudi Arabia a non-democratic monarchy. Why might this be so?

(Continued)

Are Canadians particularly "vigorous and bold," and thus more capable of self-government? Are Saudis "fearful" and indecisive, and consequently in "need" of the iron fist of a non-democratic ruler?

Such stereotyping will not get us very far. Moreover, if we were to continue to gather information, we'd quickly find countries that seem to confound Montesquieu's expectations. For example, consider Brazil and Russia. Stereotypes of Brazilians and Russians fit Montesquieu's images—"Brazilians prefer spending the day at the beach rather than working," while "Russians are dour and tough." The tropical sun in Brazil certainly "enervates the body," but Brazil is a democracy. In contrast, the Arctic cold in Russia would certainly "constrict the body's fibers," but Russia is not a democracy.

ASSESS THE HYPOTHESIS

These four cases do not confirm or disconfirm Montesquieu's hypothesis. Using Table 1.2, can you brainstorm additional countries that fit in each box? The more countries you find that fit in the "Cold and Democratic" and "Hot and Non-Democratic" boxes, the stronger the evidence in Montesquieu's favor. Conversely, the more countries that fit into the "Cold and Non-Democratic" and "Hot and Democratic" boxes, the weaker the evidence for this hypothesis.

On the one hand, you might think Montesquieu's hypothesis is far-fetched. Even if you discovered that most countries are either "Cold and Democratic" or "Hot and Non-Democratic," you might still wonder, "Why?" Many other things might explain why countries are democracies or not. Perhaps Montesquieu's hypothesis is outdated—a product of an era when stereotyping was accepted, and unbiased information about the world scant.

Yet on the other hand, scholars still take Montesquieu's basic insight about the relationship between the environment and politics seriously. The further one goes from the equator, the less common are dangerous tropical diseases such as malaria and yellow fever. Moreover, one only finds large swaths of flat and fertile land in the temperate zones of both the northern and southern hemispheres. Lands nearer to the equator are indeed too hot to support agriculture, as they are typically covered with jungle or desert. Some scholars have suggested that patterns of European settlement around the world in past centuries are related to the emergence of democracy and dictatorship today: where settlers set up farms and strong property rights, democracy later emerged. Where settlers could not survive, colonizers ruled via force—and such patterns of rule continue long after the colonies gained independence.[3] We will revisit this question again in Chapter 11.

Given this historical pattern, 250 years after Montesquieu, scholars who conduct research into questions such as why some countries are rich and others poor and why some countries are democracies while others remain non-democratic test for a connection between climate and government form by including the *latitude of a country's capital city* in their analyses. Latitude measures how far a country is from the equator—and thus serves as a rough indicator of climate. And although Montesquieu was basically stereotyping and guessing, his intuition still finds support in technically sophisticated research: since about 1800, the further a country is from the equator, the more likely is democracy to emerge. ▲

CRITICAL THINKING QUESTIONS

1. Do you think that Montesquieu might have confused correlation with causation in his original hypothesis?
2. What else might cause the observed relationship between climate and form of government?
3. Is it proper to generalize about a country's climate? Many larger countries encompass mountains, deserts, jungles, and grasslands. Most do not have "a" climate, but rather several climates. How might Montesquieu have responded to this?

TABLE 1.2 Exploring Montesquieu's Theory of Climate

	Hot	Cold
Democracy	Brazil	Canada
Non-democracy	Saudi Arabia	Russia

APPROACHES TO DOING COMPARATIVE RESEARCH

1.5 How do we obtain evidence to build arguments in comparative politics?

To meet the challenges facing comparative politics research, scholars have developed different ways to obtain evidence: quantitative and qualitative research. Let us explore these two approaches, and consider their relative advantages and disadvantages.

Quantitative Research

quantitative research ■ relies on statistical data to assess relationships between attributes and outcomes, analyzing those data using computers.

How does one do comparative politics research quantitatively? Quantitative research relies on statistical data to assess relationships between attributes and outcomes, analyzing those data using computers. Sometimes scholars use data that others create. For example, to explore the hypothesis that economic performance impacts election outcomes, we might gather dates of elections and the percent of the vote of the incumbent party from Election Resources on the Internet (www .electionresources.org) and then find information on the state of the economy in the months or years preceding the election from the World Bank (www.worldbank .org) and then correlate the economic data with the election results.

Sometimes, researchers create their own quantitative data by transforming nonquantitative information into numbers. For example, a researcher may have precise measures of ethnic diversity, but no precise measure of civil war. As you might imagine, "measuring" the presence or absence of civil war is difficult. To simplify matters, a scholar might decide that countries that experience more than 1,000 battle deaths a year can be said to be in a state of civil war, and thus classify countries based on reports of battle deaths as "1" (war) or "0" (no war). Doing so would allow statistical analysis of the relationship between the degree of ethnic diversity and the emergence of war.

Quantitative research emphasizes breadth over depth. This is because the larger the sample of quantitative data one analyzes, the lower the likelihood that any relationships you discover in the data are random, and the lower the likelihood that the sample you have gathered is biased. For example, survey researchers trying to find out who is going to win an election do not survey ten people—they survey 1,000 or 2,000 to get a "national sample," because they want to lower the probability that they have inadvertently surveyed a group that differs from the "true average" of the entire population. The more examples you study of the phenomena you're interested in, the less likely you will have a biased sample.

In going for breadth over depth, the primary advantage of quantitative research is that—in theory at least—it allows for precise assessment of the relationship between causes and effects. However, going for breadth is also the primary disadvantage of quantitative research—doing so may sacrifice depth of understanding of what is really going on, politically. Statistical data tend to be detached from the human environment, and they tend to assume that the world can be portrayed in fixed quantities, when in fact much that is interesting about politics is fluid and changing.

Qualitative Research

Not all comparative politics questions are amenable to quantitative research. For example, although there have been relatively few cases of successful revolutions in world history, many people are interested in figuring out their causes. Due to their rarity, quantitative analysis of revolutions is impossible. Moreover, quantification of an attribute or outcome may miss what is truly important or meaningful. For example, perhaps a political leader's charisma or use of cultural symbols, images, or rhetoric causes particular emotional or psychological responses that spur revolutionary mobilization. Such attributes—either a leader's charisma or the reasons why people respond to charisma—are not easily quantified, if at all.

For these reasons, we must have an alternative to quantitative research to answer many important comparative politics questions. By definition, qualitative research does not attempt to quantify attributes and outcomes. Instead, where quantitative research focuses on breadth, qualitative research focuses on an in-depth understanding of the phenomena we're interested in exploring. Because it digs deeper, using interviews, long periods of field research, and interpretation of archival records, qualitative research necessarily considers fewer cases than does quantitative research. In theory, this depth of knowledge helps to bolster causal arguments by strengthening our understanding of the mechanisms that link causes to effects.

> **qualitative research** ■ focuses on an in-depth understanding of attributes and outcomes. Privileges depth over breadth.

There are three main disadvantages with qualitative research. First, it produces a causal argument for only the cases being compared, skirting toward the problem of generalizing from the specific. Second, qualitative research can get bogged down in relatively unimportant details and degenerate into description without explanation. Without conducting a broad examination of all potentially relevant cases, qualitative research may erroneously overemphasize a causal factor unique to a particular case. For example, a focus on one revolution might highlight the importance of a rebel victory in one particular battle—but fail to notice what is less obvious but crucial to explaining all successful revolutions—the overall political weakness of the incumbent government, when compared against cases of unsuccessful revolutions. Finally, although this problem also sometimes confronts quantitative research, it is often difficult to judge the relative validity of a qualitative argument, because it is impossible to "check" a scholar's findings. After all, by definition no "hard data" exist that another scholar could gather again and re-explore with statistical analysis.

Comparative politics research is almost never conducted in a laboratory, with controlled conditions that would give us an unimpeachable answer to our question. But the fact that many challenges face comparative politics research does not mean we should throw up our hands and simply suppose that we cannot build convincing arguments about how the world works. Today, scholars often employ mixed methods approaches, using both quantitative and qualitative techniques, in an effort to build convincing claims about the relationships between attributes and outcomes. The best we can do is look for cases that are as similar as possible on certain variables and as different as possible on other variables, and then build an argument about the implications of such differences and similarities.

> **mixed methods research** ■ uses both quantitative and qualitative techniques, in an effort to build convincing claims about the relationships between attributes and outcomes.

CONCLUSION

The world is a dangerous and fascinating place, and only by learning about how politics works in other countries can we understand how best to engage those countries. We need to understand how and why politics works elsewhere in order to understand how their politics impacts us, and how their politics impact other countries, as well. Comparative politics is about the systematic search for answers to questions about how people around the world make and contest authoritative public choices. To guide that effort, we use the comparative method, a way of thinking systematically about why the same outcome sometimes occurs in cases that are very different, and why different outcomes sometimes occur in cases that are very similar. The comparative method highlights some of the many challenges to finding convincing answers to our questions about comparative politics.

Comparative politics focuses on answering questions—on explaining complex political phenomena. The challenges it confronts means that explanations using the comparative method are always provisional—a fact that may be somewhat disappointing. Yet the demand for answers is as pressing as ever, given how complex the world has become and how fast the world is changing. The world needs more and better comparative politics research—and this book gives you the tools to make that happen, by focusing your attention on useful ways of asking and answering these key questions.

Every chapter in *Comparative Politics* poses an important question about politics around the world and then explores the ways scholars have sought to answer that question, using real-world examples to ground and clarify the discussion. The book's approach differs from other texts by offering a set of key questions in lieu of a set of important countries. This approach prioritizes the questions, not the country cases, because we want to develop convincing explanations—and doing so requires gathering information from beyond the borders of a limited number of countries. Because each chapter in this book begins with a question of broad interest, you will gain experience learning how to develop arguments by comparing countries to each other.

The question that begins each chapter is posed within the context of an engaging real-world example. Consider Chapter 3: the question that chapter explores in depth is, "What is democracy?" The chapter starts off by drawing your attention to the Middle East, a region with very few democratic governments—but where protests ranging from mild to very violent have rocked autocratic governments since late 2010. No one knows whether democracy will flourish in the Middle East—but the question of what sort of democracy might emerge in region is certainly among the most important for students of politics today.

After connecting a political science question to the real world of politics, each chapter is organized around the key arguments that scholars of comparative politics offer in answer to that question. This material is presented in a particular way—each section of each chapter first poses a "smaller" question that ties back to the chapter's main question, illustrating how each section contributes to answering the chapter's larger question. This approach is designed to get you to see how political scientists do their own work—often by engaging a smaller piece of a larger puzzle—engaging, debating, and coming up with plausible arguments to the key questions about politics in the world today.

Each chapter also contains a feature box that gives you an opportunity to apply what you have learned in the chapter and engage in the process of building a political science argument. Each box describes a real-world political puzzle related to the chapter's main question. It then provides information necessary to critically engage the competing arguments and evidence that scholars have used in order to try to explain that puzzle, and lays out competing hypotheses and expectations for addressing the question. This exercise helps you to learn how a scholar of comparative politics would reason about the issue at hand, and provides you with opportunities to learn how to recognize and ultimately construct your own arguments about how politics works around the world.

The end of each chapter provides useful material for you to both review and deepen your understanding of what you've just learned. After the chapter conclusion ties everything together for you, you'll find a list of the chapter's key political science terms—which are also highlighted and defined at first mention throughout each chapter; a short set of review questions for you to use in assessing whether you've digested the chapter's main points (and that can also help you study for exams); and several annotated suggestions for additional reading, if you find the chapter's topic particularly interesting.

For readers who want more specific country information to complement the questions raised here, an accompanying country casebook is available that emulates the pedagogical approach of this survey. The ten country cases include the United Kingdom, Germany, France, Japan, Russia, China, Mexico, India, Iran, and Nigeria. Each country chapter begins with a question, just like each chapter in this book, and the material in each chapter answers that question while also providing information useful for answering the range of questions that this book asks. In short, the country casebook is designed specifically to complement this question-driven text.

The chapters in this book—and thus the chapter questions—are ordered logically. Chapter 2 begins with Hobbes's fundamental question, "How is political order established?" Considering this question sets the stage for the discussion of the purpose and evolution of the state. The next key question is, "How is power distributed within states?" Chapters 3 and 4 answer this question by focusing on the institutions of democratic and non-democratic regimes. Chapter 5 explores the question, "Why do transitions between democracy and non-democracy sometimes occur?"

The next few chapters shift the focus toward political identities, keeping in mind that identities cannot be fully separated from institutions or interests. After all, political institutions shape how identities gain representation in the formal realm of politics—and political identity is often the raw material from which individuals and groups construct their political interests. Chapter 6 asks, "What is political identity?" and focuses on explaining the conditions under which ethnicity and nationalism become politicized. Chapter 7 turns to another hot-button question—the compatibility between religious identity and democracy—while Chapter 8 explores the political consequences of changing conceptions of gender around the world.

The next two chapters turn to the general question of how and why individuals' political interests and identities are mobilized collectively. Chapter 9 explores peaceful forms of collective action—interest groups, social movements, and political parties—while Chapter 10 asks why people sometimes take up arms against the established political order. The last three chapters turn to pressing questions at the intersection of politics and economics. Chapter 11 asks. "Why are some countries rich and others poor?" and Chapter 12 explores why some countries tax and spend more than others. Finally, Chapter 13 explores the question of globalization and its impact.

In sum, this book provides the tools for you to learn how comparativists answer pressing questions about politics. It poses questions that will pique your curiosity about how politics works around the world, and leads you through the different ways that comparative political scientists have endeavored to answer those questions. The book is organized around these questions, but uses cases from the real world to demonstrate how to build arguments in political science. ▲

✓ Study and Review the Post-Test & Chapter Exam at mypoliscilab.com

KEY TERMS

politics   4
comparative politics   5
hypothesis   10
falsifiable   11
comparative method   13
method of agreement   13

method of difference   15
correlation   17
causation   17
quantitative research   22
qualitative research   23
mixed methods research   23

REVIEW QUESTIONS

1. What is comparative politics?
2. What is the difference between a falsifiable and nonfalsifiable hypothesis?
3. What is the method of agreement?
4. What is the method of difference?
5. What is the difference between correlation and causation?
6. Why is it hard to identify the true "cause" of something?
7. Why are data in comparative politics research often unreliable?
8. What is quantitative research?
9. What is qualitative research?

SUGGESTED READINGS

Fearon, James. "Counterfactuals and Hypothesis Testing in Political Science." *World Politics* 43 (1991): 169–196. Describes an important way to test arguments for which there is little or no direct empirical evidence—counterfactuals, or "thought experiments."

Geddes, Barbara. "How the Cases You Choose Affect the Answers You Get: Selection Bias in Comparative Politics." *Political Analysis* 2 (1990): 131–150. Explains why the challenges of comparative research frequently impede the development of convincing explanations for important events or processes.

Lijphart, Arend. "Comparative Politics and the Comparative Method." *American Political Science Review* 65, 3 (1971): 682–693. A classic explanation of how to employ the comparative method.

Munck, Gerardo. "The Past and Present of Comparative Politics." In *Passion, Craft and Method in Comparative Politics*, edited by Gerardo Munck and Richard Snyder, New York: Cambridge University Press, 2007. Details the evolution of the comparative politics subfield.

Wood, Elisabeth Jean. "Field Research." In Carles Boix and Susan Stokes (eds), *The Oxford Handbook of Comparative Politics*. New York: Oxford University Press, 123–146. 2007. A discussion of why it is crucial for comparative political scientists to spend extended periods of time in the places where they conduct their research.

NOTES

1. This definition of politics is owed to Harold Lasswell, in his *Politics: Who Gets What, When, How* (New York: McGraw-Hill, 1935).
2. This material can be found in Montesquieu's *The Spirit of the Laws,* Book 17.
3. See Daron Acemoglu, Simon Johnson, and James Robinson, "The Colonial Origins of Comparative Development: An Empirical Investigation," *American Economic Review* 91(5)(2001): 1369–1401.

The State

n ports that lack

? Where do "states" come from?

In April 2009, Somali pirates captured an American cargo ship and took its captain hostage aboard a small lifeboat. The U.S. Navy destroyer *Bainbridge* engaged in pursuit, and when the pirates pointed their weapons at the American hostage, U.S. Navy SEALs targeted and killed them with three shots.

Pirates flourish off the coast of Somalia because a functioning central government has not controlled that country's territory since 1991. Somalia is considered a failed state, which means that it has no effective national legal authority: no police, no army, and no legal system to pursue and punish pirates. It also means that the central government cannot police the country's 2,000 miles of coastline or surrounding waters. For this reason, some pirates claim to be acting in the best interests of their country, defending its national honor by attempting to prevent other countries' fishing fleets from illegally overfishing in Somali waters.[1]

The pirates' ranks are typically filled with unemployed young men who, given the fact that their country has been ripped apart by warfare for almost 20 years, see few alternatives in their bleak future. None of the men expect to live very long so they attack huge ships fearlessly, making high seas piracy into a big business. Ship owners typically prefer to pay the pirates' multimillion-dollar ransom demands to free their ships' crews than to have blood spilled on their decks and their cargo destroyed or sold off.

Failed though the Somalian state may be, its borders can still be located on any world map that divides the earth's territory into almost 200 states. The **state** is a political-legal unit with sovereignty over a particular territory and the population that resides within its borders, where **sovereignty** is defined as ultimate responsibility for and legal authority over the conduct of internal affairs, including a claim to a monopoly on the legitimate use of physical force—within territory defined by geographic borders.[2] It follows that a **failed state** occurs when sovereignty over claimed territory has collapsed or was never effectively established at all. Places like Somalia tend to be chaotic and poverty stricken, and they lack the infrastructure to provide their citizens with basic resources. Other contemporary examples of failed states include Sudan, Congo, Afghanistan, and Haiti.

"Failure" implies that "success" is the global norm—and that a strong government can address issues such as poverty and chaos. But **where do "states" come from?** The question that we explore in this chapter is not merely how a functioning state might emerge in Somalia, but why states exist at all. The world was not always divided into clearly delineated borders as it is today. In fact, until recent decades, no sovereign central political authority existed in many places around the world, even in theory.

As the example from Somalia suggests, a state "fails" when the central government cannot unite often conflicting individual interests and identities in order to protect and satisfy collective interests in security and civil peace. The story of state formation thus explores the forces behind the emergence of institutions, rules, and behavioral norms that balance the tension between individual and group interests. Comparative politics explores the **legitimacy** of the state—the degree to which

---

Read and Listen to Chapter 2 at mypoliscilab.com

Study and Review the Pre-Test & Flashcards at mypoliscilab.com

state ■ a political-legal unit with sovereignty over a particular geographic territory and the population that resides in that territory.

sovereignty ■ ultimate responsibility for and legal authority over the conduct of internal affairs, including a claim to a monopoly on the legitimate use of physical force—within territory defined by geographic borders.

failed state ■ a state where sovereignty over claimed territory has collapsed or was never effectively established at all.

legitimacy ■ the degree to which citizens willingly accept the state's sovereign authority to use power.

citizens willingly accept the state's sovereign authority to use power—as well as the state's effectiveness—how the institutions of the state shape citizens' lives.

In this chapter, we first explore the challenge of balancing individual and collective interests as a way to establish order in human societies. We then differentiate the state from other concepts such as nation, government, and society. Third, we compare the factors that explain state formation in early and later historical eras. Finally, we explore one way that political scientists measure states' relative strength or weakness—that is, their ability to maintain effective order. The point, as you will see, is that comparative politics provides insight into the question of where states come from. Such insight then helps us understand why some succeed and others fail to exert authority over the territory within their borders.

BALANCING INDIVIDUAL AND COLLECTIVE INTERESTS

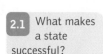 **2.1** What makes a state successful?

collective action problem ■ a situation wherein each individual has private incentives not to participate in an action that benefits all members of the group.

A successful state must first solve the problem of establishing political order among its people. Establishing political order is a collective action problem, a clash between individual and collective interests. When members of a group must choose whether to participate in a collective activity—for example, paying taxes to provide for education or participating in a protest movement against a dictatorship—problematic issues often arise. Leaders want everyone in the group to participate, but each individual is torn between incentives *not* to participate and their interests in benefiting from the group's work. From an individual's standpoint, cooperating with others can be costly in terms of time, money, or forgoing other choices. Individuals, thus, often have an incentive to let everyone else do the hard work associated with public benefits. Let's explore a classic example—the Prisoner's Dilemma—to illustrate how the tension between individual and collective desires pervades politics.

The Prisoner's Dilemma

The best-known example of a collective action problem is the Prisoner's Dilemma, which got its name from the following hypothetical situation: two criminals are arrested under suspicion of having committed a bank robbery. The police do not have enough evidence to convict either suspect, so they tell each the same thing: "Here's the deal. We admit that we don't have enough to convict you. So if both of you hold out and don't confess to robbing that bank, then we'll send you to prison for two years for violating your parole. However, if you confess to the robbery and your partner keeps his mouth shut, then you'll go free while he will get ten years in the state penitentiary. Of course, if you don't confess and he does, then we'll let *him* walk, and *you* will do the ten years. And if you both confess, you'll both get five years."

The cops have the criminals in a bind, because each will reason similarly: "If I keep quiet but my buddy rats me out, then I'm going up the river for ten years. If I confess and he does too, we both do five years. And if we both keep quiet, we both do two years. The best for me would be if I confess and he keeps quiet, because then I go free and he does the hard time. But if he thinks just like me, then he'll confess and go free, and I'll do the ten years. So no matter what he intends to do, I'm better off confessing than holding out." Since both criminals think the same way, both end up confessing—and both end up spending five years in prison.

The prisoners are in a dilemma—they cannot coordinate on their optimal collective interest, which is to both keep quiet, nor can they be sure they'll obtain their optimal individual interest, which is to go free. The incentives of the situation push them to opt for what they *think* might be the individually optimal outcome— confessing that both of them did it—in the belief that doing so will result in being released. Yet, since both prisoners face exactly the same incentives, each confesses and each does five years. Individual incentives trump the "collective good."

The Prisoner's Dilemma illustrates the tension between individual and collective interests at the core of any collective action problem. The same tension exists in politics where individual and collective interests frequently clash. For example, no one wants to pay taxes, even though everyone wants *everyone else* to pay their taxes, because the public services that the government provides—such as roads, schools, and national defense—make us all better off. If there were no penalties for tax evasion, more people might "free-ride" off the "suckers" who still willingly sent their money to the IRS.

Reconciling individual and collective interests is difficult in politics because some people want to advance their own interests regardless of how doing so might affect others' interests. Unfortunately, as the Prisoner's Dilemma illustrates, in politics our choices are often interdependent: what I choose to do may affect your ability to choose what you want to do, and vice-versa. Thus if we all act solely on our individual interests, we all might lose out on what we want. States—as the English philosopher Thomas Hobbes first told us—exist to prevent such situations from arising.

Hobbes's Problem

The collective action problem illustrates that private preferences and public choices often conflict. The fundamental challenge of politics is thus making authoritative public choices. How do governments avoid suboptimal outcomes—such as having everyone choose not to pay taxes? There are two ways to solve such collective action problems: by using coercion or by gaining consent. People can be forced to pay their taxes, or they can willingly do so. However, only coercion—or the threat of coercion—can ensure *authoritative* collective choices. Governments gain legitimacy when individuals consent to authoritative public decisions.

Thomas Hobbes (1588–1679) was among the first to recognize the clash between individual and collective interests as well as articulate a solution to it. In his book *Leviathan*, Hobbes pointed to the state as the solution to this problem. Leviathan is a metaphor for the state—the political-legal entity employed to resolve the tension between our individual interests to do as we please and our collective desire for law and order. Hobbes evoked the biblical image of a Leviathan because he believed that the state needed to be powerful enough to keep individuals in line. However, he imagined the Leviathan in human form because he did not want such authority to derive from God. Written more than 350 years ago, *Leviathan* remains a classic of Western political thought because Hobbes was among the first to articulate a justification for

In the Old Testament book of Job, the leviathan was a crocodile-like sea monster that only God could subdue. This illustration shows a typical cover of Hobbes's book, where the leviathan is imagined in human form as a giant who dominates the world and all the people in it.

political authority and legitimacy that did not rest on the divine right of kings. In addition, his justification for strong central government differed from that of previous thinkers because it required popular *consent* rather than divine right or coercion.

Hobbes wrote during a period of violent civil war, and as a result he feared that anarchy was coming to England. He believed that anarchy would be bad for everyone, including the rich and powerful. Human society, Hobbes argued, only flourishes if government provides all citizens with security of life and property. He derived this conclusion by asking his readers to imagine what life would be like in a state of nature, a mythological time before any human community or government existed. Hobbes famously described life in the anarchic state of nature as "solitary, poor, nasty, brutish, and short."

Using logic similar to that in the Prisoner's Dilemma, Hobbes argued that humans need government to avoid this dismal fate. He assumed that individuals in the state of nature would be most interested in self-preservation, and he reasoned that those who were strong enough to assure self-preservation would then be interested in acquiring power over others. Given this, the weak would have an intense interest in protecting themselves from the strong. Yet, because there is no government in the state of nature, the interests of the strong and weak would conflict. Without government, laws, contracts, law enforcement, and justice systems would not exist. In the state of nature, "might makes right": the strong do what they want, while the weak do whatever they must to survive. The solution to this problem is for the state to create order out of chaos.

state of nature ■ term coined by Thomas Hobbes to describe an imaginary time before human beings organized into governments or states for the collective good.

Hobbes's Solution

Hobbes understood that people are self-interested and that self-interest includes a desire for security. He intuited that the solution to creating order out of chaos emerges from the same sentiment he felt as civil war swirled around him: fear. Fearful for their own well-being, people would agree to limit their own freedom to do as they please, as long as everyone else agreed to the same restrictions. Hobbes believed that self-interested individuals would consent to a social contract, an agreement wherein everyone binds their own hands. Enforcing the social contract means consenting to an authority that will keep everyone in line: the Leviathan. For Hobbes the Leviathan should have freedom to use coercion, as long as it keeps the peace between people and recognizes everyone's right to self-preservation. Consenting to a strong central power—either a monarch or an assembly of some kind—resolves Hobbes' collective action problem.

social contract ■ a theoretical political agreement in which everyone agrees to limit their ability to do as they please in order to achieve some collective benefit.

All governments—including democracies—coercively limit individual freedom to some degree. The question is whether the government does so because citizens consent to such limits or because the government controls the means of coercion. Hobbes wanted to distinguish "might" from "right"—that is, to distinguish coercive, illegitimate authority from consensual, legitimate authority. Yet he was among the first to recognize that even legitimate authority must be backed by the threat of force. Politics always involves the threat of state violence against all citizens, no matter how democratic the system. Thus, for Hobbes, notions such as human rights and justice ironically depend on the brute power of the state because the threat of punishment, not moral qualms, prevents most people from violating others' rights. For Hobbes, the Leviathan should use force only to uphold citizens' freedoms. Hobbes believed that "consenting to being coerced" results in a stable *and* just social order.

Hobbes offered a philosophical answer to the question of where states come from. He suggested that states help provide law and order, and other useful services—they help people avoid contemporary Somalia's situation of near-anarchy, chaos, and political violence. In short, states offer a response to individuals' core interest in personal security—they balance individual and collective interests. Now let's look more closely at *how* the state maintains order by examining the state's attributes.

ESTABLISHING INSTITUTIONS

2.2   What do
states do?

Watch the Video
"Artificial Borders
and Tribal Conflicts in
Pakistan"
at mypoliscilab.com

Explore the Comparative
"Political Landscapes"
at mypoliscilab.com

For Hobbes, the creation of a strong central government could generate cooperative behavior that would end the "war of all against all" and resolve the prisoner's dilemma inherent in the state of nature. Ending such a war requires consenting to limitations on one's own freedoms, thereby empowering a Leviathan. Yet, what are Leviathan's characteristics? What, exactly, is the state? We turn to these defining questions in order to explain what states "do," to distinguish the institutional notions of "state" and "government" from each other, and to distinguish the state from ideas of "nation" and "society," which focus on political interests and identities rather than on political institutions.

Sovereignty

As defined earlier, a state is a political-legal entity that has sovereignty. Two characteristics of sovereignty are key to effective rule of the state. The first is centralized decision making. Ultimately, one or some individuals control the state on behalf of everyone else. Second, centralization requires the possibility of coercion, given that centralized decisions for the entire community may or may not reflect everyone's individual interests. States can force individuals to do what they do not want to do and can prevent them from doing what they want to do. Many comparative politics questions focus on the ways states and their rulers regulate what people do with their time, money, property, minds, and bodies.

Let us focus for a moment on the part of the definition of the state involving a "monopoly on the legitimate use of force." All governments use force or the threat of force to maintain order. Indeed, the threat of violence is behind every authoritative political decision. As Hobbes said, "Covenants without the sword are but words." Similarly, Columbia University political scientist Charles Tilly said, "Violence is written in the DNA of the state." Of course, even the most dictatorial of states are never perfect monopolists of violence. There will always be crime. However, states claim a monopoly on the *legitimate* use of force within their territory: authorization to use violence is ascribed to institutions or individuals only to the extent that the laws of the state permit it. All other violence, whether organized or random, is illegitimate.

Hobbes suggested we willingly submit to such authority because the alternative—anarchy—is riskier to our ability to enjoy life. The implication is profound: human communities can only improve their general welfare through the use of coercion, not simply through individual choice. This idea holds regardless of who occupies the government and regardless of whether the state is a democracy or a dictatorship—yet understanding why this is so requires distinguishing the *state* as a concept from the *government*.

State versus Government

Like the Leviathan, the state is an abstraction. You can't "touch" it, or really identify "who" the state is. In contrast, a government is a concrete organization that has the authority to act on behalf of a state, and the set of people who have the right to make decisions that affect everyone in a state. You might want to think of the difference between government and state as the difference between body and soul. The former is the body—eyes, ears, fingers, and toes—while the latter is the soul. You can have a toe amputated, or a prosthetic leg attached, but the rest of your body keeps functioning. More importantly, even without that toe, you're still essentially the same person. The state is, thus, like an image or idea of a territory and the practices, institutions, and traditions of the people within that territory. For this reason, many countries separate the "head of state" from the "head of government." In Japan, the head of state is Emperor Akihito, who publicly personifies and represents the spirit of the national community; he also upholds that community's legitimacy. In contrast, the prime minister of Japan is the chief executive officer of the government administration. To make the understanding of the state even more precise, we can also distinguish it from the nation, as well as from society.

government ■ the organization that has the authority to act on behalf of a state, and the right to make decisions that affect everyone in a state.

State versus Nation

In ordinary conversation, we often use the terms *state, nation,* and *country* interchangeably. In political science—and in this text—we will use *state* rather than *country* to refer to political units with sovereignty over territory. Yet, what's the difference between a state and a nation? As defined above, a state is a political-legal abstraction. In contrast, a nation is a form of political identity—a cultural grouping of individuals who associate with each other based on collectively held political identity. This identity can be based on shared cultural traits (such as religion or ethnicity) or a historical association with a particular territory. Given this psychological attachment to the group, members may mobilize to pursue autonomy and possibly self-government. However, nations do not have the organizational and institutional characteristics of states—for example, they do not have administrative officials, clear membership rules, or mapped boundaries. More important, they do not possess sovereignty, and they do not claim a monopoly on the legitimate use of force over their own people. Without a state, nations lack political autonomy.

nation ■ a cultural grouping of individuals who associate with each other based on collectively held political identity.

Sometimes, states and nations overlap perfectly, but this is not always the case. In Japan, the two overlap almost exactly. This is because the Japanese language is not indigenous anywhere else, and people with Japanese ancestors who live outside Japan do not consider themselves members of the Japanese nation but of other cultures—if you asked descendents of Japanese immigrants in the United States if they identify as patriotic Japanese or patriotic Americans, nearly all would affirm their allegiance to the United States.

Elsewhere, the coincidence between state and nation is looser. Especially in Africa, Asia, and the Middle East, some cultural groups are split by state boundaries, meaning that a nation can exist in more than one state. For example, ethnic Kurds are found in Turkey, Iran, and Iraq. Many Kurds consider themselves members of the Kurdish nation, rather than a member of the any other. However, "Kurdistan" exists only as "the general area where Kurds live," and no other state recognizes Kurdistan as an independent state. Where state and nation do not coincide, we often see civil conflict.

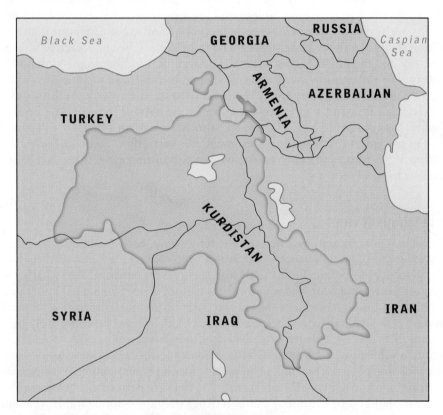

Approximate Extent of the Kurdish Ethnic Group

Turkey, Iran, and Iraq face a challenge because state and nation do not fully overlap. Ethnic Turks, Persians, and Arabs form majorities in those three countries, but ethnic Kurds—who consider themselves a distinct nationality—also inhabit each of these states.

A final important difference is that membership in a state is an objective, legal fact: you are either a citizen or not, based on where you live or were born, or what passport you carry. In contrast, nationalism, the feeling of identification with a nation, is a subjective sentiment. It is a form of political identity—a set of learned political beliefs that people can feel very deeply, like religious faith. People do not willingly lay their life on the line for their state, although nationalistic patriotism often motivates people toward valor on the battlefield. Let us now consider a final distinction, between the state that holds legal sovereignty and the society that exists within that territory.

nationalism ■ a subjective feeling of membership in a nation.

State versus Society

Society (sometimes called "civil society") is a term for the diverse forms of voluntary collective action that people engage in outside the realm of the state and its authoritative, coerced public choices. It consists of all formal and informal organizations, social movements, and interest groups that attempt to (1) remain autonomous from state control and (2) articulate their own economic, cultural, and/or political identities and interests.[3] When we speak of society, we mean the ways that people "speak, assemble, associate, and reason together on matters of public concern" and act together to influence politics.[4] This idea invokes interests and identities, rather than political institutions.

society ■ a term for all organized groups, social movements, interest groups, and individuals who attempt to remain autonomous from the influence and authority of the state.

In the United States, examples of such interest- or identity-based organizations include churches and other faith-based organizations, community groups ranging from the Boy Scouts to the Junior League to the Elks Club, American Legion, or Loyal Society of Moose; professional associations such as the American Bar Association, American Medical Association, or even the American Political Science Association; charities and other voluntary groups such as the United Way or the Red Cross; nongovernmental advocacy organizations such as the National Rifle Association, Planned Parenthood, the American Civil Liberties Union, the Federation for American Immigration Reform, or Amnesty International; labor unions such as the AFL-CIO; and business associations such as the National Association of Manufacturers or the Chamber of Commerce.

Organizations and groups such as these are clearly not part of the state. Yet, like state or nation, the concept of society is an abstraction. This makes it extremely difficult to locate the dividing line between state and society in the real world. Nevertheless, political scientists are interested in the former's capacity to use its coercive authority to influence the latter—and in individuals' and groups' capacity to influence the state and the policies its government produces. This suggests that a potential tension always exists between state and society: on the one hand, the state can become too strong, eliminating individual and group political, economic, and cultural freedoms.

On the other hand, a strong society can serve as a monitor, check, and restraint on the use of coercive authority. However, if a state is too weak in the face of powerful societal interests, it may be unable to control a part of the society. For example, in some countries, rebel groups or criminal organizations are strong enough to resist state authority. In such situations, these groups provide their own version of law and order within the state's territory. Examples include the pirates and other armed factions organized by clan that have caused such terrible chaos in much of Somalia in recent years, or armed gangs of drug traffickers that contest control over vast neighborhoods in Mexican cities near the U.S. border, such as Ciudad Juarez or Tijuana. Some states are so weak that they collapse into chaos or even anarchy.

When states are too weak, certain parts of society may also dominate the rest of society. Such situations arise when corruption is rampant, for example. In such cases, wealthy and powerful individuals or groups use their resources to control the state for their benefit, limiting the collective, public benefits that states should in theory provide to all citizens.

People organize themselves into states to resolve the inevitable collective action problems that arise in large communities, out of a desire to establish political order. In the contemporary world, the state—through the government of the day—remains the key political-legal entity that organizes the political interests and identities in nation and society. The table on the following page summarizes the distinctions between these concepts.

The discussion thus far has been conceptual. Now that we know why states exist and what they do, it's essential for us to return to the chapter's main question and try to explain where states in the real world come from—both in early eras and in more recent decades.

UNDERSTANDING EARLY STATE FORMATION

2.3 What factors explain the emergence of the world's first states?

Scholars generally date the founding of the modern world system of states to the year 1648 (Thomas Hobbes completed *Leviathan* in 1651). In that year, European leaders signed the Treaty of Westphalia, named for the German province where it was signed. The treaty ended the Thirty Years' War, which was both a religious conflict between Protestants and Catholics and a territorial dispute between rival leaders. While the details of this war are unimportant for this course, the Treaty of Westphalia is important because it established the principle that secular leaders—as opposed to a religious authorities, in this case, the pope—held ultimate authority over a given territory.

The Treaty of Westphalia serves as a convenient dividing point between "premodern" and "modern" forms of political organization, but states as we have defined them did not magically "appear" in 1648. The treaty merely highlighted a process that was centuries in the making. In fact, there was no point at which the first states all "emerged," because the process was evolutionary and occurred differently across time and place. Nevertheless, the modern state is associated with the following:

1. A decline in the legitimacy of traditional forms of political authority such as the rule of a charismatic authority figure, inherited leadership, or religious authority, and an increase in the legitimacy of depersonalized, public governance based on the rule of law;

SUMMARY TABLE

Distinctions among State, Government, Nation, and Society

Concept	Definition	Example
State	A *political-legal* unit with sovereignty over a particular territory and the population that resides in that territory.	The United Kingdom
Government	The organization that has the authority to act on behalf of a state and the set of individuals who act within the state's institutions	British Prime Minister David Cameron, his appointees, and bureaucrats accountable to his leadership
Nation	A *cultural grouping* of individuals who associate with each other based on collectively held political identity.	Scottish and Welsh— groups that live in the UK but identify with a regional cultural identity, including different accent or language, dress, food, customs, and, perhaps, religion
Society	The formal and informal organizations, social movements, and interest groups that attempt to (1) remain autonomous from the state and (2) articulate their own identities and interests independently from the influence of the state and its authorities.	British environmental, feminist, sports, or religious organizations

2. An increase in the central government's sovereignty over carefully delineated territory and a decline of decentralized and overlapping forms of sovereignty such as the traditional system of feudalism, under which several local or regional land-owning nobles claimed authority over a single piece of territory and only paid nominal allegiance to a central king or emperor;

3. An increase in the organizational complexity of central-government institutions.

Many contemporary states do not perfectly conform to these criteria of depersonalized, complex central-government sovereignty. In particular, kinship remains

feudalism ■ a form of political organization in which no single political entity or ruler held unambiguous territorial sovereignty and in which political rule involved multiple and often overlapping lines of authority.

central to the transfer of political authority in many countries. Nevertheless, these factors tend to distinguish premodern forms of rule from states. Still, the question remains, "What caused the shift from premodern to modern political organization?" Let's first consider two explanations for the early rise of the state in Europe. The two approaches diverge in terms of what each considers the most important *causal* factors associated with early state formation—political interests, or the impact of the natural environment.

Political Interests and Early State Formation

What forces explain the transformation of a situation in which authority over territory is unclear and fragmented to one in which a central government holds unambiguous sovereignty? During the Middle Ages, the kings, dukes, barons, and princes who ruled different European territories pursued their own political interests as "coercive, self-seeking entrepreneurs."[5] They were coercive because they controlled instruments of violence; they were self-seeking in their interest to protect and expand their territory; and they were entrepreneurial because they were willing to try new techniques to increase their power.

During this era, European rulers' interests in establishing uncontested authority over their own lands pushed them to compete with other rulers for political primacy. Such competition boiled down to preparing for and engaging in warfare—and warfare is extremely expensive. This means that early state formation was triggered by war preparations—competition over territory—in combination with tax-extraction. Warfare and taxation are necessary to establish and defend sovereignty over territory. Of course, rulers have been waging war and extracting taxes the world over since the dawn of time. This raises the question of why war and taxes—and a political interest in defending territory—should cause the rise of the modern state only in the 1600s in Europe. To answer that question, let us turn to the ways that the military, economic, and cultural identity contexts of the Middle Ages helped shape political interests.

The Military Context　Armies require weapons, training, food, housing, clothing, and equipment—and a desire to place heavier cannons on naval vessels at that time required investment in the development of larger, more complex fighting ships. Larger armies and navies are extremely costly. And spending on offense also meant increasing spending on defense—that is, rulers responded to improvements in siege artillery and naval weaponry by constructing more elaborate and larger defensive fortifications, which are also quite expensive. In short, changes in military technology in the Middle Ages gave rulers a powerful incentive to increase military spending. Increased military spending meant that rulers needed to raise taxes—and both war preparations and taxation require centralization of power and construction of the large, complex bureaucracies that characterize modern states. Yet other changes that drove early state formation in Europe were also afoot—an economic boom.

FRENCH GALLEY VS. BRITISH SHIP OF THE LINE

A naval galley (top) contrasted against a ship of the line (bottom). Galleys were the dominant type of naval warship for almost 2,500 years, until the 1600s. The largest weighed about 200 tons and typically carried one bronze smoothbore cannon, which was only useful at short range. The larger and more powerful vessels emerged in the 1600s as a result of technological advances in ship design and construction. A ship like this could weigh 2,000 tons and carry more than 100 rifled iron cannon, which were accurate at much longer ranges. Building just one of these ships costs as much as an entire fleet of galleys, but rulers who commanded fleets of advanced warships succeeded in consolidating state sovereignty.

The Economic Context   In addition to the growing need for tax revenue driven by rising military expenditures, broad economic changes beginning in the late Middle Ages also drove early state formation. First, a gradual increase in agricultural productivity in Europe improved standards of living and helped support general population growth. These developments permitted the raising and supporting of larger armies and navies. Yet, as noted above, increasing the size of military forces required imposing ever-larger tax burdens. Beginning in the sixteenth century, some rulers sought new sources of revenue by expanding, controlling, and extracting resources from overseas empires. Rulers in some countries also encouraged the growth of domestic industry, which offered rich new sources of tax revenue beyond the traditional taxation of land and agricultural production.

The growth of industry, trade, and commerce coincided with the rise of cities around Europe, which meant the rise of a new class of urban merchants and traders who pursued profit, political stability, and security. These budding capitalists invented new and profitable methods of finance and speculation, all of which rulers could tax. Rulers who provided favorable conditions for economic growth increased their own tax revenue. Greater tax revenue supported larger military forces, which in turn protected the domestic security of the developing state. As Europe's military and economic situation was changing, a final factor was also contributing to the early rise of the modern state—changes in the cultural context.

The Cultural Identity Context   Europe's military and economic transformations were accompanied by a monumental shift in collective and individual beliefs and political identities, which also created an environment in which modern states would emerge. For example, the feudal form of collective political identity—in which each person had a preordained station in life—declined, while the concept of individual self-interest emerged. These changes occurred as part of the Protestant Reformation and the Age of Enlightenment, both of which challenged the legitimacy of religious authorities and the divine right of kings to rule, and opened the door to the transition from premodern to modern forms of political authority. Recall that the Treaty of Westphalia broke the pope's claim of sovereignty and forced European rulers to articulate nonreligious rationales to justify their sovereignty over people and territory. Within this changing cultural and religious context, and given the changing military and economic context, the notion of the state began to take shape.

Starting about 500 years ago, European rulers' interests in consolidating authority over their territories generated intense rivalries and competition—and only the strong would survive. Rulers built up strength by extracting tax revenue to arm increasingly expensive military forces. Because modern states require complex and centralized bureaucracies, the states that emerged first were those where economic growth was encouraged, where rulers devised new ways to tax, and that were militarily successful. The decline of centuries-old cultural practices such as deference to religious authorities also opened the door for the rise of modern forms of political organization.

The Natural Environment and Early State Formation

One way to explain early state formation focuses on how changes in the military, economic, and cultural-identity contexts shaped rulers' political interests, which drove early state formation because of competition between leaders for territory and military power—and because of tension between ruler and subject over the rights of taxation. Let us now contrast this argument with one that deemphasizes politics and focuses instead on the impact of the natural environment.[6]

Competition and warfare between rival leaders have occurred throughout human history. This means that political competition by itself cannot explain the rise of the modern state in the 1600s. An alternative explanation for the emergence of the first modern states focuses on rising population density in Medieval Europe. Historically, whether in ancient or contemporary eras, the size and density of the regional population is a strong predictor of political centralization and institutional complexity. Populations increase when more babies survive into adulthood, at which point they make more babies. What causes declines in infant mortality rates? The key factor lies with the natural environment: an increase in food production. Increases in food production allowed more babies to eat well, survive into adulthood, and make more babies. An increase in food production in Medieval Europe, thus, may explain the increased population density that led to modern state formation.

If a rise in food production in Europe is all-important for explaining early state formation, a pertinent question is, "What explains the rise in food production at this time?" The best answer to that question is that Europe had good luck rather than any particular advantage in brainpower or creativity, implying there is nothing inherently superior about Western cultures. Instead, countries such as England, France, and Germany just had the good fortune to be located in a relatively flat, temperate zone where heavy pack animals, such as horses and cattle, and food crops, especially grains like wheat and oats, and potatoes, could thrive.

The idea that Western Europe's success at forming the first modern states was a determined by nature's roll of the dice has proven influential, partly because it is "politically correct." The states that emerged and consolidated first had tremendous advantages over people in other regions. These states had military, economic, and technological superiority, which explains their eventual domination or colonization of most of the rest of the world from the 1500s to the mid-twentieth century. Yet this "environmental" argument suggests Western Europeans shouldn't be proud of this accomplishment, because nothing they consciously did accounts for their superiority. They just won the global environmental lottery.

To explain early state formation, both political competition and environmental factors are important; the table on the following page summarizes the main points of this section. Geography is not always destiny—places with similar natural environments do not always have similar political systems. Because we cannot always map environmental conditions to political outcomes, we know that political interests also matter. This combination of the political and environmental contexts

SUMMARY TABLE

Explaining Early State Formation

Factor	Argument
Political Interests	In the context of changing military technology, economic growth and the decline of traditional feudal and religious cultural practices, states emerged as Medieval European rulers competed to consolidate control over territory.
Natural Environment	An increase in food production in Medieval Europe resulted in growing population density; this resulted in early state formation because larger and denser populations require more complex and centralized political institutions to govern.

shaped early state formation—and as we shall see, differences in context shaped the way that states emerged in recent decades.

UNDERSTANDING LATE STATE FORMATION

2.4 What factors explain the emergence of states in recent decades?

⊙ Watch the **Video** "Kenya's Developmental Challenge" at **mypoliscilab.com**

In 1945, the United Nations had only 51 member-states; by 2006, it had 192.[7] Many new states emerged after World War II, following the collapse of European colonial empires in Africa, Asia, and the Caribbean. Others arose in Eastern Europe when the Soviet Union collapsed in 1991. The environmental and political factors at work centuries ago created some of the world's strongest states, by any measure. By contrast, many late-forming states are among the world's weakest.

As the example of the Somali pirates illustrates, many newer states cannot effectively police their own borders or monopolize the means of violence within their territory. Many newer states also have weaker capacity to tax and extract revenue from their citizens, which results in rampant corruption, tax evasion, and poor economic growth. Finally, newer states rarely provide adequate government services to their citizens. Given this lack of effectiveness across multiple dimensions, many newer states also lack legitimacy.

What explains late-forming states' relative weakness? State formation in recent decades differs considerably from the process that unfolded centuries ago. To answer this question, we need to examine how political interests, the physical environment, and political identity have affected late-forming states.

Political Interests and Late State Formation

The concept of central-government sovereignty over territory was well established by the 1800s. However, the ability of many late-forming states to exert sovereignty varies considerably when compared against states that formed earlier. Recall the arguments regarding the military, economic, and cultural contexts as important influences in early state formation. Let's see how these elements apply to cases of more recent state formation.

The Military Context Western European states formed during centuries of international conflict. Indeed, as discussed, one of the most important factors driving state formation in early modern Europe was the international military context, which reshaped the feudal order and forced European rulers to search for new ways to finance defense spending. However, the international military context of the Middle Ages differed dramatically from the post-1945 era. The Cold War following World War II gained its name for a reason: there were relatively few interstate "hot" wars after 1945. Even after the Cold War ended in 1990, the pattern continued: the number of civil wars increased, while the number of interstate wars remained fairly low.

As a result, although rulers in both early- and late-forming states shared an interest in maintaining the territorial integrity of their borders, the international military context in recent decades did not contribute to state formation as it did in earlier eras.[8] The relative lack of military pressure from their neighbors meant that political leaders in recent decades faced weaker incentives to increase military spending, weaker incentives to increase taxation, and thus little reason to construct large, complex bureaucracies that characterize stronger states. To this military factor, we must now add the way that a different economic context shaped state formation in the recent era.

The Economic Context A relative lack of military pressure is not sufficient to explain the relative weakness of many late-forming states. States that consolidated relatively early—a few European states, the United States, and Japan—got the jump on the process of economic development. By the late 1800s, these were by far the world's wealthiest and most powerful states—and during that period, European states used their power to colonize most of Africa and much of Asia. Japan colonized Korea, Taiwan, and large parts of mainland China in the early twentieth century. Although the United States acquired few formal colonies, it informally influenced many other states, especially those in the Caribbean and Latin America.

Empires served the economic and political interests of the colonial power: exploitation of the labor and natural resources of the occupied territories. Colonial powers were uninterested in developing legitimate institutions in their colonies; instead, they were only interested in maintaining order effectively enough to dominate the locals and to extract what resources they could. As a result, when colonized states gained independence in the twentieth century, they did so almost overnight as the empires of foreign occupiers collapsed. Political leaders in newly independent states had little time to engage in state-building practices such as societal mobilization for warfare or expanding administrative and tax extraction capacity. Instead, most new states tended to be relatively poor, and their leaders were forced to work with the government institutions they had inherited from colonial authorities—institutions that had never been designed to provide effective government services in the first place. Moreover, citizens in new states understood their central government as little more than the representative of the departing and hated colonial authority, meaning that the central government also lacked legitimacy.

In short, for many late-forming states, the legacy of European colonialism was poverty and ineffective and illegitimate government institutions. Such an economic context constitutes a vicious circle: upon independence, rulers in many late-forming states inherited state institutions that did not even provide for law and order, which in turn made their country an unattractive prospect for investment and economic development. Thus, although most of these rulers did not have to mobilize resources to defend their territory from abroad, their primary political interest focused on surviving in office, by extracting resources through corruption and graft to buy political support and fend off political rivals. Relatively few would invest economic resources in the construction of effective government institutions that could provide favorable conditions for economic growth. Together with the different military and economic environments, a third difference—in the cultural context—would shape rulers' political interests and explain why late-forming states tend to be relatively weak.

The Cultural Identity Context   Understanding the sources of state weakness in newer states not only requires that we explore how the military and economic situations shaped rulers' political interests but also pushes us to consider the degree to which a single national cultural identity can be put to work generating legitimacy for the institutions of the state. Any state—new or old—tends to be weaker if there is a weak connection between state and nation. For several reasons, the coincidence between state and nation tends to be weaker in newer states.

In most cases of early state formation, states established their borders through a long process of competition with their neighbors. In contrast, nearly all states that emerged after World War II are former colonies, and few determined their own borders. When European rulers colonized Africa, the Middle East, and Asia, they often drew arbitrary lines on a map, out of ignorance of the local conditions. When they became independent, these former colonies inherited artificial boundaries that had little or nothing to do with either geography or the distribution of ethnic, religious, or linguistic identity groups. As a result, some post-colonial states mingle several identity groups that have no desire to live together under a single national flag. Elsewhere, the borders dividing one state from another drive through the middle of an identity group's historical homeland, dividing that group into two or more states. The arbitrariness of many boundaries weakens late-forming states because citizens disagree about the authority and legitimacy of the national government.

In many cases of early state formation, rulers often deliberately created and bolstered the legitimacy of a common national political identity, simultaneously weakening or destroying diverse local political identities. This process required centuries of chipping away at the legitimacy of local religious, ethnic, clan, or tribal forms of political authority, and at the same time constructing a substitute form of legitimate rule. In contrast, because the process of decolonization was so rapid for many late-forming states, political leaders in many newly independent states lacked the time and resources to grind down local-level political attachments in an effort to construct a coherent and legitimate national political identity.[9] For example, in the Muslim world many people continue to believe that religious authorities should have political primacy, not secular political leaders. And across many parts of Asia, Africa, and the Middle East, forms of political identity based on tribe, clan, or kinship group still predominate over any broader sense of national identity. In short, because of the persistent strength of non-nationalistic forms of political identity, many late-forming state institutions lack legitimacy.

A few states consolidated sovereignty by the 1800s—and these "early-forming" states remain relatively strong. In contrast, states that formed in more recent decades—such as Somalia—tend to be relatively weaker in terms of legitimacy and effectiveness. The explanation for such variation rests with differences in the way the military, economic, and cultural contexts shaped political interests in new states: although military pressures from abroad were lower in recent decades, many of these former colonies gained independence in a position of economic weakness. Moreover, in many cases, rulers could not draw upon a cohesive sense of national identity to enhance state legitimacy. The political context in recent decades raised high hurdles for state consolidation. In addition, as in the earlier era, in many cases the natural environment has also shaped trajectories of state formation in recent decades.

The Natural Environment and Late State Formation

Both political interests and the natural environment play a role in determining the relative strength of late-forming states. Many African states are precariously weak. In some cases, environmental factors do contribute to the relative weakness of late-forming states, because consolidating state authority and legitimacy is more difficult in states with mountainous or heavily forested areas, or in jungle-covered regions that many rivers crisscross, as in the Congo, or Afghanistan, for example. Such difficult terrain weakens states' capacity to control their own borders and police their own territory, provide public services, extract taxes, and prevent smuggling. Also, when the terrain is difficult, roads are more expensive to build and maintain. This lack of access makes extending the "reach" of the state more expensive. In contrast, in countries without forests or jungles and with relatively flat terrain, state building is relatively "cheaper."

Yet even among African states with similar geographical and/or environmental conditions, some are stronger than others (see the feature box, on Botswana and Zimbabwe). This suggests that—as in early-forming states—the natural environment does not fully determine state strength in late-forming states. For example, state fragility in the Saharan region ranges from "low" to "high": Morocco's state is relatively strong, while Mauritania and Niger are comparatively weak. And in

HYPOTHESIS TESTING | A Colonial Legacy Always Results in a Weak State: The Cases of Zimbabwe and Botswana

Botswana and Zimbabwe are neighboring states in southern Africa. Both are former British colonies and new states: Botswana gained independence in 1966, Zimbabwe in 1980. Both countries are similar in other ways, adding to the expectation that they would travel similar post-colonial paths. They both have subtropical climates and have relatively flat terrain that is suitable for farming. A dominant ethnic group exists in both countries, with several smaller ethnic minorities. However, the similarities between the two countries end at that: in recent decades, Zimbabwe's government has been riddled with corruption and its economy has crumbled into nonexistence, while Botswana is thriving. Can we relate colonialism to this divergent outcome? Let's first compare the situations in contemporary Zimbabwe and Botswana, to get a better handle on the differences between the two countries.

GATHER EVIDENCE

In most countries, people do not fear that that the cash in their pockets will be nearly worthless the following week. Zimbabwe's citizens have not been so fortunate of late. Between January 2007 and November 2008, Zimbabwe's inflation rate rose so high that the price of goods doubled *every day*. Cash was rendered worthless in days as the annual inflation rate soared to an unimaginable 89 *sextillion* percent— that's 89 followed by 21 zeros.[10] In a vain attempt to keep up, the government issued a bill worth 100 trillion dollars, worth about US$300 when it was first issued in January 2009. However, just three

A woman holds a handful of new 10 trillion (10,000,000,000,000) Zimbabwe dollar notes in Harare, Zimbabwe.

(*Continued*)

months later, Zimbabwe's government abandoned the nation's currency entirely. All private sector and government business is now conducted in Euros, U.S. dollars, and South Africa's currency, the Rand.

Inflation is not Zimbabwe's only problem—the economy is in such ruin that it is estimated that 95 percent of people were officially unemployed in 2009—up from 80 percent in 2005.[11] Inflation and unemployment have impoverished the vast majority of Zimbabweans. The International Monetary Fund (IMF) recently estimated that per capita income in Zimbabwe averages only $355 per year, the second-lowest in the world (only Congo is worse off)—meaning that the average person somehow manages to survive on only about a dollar a day. Given its lack of effectiveness and legitimacy, in 2008 Zimbabwe scored 16 out of 24 on the State Fragility Index (see below), putting it among the world's weakest states.

Zimbabwe has been an economic basket case for years, but its neighbor Botswana reveals a very different trajectory. Most importantly, Botswana's economy has grown consistently since independence, and per capita income reached almost $14,000 per year in 2008—about the same as in Russia or Chile today. (In the United States, per capita income is about $46,000 per year.)[12] In 2009, Botswana had an inflation rate of only 7.3 percent and an unemployment rate of 7.5 percent—lower than in the United States. Given its robust economic performance and consistent political stability, in 2008 Botswana scored 4 out of 24 on the State Fragility Index, the best score in all of Africa's approximately four dozen states, and among the top 25 percent of all states around the world, in terms of effectiveness and legitimacy. Botswana is clearly one of Africa's success stories, while Zimbabwe is one of Africa's disasters.

ASSESS THE HYPOTHESIS

From the information above, we can easily confirm that Botswana invalidates the hypothesis that colonialism always leads to a weak state. Yet is this case unique, while Zimbabwe's experience echoes that of many other post-colonial states? What accounts for the extreme variation in state capacity between these two neighboring African countries? Three

things are relatively more important than a colonial legacy for answering this question: diamonds, civil war, and political leadership.

Although Zimbabwe and Botswana share many environmental attributes, Botswana has the good fortune of being one of the world's largest producers of high-quality diamonds. Yet, this presents us with another puzzle, because in many post-colonial states, the discovery of minerals or fossil fuels has led to bad governance outcomes such as corruption, poverty, and inequality. To the surprise of some observers, Botswana has managed to avoid this fate. Having diamonds does not explain good governance—in fact, it makes Botswana's success all the more surprising. Something else must explain the country's relatively strong state.

The reason Botswana and Zimbabwe have diverged so clearly in terms of state performance has to do with civil war and political leadership rather with than the impact of colonialism or the discovery of diamonds. Before independence, Zimbabwe was wracked by 15 years of civil war between white settlers—who feared the loss of their land and other property—and black African insurgents. Many whites left after 1980, and reconciliation between the remaining whites and the country's black political leaders has been difficult.

Civil war also continued after Zimbabwe's independence between rival black insurgent groups. This conflict was partly rooted in ethnic identity, but partly also in competition between politicians eager to rule the new country. Civil war left Zimbabwe divided and economically devastated. In contrast, Botswana gained independence peacefully. An absence of civil conflict meant that national identity in Botswana was somewhat more consolidated soon after independence than in Zimbabwe and meant that Botswana did not have to repair war damage to get its economy in gear. A more peaceful transition to independence provided Botswana's state with relatively greater legitimacy than did Zimbabwe's.

Since independence, Botswana's leaders have also managed the country's good fortune extremely well. Diamonds were discovered the year after

(Continued)

independence, and the country's rulers deftly negotiated with huge and powerful multinational mining corporations to ensure sufficient government revenue. Moreover, unlike some other countries' leaders, they did not simply stash those profits in Swiss bank accounts but instead worked to provide Botswana's citizens with decent public services. In addition, politics takes place in a fairly open and democratic system, although one party has dominated elections since independence.

In Zimbabwe, on the other hand, one man has ruled since independence—Robert Mugabe. Mugabe was a hero of the black independence movement, yet his country has actually grown poorer since independence. Mugabe likes to blame foreign meddling for his country's poverty, but his unpredictable economic policies and dictatorial unwillingness to share or relinquish power helps explain his country's dire social, political, and economic situation.[13]

Botswana and Zimbabwe gained independence as extremely weak states, but colonialism cannot explain why the former offers fairly effective and legitimate state governance, while the latter represents a case of state failure. Botswana's diamonds give it a natural advantage, but other countries have squandered such good fortune. Civil war got Zimbabwe off on the wrong foot, and differences in post–independence political leadership also help explain why these two similar countries have taken such different paths in terms of state strength. ▶

CRITICAL THINKING QUESTIONS

1. What do you think is more important for explaining Botswana's success—the lack of war, diamonds, or good leadership?
2. Why do you think relatively few African countries have been able to follow Botswana's example?

southern Africa, Botswana exhibits low fragility, while its neighbor Zimbabwe is among the most fragile states in the world. This variation suggests that the natural environment can be important but does not fully determine the strength of late-forming states.

The military, economic, and cultural context in recent decades has predisposed many late-forming states toward weakness—ineffective and illegitimate governance. And in some cases, environmental conditions have made the consolidation of state authority in former colonies even harder. Do these factors doom late-forming states to weakness? At this point let us turn to the consequences of late state formation.

The Consequences of Late State Formation

For many late-forming states, such as Somalia, the timing of independence has had fateful consequences for the state's strength. Both the changed military and economic contexts as well as issues of political identity have weakened many late-forming states. When they gained independence, many inherited colonial institutions that were not originally designed to establish effective governance. Moreover, the population of these new states regarded the former colonial institutions as illegitimate, meaning that the new state rulers were only seen as legitimate because they had led successful independence movements. Such leadership is valuable, but such legitimacy dissipates when citizens discover that rulers fail to provide effective governance. Given the persistence of preexisting forms of political identity, rulers of many new states have found it difficult to establish state legitimacy. Instead, in many cases, they have relied on graft and manipulation of the political rules to stay in power—a process that perpetuates state weakness.

The tendency for newer states to be weaker has important political, social, and economic consequences. In weaker states, the rulers, the institutions of government, and even the form of government, whether democratic or not, lack both authority and legitimacy. No matter who is in charge, citizens are less likely to obey the laws, pay their taxes, or contribute to the resolution of society's many collective action problems. In some new states, the central government is so weak that it must compete with other groups for monopoly of violence—as in contemporary Somalia, for example. State weakness can, thus, result in a proliferation of armed groups outside the control of state security forces, corruption, civil conflict, and trafficking in drugs, weapons, and even humans. State weakness often becomes a vicious circle, with weakness breeding more weakness. An inability to control crime and corruption means tax evasion is high, economic investment is low, and government provision of services minimal. In such a situation, even public-spirited political leaders have few options. In the contemporary world, states that were born weak have the deck stacked against them.

Answering this chapter's main question, "Where do 'states' come from?" reveals that a state's ability to exert sovereignty over territory and people can vary a great deal. States that formed in early historical eras tend to be relatively stronger than states that formed later. The table below summarizes the main reasons why: in many cases, both political interests and the natural environment conspired against the formation of effective and legitimate state institutions. Our comparison of early- and late-forming states, however, raises an important question: how exactly do we measure differences in state strength? The next section describes one such method.

SUMMARY TABLE

Explaining Late State Formation

Factor	Argument
Political Interests	Although ex-colonies faced relatively low military threats from abroad, late-forming states tend to be relatively weak because many were extremely poor at independence and could not draw upon a coherent national identity to generate legitimacy.
Natural Environment	Late-forming states with difficult terrain find constructing legitimate and effective state institutions more expensive. States with flat and open terrain can more easily control their own borders and police their own territory.

MEASURING STATE STRENGTH

2.5 How can we measure state "strength"?

👁 Watch the Video "Somalia's Pirates" at mypoliscilab.com

An important reason that states exist is because they can provide order and foster the conditions for society to flourish. Australia, Japan, Singapore, Chile, and Norway are states that tend to achieve these goals, and they tend to perform well on measures of state strength. Other states, however, fall into chaos and violence. Examples at this end of the spectrum include Somalia, Lebanon, Iraq, Afghanistan, Congo, Pakistan, and Haiti. How can we identify the states most at risk of failure or collapse? Several scholars and international nongovernmental organizations seek to answer these questions by assessing state strength and weakness.

To gain some insight into how they do this, let's consider one such measure, which suggests that strength is a function of a state's capacity to generate order and other collective benefits through (1) the use of power—*effectiveness* and (2) voluntary compliance—*legitimacy*. This approach connects back to Hobbes's emphasis on combining coercion with consent as necessary elements for stable governance. That is, state strength is not simply an ability to carry out certain tasks; it also involves a popular perception of the state as just and fair in the way it carries out those tasks. Effectiveness and legitimacy are both necessary elements of state strength because a state may remain weak if it lacks effectiveness or legitimacy, but it is likely to completely fail only if it has lost both effectiveness and legitimacy.

The State Fragility Index

Political scientists employ a useful tool called the State Fragility Index to measure state effectiveness and legitimacy on four dimensions: security, political, economic, and social. The security dimension breaks down into two scores:

- *Security Effectiveness Score*: assesses the danger of external armed conflict, based on the intensity of international warfare in a state's recent past.
- *Security Legitimacy Score*: measures state repression of its own citizens, which ranges from "none" to "systematic."

The political dimension also breaks down into two measures:

- *Political Effectiveness Score*: a measure that combines considerations of (1) how long the political system has been in existence; (2) how long the current leader has been in office; and (3) the total number of recent attempts to overthrow the leader or the political system.
- *Political Legitimacy Score*: a measure that assesses political factionalism, ethnic group discrimination against more than 5 percent of the population, the salience of ethnicity in politics, the importance of an exclusionary ideology for those who control the government, and the overall fragmentation of the political system.

The economic dimension is based on the following:

- *Economic Effectiveness Score*, which combines (1) the most recent year's measure of the country's per capita income; (2) the average growth rate of per capita income over the past five years; and (3) the average growth rate of per capita income over the past 15 years.

■ *Economic Legitimacy Score*, which measures the share of manufactured goods as a proportion of all goods the country exports, on the theory that a reliance on primary commodities such as oil, unprocessed minerals or agricultural products indicates fewer economic opportunities for individuals and greater individual dependence on the government for survival.

And finally, the social dimension includes the following:

■ *Social Effectiveness Score*, which uses the United Nations' "Human Development Index" (HDI) score. The HDI combines measures of (1) life expectancy, (2) literacy, (3) educational attainment, and (4) GDP per capita.

■ *Social Legitimacy Score*, which isolates a country's infant mortality rate as the most obvious indicator of state failure to provide adequate health care, sanitation, and clean drinking water.

We measure each score on a four-point scale, from 0 to 3, with higher scores representing lack of effectiveness or legitimacy (in "extreme" cases, a country is awarded 4 points). Then, we add all the scores together to arrive at a single State Fragility Index score. Table 2.1 presents the findings for several countries.[14]

TABLE 2.1

Strong and Weak States in 2009

State	Fragility Index	Security Effectiveness	Security Legitimacy	Political Effectiveness	Political Legitimacy	Economic Effectiveness	Economic Legitimacy	Social Effectiveness	Social Legitimacy
UK	0	0	0	0	0	0	0	0	0
USA	2	1	1	0	0	0	0	0	0
Cuba	6	0	1	0	1	2	2	0	0
Russia	8	2	2	1	0	1	2	0	0
Venezuela	10	0	2	2	2	0	3	0	1
Haiti	14	1	2	2	1	4	0	2	2
Iraq	20	3	3	3	3	3	3	1	1
Afghanistan	22	3	3	2	1	4	3	3	3
Somalia	25	3	3	3	3	4	3	3	3

Source: Center for Systemic Peace. "State Fragility Index and Matrix. Time-Series Data, 1995-2009." Severn, MD: CSP. Available at http://www.systemicpeace.org/inscr/inscr.htm, June 23, 2011.

State Fragility in 2009

Some states—particularly those in Western Europe—that formed in earlier historical eras tend to be relatively strong, while others—particularly those in Africa and parts of Asia and the Middle East—tend to be weaker. However, even among former colonies in Africa, for example—some states are stronger than others.

How the Index Works

Keep in mind the distinction between state and government: the measure of state strength does *not* assess the stability or popularity of any particular government administration, president, or prime minister. It measures the likelihood that the state itself is either coherent or vulnerable to collapse in a given year. And although the rankings for any particular country could be debated, the cross-country pattern does reflect what we think is going on in the world, as reflected in the map above. The map's key describes which countries are most at risk of "failure" in the contemporary world.

Measuring state strength serves many purposes in comparative politics, including giving political scientists a way to make an abstract concept more concrete. We will use the concept of state strength repeatedly throughout this text—for example, when discussing civil war and when considering why some states grow rich while others remain poor.

CONCLUSION

States exert sovereignty—supremacy of political authority and a monopoly on the legitimate use of physical force within a given territory. They organize the institutions, interests, and identities of governments, nations, and societies. Where did all these states come from? To answer this chapter's main question, we first considered Thomas Hobbes's suggestion that people agree to bind their own hands and submit to authority because they fear anarchy. Individuals want to live in an orderly society; delegating power to a centralized political authority limits individual choice to some extent but is better for everyone than anarchy.

Hobbes's argument may have philosophical merit, but since no "state of nature" has never really existed, to explain why states exist in the real world we explored how political interests and the natural environment shaped rulers' interests and their ability to consolidate state authority and legitimacy. In early historical eras, European rulers fought bitterly to solidify control over their territories. The winners were those who figured out how to both grow their economies and extract more tax revenue to finance ever-increasing military expenditures. Taxing and preparing for war created complex and centralized government bureaucracies—the machinery of the modern state. A weakening of traditional religious authority in several European countries also paved the way for the rise of modern forms of political organization.

A second explanation for the emergence of early states suggests that the natural environment in particular parts of the world makes it more or less difficult for leaders to consolidate and centralize political control. In particular, environments that can support dense and growing populations are likely to see centralized forms of rule emerge. In contrast, inhospitable environments with rough terrain make consolidation of authority more difficult.

Finally, we discovered that timing matters for answering this chapter's question. Although late-forming states certainly exist as lines on a map, many have been unable to consolidate effective and legitimate sovereignty over their territory. Many new states inherited institutions from former colonial authorities—institutions that were not set up to provide effective and legitimate government, only to extract resources. Many also lacked a coherent national identity at independence, which has made the consolidation of legitimate authority harder. Governance tends to be relatively ineffective and illegitimate in late-forming states.

A universal desire for law and order underlies peoples' desire for effective and legitimate rule, but several factors have contributed to the relative success of state formation, including leaders' responses to military, economic, environmental, and cultural factors, as well as the timing of state formation: states that formed early got a head start, while most states in Africa, Latin America, and Asia that were once colonies have faced steeper challenges for consolidating legitimate and effective political authority. ◤

✓●─Study and Review
the Post-Test &
Chapter Exam
at mypoliscilab.com

KEY TERMS

state   29
sovereignty   29
failed state   29
legitimacy   29
collective action problem   30
state of nature   33

social contract   33
government   35
nation   35
nationalism   37
society   37
feudalism   39

REVIEW QUESTIONS

1. What is Hobbes's problem, and why did he propose the state as the solution?
2. What are the differences between the state, the government, the nation, and society?
3. How did political interests shape early state formation?
4. To what extent did the natural environment shape early state formation?
5. How did political interests shape late state formation?
6. To what extent did the natural environment shape late state formation?
7. Consider the elements of the State Fragility Index. Which element do you think is most important to explain state strength and/or fragility, and why?

SUGGESTED READINGS

Centeno, Miguel A. *Blood and Debt: War and the Nation-State in Latin America*. University Park: Pennsylvania State University Press, 2002. A study of the implications of civil and international warfare in Latin America on state formation.

Fearon, James, and David Laitin. "Neotrusteeship and the Problem of Weak States." *International Security* 28, 4 (2004): 5–43. Considers how the political vulnerability of newer states and the influence of stronger states perpetuate state weakness.

Hui, Victoria. *War and State Formation in Ancient China and Early Modern Europe*. New York: Cambridge University Press, 2005. Explores the case of state formation in China in great depth.

Reno, Will. *Corruption and State Politics in Sierra Leone*. New York: Cambridge University Press, 2008. Considers the relationship between the economic context and politicians' incentives in a late-forming state.

Spruyt, Hendrik. "War, Trade and State Formation." In *The Oxford Handbook of Comparative Politics*, edited by Carles Boix and Susan Stokes, 211–235. Oxford: Oxford University Press, 2007. Explains how the military and economic contexts shaped politicians' interests in state building, particularly in early-forming states.

NOTES

1. Paul Salopek, "Off the Lawless Coast of Somalia, Questions of Who Is Pirating Who," *Chicago Tribune*, October 10, 2008, accessed April 15, 2009, http://www.chicagotribune.com/news/chi-somalia-pirates_salopek1oct10,0,6155016.story.
2. See Max Weber, *Economy and Society*, vol. 1 (Berkeley: University of California Press, 1978), 54.
3. Larry Diamond, *Developing Democracy: Toward Consolidation* (Baltimore: Johns Hopkins University Press, 1999), 222.
4. Jean Cohen and Andrew Arato, *Civil Society and Political Theory* (Cambridge, MA: MIT Press, 1992), 546.
5. See Charles Tilly, "War-Making and State-Making as Organized Crime," in *Bringing the State Back In*, ed. Evans et al. (New York: Cambridge University Press, 1985), 169.
6. Jared Diamond, *Guns, Germs and Steel: The Fate of Human Societies* (New York: W.W. Norton & Co., 1997).
7. See "Growth in United Nations Membership, 1945-Present," accessed December 20, 2009, http://www.un.org/members/growth.shtml.
8. See Jeffrey Herbst, "The Creation and Maintenance of National Boundaries in Africa," *International Organization* 43, 4 (1989): 673–692.

9. See Robert H. Jackson, "Quasi-States, Dual Regimes, and Neoclassical Theory: International Jurisprudence and the Third World," *International Organization* 41, 4 (1987): 519–549.

10. Compiled by Professor Steven Hanke of Johns Hopkins University, accessed April 23, 2010, http://www.cato.org/zimbabwe.

11. Central Intelligence Agency, World Factbook, https://www.cia.gov/library/publications/the-world-factbook/fields/2129.html.

12. See the IMF's World Economic Outlook database, http://www.imf.org/external/pubs/ft/weo/2008/02/weodata/index.aspx.

13. See for example, "Country Profile: Zimbabwe," http://news.bbc.co.uk/2/hi/africa/country_profiles/1064589.stm.

14. Monty Marshall and Benjamin Cole, "Global Report 2009: Conflict, Governance, and State Fragility," Center for Systemic Peace, Center for Global Policy, George Mason University, accessed February 5, 2010, http://www.systemicpeace.org/Global%20Report%202009.pdf.

Democratic Political Regimes

? What is democracy?

In January 2011, tens of thousands of Egyptians took to the streets to protest against their government. Egypt has never experienced democracy—and the president at the time, Hosni Mubarak, had long argued that democracy would cause political chaos. His 30-year dictatorship brought stability, even as neighboring countries such as Sudan and Somalia suffered chronic violence and political disorder. Yet, the stability of his rule came with significant costs for average Egyptians, who had few legal options to express their views about politics—and if they decided to vocalize their opinions, they risked jail, torture, or worse.

When popular protests first erupted, most observers believed Mubarak's regime faced few credible threats. However, within a few weeks, the dictator found himself without a job. Very quickly the question became, "What next?" By late 2011, Egypt faced the thorny task of maintaining political stability and creating a new political system to effectively govern its diverse population. The United States and other countries pushed Egyptian leaders to negotiate—not over whom to install as a new dictator, but over a democratic constitution for the country's future—one that would promote stability but that would also respect individual rights and permit greater political representation.

Egypt's leaders face a quandary fundamental to all democracies: how to let citizens' interests and identities be heard while effectively maintaining law and order. Politicians around the world have approached this challenge in many ways, and not all experiments have succeeded. Some countries' democracies grow wealthy, educate their children, maintain law and order, preserve national security, and let a wide range of societal interests and identity groups participate in the political process. Others succumb to a cacophony of voices and demands that result in deadlock and economic stagnation. When democracy fails to provide good governance, citizens often lose faith—not just in their leaders but also in the form of government—a situation that has in some cases led to a collapse back to dictatorship. The challenge of democracy in Egypt in 2011 is anything but simple.

But *what is democracy?* Democracies embody limited government, which means that the state's power is relatively weak and citizens are given wide latitude in terms of expressing their personal political interests and identities. In contrast, non-democratic governments like Mubarak's Egypt have greater ability to manipulate, restrict, or prohibit citizens from making political, economic, or even social choices. Simultaneously balancing limited government with effective government is a tricky business. Here in the United States, we take democracy for granted. Yet, given the potential coercive power of the state, some consider the existence and maintenance of limited government nothing short of miraculous.

We begin to answer this question by first defining democracy as accountability through institutionalized participation and contestation. We then discuss the institutional requirements necessary to support participation and contestation. Once we've laid the groundwork with this definition, we consider why a tradeoff between limited and effective government is inherent to democracy, and then we compare the ways political institutions around the world can concentrate or disperse political power, seeking to find the best balance between limited and effective government.

☐ Read and Listen to Chapter 3 at mypoliscilab.com

✓ Study and Review the Pre-Test & Flashcards at mypoliscilab.com

democracy ■ a political system in which the rulers are accountable to the ruled.

DEFINING DEMOCRACY

3.1 What differentiates a democratic from a non-democratic form of government?

👁 Watch the **Video**
"Party Politics in Scotland"
at **mypoliscilab.com**

One way to answer the question "What is democracy?" is to return to its origin. The idea of "rule by the people" goes back thousands of years to ancient Greece, but our contemporary definition of democracy is a fairly recent invention that has changed over time. For example, in 1832, only about 5 percent of the adult population could vote in the United Kingdom. Such a proportion sounds elitist, yet today we venerate the UK as one of the world's oldest democracies.

The definition of democracy continues to evolve, and no country perfectly fits the definition. But if this is true, where's the dividing line? How can we tell whether a country is a democracy or not? A country is deemed a democracy if it enacts three principles: accountability, participation, and contestation. Let us consider these principles and their relationship to each other.

Accountability

The first element of the definition is that democracy is a political system in which the rulers are accountable to the ruled. In theory at least, a democratic government serves at the pleasure of the citizens, and not vice versa. Given this, we define accountability as a political mechanism that offers citizens regular and realistic opportunities to remove the rulers from office, through peaceful, legal means. Removing a leader via massive protest, as occurred recently in Egypt—is not a "regular" opportunity, nor did the process follow constitutional guidelines. In a democracy, citizens can elect the government and then—at the next election—they can also remove it. Accountability includes voting incumbent politicians out of office, and it also can include impeaching elected officials or firing bureaucrats who violate the law or who do not perform their jobs well. Defining accountability as the opportunity to remove rulers is fairly narrow; the possibility of accountability in this sense does not guarantee it in a broader sense of "good government" or "responsiveness" to citizens' demands. Still, it does offer the possibility of removing leaders peacefully while maintaining overall political stability. To understand how such outcomes are possible, we need to understand how participation and contestation faciliate accountability.

accountability ■ a political mechanism that offers citizens regular and realistic opportunities to remove the rulers from office through peaceful and constitutional means.

Participation

The first element in the definition of democracy is that the rulers are accountable to the ruled. To this we must add two additional principles: participation and contestation. To guarantee accountability in a democracy, political participation must be institutionalized, suffrage must be universal, and participation must be unforced. By institutionalized, we mean that clear and consistent rules define membership in the electorate—the group of citizens eligible to participate in the election of government leaders—and by universal suffrage, we mean that everyone must have the right to participate in the process that selects and removes government leaders. Acceptance of universal suffrage as a basic requirement for democracy has evolved only gradually. For example, the United States only granted women the right to vote in 1920. Egypt granted women the vote in 1956, and Saudi Arabia did just in 2011.[1]

electorate ■ a group of citizens eligible to participate in the election of government leaders.

universal suffrage ■ wherein all adult citizens have the right to participate in the electoral process that selects and removes government leaders.

Finally, by unforced, we mean that the government cannot require citizens to participate in politics in particular ways against their will, such as voting for or against particular parties or candidates. A country is a democracy only if all adults are treated as equals; no one can have more political rights than others, no one can be legally excluded from participating in politics, and everyone must have equal ability to freely express their political preferences. When political participation is unforced, accountability in a democracy is made possible. Still, without contestation, democracy is not complete.

Contestation

Participation is not the only requirement to generate accountability in democracy. In addition, political contestation for power must also be institutionalized and not manipulated or controlled by the government. This means there must be real competition for power: democracy requires that the number of competitors for power must be greater than one; there must be at least one alternative group of potential rulers willing to replace the incumbents.

However, having more than one group compete for power does not make a country a democracy. Non-democratic governments frequently hold elections, even though the outcomes are foregone conclusions. It is the nature of political contestation that defines democracy: open competition between rivals within established rules is a normal part of politics. In a non-democracy, those who hold power fear contestation and attempt to limit or suppress it. When open contestation for power does occur in a non-democratic system, it is often not organized but chaotic and bloody.

Figure 3.1 shows that without participation and contestation, accountability is impossible—and, thus, a country cannot qualify as a democracy.[2] If we were to place countries on this figure, democracies would fall somewhere in the upper-right quadrant. Countries in the lower-left see neither contestation nor participation. Monarchies such as Saudi Arabia fall here, as would such non-democracies as North Korea, where a single leader or a very small clique dominates politics.

Some countries—such as Egypt prior to 2010—fall on the lower-right. These countries have a veneer of popular participation, because elections are regularly held. However, incumbent leaders limit contestation and make a sham of these elections by impeding opposition parties' ability to campaign and win votes. In 2011, in the span of three weeks, Egypt went from having almost no open contestation to a great deal. The speed and strangeness of seeing massive street protests illustrates the fact that Egypt remained a non-democracy: citizens had no regular and legal means to protest or remove government leaders, so they took to the streets. It remains to be seen whether Egypt can institutionalize political participation and contestation over the long run and truly become a democracy.

As for systems in the upper-left, very few real-world examples exist. A country that experiences intense political contestation but no popular participation is witnessing a battle between political elites for power in which average people have no influence over the outcome. Rebels might defeat the incumbents, removing the rulers from office—but that is not the sort of accountability one sees in a democracy, since citizens played no part. The key point remains: without both participation and contestation, a country is not a democracy.

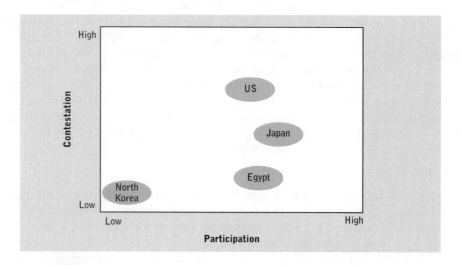

FIGURE 3.1

Defining Democracy via Contestation and Participation

Democracy requires permitting high levels of both political contestation and participation.

"How much" participation and contestation are necessary to make rulers accountable to the ruled? There is no precise answer to that question. Broadly speaking, democracies fall in the upper-right quadrant of Figure 3.1. Considerable variation exists within democracies in terms of the amount of participation and contestation. Some have relatively low degrees of contestation. For example, Japan is a democracy. Yet, even though its elections are free and fair, a single party has held power for all but six years since the country's post–World War II constitution was enacted. Likewise, the United States is a democracy, but political participation—as defined by the proportion of citizens who vote in national elections—is comparatively low. Moreover, unless a presidential candidate is from either the Democratic or Republican party, he or she has little chance of winning. This suggests that contestation is limited.

Democracy is a form of government that offers citizens regular and realistic opportunities to remove rulers from office, through institutionalized participation and contestation. To qualify as a democracy, all adults must be eligible to participate in politics, and the government cannot force citizens to vote in certain ways. Democracy also requires that the number of viable competitors for control of government is greater than one. Non-democratic systems can have either participation or contestation, but they won't combine both—meaning that citizens have no way to hold their government accountable and bring in new leaders. This definition is useful for comparing and contrasting across countries. However, to improve our ability to distinguish democracies from non-democracies, we need to explore the political and legal requirements that help institutionalize and maintain participation and contestation over the long run.

Elements of Democracy

Accountability	A way for citizens to remove rulers from office.
Participation	Clear rules must institutionalize universal suffrage; political choices must be unforced.
Contestation	Real competition for power must exist; there must be more than one group competing for power.

REQUIREMENTS FOR DEMOCRACY

To determine whether a country is a democracy or not, we need to take a closer look at how its political institutions support contestation and participation. It seems relatively simple to judge a country democratic or not based upon whether (1) elections open up the possibility of removing those in power, (2) everyone can freely participate in those elections, and (3) more than one party or candidate contests the elections. Yet these core principles of democracy require further elaboration. Several rules are necessary to support accountability; if such requirements are not met, participation and contestation will be distorted in an anti-democratic fashion, there will be no accountability, and the system will not be a democracy.[3] There are three key requirements that explain how to judge whether a country is a democracy or not: elected government, civil liberties, and fair elections.

3.2 What political rules are necessary for institutionalized participation and contestation?

Explore the Comparative "Constitutions" at mypoliscilab.com

Elected Government

Participation or contestation alone is insufficient to make accountability possible—they must be combined in an electoral process. It may seem obvious that elections should be part of the definition of democracy. Yet a good question is, "How many government officials must be elected for a country to be considered democratic?" In the United States, for example, only about 1 out of 40 "government officials" is elected. In any country, most people who work for the government—from police officers to mail carriers to tax collectors—are not elected. They are appointed or take a test to get their job. Given this, we can say that to qualify as a democracy, all government officials must either be elected by the entire adult population or in one sense or another accountable to an elected official who is in turn accountable to all citizens. Without this sort of accountability, a country cannot be considered a democracy.

Civil Liberties

Holding elections does not automatically qualify a country as democratic. True democracies must also protect certain key individual and group rights. The first is freedom of expression. This is not an absolute freedom—the U.S. Constitution protects freedom of speech, but does not give people license to say whatever they want, regardless of the consequences. These days, one certainly cannot say, "I have a bomb," while traveling on an airplane, even in jest. Democracies all over the world face similar quandaries about the limits of free speech. For our purposes, freedom of expression means that the government cannot prohibit anyone from criticizing the government or impede anyone's attempt to influence others' opinions about the government.

Democracies must also allow citizens freedom of assembly—the right to join and/or form organizations that are independent of state control. Membership in organizations allows people to meet and talk with others who share their opinions, acquire new information, encounter different viewpoints, and also to publicly express their political preferences—either in support of or opposition to the government.

Finally, democracy requires freedom of the press—the government cannot control the information conveyed to members of society. To form their own political opinions, citizens must be able to access competing viewpoints and different sources of information. Freedom of the press, thus, requires that mass media—TV, newspapers, radio, the Internet, etc.—be available in some form that is free from state control. And such media must be able to present information independently of what the government of the day might prefer. When political rules of the game protect individual and group rights, elections take on more meaning.

Fair and Frequent Elections

To qualify as a democracy, a country must combine the requirements of elected government and civil liberties to guarantee "fair and frequent" elections. "Fair" elections mean that the government does not meddle in the election process to favor certain candidates and discriminate against others. As for elections' frequency, a good question is, "How frequent is frequent enough?" The length of a politician's term in office must strike a balance between limited and effective government. On the one hand, a lengthy term is an invitation for abuse of power and for a politician to ignore the public. On the other hand, we want politicians to have enough time to formulate and implement policies that are useful.

It is difficult to know where the "sweet spot" lies in terms of striking this balance; common sense suggests that holding elections every few years qualifies a country as democratic. In the real world, the average term for directly elected executives and legislators is about four years. The upper limit for presidents' terms is six years (Mexico, for example) and for legislators' terms eight years (Brazilian senators). Anything longer than that suggests that the government is moving away from "frequent" elections.

Assessing the "Quality" of Democracy

Democracy requires that citizens and politicians respect rules that guarantee elected government, universal suffrage, civil liberties, and fair and frequent elections. Determining how well countries respect these rules is not always clear-cut. While we can easily call Norway a democracy but not so North Korea, other countries are much harder to classify one way or the other. To help students, scholars, and policymakers make such judgment calls, a non-governmental organization established in 1941 called Freedom House assesses the quality of democracy in every country in the world.

Freedom House "grades" countries based on answers to a series of questions about political rights and civil liberties.[4] The questions range from, "Is the head of government elected through free and fair elections?" to "Is there freedom of assembly, demonstration, and open public discussion?" Analysts at Freedom House do not simply read a country's constitution to make their assessment. Instead, because what's written in the law does not always capture the true distribution of power, they gather evidence from a variety of sources in an effort to capture the essence of real-world politics—the extent to which each country guarantees political equality, enforces civil liberties, and offers the possibility of accountability by respecting the fairness of political participation and contestation. In 2011, 45 percent of the world's countries were classified as "free" democracies, 24 percent were "not free" non-democracies, and 31 percent were "partly free."[5]

As Figure 3.2 suggests, the definition of democracy requires both participation as well as contestation—which in turn require guarantees of elected government, civil liberties, and fair and frequent elections. Although assessing the extent to which countries live up to these standards is often difficult, we know that democracies tend to promote limited government, and protect individuals' and groups' rights to participate in politics. Still, citizens in a democracy do not want only limited government—they also want government to be effective. Simultaneously balancing these two goals can be a tricky business, given the state's overwhelming capacity for coercion. How do democracies successfully balance limited and effective government? If power grows too centralized, democracy may become endangered. Yet if government grows too weak, it may be unable to get anything done. In the next section we explore this dilemma in more depth, so that we can then turn to the different ways that democracies around the world attempt to strike a balance between limited and effective government.

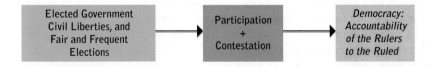

FIGURE 3.2

The Core Elements of Democracy

A set of political institutions are necessary to support participation and contestation, which are required for democracy.

MADISON'S DILEMMA: BALANCING LIMITED AND EFFECTIVE GOVERNMENT

3.3 How do democracies balance the tension between limited and effective government?

"What is democracy?" In addition to government institutions that protect the principles of accountability, participation, and contestation, every democracy faces the challenge of balancing limited and effective government. In theory, concentrating power enhances a government's ability to get things done, while splitting it makes coordinating and implementing policies more difficult. Non-democratic states structure authority to enforce the government's version of law and order—a key aspect of effective government—at the expense of limits on government power. Yet democracies are different. Citizens in democratic states want government to get things done, while also ensuring that liberty does not give way to tyranny.

constitution ■ a set of key laws and principles that structure the extent and distribution of government authority and individual rights, by setting up the rules of the political game.

👁—|**Watch** the **Video** **"Reforming the House of Lords"** at **mypoliscilab.com**

A constitution is a set of key laws and principles that structure the extent and distribution of government authority and individual rights by setting up the rules of the political game.[6] For example, the U.S. government might allow the Federal Bureau of Investigation (FBI) to freely wiretap and listen in on our private conversations to protect the country against terrorism, but what individual freedoms would be lost when the government has such power? Such tradeoffs are inherent in democracies, and we call this tension "Madison's Dilemma." James Madison was the main author of the U.S. Constitution and the fourth U.S. president. In 1787, he also co-authored a series of widely distributed pamphlets known as the *Federalist Papers*, which articulated the difficulties facing a young country: "If men were angels, no government would be necessary. . . . In framing a government . . . the great difficulty lies in this: you must first enable the government to control the governed; and in the next place oblige it to control itself."

Why is it so hard to write a constitution that fosters both effective and limited government? Consider the quote: "*If* men were angels, no government would be necessary." Madison assumed that none of us—and this holds especially for politicians—are angels. We hope that politicians will be competent, honest, and inspiring leaders, but they often fall far short of this ideal. Madison assumed that politicians are self-interested and ambitious, and he drafted the U.S. Constitution precisely to avoid a repeat of the situation that had caused the American Revolution: a belief that the British government oppressed the American colonies. He argued that democratic constitutions must minimize the potential for politicians' self-interested hunger for power to result in ineffective, corrupt, or even tyrannical government. Certain institutional structures, he argued, could both limit politicians' power and maintain government stability and effectiveness.

To find a balance between limited and effective government, Madison famously advocated establishing political institutions that "check and balance" politicians' ambitions against each other, so that no one person or group could concentrate enough power to overwhelm individual freedoms. This idea is fundamental to the U.S. Constitution, and as a result, political institutions in the United States tend to fragment, decentralize, and consequently weaken the central government's power. Other democracies address the tension of limited yet effective government in different ways.

Four key constitutional rules work to concentrate or disperse political power: (1) unitarism versus federalism, (2) separation or fusion of powers, (3) judicial review versus parliamentary supremacy, and (4) a majoritarian or proportional electoral system. These principles of constitutional design help us understand the different ways democracies address Madison's Dilemma.

UNITARY VERSUS FEDERAL CONSTITUTIONS

Democracy requires rules that support participation and contestation. Yet it also demands that citizens and politicians make a decision about Madison's Dilemma: what's the best way to balance limited and effective government, by concentrating power or dispersing it? The first key decision focuses on whether the constitution should be unitary or federal.

A unitary state is one in which the constitution grants the central government exclusive and final authority over policymaking across the entire national territory. Unitary constitutions tightly circumscribe local, state, or regional governments' responsibilities and authority by granting the central government veto power over subnational governments' decisions. Under unitary constitutions, local governments have no autonomous authority to make policy. Unitary constitutions, thus, clearly concentrate power at the national level— meaning that they concentrate power in the hands of whatever politician or party controls the national government. France, Chile, Japan, Israel, and the UK are examples of democracies with unitary constitutions.

In contrast, in a federal state, the constitution grants two or more governments overlapping political authority over the same group of people and same piece of territory—for example, a state or provincial government as well as the national government. To qualify as a federal state, the constitution must grant governments at the local, state, or provincial level exclusive control over at least one policy area. This could include education or healthcare policy, or the authority to impose certain forms of taxes, for example. In federal systems, the central government cannot veto policy decisions that fall under subnational governments' control. Given this, federal constitutions tend to disperse and fragment political power relative to unitary constitutions.

The map below shows all 26 federal systems in the world as of 2010. Although most democracies are unitary, many of the world's most populous democracies are federal, including the United States, India, Brazil, Mexico, and Germany. Thus, although only about 40 percent of the world lives in a federation, more than half of all people in the world who live in a democracy live in a federation.

In both theory and practice, unitary constitutions concentrate political power in the hands of politicians who control the central government. However, the degree to which federal countries grant autonomous powers to subnational governments varies considerably. For example, the United States is perhaps the most politically decentralized federation in the world. State governments in the United States have considerable taxing and policymaking powers. Moreover, the Tenth Amendment to the U.S. Constitution says, "The powers not delegated to the [national govern-

3.4 How do unitary and federal constitutions address Madison's Dilemma?

unitarism ■ the constitution grants the central government exclusive and final authority over policymaking across the entire national territory.

federalism ■ the constitution grants two or more governments overlapping political authority over the same group of people and same piece of territory.

✷ Explore the Comparative "Federal and Unitary Systems" at mypoliscilab.com ment of the] United States by the Constitution, nor prohibited by it to the States, are reserved to the States respectively, or to the people." Most federations do not give subnational governments such political autonomy. For example, although Brazil's constitution is federal, its states have few autonomous powers.

Why are some countries federal, while others are unitary? As you can see from the map, many federal countries are quite large. By maintaining a government presence in outlying areas, federalism can be a useful administrative tool to maintain political order—effective government—across wide swaths of territory. Yet the map also shows that several smaller democracies are federal. This suggests that countries do not adopt federalism primarily to establish effective government. Instead, they adopt federalism to disperse power and limit the central government's authority—that is, to foster limited government.

Reasons to empower subnational governments include citizens' preferences for limited government (as in the United States), or a concern over protecting the rights of ethnic, linguistic, or religious minority identity groups that live predominantly in certain regions, states, or provinces. For example, Canada's federal constitution provides the French-speaking province of Quebec with some measure of autonomy from the central government, which is dominated by politicians from the English-speaking provinces. Federalism also works to limit political tension in India, an ethnically, linguistically, and religiously diverse country. Under a unitary constitution, minority groups in India, Canada, or elsewhere might fear loss of their group's autonomy to set education policies or worship as they please, for example.

In contrast, by concentrating power in the hands of the national government, unitarism tends to promote effective government. Under what political conditions

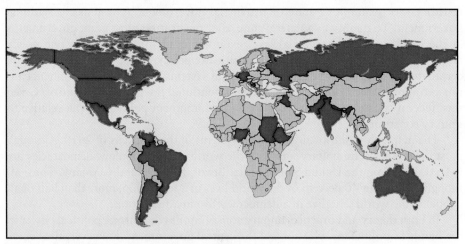

Unitary and Federal Systems around the World as of 2010

Only 26 countries are federal; the rest are unitary. However, this map shows that many federal systems—such as the United States, Canada, Mexico, Brazil, Russia, Germany, and India—are among the world's largest and/or most populous countries.

is a unitary constitution therefore most appropriate? Scholars suggest that unitarism works best in relatively homogenous societies—that is, countries that do not have problematic political divisions between ethnic, religious, or linguistic identity groups that might demand national self-determination if they believed the majority were trampling their rights. In a homogenous society, a unitary constitution may help promote effective government without sacrificing much in terms of limiting government.

In theory, then, federalism assumes that by giving minority groups some voice at the local level, they will be more willing to negotiate on other issues at the national level. A federal constitution can, if designed well, promote political stability in a country that has multiple competing ethnic, religious, or other political identity groups—a country that might otherwise collapse into civil war or split into several smaller, weaker countries. There are several other important ways democratic constitutions address Madison's Dilemma; let us now turn to the question of the relationship between the executive and legislative branches of government.

EXECUTIVE–LEGISLATIVE RELATIONS

In both unitary and federal democracies, the relationship between the executive and legislative branches of government shapes the distribution of power. Nearly every democratic constitution around the world organizes these branches in one of three ways: presidential, parliamentary, or semi-presidential hybrid. There are two ways to distinguish these three systems—(1) by considering whether they exhibit what we call "separation of origin" and "separation of survival," and (2) by discussing the degree to which each system concentrates or disperses political power.

Presidentialism

In a presidential system such as that in the United States, the executive and legislative branches enjoy both separation of origin and survival. Separation of origin means that the voters directly elect the members of the legislature *and* cast a separate ballot directly electing the chief executive, the president. The two branches of government—executive and legislative—thus "originate" through separate electoral processes. The president then appoints a cabinet, and together the president and his or her cabinet secretaries (sometimes called ministers) run the departments of the government.

Separation of survival means that members of both the executive and legislative branches serve for fixed terms of office. Both branches "survive" until the end of the term because neither the executive nor the legislative branch can "fire" the other before the next scheduled election, except in constitutionally extraordinary circumstances that might result in a president's impeachment. These characteristics define a presidential democracy. Let us now see what

> **3.5** How does the relationship between executive and legislative branches of government address Madison's Dilemma?

> ✷ Explore the Comparative "Legislatures" at mypoliscilab.com

presidential system
■ a constitutional format in which the executive and legislative branches enjoy both separation of origin and survival.

separation of origin
■ voters directly elect the members of the legislature and also cast a separate ballot directly electing the chief executive, the president.

**separation
of survival** ■
members of both the
executive and legisla-
tive branches serve for
fixed terms of office.

**parliamentary
system** ■ a constitu-
tional format in which
the executive and leg-
islative branches have
neither separation of
origin nor separation
of survival.

prime minister ■ the
chief executive in a
parliamentary system.

no-confidence vote
■ a parliamentary
vote which, if suc-
cessful, terminates
the prime minister's
appointment.

**semi-presidential
hybrid** ■ a consti-
tutional format in
which the president
and parliament enjoy
separation of origin,
but only the president
enjoys separation of
survival.

happens when we take a different approach to separation of origin and survival and explore parliamentarism.

Parliamentarism

In a parliamentary system such as that in the UK, we see neither separation of origin nor separation of survival. Voters directly elect members of the legislature, called the parliament. Those legislators then elect the chief executive, known as a prime minister (PM). In turn, the PM appoints a cabinet, and together the PM and the cabinet run the executive-branch departments, sometimes called ministries. There is no separation of origin because one branch of government (the executive) originates from within the other (the legislature). In contrast to presidential systems, in parliamentary systems citizens have only an indirect voice in selecting the executive.

Parliamentarism also differs from presidentialism in that there is no separation of survival, because neither the executive nor the legislative "branches" enjoy a fixed term. Under certain conditions, prime ministers can call early legislative elections, thereby threatening the jobs of all members of parliament. Yet the prime minister also serves at the pleasure of the parliamentary majority: if he or she loses majority support, a no-confidence vote can be called, which, if successful, terminates the prime minister's appointment. In such cases, parliament must choose a new PM and cabinet or call early elections to let the voters decide who should run the next government. Thus, in contrast to a presidential system, under parliamentarism, the two branches of government (the PM and the parliament) depend on each other for survival in office until the next scheduled election. Let's now turn to the third major way to structure the relationship between the executive and legislative branches of government: the semi-presidential hybrid format.

Hybrid Systems

Presidentialism embodies separation of origin and survival, while parliamentary systems have neither. As the name implies, the third constitutional format—the semi-presidential hybrid such as that found in France—combines features of both presidentialism and parliamentarism. First, like presidentialism, in hybrid systems the president and parliament enjoy separation of origin: voters directly elect both the president and the members of the legislature. Second, unlike in presidential systems, parliament in hybrid systems elects a prime minister, whom the president typically must also approve. The PM heads the cabinet, which runs the executive-branch ministries. Thus, in a hybrid system, executive power is shared between the president and the prime minister.[7] Semi-presidential hybrid constitutions often go into considerable detail about how authority and responsibilities will be divided. In some countries, presidents have very little authority beyond nominating the PM. In other countries, presidents control foreign affairs or can issue decrees with the force of law, all of which has the effect of reducing the PM's influence.

Third, as in presidential systems, in semi-presidential hybrid systems the president sits for a fixed term, enjoying separation of survival as well as separation of origin. However, as in a parliamentary system, in hybrid systems neither the legislature nor the PM and his or her cabinet sit for a fixed term. As in parliamentarism, the PM in hybrid systems is accountable to the parliamentary majority; that majority can call a no-confidence vote and replace the PM if necessary. Yet given the dual executive—an executive branch of government characterized by a division of authority and responsibility between a president and a prime minister—presidents also have the power to dismiss the PM, and in some cases presidents can even call early elections, thereby putting the jobs of all the members of parliament at risk as well.

dual executive ■ in hybrid democratic regimes, an executive branch of government characterized by a division of authority and responsibility between a president and a prime minister.

Differences in the separation of origin and survival define the basic distinctions between parliamentary, presidential, and hybrid systems. The world's democracies are fairly evenly divided between these three ways of organizing executive–legislative relations, as Table 3.1 illustrates. Parliamentarism tends to dominate in Western Europe; presidentialism dominates in Latin America, while hybrid systems dominate in Eastern Europe and in Africa.

▶ **TABLE 3.1**

Presidential, Parliamentary, and Semi-Presidential Democracies

Region	Parliamentary	Presidential	Semi-Presidential	Other Hybrid
European Union/Western Europe and Mediterranean	Belgium, Czech Republic, Denmark, Estonia, Finland,* Germany, Greece, Hungary, Ireland,* Israel, Italy, Latvia, Netherlands, Norway, Slovenia,* Spain, Sweden, Turkey, United Kingdom	Cyprus	Austria, France, Lithuania, Poland, Portugal, Slovakia	Switzerland

(Continued)

TABLE 3.1 (CONTINUED)

Region	Parliamentary	Presidential	Semi-Presidential	Other Hybrid
Post-Communist (but not EU)	Albania, Moldova		Armenia, Belarus, Bosnia-Herzegovina,** Bulgaria, Croatia, Georgia, Macedonia, Mongolia, Romania, Russia, Serbia and Montenegro,*** Ukraine	
Americas	Canada, Jamaica, Trinidad and Tobago	Argentina, Brazil, Chile, Colombia, Costa Rica, Dominican Republic, Ecuador, El Salvador, Guatemala, Honduras, Mexico, Nicaragua, Panama, Paraguay, United States, Uruguay, Venezuela	Peru	Bolivia, Guyana
East and South Asia/ Pacific	Australia, Bangladesh, Fiji, India, Japan, Malaysia, Nepal, New Zealand,	Indonesia, Philippines, South Korea	Sri Lanka, Taiwan	

(*Continued*)

Region	Parliamentary	Presidential	Semi-Presidential	Other Hybrid
	Papua New Guinea, Thailand	Indonesia, Philippines, South Korea	Sri Lanka, Taiwan	
Africa	Botswana, Lesotho, Mauritius, South Africa	Benin, Ghana, Malawi, Nigeria	Burkina Faso, Madagascar, Mali, Mozambique, Namibia, Niger, Senegal	

TABLE 3.1 (CONTINUED)

Notes: Includes countries of at least 500,000 population with Freedom House political rights score of 4 or better, averaged throughout the period 1990-1991 to 2004, or for each year since 2000. Belarus and Bosnia-Herzegovina do not meet these conditions, but are included so as to cover all Europe. Malaysia is also included for having consistently held semi-competitive elections.

*Indicates presence of elected president lacking any significant constitutional powers (government formation, dissolution, or veto).

**Collegial (three-person) presidency.

***Each autonomous republic retains an elected presidency, although the federal presidency is no longer elected.

Source: Matthew Shugart, 2006. "Comparative Executive-Legislative Relations." In R. A. W. Rhodes, Bert Rockman, and Sarah Binder. *Oxford Handbook of Political Institutions*. (Oxford, Oxford University Press, 2008): 351.

Addressing Madison's Dilemma

Differences in terms of separation of origin and survival define the distinction between presidentialism, parliamentarism, and semi-presidential hybrid constitutional formats. How do these distinctions affect the concentration or dispersion of political power? In all democracies, voters theoretically hold power over government officials; they can reward politicians with reelection when times are good, or kick them out of office when times are bad. Of course, in reality, voters' influence is limited. In between elections, power lies firmly within government institutions. The question, therefore, turns on the degree to which constitutions permit concentration or dispersion of power within these institutions. As we shall see, the extent to which power is concentrated in reality depends on two factors: (1) the formal constitutional rules we described above, and (2) the relationship between the executive—whether a president or a prime minister—and the political parties in the legislature. Let's examine the way these two factors interact to concentrate or disperse power.

Power under Presidentialism   In a presidential system, voters delegate control over government to two separate sets of politicians: a president, who controls the day-to-day implementation of policy, and a majority in the legislature, which may or may not come from the president's party. Thus, on the one hand, presidential systems concentrate tremendous power in the hands of an autonomous president. Most important, because of the separation of survival, a legislative majority cannot "fire" a president, no matter how badly he or she performs. In addition, presidents control the cabinet and the executive-branch bureaucracy, even if they don't control the legislature.

On the other hand, presidential systems counterbalance the president's autonomous power by separating the executive and legislative branches. All else being equal, constitutions with separation of origin and survival disperse power compared to parliamentary systems. Separation of origin means that presidents and legislative majorities possess independent bases of authority and legitimacy—but this also means that they may not always see eye to eye. And because of the separation of survival, both the president and the legislature can survive in office without the assent of the other. Given this institutional arrangement, when the president and the legislative majority disagree about policy proposals, the result might be government deadlock—that is, ineffective government. To get anything done, the president and the legislative majority must negotiate across constitutionally separate branches, not merely within the legislature, as in a parliamentary system.

Smooth negotiations—and, thus, effective government—across branches tend to follow when the president and his or her party not only control a legislative majority, but when they agree on policy proposals. Presidents have a legislative majority about 60 percent of the time under presidentialism. The other 40 percent of the time, the separation of executive and legislative branches under presidentialism tends to disperse political power because the executive faces a legislature controlled by a party or coalition of parties other than his or her own, a situation known as divided government.[8] Such a situation arose, for example, after the 2010 mid-term elections in the United States, when the Republicans took over control of the House of Representatives in the legislative branch, while Democratic president Barack Obama remained in control of the executive branch.

divided government
■ occurs in presidential systems when the president comes from one party but a different party controls the legislative branch.

Even though presidents concentrate considerable authority, presidential constitutions force the executive and legislature to negotiate across branches to accomplish anything, thereby embodying the limited-government principle of "checks and balances." The checks and balances created by the separation of survival often force presidents to negotiate with their own parties and make life even more difficult for presidents who do not control a legislative majority.

Power under Parliamentarism   In contrast to presidentialism, parliamentary systems have no "checks and balances." Instead, they give members of parliament the authority to form the executive branch of government. This means that the majority that controls parliament concentrates political power in its hands. That majority both nominates and controls the fate of the prime minister and the cabinet. PMs lack the separation of origin and survival that presidents enjoy, but as long as the PM leads a solid parliamentary majority, in day-to-day practice they have considerable power over their cabinet ministers as well as over the rank-and-file in their party. All else being equal, when only one party controls a legislative majority, parliamentary systems concentrate power more than presidential systems, embodying the principle of effective government.

Although parliamentary constitutions afford no formal separation of executive and legislative powers, they can and often do disperse power *within* the legislature. This occurs when no single party holds a legislative majority. In this situation, parties must form a coalition government, a situation in which multiple parties formally agree to divvy up positions in the cabinet and nominate a prime minister, who usually comes from the largest party. Coalitions are frequent worldwide, occurring about 50 percent of the time under parliamentarism.[9] For example, following the May 2010 elections, Britain's Conservative Party won the most seats—but did not win a parliamentary majority. As a result, the new Conservative PM, David Cameron, had to form a coalition with the third-place party, the Liberal Democrats, in order to obtain a majority of seats in parliament.

Just like when a president faces an opposition-controlled legislature, when we see a coalition under parliamentarism, the PM must negotiate with other parties to get anything done. Because negotiations can be difficult, coalitions sometimes col-

Liberal Democratic leader Nick Clegg engages Conservative Party leader David Cameron, while Labour leader Gordon Brown awaits his turn to respond in a televised debate just prior to the UK's 2010 election. The election results gave Cameron's party the largest share of seats in parliament—but to obtain a governing majority, the Conservatives had to form a coalition government with the Liberal Democrats.

lapse, in which case a new government must be formed with different parties—and often with a different prime minister. Sometimes, coalition collapse leads to new elections, forcing politicians to face the voters. In short, as in presidential systems, whether the chief executive's party controls a majority on its own or whether other parties are large enough to force the chief executive to negotiate can determine the real degree of concentration or dispersion of power in the political system, independently of the formal constitutional format.

Power under Semi-Presidential Hybrids   Parliamentary systems tend to concentrate power relatively more than do presidential systems, though the structure of the political party system has the potential for dispersing authority. In theory, semi-presidential hybrid constitutions occupy a middle ground. As in parliamentary systems, in hybrid systems a parliamentary majority elects the prime minister, and a parliamentary majority can remove the PM. Yet as in presidential systems, the directly elected president also plays a powerful role. The dual executive works to disperse executive power, because both the president and the PM must work together to implement policy.

In practice, however, two factors tend to concentrate power in most hybrid systems. First, many constitutions give presidents special unilateral powers. In a few hybrid systems, presidents are mere figureheads, such as those in Austria and Ireland; such countries function essentially as parliamentary systems. Yet many other hybrid regimes give presidents substantially more power than the PM. For example, in Taiwan, the president can name and dismiss the PM and/or the cabinet, enact certain laws without parliamentary assent, and even dissolve parliament and call new elections. When presidents possess this kind of authority, political power is more concentrated than under a parliamentary constitution.[10]

Second, as in both presidential and parliamentary systems, the relative concentration or dispersion of political power depends on the size of the president's party relative to other parties. In hybrid systems, presidents tend to dominate their own party informally, independently of the formal authority they derive from the constitution. Indeed, if the president and PM come from the same party, the PM is usually subordinate to the president. For example, in France, the constitution specifically gives the president the power to nominate the prime minister. However, it is vague about whether the president can dismiss the PM. In practice, French presidents frequently dismiss PMs, because the president is regarded as the party's leader and the PM is regarded as second-in-command. When French president Nicholas Sarkozy won election in 2007, he immediately replaced Dominique de Villepin as PM, even though Villepin and Sarkozy came from the same party. Sarkozy then nominated another member of his party, François Fillon to be "his" representative in parliament. This pattern occurs in most hybrid systems.[11]

The combination of formal and informal authority means that when the president's party (or coalition of parties) forms a parliamentary majority, the president rather than the PM becomes the linchpin of the entire political system. In turn, this implies that hybrid constitutions tend to disperse political power and embody limited government only when the president and the PM come from opposing parties, a situation which occurs only when the president and the parliamentary majority come from opposing parties, much like cases of "divided government" in presidential systems. In France, for example, such a situation occurred most recently between 1997 and 2002. At that time, Jacques Chirac of the conservative Rally for the Republic party was president, while Lionel Jospin of the leftist Socialist Party was prime minister. Episodes like this are relatively rare in hybrid systems, occurring only about 15 percent of the time.[12]

In sum, the relative concentration or dispersion of power in hybrid systems depends on the extent of unilateral powers the constitution gives to the president, and on whether the president's party controls a parliamentary majority. When the president's party dominates the legislature, hybrid constitutions tend to concentrate power even more so than in either presidential or parliamentary systems, and enhance the capacity for effective government. Only when the president and the prime minister come from opposing parties do we have a balance between branches and, thus, more of an emphasis on limited government, because both the president and the PM must share power.

Differences in the separation of origin and survival define the basic distinctions between parliamentary, presidential, and hybrid systems, and offer basic guidelines for understanding the degree of concentration or dispersion of power within each system. The table below sums up these differences. Presidential systems have separation of origin and survival of both branches of government. Parliamentary systems have neither separation of origin nor survival, because the executive emerges from within the legislative branch. And semi-presidential hybrids have separation of origin for both branches, but the PM remains accountable to the parliamentary majority, meaning that only the president enjoys separation of survival. The fine print of democratic constitutions around the world depart from these guidelines in various ways, but these two principles provide the foundation for understanding a crucial power relationship within each system.

► SUMMARY TABLE

Democratic Constitutional Formats

Type of Government	Separate Origin of Both Branches	Separate Survival of Both Branches	Concentration of Power in Theory
Presidentialism	Yes	Yes	Low
Hybrid	Yes	No	Medium
Parliamentarism	No	No	High

Executive–legislative relations are organized in three basic ways under democratic constitutions. Yet there is one remaining branch of any government—the judiciary—that influences the give-and-take between limited and effective government.

JUDICIAL REVIEW VERSUS PARLIAMENTARY SUPREMACY

3.6 How does judicial review versus parliamentary supremacy over the judiciary address Madison's Dilemma?

judicial review ■ the ability of a country's high court to invalidate laws the legislature has enacted by declaring them unconstitutional.

parliamentary supremacy ■ a principle according to which judges' decisions remain subordinate to decisions of the legislative majority.

✷–[Explore the Comparative "Judiciaries" at mypoliscilab.com

In addition to the question of federalism or unitarism and the issue of the way to organize relations between the executive and legislative branches of government, democratic constitutions can concentrate or disperse power through decisions about how to the structure the legal system. Judicial review is the ability of a country's high court to invalidate laws the legislature and/or executive have enacted by declaring them unconstitutional. This approach contrasts with the principle of parliamentary supremacy, in which judges' decisions remain subordinate to decisions of the legislative majority.

Countries that enact the principle of judicial review give courts power to invalidate laws in one of two ways: either through the country's regular court system—as with the U.S. Supreme Court, for example—or through a specially designated constitutional court. This latter type of court is separate from the rest of the court system and only adjudicates the constitutionality of legislation—the court has no jurisdiction over civil or criminal cases. As of the mid-2000s, the constitutions of 71 percent of the world's democracies include provisions for judicial review of legislation.[13] Democracies that do not allow for judicial review include Denmark, the Netherlands, Switzerland, and the UK.

Judicial review tends to disperse political power. Recall that Madison feared majority tyranny—that once elected, a majority party might pass laws in its own interest, endangering limited government. Judicial review tempers the power of majorities, protecting individuals, minority groups, and subnational governments in federal systems against laws that violate their constitutional rights. Judicial review thus supports limited government, because it creates an independent "brake" on majority control. Many suggest that judicial review is key to the very definition of democracy: without it, so the argument goes, elections provide insufficient insurance against the whims of a temporarily popular majority.

Arguments against judicial review exist. For one, giving judges independent authority potentially sacrifices effective government on the altar of limited government. During a serious national crisis, for example, perhaps an elected government should be allowed to try something—*anything*—without worrying whether a Supreme Court will overturn its proposals. Others object that giving unelected and unaccountable judges the power to invalidate legislation actually violates the definition of democracy as a political system in which the rulers are accountable to the ruled. Opponents of judicial review argue that democracy requires that elected officials interpret the constitution, not unelected judges. They also suggest that it is naïve to assume that unelected judges will be politically impartial. After all, elected politicians from one political party or another typically appoint those judges in the first place—and politicians tend to nominate judges who share their political interests. Because voters neither hire nor fire judges, judicial review insulates a set of political actors from both voters and elected officials.

Judicial review in the United States goes back to 1803, in the case of *Marbury v. Madison* (yes, that James Madison). At that time, the U.S. Supreme Court established that the judicial branch had the authority to undertake judicial review. However, until recent decades, few other countries employed this constitutional principle. In Europe, most democracies emerged with the tradition of parliamentary supremacy, which concentrates power in the hands of the parliamentary majority and gives elected politicians an advantage over unelected judges. This may sound democratic, but European countries began to embrace judicial review after the rise of fascist dictatorships in Nazi Germany, Spain, and Italy made it clear that parliamentary majorities could not be trusted to uphold limited government. In fact, under pressure from fascist movements like Hitler's Nazi party, parliaments sometimes eagerly passed legislation that eliminated existing constitutional liberties.

The horrible consequences of fascism prompted politicians and activists in Europe and elsewhere to seek stronger safeguards against future collapses of democracy. To escape the longstanding tradition of judicial subordination to parliament, they institutionalized the principle of judicial review. And as more and more countries adopted democracy in the last quarter of the twentieth century, many adopted judicial review for similar reasons—to promote limited government, and prevent the recurrence of dictatorship. These countries' new democratic leaders sought to enshrine checks and balances and ensure that courts could protect individual human rights.

Judicial review is now seen around the world as a key factor for defending the principles of individual and minority group rights, because it tends to disperse political power. In contrast, the principle of parliamentary supremacy maintains judicial power relatively concentrated in the hands of the legislative majority. Let's now consider the final important way that democratic constitutions can concentrate or disperse political power—through the electoral process.

Marbury v. Madison
■ A U.S. Supreme Court case, which established that the judicial branch had the authority to undertake judicial review of laws passed by Congress and signed by the president.

MAJORITARIAN VERSUS PROPORTIONAL ELECTORAL SYSTEMS

The last important way democratic institutions address the tension between limited and effective government is through the electoral process. The **electoral system** is the political rules that translate citizens' votes into legislative seats and/or control of a directly elected executive. Let us focus on the way in which those rules tend to (1) manufacture majority control of the legislature, giving one party control; or (2) promote proportional representation in the legislature, thereby giving ethnic, religious, or other political minorities some power.

Electoral systems that tend to give one party control over representative institutions concentrate power and emphasize the benefits of effective government. In theory, such institutions should not completely sacrifice limited government because voters can always hold that party accountable at the next election. Still, in contrast, electoral systems that give minorities some representation address Madison's

3.7 How do different electoral systems address Madison's Dilemma?

electoral system ■ the political rules that translate citizens' votes into legislative seats and/or control of a directly elected executive.

> **TABLE 3.2**
>
> ### UK 2005 Parliamentary Election Results
>
> | Party | Percent of Votes | Percent of Seats |
> |---|---|---|
> | Labour | 35.2 | 55.1 |
> | Conservative | 32.3 | 30.5 |
> | Liberal Democrats | 22.0 | 9.6 |
> | Others | 3.8 | 0.9 |
>
> Source: BBC News, "Blair Wins Historic 3rd Term—Majority of 66." Accessed July 7, 2011, http://news
> .bbc.co.uk/2/hi/uk_news/politics/vote_2005/constituencies/default.stm.

Dilemma by dispersing political power, hoping to enhance limited government without completely sacrificing effective government. Let us illustrate the different extent to which four electoral systems generate majority control or give political minorities some representation: plurality rule, majority rule, proportional representation, and mixed electoral rules.

Plurality Rule

plurality rule ■ the candidate who receives the largest share of the votes in the district wins, even if that share is less than a majority of 50 percent +1 of the votes.

Under plurality rule, the candidate who receives the largest share of the votes in the electoral district wins the seat, even if that share is less than a majority of 50 percent +1 of the votes. This system is used for elections to the U.S. House of Representatives and in legislative elections in the United Kingdom, for example. Because only one seat is at stake in each electoral district in such elections, plurality rule tends to generate distortions between the percentage of votes received and the percentage of seats received: the best-performing party at a given election tends to do "better" than its vote percentage might suggest, while smaller parties are penalized and do "worse" than their vote percentage might suggest. Given this, plurality rule tends to manufacture majority control of the legislature, even if the best-performing party does not win an actual majority of all the votes. Table 3.2 illustrates this dynamic, with results from the 2005 parliamentary election in the UK.

This election illustrates how plurality rule tends to manufacture majority control of the legislature out of less than a majority of all the votes. Labour benefited to such a degree because at this election voters preferred it to the other party that was competitive across almost the entire country, the Conservatives. In contrast, the Liberal Democrats and other small parties managed to win a plurality of votes in relatively few of the UK's 646 electoral districts, and, thus, were heavily penalized and won relatively few seats. In general, the plurality system tends to discriminate against smaller parties. However, as this chapter's feature box indicates, when parties are strong in particular regions, plurality rule may not discriminate against them.

HYPOTHESIS TESTING | Plurality Rule Discriminates against Small Parties: Comparing the UK and India

The UK and India are culturally, religiously, economically, and socially very distinct societies: predominantly Protestant versus predominantly Hindu; rich versus poor; Europe versus Asia. Yet, India inherited many of its institutions from the UK when it became independent in 1947, and to this day, electoral systems in both countries remain the same: plurality rule. Plurality rule tends to generate majoritarian representational outcomes that enhance effective government, while proportional systems enhance limited government by empowering diverse interest groups in society. But to what extent does a plurality rule electoral system *always* generate a majoritarian outcome?

GATHER EVIDENCE

Like the United States, British election results typically support the idea that plurality rule favors larger parties and discriminates against

smaller parties. Two parties—Labour and the Conservatives—have dominated elections and traded off control of government for nearly a century.

In the 2010 election, it seemed that the Labour and Conservative parties would dominate once more, but because the Conservatives won only 47 percent of the seats, for the first time since 1974—and for only the second time since 1929—plurality rule did not "manufacture" a parliamentary majority. The Conservatives fell 19 seats short, and had to form a coalition government with the third-place Liberal Democrats. Although the election failed to generate a clear majority, it came close—working as predicted to favor some and discriminate against other parties.

A similar dynamic initially characterized Indian elections. Confirming the expectation that plurality rule is associated with majoritarian outcomes, in

TABLE 3.3   UK Election Results, 2010

Party	Percent of Votes	Percent of Seats
Conservative	36.1	47.1
Labour	29.0	39.7
Liberal Democrats	23.0	8.8
UK Independence Party	3.1	0.0
British National Party	1.9	0.0
Democratic Unionist	0.6	1.2
Scottish Nationalist	1.7	0.8
Sinn Féin	0.6	0.8
Plaid Cymru	0.6	0.5
Social Democratic and Labour	0.4	0.5
Others	5.0	0.6
Total	100.0	100.0

Source: "Election 2010, National Results." BBC Mobile, accessed July 7, 2011, http://news.bbc.co.uk/2/shared/election2010/results.

(*Continued*)

Supporters await the start of a political rally for the Bahujan Samaj Party in April 2009. The BSP is a regionally strong party, gaining nearly all of its votes among poor people in India's most populous state, Uttar Pradesh.

the first eight parliamentary elections following its independence from the UK in 1947, a single party dominated the majority of seats. However, starting with the 1989 election, no party has managed that feat again—every government since that year has required a coalition between multiple parties. Moreover, India's party system now exhibits far greater fragmentation than does the UK party system. There are two relatively large parties, which won almost 60 percent of the seats between them in 2009. However, almost 40 other parties—and numerous independent candidates not affiliated with any party at all—split the remaining 40 percent of the seats, with most winning just a few seats with a small fraction of the vote.

ASSESS THE HYPOTHESIS

The resulting coalition government from the 2010 UK election might be an aberration, but the consistent fragmentation of the Indian party system since the late 1980s undermines the hypothesis

that plurality rule always tends to manufacture parliamentary majorities, favoring effective government. When will plurality rule *not* discriminate against smaller parties?

The 2010 results from the UK point toward an answer: when parties can compete effectively in particular regions. For example, the Democratic Unionist party and Sinn Féin compete only in Northern Ireland; the Scottish Nationalist party competes only in Scotland, and Plaid Cymru competes only in Wales. Under the UK's plurality system, these parties are viable—on a small scale, at least—because they concentrate all their votes in particular geographic regions. In contrast, the Liberal Democrats spread their vote around the whole country, doing well enough to win the plurality in only a few districts.

Plurality rule will not discriminate against smaller parties when those parties concentrate their votes in confined geographic regions. Many small parties around the world target religious, linguistic,

(*Continued*)

or ethnic groups that live only in a particular area, rather than attempt to appeal to voters across the whole country. When support for such regional identities is strong, small parties may win the plurality of votes *in the electoral districts in those regions*.

India epitomizes this outcome. In the 1980s, regional-based parties increased their success, much to the chagrin of the leaders of the country's larger parties. Today, India's system is fragmented precisely because many parties gain support from identity groups with a strong presence in only particular regions of the country. For example, the Bahujan Samaj (BSP) and Samajwadi parties— which finished fourth and sixth in India's 2009 elections, as shown in Table 3.4, are strong only in the Indian state of Uttar Pradesh, while the Telugu Desam party, which finished eighth, is strong in Andhra Pradesh. Having a concentrated support base allows these parties to win a plurality of the vote in some districts in those states, but they win almost no votes elsewhere in India.

In order to understand why a party system has a certain number of parties, one cannot consider the electoral system alone, but rather one must take into account both the institutional and identity contexts. Institutions alone do not determine the number of parties in a party system: in fact, the institutions and regional identities interact. Outcomes in these two countries show that electoral rules alone do not determine election outcomes. Outcomes are a function of the rules as well as of the distribution of support for particular parties. If parties can compete effectively in every electoral district, plurality rule will be associated with only two parties. But if regional parties can build up their support, they stand a good chance of gaining some degree of representation.

CRITICAL THINKING QUESTIONS

1. If India were to adopt a proportional representation electoral system, would fragmentation in the parliament increase, decrease, or stay about the same?
2. If the United States were to adopt a proportional representation electoral system, would fragmentation in the parliament increase, decrease, or stay about the same?

TABLE 3.4   India Election Results, 2009

Party	Percent of Votes	Percent of Seats
Indian National Congress	29	38
Bharatiya Janata Party	19	21
Communist Party of India (Marxist)	5	3
Bahujan Samaj Party	6	4
Independents	5	2
Samajwadi Party	3	4
All India Trinamool Congress	3	3
Telugu Desam Party	3	1
Nationalist Congress Party	2	2
31 Other Parties	24	22
Total	100	100

Source: Electoral Commission of India, "Statistical Reports of Lok Sahba Elections–2009." Accessed July 7, 2011, http://eci.nic.in/eci_main/archiveofge2009/statistical_report.asp.

> ### TABLE 3.5
>
> **France 2007 Parliamentary Election Results**
>
> | Party | Percent of Votes (First Round) | Percent of Seats |
> |---|---|---|
> | Union for a Popular Movement + allies | 45.6 | 59.8 |
> | Socialist Party + allies | 35.6 | 39.3 |
> | Democratic Movement | 7.6 | 0.5 |
> | Other Parties | 11.2 | 0.4 |
>
> Source: Ministry of the Interior of France, "Legislatives 2007." Microsoft Excel file, accessed July 7, 2011, http://www.interieur.gouv.fr/sections/a_votre_service/elections/resultats/accueil-resultats/downloadFile/attachedFile_2/Leg_07_FE_METRO_OM.xls.

Majority Rule

majority rule ■ requires that candidates obtain a majority of 50 percent +1 of the votes in the district to win.

In contrast to plurality rule, majority rule requires that candidates obtain an actual majority of 50 percent +1 of the votes in an electoral district to win. Sometimes—in a three-way race, for example—no candidate obtains 50 percent +1 of the votes. When this occurs, countries that use majority rule then have a second round of elections that pit the top two vote-getters from the first round against each other. This necessarily results in a majority winner.

Majority rule and plurality rule do have something in common: because only one seat is at stake in each electoral district, majority rule electoral systems also tend to reward larger parties and penalize smaller parties. Consider the results in Table 3.5, from the 2007 parliamentary elections in France, which uses the two-round majority-rule system.

Because the Union for a Popular Movement (UMP) and the Socialists were by far the largest parties in their coalition, we can consider them to be single parties. At this election, the smaller parties were heavily penalized—the Democratic Movement and smaller parties obtained almost 20 percent of the votes, but less than 1 percent of the seats! This result gave the two larger parties—the Socialists and, especially, the UMP—considerably more seats than their vote percentage might suggest. As Table 3.6 illustrates, like the plurality rule, legislative elections using majority rule tend to concentrate control over representative institutions in the hands of one party.

Proportional Representation

proportional representation ■ an electoral system that distributes seats proportionally to the vote each party receives.

In countries that use plurality or majority electoral rules, there is typically one seat at stake in every electoral constituency or district. Just more than half of the world's democracies use some form of plurality or majority rule, but about one in three use some form of proportional representation (PR) to translate votes into legislative seats. In countries that use PR, there must be more than one seat at stake in each

TABLE 3.6

Seat Distribution under Different Electoral Rules

Party	Vote Share	Seat Share if One Seat Is at Stake (Plurality or Majority Rule)	Seat Share if 10 Seats Are at Stake (PR)
1	51%	100%	50%
2	39%	0%	40%
3	10%	0%	10%

electoral district. And as the name implies, this electoral rule distributes those seats proportionally to the vote each party receives in each district.

To illustrate how PR differs from plurality or majority rule electoral systems, consider two examples in Table 3.6. First, suppose three parties run a candidate in a district with only one seat at stake, using either plurality or majority rule. Party 1 gets 51 percent of the vote, Party 2 gets 39 percent, and Party 3 gets 10 percent. If there is only one seat at stake, then Party 1 wins "all" the seats, and Parties 2 and 3 get nothing. Now suppose that there are, instead, ten seats at stake in this electoral district and that the electoral rule is PR. If the parties got the same proportions of the vote, Party 1 would get five seats, Party 4 would get four, and Party 3 would get one.

In contrast to the concentration of political power that tends to result in elections using plurality or majority rule, PR tends to disperse political power somewhat more. Consider the results from Portugal's 2009 parliamentary election using PR in Table 3.7. In Portugal, there are 22 electoral districts, the smallest of which elects two members to parliament and the largest 47. In contrast to the result from the UK in Table 3.2, the results in this system do not give as much of a "bonus" to the largest party, and they do not discriminate as much against the smaller parties.

TABLE 3.7

Portugal 2009 Parliamentary Election Results

Party	Percent of Votes	Percent of Seats
Socialist Party	36.6	42.2
Social Democrats	29.1	35.2
People's Party	10.4	9.1
Leftist Bloc	9.8	7.0
Communist/Green Coalition	7.9	6.5

Source: Comissão Nacional de Eleições, "Resultados Eleitorais, Assembleia da República." Accessed July 7, 2011, http://eleicoes.cne.pt/vector/index.cfm?dia=27&mes=09&ano=2009&eleicao=ar.

TABLE 3.8

Israel 2009 Parliamentary Election Results

Party	Percent of Votes	Percent of Seats
Kadima	22.5	23.3
Likud	21.6	22.5
Yisrael Beiteinu	11.7	12.5
Labor	9.9	10.8
Shas	8.5	9.2
United Torah Judaism	4.4	4.2
United Arab List	3.4	3.3
National Union	3.3	3.3
Hadash	3.3	3.3
New Movement-Meretz	3.0	2.5
The Jewish Home	2.9	2.5
Balad	2.5	2.5

Source: Israel Ministry of Foreign Affairs, "Final Election Results." Available at http://www.mfa.gov.il/MFA/History/Modern+History/Historic+Events/Elections_in_Israel_February_2009.htm#results, accessed July 7, 2011.

Other PR systems generate even more proportional results. Consider the results of the 2009 parliamentary elections in Israel, where all members of parliament are elected in a single, nationwide electoral district with 120 seats at stake. Under this system, even the smallest parties can win a seat. As Table 3.8 shows, the vote and seat percentages are quite similar, meaning that the system barely favors large parties and hardly discriminates against small parties. This system disperses political power about as much as can any electoral system.

Mixed Electoral Rules

mixed electoral rules
■ combine a plurality or majority electoral rule to elect some members of the national legislature with a PR electoral rule to elect the remainder.

The last electoral system to discuss also tends to disperse political power, but not as much as proportional representation. About 13 percent of all democracies employ mixed electoral rules.[14] Mixed electoral rules combine a plurality or majority electoral rule to elect some members of the national legislature, with PR to elect the remainder. In Germany, for example, the parliament has 598 members, half elected by plurality rule in single-member districts, and half elected in each of Germany's 16 states (Germany is a federal system) via PR.[15] At each parliamentary election, voters cast two votes: one for a candidate using the plurality rule in their home electoral district (similar to U.S. House elections or UK parliamentary elections), and a second for a party's entire list of candidates in a PR election.

As the name implies, mixed electoral rules are designed to find a middle ground between the majority-enhancing effects of plurality or majority-rule electoral systems and the power-dispersing effects of PR systems. In practice, the results of elections using mixed electoral rules often tend to resemble elections under PR. Consider the results in Germany's 2009 parliamentary elections, in Table 3.9. In contrast to the results for the UK, even using plurality rule to elect half of the parliament only gives the largest party a small bonus. Yet in contrast to the results for Israel, the results do discriminate against the very smallest political parties.

Electoral rules address Madison's Dilemma in different ways. Plurality and majority-rule electoral systems focus on promoting effective government by tending to give one political party majority control over representative institutions. In contrast, PR and mixed electoral systems focus on limiting government power by giving smaller parties relatively greater ability to win some legislative seats. Because passing a bill in a legislature always requires at least a majority of legislators' votes, PR and mixed systems tend to force larger parties to compromise with smaller parties in order to get anything done.

As with the impact of federalism and the separation of powers, the impact of electoral systems on the balance between effective and limited government depends in part on the relative balance of political interests and identity groups in society, and in particular on the question of what political interests and identities are mobilized into the party system. In an ethnically, linguistically, or religiously homogenous country, an electoral system that promotes majoritarian representational outcomes may work best because there is less worry that minority interests will be sacrificed in the name of effective government. Yet, in a more ethnically, linguistically, or religiously diverse society, electoral systems that allow for PR may offer a better prescription for overall democratic performance because minorities may have more to fear from majority dominance.

TABLE 3.9

Election Results in Germany 2009

Party	Percent of Party List Votes	Percent of Total Seats
Christian Democrats/Christian Social Union	33.8	38.4
Social Democrats	23.0	23.5
Free Democrats	14.6	15.0
The Left	11.9	12.2
Alliance '90/Greens	10.7	10.9
Others	6.0	0.0

Source: Federal Returning Officer of Germany, "Final Result of the Election to the German Bundestag 2009." Accessed July 7, 2011, http://www.bundeswahlleiter.de/en/bundestagswahlen/BTW_BUND_09/ergebnisse/bundesergebnisse/index.html.

CONCLUSION

Democracy is a political system in which the rulers are accountable to the ruled. We refined this definition by noting that accountability requires the combination of institutionalized participation and contestation, and then by tallying the institutional requirements necessary to make accountability possible and support open participation and contestation: elected government, civil liberties, and free, fair, and frequent elections.

This definition of democracy focuses on how political institutions can limit government power, to preserve individual rights and freedoms. Limiting government power is no easy task: citizens of democracies want to prevent tyranny, but also want to concentrate enough power so that government can get things done. The question then turns to Madison's Dilemma: how democracies attempt to strike a balance between effective and limited government.

Democratic institutions address this tension in multiple ways, choosing between (1) federalism and unitarism; (2) presidential, parliamentary, and hybrid semi-presidential systems; (3) judicial review or parliamentary supremacy; and (4) plurality or majority-rule electoral systems versus proportional representation and mixed electoral systems. Each of these four elements of democracy illustrates the tradeoff inherent in Madison's Dilemma: concentrating power might enhance effective government, but it tends to eliminate checks and balances. In contrast, dispersing power might reduce the effectiveness of government, but it offers greater checks on majority rule. Madison sought to establish both effective *and* limited government, but he feared the tyranny of the majority more than he feared ineffective government—hence, his recommendations for institutions that tend to disperse power such as presidentialism and federalism. The summary table below highlights the key findings: unitarism, parliamentarism, judicial subordination to parliament, and plurality or majority rule all tend to concentrate political power, while federalism, presidentialism, judicial review, and PR or a mixed electoral rule tend to disperse power.

Around the world, politicians continue to consider these tradeoffs when designing their own country's constitution. When a country decides to adopt or change democratic institutions, what political, social, or economic conditions encourage politicians to choose institutions that centralize or decentralize political power? How will Egyptians choose to balance limited and effective government as their country takes steps toward democracy, for example? The answer to that question depends in part on the *informal* balance of forces within any society—on the nature

SUMMARY TABLE	
Power in Government Institutions	
Tendency to Concentrate Power	**Tendency to Disperse Power**
Unitarism	Federalism
Parliamentarism	Presidentialism
No Judicial Review	Judicial Review
Plurality or Majority Rule	PR or Mixed Electoral Rule

of interest group representation and the number, relative size, and type of parties that can effectively compete for votes.

No one knows which mix of institutions offers the 'best' balance between limited and effective democratic government. In practice, the question is resolved through trial and error, political debate, and through the electoral process. That is, supporters of each political viewpoint believe that their approach best promotes effective government while also preserving limited government. Ultimately, the question of what sorts of institutions promote both limited and effective government is intimately related to the balance of a society's political, social, economic and cultural interests and identities. ◣

✓ Study and Review
the **Post-Test &**
Chapter Exam
at **mypoliscilab.com**

KEY TERMS

democracy   59
accountability   60
electorate   60
universal suffrage   60
constitution   66
unitarism   67
federalism   68
presidential system   70
separation of origin   70
separation of survival   70
parliamentary system   70
prime minister   70

no-confidence vote   70
semi-presidential hybrid   71
dual executive   71
divided government   74
judicial review   78
parliamentary supremacy   78
Marbury v. Madison   79
electoral process   79
plurality rule   80
majority rule   84
proportional representation   84
mixed electoral system   86

REVIEW QUESTIONS

1. Why does democracy require both participation *and* contestation?
2. What institutional rules are necessary to guarantee participation and contestation and offer the possibility of accountability?
3. What is "Madison's Dilemma"?
4. What institutions of democracy tend to concentrate political power, and why?
5. What institutions of democracy tend to disperse political power, and why?

SUGGESTED READINGS

Dahl, Robert. *Democracy and Its Critics*. New Haven, CT: Yale University Press, 1989. A classic study of the evolving nature and definition of democracy.

Ginsburg, Tom. "The Global Spread of Constitutional Review." In *The Oxford Handbook of Law and Politics*, edited by Keith Whittington and Daniel Keleman. New York: Oxford University Press, 2008. Explores the evolution and impact of the spread of judicial review around the world.

Przeworski, Adam et al. *Democracy and Development*. New York: Cambridge University Press, 2000, Chapter 1. Considers the best way to define and measure democracy.

Samuels, David. "Executive-Legislative Relations." In *The Oxford Handbook of Comparative Politics*, edited by Carles Boix and Susan Stokes. New York: Oxford University Press, 2006. Reviews many of the contemporary issues in the study of executive–legislative relations.

Schmitter, Philippe, and Terry L. Karl, "What Democracy Is ... and Is Not." *Journal of Democracy* 2 (1991); 75–88. A thought-provoking exploration of various definitions of democracy.

NOTES

1. See the Inter-Parliamentary Union's website on "Women's Suffrage," http://www.ipu .org/wmn-e/suffrage.htm, accessed November 21, 2008.
2. This figure is based on Robert Dahl's famous conceptualization of democracy in his book *Polyarchy: Participation and Opposition* (New Haven, CT: Yale University Press, 1971).
3. See Robert Dahl, *On Democracy* (New Haven, CT: Yale University Press, 1998).
4. See http://www.freedomhouse.org.
5. See http://www.freedomhouse.org/images/File/fiw/historical/CountryStatusRatings Overview1973-2011.pdf, accessed April 1, 2011.
6. Nearly all democracies have written constitutions. The UK and Israel are exceptions—there is no single document called a "constitution." Rather, they rely on a set of important laws to establish the basic rules of politics.
7. Some parliamentary systems—such as Germany and Italy—have unelected presidents whose role is largely symbolic and who have little real authority. Only systems with directly elected presidents qualify as hybrid systems.
8. José Antonio Cheibub et al., "Government Coalitions and Legislative Success Under Presidentialism and Parliamentarism," *British Journal of Political Science*, 34 (2004): 565–587.
9. Kaare Strøm and Benjamin Nyblade cite a figure of 62 percent for Western European parliamentary countries (787). "Coalition Theory and Government Formation," in *Oxford Handbook of Comparative Politics*, ed. Carles Boix and Susan Stokes (Oxford: Oxford University Press, 2007: 782-804).
10. See Matthew Søberg Shugart, "Semi-Presidential Systems: Dual Executive and Mixed Authority Patterns," *French Politics* 3, 3 (2005): 323–351; or Robert Elgie, ed., *Semi-Presidentialism in Europe.* (Oxford: Oxford University Press, 1999).
11. See David Samuels and Matthew Shugart, *Presidents, Parties and Prime Ministers.* (New York: Cambridge University Press, 2010), chapter 4.
12. Samuels and Shugart, *Presidents, Parties and Prime Ministers.*
13. Calculated from the Comparative Constitutions Project, www.comparativeconstitutionsproject.org. I thank Zach Elkins, James Melton, and Tom Ginsburg for help on this question.
14. See International IDEA, *Electoral System Design: the New International IDEA Handbook* (Stockholm: International IDEA, 2005), 30. Available at www.idea.int.
15. The German electoral system also has what are known as "overhang" seats, but this detail need not concern us.

Non-Democratic Political Regimes

Kim Jong Il (right), who ruled North Korea from 1994 until his death in 2011, is shown here applauding a military parade. His son and apparent successor, Kim Jong Un, stands in front of an array of high military authorities. Leadership succession

? What is non-democracy?

Read and Listen
to Chapter 4
at mypoliscilab.com

Study and Review
the Pre-Test & Flashcards
at mypoliscilab.com

In late 2008, rumors of failing health swirled around North Korea's "Dear Leader," Kim Jong-Il, ruler of the country since 1994. Following allegations that he had suffered a paralyzing stroke earlier that year, Kim disappeared from public view for several months. Intelligence analysts around the world whispered that Kim was receiving treatment in a Chinese hospital, that he was in a permanent coma—or even that he had died in 2003 and that a series of Kim impersonators kept up a pretense that the Dear Leader continued to control North Korea's government. Government officials in North Korea released photos allegedly showing Kim at concerts, soccer games, and military parades, but such efforts only encouraged curious observers to scrutinize the photos for irregularities—finding, for example, green leaves on trees in photos supposedly taken in early winter.[1]

Kim's good health was crucial to North Korea because the entire system of government hinged on his authority. Kim Jong-Il's father Kim Il-Sung proclaimed the country an independent state in 1948, and he ruled the country with an iron fist until his death in 1994. The elder Kim's absolute control rested on his command of the country's military and on his leadership of the North Korean Communist Party. Yet to solidify popular support for his rule, Kim Il-Sung also developed a cult of personality around himself—a form of hero worship. Popular songs glorified the elder Kim's exploits, and artists were encouraged to portray him in a heroic light in painting, sculpture, and film. To this day, North Korean children are taught to revere Kim Il-Sung almost as a god—"Thank you, Father Kim Il-Sung" is the first phrase North Korean parents are instructed to teach their children.[2]

After publicly announcing that he would pass power to his son, Kim Il-Sung began transferring to him this cult of personality. As with the father, the son's birthday is also a national holiday. Popular songs praise Kim Jong-Il's leadership and even proclaim that, "There is no Motherland without you." When Kim Jong-Il died suddenly in December 2011, a potential succession crises emerged, because Jong-Il had not begun to transfer this cult of personality to his son, Kim Jong-Un.[3]

North Korea is an example of a totalitarian regime—a type of non-democratic government that attempts to shape the interests and identities of its citizens through the use of ideology, coercive mobilization, and severe repression. However, because North Korea's leaders are wary of outsiders, they keep as much information secret as possible. The true nature of North Korean politics remains a mystery. When Kim died, outsiders were mystified as to how power would be transferred to his apparent successor, his 28-year-old son, who had little governing experience--and whether North Korea would remain stable or collapse into chaos. The mysteries of North Korean politics raise the question of how we should compare and contrast different non-democratic regimes.

What is non-democracy? A regime is a word for the basic form of a state's government. In this book, we talk of democratic and non-democratic regimes—and in this chapter we shall discuss varieties of non-democratic regimes. The case of Kim

regime ■ the basic form of a state's government.

Jong-Il calls attention to two key aspects of politics in non-democratic regimes: the relationship between state and society, and the institutions of the regime itself. The first focuses on the extent to which the government uses institutions of the state to shape citizens' interests and identities, while the second aspect considers how—in the absence of truly competitive elections—non-democratic leaders are selected and removed from office. These key principles, which we shall describe in more detail in the next section, define non-democratic regimes. With these two principles to guide this chapter's exploration, we shall then differentiate between totalitarian and authoritarian regimes, and finally distinguish the ways non-democratic regimes select and remove leaders.

UNDERSTANDING THE PRINCIPLES OF NON-DEMOCRACY

Democracy reigns in almost half the world's states as of 2011. And as you can see in Table 4.1, the number of "Not Free" countries has declined over the past few decades. Still, almost one in four states today still have a non-democratic form of government, and most are found in the Middle East, Africa, and Asia. (Until the 1990s, Latin America and Eastern Europe also had many non-democracies.)

What defines non-democratic regimes? In a non-democracy, individuals and groups in society are subject to the hierarchical authority of the state. Figure 4.1 points to the two key principles defining non-democratic regimes. Note that in opposition to the flow of power in a democracy, the large arrow only flows from the state to society. For this reason, citizens are referred to as "subjects," to highlight the fact that in a non-democratic regime individuals and groups lack the opportunity to hold rulers accountable as they can in a democratic regime: they are subject to the regime's authority. This first key facet of non-democratic regimes focuses on the way in which the government attempts to use the institutions of the state to enforce hierarchical control over citizens in society.

4.1 What defines non-democratic regimes?

Explore the Comparative "Chief Executives" at mypoliscilab.com

TABLE 4.1			
Types of Government Around the World			
Year	**Democracies**	**Semi-Democracies**	**Non-Democracies**	**Total Number of Countries**
1972	29% (44)	25% (38)	46% (69)	149
1986	34% (57)	34% (57)	32% (53)	167
1996	41% (79)	31% (59)	28% (53)	191
2011	45% (87)	31% (60)	24% (47)	194

Source: Freedom House, "Freedom in the World Country Ratings." http://www.freedomhouse.org/images/File/fiw/historical/CountryStatusRatingsOverview1973–2011.pdf, accessed July 9, 2011.

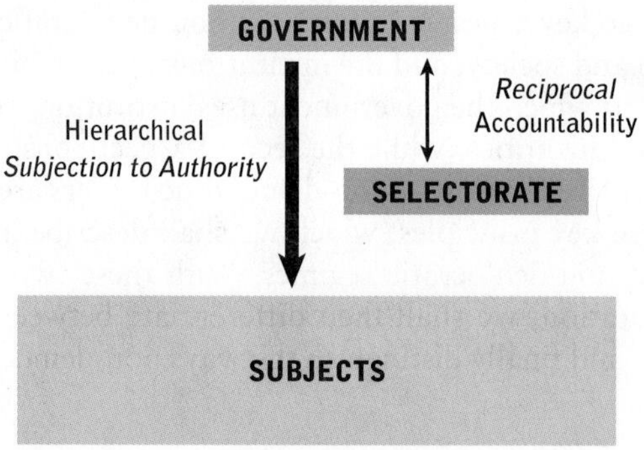

FIGURE 4.1

Accountability under Non-Democracy

Two key principles define non-democratic regimes. First, the large arrow indicates that citizens are only subject to the regime's authority—they lack the opportunity to hold rulers accountable, as in a democracy. The smaller arrow indicates the two-way relationship of reciprocal accountability in which the selectorate chooses and removes the leadership, but the leadership also selects and removes the members of the selectorate.

selectorate ■
in non-democratic regimes, a subset of the population that chooses and removes the leader or leaders.

reciprocal accountability ■
the selectorate chooses and removes the leadership, but the leadership also selects and removes the members of the selectorate.

The second defining facet of non-democratic regimes involves the nature of leadership selection and deselection. In a democracy, leadership selection and deselection rely on a clear and non-arbitrary rule: universal suffrage exercised through regular elections. In contrast, in non-democratic systems, either there is no electorate of adult citizens or the electorate has no real role in choosing national leaders. Instead, a selectorate of some small subset of the national population exists that chooses and removes the leader or leaders. It is important to note the two-way arrow between the selectorate and the leader, which implies a relationship of reciprocal accountability. Reciprocal accountability means that the selectorate chooses and removes the leadership, but the leadership also selects and removes the members of the selectorate. Neither the selectorate nor the leader or leaders possess definitive political authority.

All non-democratic regimes exhibit a hierarchical relationship between state and society and have a selectorate rather than an electorate. As in North Korea, some non-democratic regimes may go to extraordinary lengths to mobilize and coerce their citizens. Likewise, leadership selection processes in non-democracies can be unclear to an outside observer because membership in the selectorate is often determined by political favoritism or membership in a particular family or ethnic or religious group. However, not all non-democracies are as repressive as North Korea, and leadership selection processes can also be fairly clear, even if they remain closed to average citizens. In the remainder of this chapter, we explore variation across different types of non-democracies. We focus first on categorizing state–society relationships in totalitarian and authoritarian regimes, and then turn our attention to the institutions of non-democratic governments to understand the different relationships between leaders and the selectorate.

DIFFERENTIATING TOTALITARIAN AND AUTHORITARIAN REGIMES

In all non-democratic regimes, governments use the institutions of the state to control society. Yet non-democracies use this authority in very different ways, and we can classify them as either totalitarian or authoritarian, based on the way rulers establish hierarchical authority and relate to citizens and society. Three characteristics distinguish totalitarianism from authoritarianism:

1. use of ideology,
2. the extent of coercive mobilization, and
3. the degree of social and political pluralism permitted.[4]

Of the two types of non-democracies, totalitarian regimes tend to engage in more severe repression.

- A totalitarian regime is defined as one in which the government attempts to shape the interests and identities of its citizens by articulating a coherent ideology, employing extensive efforts to coercively mobilize support for the regime, and imposing tight restrictions on both social and political pluralism.
- An authoritarian regime concentrates on using coercion to limit *political* pluralism in order to remain in power, but relative to a totalitarian regime, an authoritarian regime permits some *social* pluralism. An authoritarian regime does not use ideology or coercive mobilization to shape citizens' interests, identities, or support for the regime.

Today, most non-democratic regimes are authoritarian. However, totalitarian regimes have played a critical role in shaping world politics since the 1930s. Nazi Germany is perhaps the best-known example; totalitarian regimes also dominated Russian and Chinese politics for decades, as we will discuss below. The three key differences in the ways that non-democratic regimes relate to society distinguish authoritarianism from totalitarianism. Let's examine the use of ideology first.

Use of Ideology

An ideology is a set of political beliefs or ideas that structures and gives meaning to our political interests and that motivates people to act politically in particular ways. In a totalitarian regime, leaders believe that their interests include implementing their ideology's tenets and spreading and deepening its influence both at home and abroad. In contrast, authoritarian governments spend less time and government resources promulgating an official ideology. This is not to say that authoritarian governments do not repress dissent, but that they devote more resources to maintaining order and less on drilling ideological purity into their subjects.

Totalitarian ideologies are distinct in five ways:[5]

- Totalitarian ideologies are overt: national leaders write them down and broadcast them publicly.
- Totalitarian ideologies are systematic: governments discuss and update a highly detailed set of integrated ideological principles.

4.2 What is the distinction between totalitarianism and authoritarianism?

Explore the Comparative "Civil Rights" at mypoliscilab.com

ideology ■ a set of political beliefs or ideas that structures and gives meaning to political interests and that motivates people to act politically in particular ways.

- Totalitarian ideologies are institutionalized: leaders empower bureaucrats to serve as official ideologues, whose job it is to constantly articulate and update the regime's ideology, and spread government propaganda.
- Totalitarian ideologies are dogmatic: Regimes create and impose their own official political views on every citizen and brook no dissent. Anyone who suggests the government's view is wrong or who proposes an alternative interpretation of the regime's ideology is repressed.
- Finally, totalitarian ideologies are totalizing: they provide individuals with behavioral guidance for all aspects of their lives and even seek to reshape individuals' interests and identities in the regime's image. For example, ideology in Russia under the Soviet Union (USSR) (1922–1991) extolled the virtues of the "New Soviet Man," one who enthusiastically supported the regime and its ideological goals and repudiated all personal ambitions and desires.

Totalitarian ideologies resemble cults. The Soviet regime went to extraordinary lengths to socialize children to support the government and its communist ideology. From primary school through college, students were required to take courses on political knowledge and ideology. (How would you feel if a course titled "Proper Political Thought" was a requirement for graduation?) The government determined the content of these courses, designed teaching methods to eliminate students' individual personalities, and encouraged students to see themselves only as members of the collective.

Leaders of totalitarian regimes devote so much energy to indoctrination partly because they may believe their own propaganda, and partly because doing so advances their political interest in retaining power. Wanting to hold onto power is hardly exclusive to totalitarian regimes; democratic and non-democratic leaders all wield power in an effort to influence people's political values, goals, and preferences. Yet totalitarian regimes are distinguished by their strenuous efforts at coercive ideological indoctrination.

Extent of Coercive Mobilization

Together with the elaboration and propagation of an elaborate ideology, totalitarianism differs from authoritarianism in terms of the extent to which rulers use their power to coercively mobilize support for the regime. Democracies do not coercively mobilize their societies except in cases of national emergency or war, when the government may force citizens to move from their homes or serve in the armed forces. Likewise, authoritarian regimes do not engage in much coercive mobilization in support of the regime; typically, they are more interested in demobilizing society and discouraging people from becoming politically engaged.

In contrast, totalitarian regimes engage in extensive coercive mobilization, by forcing people to labor (often literally) toward the regime's goals or to publicly demonstrate their support for the regime through participation in mass demonstrations and marches. Totalitarian regimes institutionalize and spread this ideology through a political party. This party seeks to control all aspects of society and to politicize all forms of social and cultural life, mobilizing individuals to support the regime, its goals, and its ideology. To advance in any profession, citizens living under totalitarian governments must become members of this government party and pledge complete obedience to the regime's ideology and party leaders.

To illustrate coercive mobilization further, let's return to the example of the Soviet Union. To supplement the ideological indoctrination students learned in school, the government created and controlled special youth organizations called the "Young Pioneers," designed to enhance the socialization process and transform children into reliable regime supporters. Unlike the Boy Scouts or Girl Scouts or similar organizations in the United States and elsewhere, kids in the Soviet Union were required to join the Pioneers at a young age and continue on through high school. And also unlike the Scouts, Soviet youth organizations were instruments of the government, designed to reinforce ideological indoctrination, mobilize peer pressure, and manufacture absolute conformity with government dictates.

Once students entered university, they faced pressure to join another government-controlled organization called the *Komsomol*—in Russian, an abbreviation for Communist Youth Union—which at one time had millions of members. Job prospects and career advancement—especially in government jobs—often depended on having demonstrated a commitment to the organization. *Komsomol* leaders, supported by the Communist Party, acted like power-mad dormitory resident assistants.

A painting of militarized *Komsomol*, the communist youth organization under the USSR. Powerful incentives drove millions of teenagers and young adults to join—an example of a totalitarian government using institutions to coercively mobilize support.

They conducted hygiene inspections, enforced rules for proper decorum, kept an eye out for individuals who were thought to be politically suspect or who were acting with too much individuality, and even patrolled parties to keep boys and girls from dancing too closely—all in the name of supporting the Soviet government. Youth and students who exhibited zeal in the Young Pioneers or the *Komsomol* were recruited into the Communist Party.[6] This example illustrates how obsessively totalitarian regimes employ state institutions to coercively mobilize individuals to support the regime.

Degree of Social and Political Pluralism

Totalitarian regimes couple the use of ideology and coercive mobilization with a third characteristic, a strenuous effort to minimize the degree of social and/or political pluralism. Democracies tolerate social and political diversity, meaning that interest and identity groups are allowed to organize and participate in politics. Authoritarian regimes tolerate some degree of *social* freedoms—for example, by allowing people to mobilize and collectively organize along cultural or other nonpolitical forms of identity or interests, such as sports clubs or musical, artistic, or religious groups. However, they limit *political* pluralism—for example, by impeding the transformation of non-political societal groups such as a hiking club into an environmental protest movement and by using the police and armed forces to repress political opposition.

In contrast, totalitarian regimes tolerate no social or political pluralism. In a totalitarian society, the central government subordinates all facets of social, economic, and political power. That is, totalitarian regimes abolish not just organized civil society but often go to bizarre lengths to control every aspect of individual citizens' private lives, including what clothes people can wear and even how they wear their hair. For example, in 2005, the *New York Times* reported that the government of North Korea had begun to require men to visit a barber twice a month, because long hair "consumes a great deal of nutrition" and "robs the brain of energy." This policy was encouraged by commercials on government-controlled television (the only channel available), via a series called "Let Us Trim Our Hair in Accordance with Socialist Lifestyle."[7] In a totalitarian regime, every facet of human existence can become a public matter, subject to government control—family life, education, friendship, work and leisure, even romance.

Totalitarian regimes have two tools they use to implement such monopoly control. The first is the official regime party. The regime party is not merely a tool of coercive mobilization; it also centralizes control over the state as well as society. Party members infiltrate the military and the police to indoctrinate members and turn them into tools of the regime. The government, through the party, also establishes control over the economy, by assuming either ownership or decision-making power over private enterprises and important businesses. Members of the government party also infiltrate and establish control over all mass media, including radio, TV, newspapers, and the Internet.

The second tool is the threat of violence. As noted above, authoritarian regimes sometimes use violence to control political pluralism. Totalitarian regimes use

SUMMARY TABLE

State–Society Relations in Different Political Regimes

Key Characteristic	Democracy	Non-Democracy	
		Authoritarianism	Totalitarianism
Use of ideological indoctrination	None	Limited	Extensive
Extent of coercive mobilization	None	Limited or minimal; *de*-mobilization emphasized	Extensive
Degree of Social or political pluralism permitted	Extensive	Limited	None
Examples	Canada, Japan, Israel	Brazil (1964–1985), Mexico (1929–2000), Greece (1967–1974), Egypt (1952–2011)	USSR (1917–1991), Nazi Germany (1933–1945), Italy (1922–1943), North Korea

violence to control both political *and* social pluralism. They typically create special police forces that have the authority to invade every aspect of individuals' personal and social lives. They also use informers, encouraging citizens to report on each other's activities. Fear of prison or personal harm divides individuals from each other and creates suspicion. When distrust and fear prove insufficient to suppress pluralism, the police jail or violently crush opponents. The use of coercion deters political and social pluralism and keeps citizens in line.

George Orwell's famous notion from his book *1984* that "Big Brother is watching you" reflects the key idea behind totalitarianism: the government tolerates absolutely no opposition, has eyes and ears everywhere, and is willing and able to whisk you away if you behave in a politically "inappropriate" manner. In places like North Korea today, or Hitler's Germany or the Soviet Union in the past, totalitarian regimes have used the institutions of the state to indoctrinate individuals with an ideology, in an effort to shape their interests and identities in support of the regime—and they have followed through on their threat to use violence against those who resisted. Totalitarian regimes emphasize ideological indoctrination and coercive mobilization, and attempt to eliminate any and all social and political pluralism. By contrast, authoritarian regimes can seem almost benign, although their interest in de-mobilizing the population certainly opens the door for extensive use of repression and coercion. The table above summarizes the distinctions between democratic, authoritarian, and totalitarian systems in terms of state–society relations and provides examples of each type. In the next section, we explore the two most important ideologies totalitarian regimes employed to indoctrinate and mobilize their populations: fascism and communism.

DIFFERENTIATING COMMUNIST AND FASCIST IDEOLOGIES

4.3 What defines the distinction between communism and fascism?

A key difference between totalitarian and authoritarian regimes is that the former attempts to shape citizens' interests and identities by articulating and imposing an official ideology. Two distinct types of totalitarian ideologies had tremendous influence in world politics during the twentieth century: communism and fascism. Communist ideology holds that under capitalist economic systems, the wealthy exploit the workers and the poor. Communists believe that efforts should be made to redistribute economic wealth as much as possible, and that a single political party should direct the government and control the state. In contrast, fascism is a totalitarian ideology based on racist principles that glorified militarism, violence, nationalism, and the state over individual interests and identities and that exalts a charismatic individual political leader.

Fascism provided the ideological foundations of Hitler's Nazi regime before and during World War II, while communism motivated the Russian (1917) and Chinese (1949) revolutions and shaped the course of the Cold War, a period of international conflict lasting from 1945 to 1990, which opposed democratic capitalist countries against non-democratic communist countries. These two ideologies illustrate the true nature of totalitarianism, and how totalitarian and authoritarian regimes differ. Let us attempt to clarify the meaning of these often-heard but frequently misunderstood terms.

communism ■ holds that under capitalist economic systems, the wealthy exploit the workers and the poor. Communists believe that efforts should be made to redistribute economic wealth as much as possible, and that a single political party should direct the government and control the state.

fascism ■ a totalitarian ideology based in racist principles that glorified militarism, violence, nationalism, and the state over individual interests and identities, usually led by charismatic individual political leaders.

Cold War ■ a period of international conflict lasting from 1945 to 1990, which opposed democratic capitalist countries against non-democratic communist countries.

Communism

Communism served as the guiding principle behind the Russian and Chinese revolutions, and communist regimes' political and economic opposition to democracy and capitalism served as the basis for international conflict during the Cold War. Until the end of the 1980s, communism was the official ideology of numerous states from Central Europe to Southeast Asia, including Poland, the Czech Republic, Romania, Russia, Ukraine, Lithuania, Kazakhstan, Mongolia, China, Cambodia, and Vietnam. Other communist regimes emerged in Yemen, Cuba, Ethiopia, Angola, and Mozambique. At the end of the 1980s, most of the world's communist governments collapsed.

Communism was not conceived as a totalitarian ideology. Communist regimes were guided by ideological principles first laid down by German philosophers Karl Marx (1818–1883) and Friedrich Engels (1820–1895). The first key idea behind communism is that in capitalist or free-market economic systems, the wealthy exploit the workers and the poor. According to Marx and Engels' version of communist ideology, the poor should work towards establishing a society in which economic hierarchies no longer existed, and in which everyone participated in political and economic decision making. This implied considerable economic redistribution from the rich to the poor. In fact, to create a society in which everyone could live as social and economic equals, Marxist theory suggested the government replace the capitalist economic system, in which individuals hold and invest property, with a system that eliminates private property altogether.

capitalism ■ an economic system in which individuals hold and invest property.

Marx never provided details as to how a communist political system would actually function in the real world. It was left to Russian revolutionary Vladimir Lenin (1870–1924) to elaborate on Marxist ideology after he led the overthrow of Russia's monarchy in 1917 and established the Soviet Union. Lenin considered average citizens incapable of constructive political engagement and argued that a communist revolution requires a select elite to lead a tightly controlled, highly disciplined political party trained to combat entrenched political forces on behalf of the rest of society.

Lenin also asserted that after a successful communist revolution, party leaders would assume control of all state institutions and use coercion to completely transform society according to communist ideological principles. For example, he argued that the most effective way to promote a classless society of economic equals is to eliminate private property entirely, and he also held that the most effective way to accomplish that goal is to give the central government complete control over all economic activity. Under the communist regime he eventually set up in Russia, private citizens could not own property of any kind; everything belonged to the state.

Lenin and his successor Josef Stalin (1878–1953) were responsible for creating a fully totalitarian regime in the Soviet Union. They elaborated communist ideology in great detail and used fear-mongering and extensive coercion to enforce conformity with the regime's dogmatic ideological principles. Thus, although communist ideology as Marx defined it advocated equality, in practice, members of the Communist Party became a privileged class, enjoying perks that other citizens did not enjoy and enforcing totalitarian control over all aspects of society.

During the Cold War, the clash between communist dictatorships and capitalist democracies drove the world to the brink of nuclear holocaust. Today, communist parties remain in power only in Cuba, North Korea, Laos, Vietnam, and China. In all five of these countries, a single party remains in power and tolerates no political opposition. However, Laos, Vietnam, and China abandoned communist economic principles after the collapse of the Soviet Union. The Chinese Communist Party has gone so far as to wholeheartedly embrace capitalism—even suggesting that getting rich is every Chinese citizen's patriotic duty. Marx and Lenin are probably spinning in their graves!

These regimes have moved away from totalitarianism, yet they all remain authoritarian because they continue to limit political pluralism and to punish political dissent. North Korea has engaged in neither economic nor political reforms and remains the contemporary world's best example of a fully totalitarian regime.

Fascism

Totalitarian communist regimes dominated governments from Eastern Europe to Southeast Asia for much of the twentieth century. Fascism was a second important totalitarian ideology, and fascist regimes emerged early in the twentieth century in Italy, Germany, and Spain. Fascist movements also gained prominence in the UK, France, Brazil, Japan, and elsewhere.

Several principles unite fascist ideology. First, Fascism drew intellectual inspiration from popular nineteenth-century racist theories of Social Darwinism—the

Watch the Video "Castro's Cuba" at mypoliscilab.com

Social Darwinism ■ the idea that certain races are inherently superior to others and that the superior races would inevitably conquer the weaker ones.

notion that certain races are inherently superior and would inevitably conquer the weaker ones. For example, fascist leaders in Nazi Germany argued that the world's races could be ranked hierarchically, with Aryans at the top. Aryans include Germans and other northern Europeans as well as the lighter-skinned upper castes in India. Nazis believed that other races parasitically borrowed their cultural identity from Aryans. The racist theories Nazis and other fascists shared were violently anti-Semitic, believing Jews to be the "most parasitic" of all races; this form of nationalism eventually justified the genocide of the Holocaust.

In addition to racism, fascism emphasizes an extreme form of nationalism, which glorifies the nation's mythical, warlike history. Thus, Italy's Benito Mussolini linked his regime to the ancient Roman Empire, while Adolf Hitler sought to evoke the German Teutonic Knights of the Middle Ages. Fascism emphasizes the importance of the national community and the state over individual interests and identities. Proponents held that individuals could only realize their true purpose in life by subsuming their interests and desires to those of the entire nation; individualism was denigrated as selfishness. Mussolini wrote that for a fascist, "Everything is in the State, and nothing human or spiritual exists, much less has value, outside the State . . . the individual, through the denial of himself, through the sacrifice of his own private interests, through death itself, realizes that completely spiritual existence in which his value lies."[8]

Third, fascism glorifies charismatic, personalistic leaders who supposedly embody the "national will." According to fascist ideology, leaders who embody the principles of the nation and its race emerge naturally, given their innate charismatic qualities. Fascism rests on an almost mystical bond between a leader and the community—a connection that seeks to sweep followers into the movement. Moreover, because fascism emphasizes the subjection of individual political interests and identities to the movement, it justifies repressive non-democratic forms of government in which individual and minority rights are of little concern.

Finally, fascism justifies the use of violence to achieve the nation's goals, reflecting its racist and nationalist Social-Darwinist roots. Fascist ideology glorifies conquest through warfare, because war inspires heroism and acts of self-sacrifice, binding the nation more tightly together.

Fascism mobilized millions to engage in politics across Europe and elsewhere in the early twentieth century. However, the Allied victory in World War II ended the main examples of fascist governments—Hitler's Germany and Mussolini's Italy—and fascism was discredited as an ideology. No truly fascist regimes have emerged since the end of World War II.

Comparing Totalitarian Ideologies

Like all totalitarian ideologies, both communism and fascism devalue individual rights, regard democracy as weak and ineffective, and rationalize an all-powerful state. Yet, it is important not to equate communism and fascism. Communism downplays nationalism and emphasizes commonalities between workers across nations, while fascism stresses the importance of the national community. Communism also rejects private property and capitalism, while fascism does not.

SUMMARY TABLE

Comparing Communism and Fascism

	Communism	Fascism
Core Elements of Ideology	Economic: capitalism exploits the poor; communism justifies elimination of private property, redistributes wealth to the poor, and advocates government control of the economy.	Racism and nationalism: certain races are inherently superior to others and will naturally come to dominate. Extreme nationalism justifies the use of repression and violence.
Nature of Leadership	Elite party leads the revolution and then controls the state.	Charismatic leader embodies the national will.

In turn, fascism rejects communism's emphasis on economic class identity and class conflict and emphasizes nationalism as the most important form of political identity. The summary table above highlights some of the key differences between fascism and communism.

Fascism arose in opposition to communism in early twentieth-century Europe. It was most popular with people who felt left behind by advances in modern technology and by the growth of large-scale industrial capitalism. This could include just about anybody—small farmers, craftsmen, shopkeepers, or even traditional landowning conservative elites—who felt threatened by urbanization and the rising power of industrial workers. In turn, communism appealed to those industrial workers who sought political change to protect their rights as workers and to provide greater social welfare protections. These political appeals help explain why fascism is associated with nostalgic, backward-looking extreme right-wing conservative politics, while communism is associated with utopian, forward-looking extreme left-wing radical politics—even though both are totalitarian ideologies.

In sum, totalitarian governments try to completely dominate individuals and society by developing an ideology and using the institutions of the state to shape or reshape individual and group interests and identities. This effort at total domination differentiates totalitarian from authoritarian non-democracies. To be sure, no matter how repressive, no non-democratic government has exactly corresponded to our definition of a totalitarian regime. Even in Hitler's Germany or Stalin's Soviet Russia, individuals still retained some private life. Still, like many political science concepts, totalitarianism is useful because we can apply it to real-world cases. Although there is no clear way of measuring precisely how totalitarian any society is, we can compare systems against each other, or consider how regimes evolve over time and decide whether a non-democratic system exhibits the main traits of a totalitarian regime.

Totalitarian regimes have become increasingly rare, but some authoritarian regimes have attempted to employ totalitarian methods. For example, rulers in contemporary Syria and in Saddam Hussein's Iraq have made efforts to coercively mobilize citizens in support of their regimes. However, most existing authoritarian regimes fall far short of totalitarianism, either because they lack the capability to abolish all aspects of the private sphere or because they have no desire to be totalistic—as in the cases of contemporary China or Vietnam, where the government deliberately encourages the private-sector economy to grow and allows a good measure of societal pluralism, as long as such interests and identities do not threaten the political stability of the regime.

So to return to our chapter question, "What is non-democracy?"—the first key element of all non-democratic regimes is the nature of the hierarchical relationship of authority between the state and its subjects in society. In totalitarian systems like North Korea, the government attempts to completely dominate all aspects of individuals' lives, using ideology to indoctrinate and coercively mobilize people to support the regime, while eliminating societal as well as political pluralism. In contrast, state–society relations in authoritarian regimes focus more narrowly on the government's efforts to demobilize citizens and control political pluralism. Yet, there is a second key element of non-democratic regimes we must consider: the nature of the institutions that govern leadership selection and deselection. We now turn away from state–society relations and focus on the institutions of non-democratic regimes.

COMPARING INSTITUTIONS OF NON-DEMOCRATIC REGIMES

4.4 What distinguishes the types of non-democratic regimes from each other?

👁—Watch the Video **"Iran's Hybrid Regime"** at **mypoliscilab.com**

One crucial distinction among non-democracies is whether the regime is totalitarian or authoritarian. The difference between these two types focuses on the nature of the relationship between the state and society. In both regimes, the leaders are not accountable to the electorate—the full body of a nation's citizens (see Figure 4.1). However, they may be accountable to a narrower subset of the population called the selectorate. Another answer to this chapter's main question turns away from the state–society relationship and focuses our attention on relationships of power within the state—between the selectorate and the leader or leaders. To distinguish types of non-democratic regimes, we compare and contrast along four characteristics:

1. Size of the selectorate;
2. Criteria for admission to the selectorate;
3. Rules for selection of leaders; and
4. Rules governing the use of power—that is, whether the relationship between the selectorate and the leader(s) is based on formal rules and procedures, including lines of succession, party rules, and military chain of command, or whether this relationship is based on informal personal connections or networks including friends and family members.

With these four characteristics in mind, we can distinguish six types of non-democratic systems: monarchy, single-party regimes, military regimes, oligarchy, theocracy, and personalistic regimes.

Monarchies

Monarchies are non-democratic systems in which rulers assume power via birthright and are removed from power when they die. In pre-modern Europe, kings and queens were accountable only to God and had absolute power—meaning they had final authority to determine the content of the law. In theory, no selectorate exists for absolute monarchies, since no one selects the monarch. But in practice, the selectorate in monarchies consists of members of the royal family as well as powerful political groups, such as land-owning nobles and/or the military, all of whom have some leverage over the monarch. Even so, the selectorate's power to determine political succession is often limited because family bloodline determines the rules of succession when a monarch dies. This means that the relationship between the leader and the selectorate is institutionalized, even though the rules for selection of leaders depend on a family connection.

Some absolute monarchies survive in contemporary states, including Brunei, Kuwait, Lesotho, Morocco, Oman, Qatar, Saudi Arabia, Swaziland, Tonga and the United Arab Emirates, but constitutional monarchs are more common. In a constitutional monarchy, a constitution sets formal limits on the monarch's powers. A contemporary example is King Abdullah II of Jordan. Abdullah assumed power when his father Hussein died in 1999, and he is latest in the long line of the Hashemite dynasty. Abdullah and his family derive their legitimacy as rulers over Jordan on the basis of their claim of direct descent from Islam's founding prophet, Muhammad. Abdullah is a forty-third-generation descendant of Muhammad, and he can trace his ancestry back to the sixth century. However, Abdullah does not rule absolutely: elections are held, and a bicameral parliament exists. Still, the king retains considerable political power. He is chief executive of government, and parliament needs a two-thirds majority to override his veto. This means that Abdullah rules as a very powerful unelected president-for-life—a position his son will inherit when he dies.

Monarchy as a form of government is becoming increasingly rare. Many monarchies have been overthrown or have simply died out over the past few decades, replaced by either democracy or some other form of non-democracy, and no new monarchies have emerged. For example, in 2007, the parliament of Nepal decided to abolish the country's monarchy and move toward democracy. Likewise, in 2008, in nearby Bhutan, the king himself urged his subjects to vote in democratic elections that would end the monarchy's absolute reign. Many monarchies have evolved into constitutional monarchies, in which the ruler has little or no formal authority, and serves only as a symbolic head of state—as is the case, for example, with the king or queen of England.

Single-Party Regimes

A second form of non-democratic government is the single-party regime, in which a single political party dominates all government institutions and restricts political competition to maintain itself in power. The size of the selectorate in single-party regimes depends on the nature of power within the ruling party, but it is typically limited to the highest-ranking members of that party. Criteria for admission to this

monarchy ■ non-democratic systems in which rulers assume power via birthright and are removed from power when they die.

absolute monarchy ■ a monarchy in which no selectorate exists, meaning the ruler answers to no one.

constitutional monarchy ■ a system in which the constitution sets formal limits on the monarch's powers.

single-party regime ■ in which a single political party dominates all government institutions and restricts political competition to maintain itself in power.

group also vary across regimes and can include everything from charisma to personal connections to an ability to get things done in government.

In all single-party regimes, control over and transfer of political power takes place entirely within the top ranks of the ruling party. The highest-ranking members of the party determine access to their little club and also determine who gets appointed as national leader from within their members. This means that in single-party regimes, we see reciprocal accountability more clearly at work than in monarchy. In single-party regimes, the leader owes his or her job to and is accountable to the selectorate, but the selectorate is also accountable to the leader. If those who choose the leader fail at their jobs, the leader can demote them and take away their right to participate in choosing the next leader.

Single-party regimes can be either totalitarian or authoritarian. Examples of the former include Nazi Germany and the Soviet Union, while examples of the latter include Mexico, where a single party ruled from 1929 to 2000, and Taiwan, where a single party ruled from 1950 to 2000. Sometimes, as in the Soviet Union or Mexico, single-party regimes hold elections. Often, the ballots in such elections only allow citizens to vote for the party already in power, but sometimes other parties are allowed to place candidates on the ballot. Either way, in single-party regimes, elections usually just rubber-stamp the ruling party's choices for leadership, with no real contestation for power. Elections in the Soviet Union, for example, typically revealed 99.99 percent support for the ruling Communist Party.

Several single-party regimes exist today, as in Cuba, North Korea, Laos, and Vietnam, but the most prominent single-party regime in the contemporary world is the People's Republic of China. In China, a country with a population of 1.3 billion, the top leadership of the Communist Party selects and can dismiss about 5,000 top officials—including all provincial governors, heads of central-government bureaucracies, senior military officers, and top members of the National People's Congress. However, this relationship is not purely hierarchical. According to party rules, the Communist Party's Central Committee—which consists of about 300 of the highest-ranking party, government, and military officials—has the power to choose the approximately two dozen members of the *politburo*, an executive council of the Central Committee. Yet here is where we see the relationship of reciprocal accountability, because the politburo members also choose the members of the Central Committee! This means that politburo members owe their jobs to the Central Committee, while Central Committee members also hold their positions at the pleasure of the politburo. The lines of accountability run both ways within China's top leadership.[9]

military regime ■ a non-democratic regime in which the selectorate is typically limited to the highest ranks of the military officer corps.

junta ■ the group of leaders of a military regime.

Military Regimes

Military regimes are distinct from monarchies and single-party regimes in that the selectorate is typically limited to the highest ranks of the military officer corps. This group selects and removes the leader or junta (meaning a group) of leaders (pronounced *HUN-ta*). Admission to the selectorate is restricted to those who rise through the military ranks, and selection of the national leader is typically a function of military protocol. That is, the relationship between the leader and the selectorate is highly institutionalized, perhaps even more so than in single-party regimes, because the rules for advancement are fairly clear. Even so, one can never rule out informal politics in a military regime. For example, once in office, junta members might attempt to consolidate their rule by promoting their allies and removing their enemies from the very same corps of officers that selected *them*.

When military leaders decide to enter politics by overthrowing a civilian government (whether a democratic government or not), they have two distinct advantages: overwhelming firepower and a highly institutionalized structure of command and control. The question is why military leaders decide to engage in politics.

There are multiple reasons. Some military leaders—just like monarchs, party leaders or charismatic leaders like Hitler—are simply power-hungry. In other cases, they fervently believe that civilians are incapable of ruling or have brought shame to the nation. Given that effective use of a military force requires top-down command and control, officers and enlisted personnel often favor political order and dislike the chaos of protests and radical change—and they may project this desire for law and order into civilian politics, which they sometimes see as unnecessarily disorderly. Military leaders also view the armed forces' identity as selfless and their mission as universalistic—their job is to defend the entire country—whereas they see politicians as selfish, interested in defending only narrow interests or identity groups.

Given that such a self-image is probably common to all armed forces around the world, the question is why military leaders only sometimes intervene in politics. Three factors contribute. The first is the politicization of the officer corps, which can happen when civilian political organizations—especially political parties—gain influence within the ranks. This occurred after Hitler's Nazi regime took power in Germany, for example. There, the Nazi Party sought to build a network of like-minded supporters among soldiers and officers. Successful efforts such as the one in Germany tend to politicize the military, which has the often-unintended consequence of encouraging its involvement in civilian politics, or building support for would-be dictators.

A second factor encouraging military leaders to enter politics is self-interest in defending their organizational interests. The most important interest is a perceived threat to the military's autonomy. Officers tend to resist civilian interference in their affairs, especially in terms of making purchasing decisions, awarding promotions, and designing and implementing training programs. Military interests also extend to defending their share of the national budget, and not surprisingly, political interventions by a country's armed forces tend to be followed by massive increases in weapons spending. Finally, military interests may revolve around resisting threats or perceived threats to their control over the means of coercion. Civilian leaders sometimes create or enhance the power of secret police, independent militias, or presidential guards. To the extent that such organizations gain budget resources and access to weapons, officers may view them as political threats, and they may act to forestall their creation or eliminate them—and the politicians who created them.

The third factor that may give rise to military regimes has less to do with the interests of leaders of the armed forces and more to do with civilian institutions. When both soldiers and average citizens perceive civilian political institutions as legitimate, military leaders are less likely to overthrow the existing system. Yet, when officers and enlisted personnel begin to believe that civilian leaders and civilian institutions have forfeited their claim to legitimacy—whether due to corruption, generalized political disorder, loss in war, disastrous economic policies, or an inability to end political deadlock—their self-perception as defenders of the homeland leads them to conclude that they must enter politics to fulfill their oath of office. And in such situations, the weakness and illegitimacy of civilian political institutions means that the population may acquiesce or even support intervention by the armed forces. In short, military regimes are more common in weak states because the army may be the only strong institution remaining.

Military regimes have been quite common throughout history, in almost every area of the world. One recent example is Myanmar (formerly known as Burma), an extremely poor and isolated country in Southeast Asia where the armed forces controlled all institutions of government from 1962 to 2011. Twelve military commanders comprised the junta, called the State Peace and Development Council.[10] The armed forces repressed opposition parties, social movements, and NGOs; controlled access to all forms of mass media, including the Internet; and engaged in widespread human rights violations against ethnic and religious minorities and political opponents.[11] Elections were held in 2011, but pro-democracy opposition parties refused to participate and alleged fraud. Myanmar's current president and many of its top officials are former generals, and the military retains tremendous influence in politics.

Oligarchies

oligarchy ■ a non-democratic regime in which the selectorate consists of a small social, economic, or political elite, which selects a leader to represent their interests.

A fourth form of non-democratic government is oligarchy, which means, "Rule by the few." In oligarchies, the selectorate consists of a small social, economic, or political elite, who select a leader to represent their interests. Criteria for membership are often informal, as are the group's rules for selecting the leader. In contrast to a monarchy, in an oligarchy, family connections do not necessarily determine membership in the selectorate. The ruling elite may be powerful economic actors, such as landholders or financial or corporate elites, who appoint a ruler who mainly serves their interests.

In contrast to a monarchy, a single-party regime, or a military regime, the relationship between the leader and the selectorate in an oligarchy is less institutionalized, and more informal. That is, members of social, economic, or political elites may not have direct and formal control over selecting government leaders, but they do exert disproportionate informal influence relative to the rest of the population. Similarly, the ruler may not formally determine who gets to be a member of the oligarchy. Rather, government leaders may use their control over the apparatus of government to play aspirants for wealth and power off of each other, thereby obtaining more support for themselves. Several modern democracies—such as the UK, Chile, and Costa Rica—emerged out of oligarchies. In the contemporary world, true oligarchy in which only a small minority of the population has formal authority over the composition of government is unknown.

However, oligarchy still informally characterizes politics in some states. For this reason, many observers considered Russia in the 1990s an oligarchy, due to the informal power of a small group of wealthy business leaders and high-level government bureaucrats. In an oligarchy, influential people profit from their personal and family connections, often without having formal control over the apparatus of government. During Boris Yeltsin's presidency in Russia in the early 1990s, a small group of entrepreneurs profited from a combination of free-market reforms and widespread corruption, growing fantastically rich in a short period. They subsequently used their wealth to influence politics, contributing heavily to their favored candidates in elections and using bribes to influence policy. They then obtained insider information about government decisions in order to further expand their wealth and influence, and they exploited corruption by skimming off the top of lucrative government contracts, obtaining sweetheart deals for purchase of government properties, and engaging in tax evasion. The oligarchs' ability to flout the law reflected the Russian government's inability to enforce the law and the fact that some government leaders colluded, out of self-interest, with the oligarchs in the first place.[12]

Theocracies

Theocracies are distinct from all the other forms of non-democracy discussed thus far, in that their leaders claim divine guidance to hold the authority to rule. Such leaders acquire their positions by rising through a religious clerical hierarchy. Therefore, in a theocracy, the selectorate consists of high religious authorities. However, it is difficult to characterize the relationship between the selectorate and the ruler under theocracy, simply because that relationship will depend on which religion guides the theocratic rulers. A Jewish, Christian, Buddhist, Hindu, or Muslim theocracy would have different government institutions because each faith approaches the relationship between God and human society differently. Moreover, because each faith is internally divided, we cannot even identify what a "Christian" or "Muslim" theocracy might look like. For example, Catholicism has rigid hierarchical governance structures with the pope at the top. In contrast, Protestants are divided into numerous Christian sects (e.g., Episcopalians, Baptists, Presbyterians), which recognize no central religious authority.

Similarly, Islam is divided into two main sects—Sunnis and Shiites—which disagree vehemently about fundamental religious tenets, such as whether religious authority should go to direct descendants of the prophet Muhammad (Shiites) or to leaders who piously follow Islamic tenets (Sunnis). (Approximately 85 percent of the world's Muslims are Sunni, and most of the Shiites are in Iran.) In practice, this means that like Protestant Christianity, religious authority in the Sunni Muslim

theocracies ■ non-democratic regimes in which leaders who claim divine guidance hold the authority to rule.

community is highly decentralized, with no hierarchy of religious authorities. In contrast, Shiites have a more hierarchical clergy, with "grand ayatollahs" at the top and "ayatollahs" outranking other clergy, much like the pope outranks cardinals in the Catholic Church.

Because theocratic governance is guided by religious principles, theocracy also embodies elements of totalitarianism. First, in a theocracy, religion is analogous to a totalitarian ideology. After all, religious authorities in a theocracy are concerned with using the institutions of the state to reshape society—to remake individuals' identities and interests according to their religion's dictates. Second, in principle, religious authorities in a theocracy would not seek to demobilize citizens but would seek to encourage, spread, and deepen their faith. That is, a truly theocratic government would engage in some degree of coercive mobilization, forcing individuals to actively engage in and publicly proclaim their faith. Finally, a true theocracy—in which religious authorities believe that nonbelievers are heretics—would, at a minimum, have an uneasy relationship with religious and other political minorities. This means that any theocracy tends toward the "totalitarian" end of the spectrum, in terms of permitting social and/or political pluralism.

In the contemporary world, religious authorities have considerable power and comprise an important part of the selectorate in several Islamic states—for example, Saudi Arabia. However, religious authorities do not rule in those states. Instead, monarchs or other secular authorities do. In today's world, only the Vatican City (where the pope rules) is a true theocracy, and Iran comes close. However, many question the degree to which Iran approximates this type of non-democratic regime.

Personalistic Regimes

personalistic regime ■ a system built around the glorification and empowerment of a single individual.

The last form of non-democratic regime is a personalistic regime, a system built around the glorification and empowerment of a single individual. This may sound familiar, given the previous description of the personality cults that glorify the two Kims of North Korea. The key characteristic of this kind of regime is a lack of institutionalization—that is, the absence of clear rules governing politics and, in particular, governing the transfer of political power. In a personalistic regime, rulers arbitrarily intervene in individuals' lives, and their whims decide government policy. Sometimes leaders are popular, but more often they rule through cunning, guile, and a willingness to use violence.

All forms of non-democracy—including both totalitarian and authoritarian regimes—can be personalistic to some degree, if a charismatic leader is the ruler. However, the degree to which a non-democratic regime corresponds to this type versus one of the others is a function of the degree to which leadership selection and succession is institutionalized or not. In a purely personalistic regime, leadership selection and succession is informal and based on personal connections or the leaders' whim. In contrast, monarchies, military regimes, and one-party non-democratic regimes can have highly institutionalized and relatively stable leadership succession. This high degree of institutionalization helps explain why single parties managed to rule for decades in Russia (as the Soviet Union) from 1922–1991, in Mexico from 1929–2000, and in China from 1949 to the present, for example. In these institutionalized, non-democratic systems, transfers of power can go smoothly because the selectorate follows established guidelines.

In contrast, where the regime's political institutions are weak or nonexistent, politics tends to be dominated by individuals, families, and friends. In a personalistic regime, politics centers on an informal dynamic: the leader handpicks cronies to help him (or, rarely, her) run the country. This group might be considered the selectorate, but the absence of clear rules regulating succession makes politics and especially leadership succession in personalistic regimes particularly unstable and prone to violence.

Given the lack of institutionalized rules governing politics, rulers expend considerable energy building up their allies, playing their allies off each other, and tying the hands of their enemies. They do so by building a cult of personality; creating an organization that makes major social, economic, and political actors dependent on the ruler; and using corruption to distribute payoffs or reward faithful allies with plum bureaucratic positions or government contracts. They may also intimidate, harass, or repress opponents and seek to pass laws that regulate political speech or freedom to organize opposition groups or political parties. This means that the selectorate is constantly in flux. No one, including the leader, has

Jean-Bédel Bokassa at his coronation as "Emperor" of the Central African Republic in December 1977. Bokassa modeled himself after Napoleon Bonaparte, and this ceremony was rumored to have cost more than $20 million.

an institutionalized power base, because all politics is based on "who you know" and fueled by patronage and corruption. Personal loyalties structure transfers of power from one ruler to the next, which means that political contestation takes the form of rivalries, plots, conspiracies, and violent attempts to overthrow the ruler. Thus, the only path to power is to forcibly remove the leader, or fight it out when the leader dies.

Personalism in non-democratic regimes is common, but few regimes perfectly fit the stereotypical image of a regime dominated by a megalomaniac leader whose sole concern is perpetuating himself in power. One example that does approach this image is the reign of Jean-Bédel Bokassa in the Central African Republic (1966–1979). Bokassa, an army colonel, overthrew his own cousin to take power. He promoted himself first to general, then to president for life, and then declared the Central African Republic a monarchy, with himself as its first emperor, "His Imperial Majesty Bokassa I." Bokassa was notoriously unpredictable and cruel— so much so that he was rumored to be a cannibal and literally insane. Bokassa's personalistic regime was noted for its corruption, waste, and human rights abuses.[13]

In sum, a focus on the selectorate helps us distinguish the main institutions of non-democratic governments. The table on the following page summarizes these differences, focusing on the size of the selectorate, membership criteria, the rules for leadership selection, and the relationship between the leader and the selectorate. In all non-democratic regimes, the selectorate is always smaller than what the electorate would be under a democracy. Yet the size of the selectorate can vary from very few people—the ruler's family, for example—to several hundred in a single-party regime. The other three characteristics vary as a function of their clarity or opacity: criteria for membership in the selectorate can vary from completely unclear—as in a personalistic regime—to fairly transparent, as in a military regime. The same holds for membership rules—sometimes it's pretty obvious how people can gain entry into the selectorate—by being a family member or by rising through the ranks of a party or military, for example—while sometimes the process remains a mystery, as in an oligarchy or personalistic regime. Similarly, the way non-democratic regimes select rulers can vary from completely opaque—as in North Korea—to fairly clear, as in a monarchy.

Understanding the nature of a non-democratic regime's selectorate allows you to take Freedom House's list of "Not Free" countries and place each into one of the five categories of non-democracy. Yet, as with the sometimes-blurry distinction between democracy and non-democracy itself, were you to undertake this exercise, you'd quickly see that some non-democratic regimes couldn't easily be categorized. Some one-party regimes, for example, are also personalistic regimes. This is clearly the case with contemporary North Korea, which technically is a totalitarian single-party regime, but also exhibits strong traits of a personalistic regime—and even exhibits features of monarchy, given the transfer of power from Kim Il-Sung to Kim Jong-Il, as well as rumors that Kim Jong-Il plans to transfer power to *his* son upon his death. Many personalistic leaders are also military officers, making the line between personalistic and military regimes hard to identify precisely. The concept of the selectorate provides a useful starting point for classifying a non-democratic regime but not a definitive one.

SUMMARY TABLE

Characteristics of the Selectorate in Non-Democratic Regimes

Type of Non-Democracy	Size	Membership Criteria	Rules for Leadership Selection	Relationship between Leader and Selectorate	Examples as of 2011
Monarchy	Ruler's family	Family relationship	Family descent	Institutionalized, limited reciprocal accountability	Saudi Arabia, Brunei
Single-Party Regime	Variable	Party membership; rise through ranks	Determined by party rules	Institutionalized reciprocal accountability	Cuba, China, Vietnam
Military Regime	Typically limited to high officer corps	Military member; rise through ranks	Determined by military high command	Institutionalized reciprocal accountability	Myanmar, Fiji, Mauritania
Oligarchy	Small	Informal	Unclear and informal	Informal reciprocal accountability	1990s Russia
Theocracy	Variable	Member of a religious order; rise through the ranks	Variable	Variable	Vatican City, Iran
Personalistic Regime	Limited to ruler's cronies	Leader hand-picks	Unclear and Informal	Reciprocal accountability, but unclear and unstable	Libya (until 2011), Burkina Faso, Belarus

CONCLUSION

What is non-democracy? The answer turns on two key distinctions. First, consider the way in which the non-democratic state relates to society. Although all non-democratic forms of government lack accountability and involve a hierarchical relationship in which the state dominates society, compared with authoritarian regimes, totalitarian regimes go to extremes to shape the interests and identities of their subjects. Totalitarian regimes dominate, coerce, mobilize, and indoctrinate their citizens to accept the official state ideology. In contrast, authoritarian leaders are mainly preoccupied with *de*-mobilizing citizens to solidify their hold on power.

Communism and fascism were the dominant totalitarian ideologies of the twentieth century. Both are similar in that they devalue individual rights, dismiss democracy, and rationalize an all-powerful state. However, important distinctions between these ideas place their proponents on opposite sides of the political spectrum. Communism downplays nationalism and emphasizes the interests among workers across nations, while fascism stresses the importance of national community, militarism, and a strong charismatic leader. No truly fascist regimes have emerged since the end of World War II, and most countries where communist parties remain in power have become authoritarian regimes.

Following state and society, we considered the nature of the institutions of non-democratic regimes. A focus on the extent to which membership criteria in the selectorate and the relationship between the selectorate and the leader are institutionalized helps distinguish several forms of non-democratic government from each other—monarchy, oligarchy, single-party states, theocracies, military regimes, and personalistic regimes.

Almost one in four states today have some type of non-democratic regime. In particular, non-democracies still rule over most states in the Middle East, Africa, and Asia. Such governments consistently violate citizens' economic and social rights, as well as their individual liberties. However, as the information from Freedom House implies, in recent decades, many "Not Free" governments have shifted away from non-democracy and into the "Partly" or fully "Free" categories. In the next chapter, we turn to the question of why governments sometimes transition between democratic and non-democratic regimes. ▲

✓●─ Study and Review the Post-Test & Chapter Exam at mypoliscilab.com

The Democratic Republic of the Congo (DRC) and the People's Republic of China are very different. The DRC, in central Africa, is both one of the world's poorest countries and one of the world's weakest states—only Somalia is weaker.[14] Its government does not fully control the national territory, and insurgent violence continues to plague the country. In contrast, although the average Chinese person remains relatively poor compared to the average American, China's economy has been growing rapidly for 20 years, and the country is rapidly becoming a global superpower. China's state is also relatively strong. Both countries do share one key attribute—they are both non-democracies. However, the DRC is a personalistic regime, while China is a single-party system. Perhaps this difference explains why corruption—the illicit use of public authority to achieve private gain—is much worse in the DRC than in China.

It is possible that this distinction in terms of the "amount" of corruption in personalistic and single-party non-democratic regimes holds more broadly. To find out, let's consider the hypothesis that *corruption will be higher in personalistic non-democracies as opposed to single-party regimes.*

GATHER EVIDENCE

Corruption can occur when private-sector actors bribe government officials, when government officials abuse their power to extort payoffs from the private sector, or both. Every year, the World Bank assesses the level of corruption in each country around the world. The bank derives its measure by surveying business leaders, citizens, and experts about the perceived extent of corruption in their country.[15] In 2011, Denmark and New Zealand won the "clean government" award for having the least corruption, while Myanmar and Somalia were marked as the world's most-corrupt countries. Out of approximately 200 states, the DRC ranked 194th, while China ranked 123rd. By comparison, the United States ranked 30th from the top. In general, democracies

see less corruption than non-democratic regimes: the average Freedom House score for the 20 countries with the least corruption was 1.4 ("Free"), while the average for the 20 most-corrupt countries was 6.0 ("Not Free"). If we examined the World Bank's assessment of corruption in all non-democracies, would the contrast between the DRC's personalistic regime and China's single-party regime hold?

ASSESS THE HYPOTHESIS

Democracies are less corrupt on average than non-democracies because they tend to protect individual property rights and the rule of law better than non-democracies. We can extend the logic of this distinction between democracies and non-democracies to consider differences between different types of non-democratic regimes. In a democracy, politicians expect the basic rules of politics to be respected, whether their party wins or loses. In a non-democracy, no one can take such basic political stability for granted. Even so, a regime's relative degree of institutionalization may impact the level of corruption. A difference exists between dictators who can reasonably expect to remain in office over the long run versus those who fear losing their job—or even their head—from week to week. How might dictators' different perspectives on their job security impact corruption?

Non-democratic rulers who do not fear being tossed from office have stronger incentives to respect property rights and to refrain from stealing from those in the private sector. Indeed, perhaps the reason they do not fear being tossed from office is because they engage in relatively less corruption and provide some benefits to the general population. China's ruling Communist Party has been in power since 1949, and faces no credible threats to its authority. In China's single-party regime, corruption is balanced out by the government's concerted effort to grow the economy, encourage private-sector economic investment,

(*Continued*)

Corruption is widespread in China—but the Communist Party often makes a visible show of catching, prosecuting, and harshly punishing perpetrators. In this case, the mayor of Chongqing, a large city in central China, led an anti-corruption crusade that resulted in the arrest of more than 1,500 suspects, including police officers and government officials.

public—which means relatively fewer resources are available for corrupt officials to skim off the top as corruption.

In contrast, dictators who have good reason to fear losing power in the short term have stronger incentives to extract wealth as fast as possible through corruption. Faced with a likely loss of power in the near term, rulers—and their entourages—will grab what they can. The DRC's president, Joseph Kabila, gained power in 2001, after his father was assassinated by his own bodyguards. (In fact, his father had overthrown the DRC's previous president just four years earlier.) Since 2001, armed groups have attempted to assassinate Kabila at least five times, most recently in February 2011.[16] Widespread civil conflict continues in the country's vast eastern region, contributing to an overall context of political instability.[17] Since assuming office, Kabila has claimed fighting corruption would be a government priority,[18] but efforts have not improved matters at all—bribery and extortion remain rampant. Meanwhile, despite possessing vast stocks of valuable natural resources, the country's economy remains stagnant and

and improve government services such as education. From time to time, the government also makes a great show of publicly prosecuting—and sometimes executing—government officials convicted of corruption. This means that compared to a place like the DRC, in China relatively more government resources are devoted to the general

the government does little to improve the lives of average citizens.

Scholars have confirmed that the intuition from this comparison of the DRC against China holds up more generally: corruption is worse in non-democratic regimes where rulers have good reason to fear for their jobs—in personalistic

(*Continued*)

regimes, where politics is highly fluid and unstable—compared to single-party regimes, which tend to be characterized by much greater stability.[19] Where non-democratic regimes impose the fewest constraints on the individual ruler, we see more frequent abuses of power—including more pervasive corruption. ◢

CRITICAL THINKING QUESTIONS

1. Why is corruption relatively higher in personalistic non-democracies, compared to single-party regimes?
2. Would you expect military regimes to have relatively more or less corruption than personalistic regimes? Why?

KEY TERMS

regime   92
selectorate   94
rciprocal accountability   94
totalitarian regime   95
authoritarian regime   95
ideology   95
communism   100
fascism   100
Cold War   100
capitalism   100
Social Darwinism   101

monarchy   105
absolute monarchy   105
constitutional monarchy   105
single-party regime   105
military regime   106
junta   106
oligarchy   108
theocracy   109
personalistic regime   110
corruption   115

REVIEW QUESTIONS

1. What is the key difference between democratic and non-democratic regimes?
2. What is the key difference between authoritarianism and totalitarianism?
3. What are the main ways that communist and fascist ideologies differ?
4. What are the key differences between the rules of leadership succession in non-democratic regimes?
5. What is the most important way in which the relationship between the leader and the selectorate differs in non-democratic regimes?

SUGGESTED READINGS

Brownlee, Jason. *Authoritarianism in an Age of Democratization.* New York: Cambridge University Press, 2007. An overview of the nature of contemporary non-democratic regimes, focusing on the importance of a single-party system.

Friedrich, Carl, and Zbignew Brzezinski. *Totalitarian Dictatorship and Autocracy.* Cambridge, MA: Harvard University Press, 1965. A classic description of the characteristics of totalitarian regimes.

Griffin, Roger, and Matthew Feldman, eds. *Fascism: Critical Concepts in Political Science.* New York: Taylor and Francis, 2004. Explores fascist ideology and differences across fascist regimes.

Kang, Chol-hwan. *The Aquariums of Pyongyang: Ten Years in the North Korean Gulag.* New York: Basic Books, 2005. An autobiographical account of life in totalitarian North Korea.

Levitsky, Steven, and Lucan Way, eds. *Competitive Authoritarianism: Hybrid Regimes after the Cold War*. New York: Cambridge University Press, 2010. Brings in international factors to help explain how non-democratic rulers manipulate elections to their advantage.

NOTES

1. See for example, Choe Sang-Hun, "North Korea Tries to Show Its Leader Is Healthy and in Control," *New York Times,* November 7, 2008, A6.
2. See David Hawk, "Thank You Father Kim Il-Sung: Eyewitness Accounts of Severe Violations of Freedom of Thought, Conscience, and Religion in North Korea," United States Commission on Religious Freedom, accessed February 10, 2010, http://hirc.house.gov/archives/109/NKwitnesses.pdf.
3. See Chol-Hwan Kang and Pierre Rigoulot, *The Aquariums of Pyongyang: Ten Years in the North Korean Gulag* (New York: Basic Books, 2005).
4. See Juan Linz, *Totalitarian and Authoritarian Regimes: with a Major New Introduction* (Boulder, CO: Lynne Rienner Publications, 2000).
5. Zbigniew Brzezinski and Samuel Huntington, *Political Power: USA/USSR* (New York: Viking Press, 1964).
6. See for example "Reviving the *Komsomol,*" *Time,* November 4, 1968. http://www.time.com/time/magazine/article/0,9171,902498,00.html.
7. *New York Times,* January 12, 2005. http://query.nytimes.com/gst/fullpage.html?res=9A00EED81638F931A25752C0A9639C8B63.
8. From *The Doctrine of Fascism*, by Benito Mussolini and Giovanni Gentile, 1935. The full text can be found at www.historyguide.org/europe/duce.html.
9. This description comes from Susan Shirk, *The Political Logic of Economic Reform in China* (Berkeley: University of California Press, 1993).
10. See http://www.irrawaddy.org/research_show.php?art_id=454, accessed November 13, 2008.
11. Up-to-date information on Myanmar can be found at *The Irawaddy* website, http://www.irrawaddy.org/. *The Irawaddy* is a newsmagazine published by Burmese exiles living in Thailand.
12. See for example, David Hoffman, *The Oligarchs: Wealth and Power in the New Russia* (New York: Public Affairs, 2003).
13. See Kwame Anthony Appiah and Henry Louis Gates, Jr., eds., *Africana: The Encyclopedia of the African and African American Experience.* (New York: Basic Books, 1999).
14. See State Failure Task Force Global Report, accessed May 25, 2011, http://www.systemicpeace.org/Global%20Report%202009.pdf.
15. See World Bank Governance Indicators, accessed May 24, 2011, http://info.worldbank.org/governance/wgi/index.asp.
16. See "DR Congo: Six killed in 'coup bid' against Kabila," accessed May 25, 2011, http://www.bbc.co.uk/news/world-africa-12591259.
17. See "Q&A: DR Congo Conflict," accessed May 25, 2011, http://www.bbc.co.uk/news/world-africa-11108589, accessed May 25, 2011.
18. See "DR Congo Leader Kabila Sacks 3,000 Civil Servants," accessed May 25, 2011, http://news.bbc.co.uk/2/hi/africa/8442193.stm.
19. See Eric Chang and Miriam Golden, "Sources of Corruption in Authoritarian Regimes," *Social Science Quarterly* 91, 1 (2010): 1-20.

Regime Change

Chileans take to the streets to advocate an end to General Augusto Pinochet's 15-year dictatorship. These people were taking great personal risks, as the government had murdered more than 2,000 of their fellow citizens during its regime, and imprisoned thousands of others. Their efforts proved successful in defeating Pinochet's efforts to win

? What are the causes of regime change?

Read and Listen
to **Chapter 5**
at **mypoliscilab.com**

Study and Review
the **Pre-Test & Flashcards**
at **mypoliscilab.com**

In 1970, Salvador Allende won Chile's presidential election. Allende was a Socialist, and because of Chile's plurality electoral system for presidential elections, he was able to win with little more than one-third of the vote. This meant that a majority of voters opposed Allende and his policies. But Chile had held free and fair democratic elections since before World War II, and although all of its neighbors were governed by military regimes at the time, Chile's military leaders did not impede Allende from taking office. However, three years later, in the midst of political and economic chaos, the military decided to intervene. Troops murdered Allende, and leaders of the armed forces assumed power. For 15 years, the leader of the Chilean army, General Augusto Pinochet, ruled the country with an iron fist. Chilean democracy had collapsed into military dictatorship.

During Pinochet's rule, thousands of Chileans were imprisoned, tortured, killed, or "disappeared." However, in the face of increasing international pressure to restore democracy, on October 5, 1988, Pinochet sent Chileans to the polls and gave them two options: "Yes" or "No." According to Chile's 1980 constitution—which Pinochet himself had helped to write—a majority for "No" would require Pinochet to call free and fair presidential elections in 1989 and then relinquish the presidency in 1990. A majority for "Yes" would have given Pinochet another eight-year term as president. Fifty-six percent of Chileans overcame their fear of Pinochet's brutal regime and voted "No."[1] With these results, the dictator faced a dilemma: abide by the rules of his own constitution, or ignore the result and remain in power.

In his hands, Pinochet had the tools to maintain political order—particularly the coercive power of the military, police, and judicial authorities. Yet, he surprised many observers when he conceded defeat and relinquished power. Today, Chile has a thriving and stable democracy. In contrast to 1973, Chile in 1990 represents a case of democratization—the shift from non-democracy to a democratic form of government.

democratization ■
a shift from a non-democratic to a democratic regime.

What are the causes of regime change? Governments and leaders come and go; this is normal in both democratic and non-democratic states. Yet, a more fundamental political question asks why states sometimes change political *regimes*. A political regime refers to the fundamental form state institutions take: It is either a democracy or a non-democracy. Why would Allende's democratic regime collapse into non-democracy—and why would Pinochet's military regime give up power and reestablish democracy?

The Chilean regime changes in 1973 and 1990 raise the questions of why democracy emerges or collapses in some countries and not in others. How can we explain such transitions between regime types? This chapter's question is critically important for the future of global politics: people who live in democracies are likely to live healthier, longer lives because the government is less likely to repress dissent with violence; democratic regimes also perform better on a variety of measures such as providing health care, education, and other benefits that promote citizens' general welfare.[2]

There are no easy explanations for changes in political regimes, because global developments such as the spread or decline of democracy often have multiple causes. In addition, the causes of regime change in one country at one particular moment in time may be relatively unimportant in another country 20 years later. To get a handle on this chapter's question, we first review the frequency of regime change between democracy and non-democracy over time. We then explore the domestic and international political factors that appear to be systematically associated with transitions between regime types and assess the likelihood that democracy will continue to spread throughout the world—or be undermined by emerging global political dynamics.

HISTORICAL TRENDS

A first step toward understanding the causes of regime change comes from looking at historical trends both toward and away from democracy. At a very broad level, the world has experienced three "waves" of democratization, two of which were followed by "reverse waves" of regime change in which many democracies collapsed into dictatorship.[3] In each wave and reverse wave of regime change, a number of countries make the same transition from one regime type to the other. As Table 5.1 indicates, the First Wave began in the early 1800s with the emergence of

5.1 What proportion of the world's states have been democracies, historically?

TABLE 5.1

Waves of Regime Change

Wave	Time Period (Approximate)	Democracies as Percent of Total Number of Countries	Examples of Regime Change
First Wave of Democratization	1825–1925	22/67 (33%)	US, UK, France, Germany
First *Reverse* Wave	1925–1945	16/71 (23%)	Germany (1933)
Second Wave of Democratization	1945–1960	34/110 (31%)	Germany, Italy, Japan (~1945)
Second *Reverse* Wave	1960–1974	36/140 (26%)	Brazil (1964), Chile (1973)
Third Wave of Democratization	1974–1995	76/160 (48%)	Brazil (1985), Chile (1989)

Source: Center for Systemic Peace, 2011. "Polity IV Annual Time-Series 1800–2010." Available at http://www.systemicpeace.org/inscr/inscr.htm, July 10, 2011.

democracy in several countries in North America and Western Europe, including the United States and the UK.[4] In the late 1920s, the first "reverse wave" began, as several of these countries—most notably Germany—collapsed into dictatorship.

In 1945, the defeats of Hitler's Nazi regime and the Japanese and Italian dictatorships brought about the second wave of democratization. The Allied victors of World War II imposed democracy in Germany, Japan, and Italy and restored it to a few other European countries. Several Latin American countries and newly independent states such as Israel and India also adopted democracy. Still, many countries remained non-democratic, including several communist dictatorships in Eastern Europe.

A second "reverse wave" began in during the Cold War era, when several newer democracies—such as those in Latin America—then collapsed. However, the "Third Wave" of democratization began in the mid-1970s with the collapse of a longstanding dictatorship in Portugal—ironically, just a year after Allende's overthrow in Chile. As Table 5.1 indicates, by the 1990s, dozens of countries across the planet had adopted democracy, including Chile. Since the mid-1970s, most changes to democracy have occurred in Latin America and Southern and Eastern Europe. A few countries in Africa and Asia also began to shift toward democracy, but large swaths of the world remain dominated by "not free" non-democratic regimes.

Regime change—when a non-democratic state adopts democracy or the reverse—is common. Indeed, the Third Wave of regime change involved an unprecedented number of transitions to democracy in a relatively short period of time. The recent spread of democracy around the world returns us to this chapter's main question: *What are the causes of regime change?* The geographic spread of democracy also raises additional questions: why did some countries experience regime change to democracy during the Third Wave, while others never did? In the future, will countries that recently democratized collapse back into dictatorship? These are the sorts of questions we will consider in the remainder of this chapter, which explores the domestic and international factors that explain why countries experience regime change.

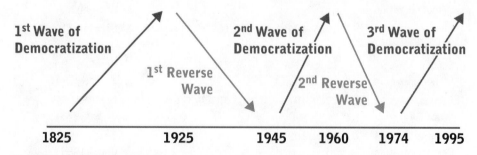

FIGURE 5.1

Waves of Regime Change

History has seen several "waves" of regime change, with the adoption of democracy being more frequent during some periods and transitions to non-democracy dominating in other eras.

DOMESTIC CAUSES OF REGIME CHANGE

When we speak of domestic factors that drive regime change, we refer to aspects of a country's history and culture, the political interests in society, and its institutions. Our goal is to determine which of these factors are associated with regime change: which seem to cause states to adopt democracy, and which seem to perpetuate non-democracy? Domestic background conditions and historical trajectories make some political outcomes more likely and others improbable or even impossible. The challenge is to identify those trajectories, and then to explain how they lead to democracy—or away from it.

Religious, linguistic, and economic conditions that exist in any particular country emerge out of long-term historical processes. Historical developments establish a set of conditions that can preclude or permit some sort of political change. In this section, we consider the impact of three pre-existing domestic conditions as they pertain to regime change: an element of political identity that we refer to as civic culture; changes in political interests and culture that result from economic development; and the armed forces' attitude toward civilian political institutions.

> **5.2** What are the domestic-level political sources of regime change?
>
> ◉ Watch the **Video** **"The End of Apartheid"** at **mypoliscilab.com**
>
> ✳ Explore the **Comparative** **"Violence and Civil Wars"** at **mypoliscilab.com**

The Civic Culture

Does the nature of a country's culture make regime change more or less likely? This idea seems plausible: After all, if a country's culture has historically supported the divine right of kings, then democracy may not flourish.[5] The core claim of a cultural approach to regime change can be stated quite simply: "No democrats? Then no democracy." The "d" in democrats is deliberately lower-case, because the claim is not a partisan statement in favor of one American political party over the other. It simply asserts that if a country's citizens value political equality and individual freedoms, then a democratic regime is more likely to emerge than if they do not hold those values. Many hold up the United States as a society with strong elements of what we call a civic culture, which is defined by three specific elements: high civic engagement, political equality, and solidarity.

Elements of Civic Culture Civic engagement refers to the degree of citizens' active participation in public affairs, such as by voting or participating in social movements, interest groups, or political parties. In other words, in cultures with high civic engagement, citizens do more than pursue their own private business or family affairs. In contrast, citizens in cultures with low civic engagement are less likely to express their interests publicly in the political arena. For example, the United States has long been noted for having multiple organizations, social movements, and interest groups. In contrast, an "uncivic" culture would have few such associations.

In a civic culture with political equality, citizenship offers both equal rights and obligations. Citizens in such communities believe that no one should be above the law. They do not tolerate giving some people political rights while excluding others, and they view non-democratic regimes as illegitimate. The more a political culture approximates this ideal of political equality, the more predisposed it is to

civic culture ■ a key aspect of a county's cultural identity defined by three characteristics: high civic engagement, political equality, and solidarity.

civic engagement ■ the degree of citizens' active participation in public affairs, such as by voting or participating in social movements, interest groups or political parties.

political equality ■ citizenship offers both equal rights and equal obligations.

democracy. In contrast, a society in which people believe that some people should have more rights than others, or that some people are by their nature above the law, is one in which political inequality is valued. Individuals in some cultures are relatively more deferential to religious or political authorities, for example. The less a political culture values equality, the less it is predisposed to democracy.

solidarity ■ the feature of a civic culture related to a general trust and respect among citizens, and a willingness to lend a helping hand, even when they might disagree on matters of public policy.

Finally, in a civic culture with solidarity, citizens generally trust and respect one another and are willing to lend a helping hand, even when they might disagree on matters of public policy. This is not to say that a civic community lacks conflict over what public policies to adopt, but it suggests that citizens tolerate divergent views because they trust that even their opponents have the best interests of the community in mind. In contrast, in an "uncivic" culture, citizens tend to distrust one another, are intolerant of different views, and less willing to lend a hand to communal endeavors. An uncivic society is one in which relatively few people join organizations or participate in organized activities outside their household, passively accepting that only the state can organize society, typically through the use of coercion.

Measuring Civic Culture   To what extent does regime change depend on the degree to which the citizens embody a civic culture? To assess this argument, we first need to know how we might measure the degree to which a community is civic. Only then might we compare societies to discover whether this sort of culture is associated with the emergence or collapse of democracy.

A key indicator of a society's civic engagement is its individuals' willingness to form and join social and political organizations. Such organizations need not be political: church choirs, bird-watching clubs, and even bowling leagues are good examples. Participation in such groups contributes to democracy by encouraging patterns of cooperation, respect for others' views, a spirit of public-mindedness, an ability to work with strangers, and feelings of trust and shared responsibility for the fate of the community. Participation in groups promotes unselfish behavior and the expectation that others should behave similarly.

Overall "civic-ness"—and, thus, the quality of democracy—can be measured by the density of a society's network of societal groups and associations. The higher the ratio of groups to the total population, the greater the civic qualities of that society's political culture and the greater the likelihood that the country will experience regime change to democracy.

Problems with the Civic Culture Argument   This civic culture argument confronts at least two challenges. First, although the density of social groups certainly indicates that citizens are engaged, not all organizations have similar goals. For example, some organizations and their members—such as the Red Cross, the local PTA, or the Eagle Scouts—promote engagement and concern for others in the community, and we might agree that people active in such groups do contribute to the development of effective social collaboration. However, other organizations are exclusive—and they can also be disdainful, intolerant, or even violent toward nonmembers. Examples include elite country clubs, the KKK, skinhead groups, and street gangs.

The differences between "good" and "bad" social engagement suggests that the density of organizational membership does not accurately measure a society's degree of civic-ness. Instead, the reasons why people mobilize are more important for the emergence of democracy than is the raw number of groups. This problem is illustrated by the case of Germany. Although a dense network of groups and associations emerged by the 1920s and 1930s, this culture of civic engagement still enabled the rise of Hitler's Nazi Party.[6]

A second issue is the chicken-and-egg problem. Does a citizenry oozing with "civic-ness" cause democracy to emerge, or does having a democracy cause citizens to become more civic? If the latter is true, then the idea that a civic culture *causes* democracy to emerge may not be true. This problem is illustrated by the case of the UK—one of the world's oldest democracies, but also a country of royalty and nobility, a place of longstanding elite snobbery against those in the working and lower classes, and a country that colonized much of the world. How did democracy emerge from an aristocratic system in which political elites treated the masses both at home and abroad with such contempt? If democracy can emerge in that cultural context, then perhaps it can emerge in any cultural context. The example of the UK suggests that a civic culture may reflect democracy, but not cause it to come about. Given these two problems, an argument that emphasizes the causal importance of political culture is at best incomplete, and we need to consider alternative explanations for regime change. Instead of political culture, let's consider the possibility that broad economic change—such as that caused by widespread industrialization—can bring about political change.

Economic Change

A country's economic transformation from poor to rich may cause a political transformation from dictatorship to democracy. Why would this be so? To answer this question, we can look to the political consequences of the Industrial Revolution—which began around 1800—and the related process of economic modernization in Western Europe. Those countries that industrialized changed rapidly from primarily rural to primarily urban, and they experienced breathtaking technological changes and improvements in quality-of-life indicators such as education and infant mortality.

The processes driving economic modernization transformed or even destroyed preexisting social and economic structures across Western Europe. Because such changes occurred in what were at that time all non-democratic regimes, scholars have long suspected that such socioeconomic changes might also transform political structures and bring about regime change to democracy.

There are two ways economic change leads to political change. The first approach focuses on interests—specifically, the way economic development can bring about the rise of new social classes, who then have strong desire to fight for access to political power. The second approach emphasizes identities—specifically, the way economic modernization changes people's values so that they grow more supportive of democracy.

Class Conflict Causes Regime Change   The first economic hypothesis about regime change suggests that democratization is more likely when widespread economic development reduces the influence of elite classes and increases the relative influence of newly emergent middle and working classes. Prior to the Industrial Revolution, the dominant economic system in Europe was feudalism. Under feudalism, the nobility owned agricultural land, from which they derived their wealth and power. The rest of the population worked land they did not own and had little if any political power. In such societies there was no real middle class—the wealthy upper-class landowners dominated politics, lording it over the huge mass of impoverished lower-class agricultural laborers.

The demise of agricultural feudalism and the rise of industrial capitalism had a tremendous impact on both economic growth and political organization. The onset of the Industrial Revolution and capitalism brought about the rise of a middle class, which included entrepreneurs who made their living through trade and commerce and applied their profits to furthering their industrial, financial, or commercial investments. With newly realized economic influence, members of the middle class in growing urban areas were keenly aware that they still lacked corresponding political rights. In turn, the established upper classes fought to retain their privileged positions and to limit other groups' access to power.

The logic of this argument with regard to regime change depends on the strength of established versus emerging economic groups. In some countries, the wealthy landowners managed to survive and thrive. To the extent that landowning elites retained power even as industrialization advanced, regime change to democracy was less likely because the wealthy could continue to block regime change. In contrast, if landowning elites grew weaker as industrialization advanced, democratization was more likely. Similarly, if the middle classes grew in numbers and became organized into political parties, unions, or interest groups, regime change to democracy was also more likely. If, however, the middle classes remained small and disorganized, regime change was less likely.

The hypothesis linking economic development to democratization through class conflict most clearly applies to a few European cases in the first wave of regime change. For example, in the 1800s and early 1900s, non-democratic regimes evolved into stable democracies in the UK, Sweden, and the Netherlands, where landowning elites grew economically less important and the middle classes grew in size and strength. In contrast, where landowning elites remained economically important even as the middle classes grew in strength, as in Spain and Germany, weak democracies emerged only to collapse back into non-democracy. These different outcomes underscore the key premise of the class-conflict argument: regime change to stable democracy depends on the emergence of a sizable middle class and a weakened wealthy landowning elite. Where the middle classes were weak and/or the landowning elite remained powerful, stable democracy was unlikely to emerge.

The class-conflict argument works well where conflicting interests of clashing economic groups has been intense. Unfortunately, it is less helpful in explaining more recent cases of democratization. This is because in recent decades many countries adopted democracy despite weak or nonexistent middle classes. This was the case with another South American country, Paraguay in 1989, for example, which experienced democratization despite widespread poverty and inequality, no industrialization, and a relatively tiny middle class. The existence of several cases that democratized without strong middle classes means that—like the civic culture argument—we cannot rely on class conflict to explain all cases of regime change. The argument appears to best apply to transitions that occurred in the First Wave of democratization, but not to others.

Modernization and Regime Change   What alternative stories might explain more recent cases of regime change? It is true that democracy remains more common in richer countries, while non-democracy is more common in poorer countries. The association between level of economic development and the likelihood that a country is a democracy is among the strongest empirical relationships you will ever see in a social science class. Given this correlation, a second version of this economics and politics story downplays class conflict and political interests and returns to political culture. This argument, known as modernization theory, suggests that democracy is not simply a function of economic growth, but rather that it is a function of the cultural changes that accompany economic growth. In contrast to the class-conflict argument, which points to the growth of a strong middle class as a key cause of regime change, modernization theory suggests that economic development encourages citizens' values to be more supportive of democracy and less supportive of non-democracy.

> **modernization theory** ■ suggests that democracy is not simply a function of economic growth but rather that it is a function of the cultural changes that accompany economic growth.

Economic modernization tends to result in more complex societies, largely due to the growth of large cities. Growth is also associated with better education and literacy, and greater exposure to the mass media, which encourages citizens to develop greater awareness of and concern for politics and public affairs. As a consequence of economic development, growing proportions of the population come to possess pro-democratic interests, such as aspirations for greater participation and the idea that every individual should have equal rights to participate in politics.

The key element of modernization theory is the connection between economic development and changes in citizens' understanding of politics. Poorer, less-developed societies maintain their traditional rigid and hierarchical political cultures, in which the poor remain deferential to established authorities. Yet, as a country grows wealthier, its citizens' attitudes toward political authority change. For example, some observers suggest that recent (and as yet unmet) demands for democracy in countries such as Tunisia and Egypt follows from the emergence of a new, educated middle class that values political freedoms historically unknown in those countries.[7]

In global perspective, the evidence for modernization theory appears to fit the facts: country wealth is highly correlated with whether a country is democratic. However, just as with the cultural and class-conflict arguments we've already discussed, modernization theory leaves some difficult questions unanswered. Many dictatorships remain intact even after they have become quite wealthy. In fact, in the early twentieth century, modernization in countries such as Germany and Japan generated support for *non-democracy*, precisely the opposite of what modernization theory predicts! Stable democracies only emerged in those countries because the United States and its allies imposed it after World War II. In the contemporary world, too, we find many exceptions. For example, Saudi Arabia retains a hierarchical political culture and appears in no danger of democratizing, no matter how wealthy it grows. At the same time, democracy has emerged and survived in several impoverished countries. India, for example, confounds modernization theory: it adopted democracy upon independence in 1948, even though it was one of the poorest countries on earth. If modernization theory were true, India should not be a democracy.

The existence of wealthy non-democracies and of poor democracies show that while economic modernization may explain some instances of regime change, it cannot provide a complete answer to this chapter's question about why some countries experience regime change. Even though wealthy countries do tend to be democracies and poor countries tend not to be, exceptions suggest that the relationship between economic development and regime change is not as straightforward as modernization theory implies. This, in turn, points us to other important factors of regime changes besides aggregate economic growth.

One twist on modernization theory focuses on the *nature* of a country's economy—whether it is diverse or whether it depends on one single valuable commodity, such as oil or diamonds. Exceptions to modernization theory lead us to ask if there is a certain *kind* of economic growth that is a prerequisite for regime change: in fact, non-democracies that develop diverse economies are more likely to see the emergence of a middle class that wants to participate in politics. In contrast, non-democracies that rely on a single commodity for their wealth fall victim to what is called the resource curse, which suggests that economic growth that relies on only one valuable resource may have problematic political consequences.

resource curse ■ hypothesizes that economic growth that relies on one valuable natural resource is unlikely to result in an equitable distribution of wealth, which creates problematic political consequences.

The logic of the resource curse is as follows: governments in countries with one abundant natural resource have strong interests in retaining tight, centralized control over the production, sale, and taxation of that commodity. Governments sometimes become addicted to the revenue this valuable commodity generates, and use that revenue to purchase political support. Because control of the resource generates such easy money, governments have few incentives to invest in other sectors of the economy. In the end, because economic development depends on government control of the main engine of the economy, a diverse market does not fully develop.

This argument helps explain why economic modernization plays a smaller role in the democratization of many Third Wave cases (1970s–1990s). During the Third Wave, transitions to democracy were more likely in countries with diversified economies than in countries that produce oil or any other single valuable natural commodity. With this hypothesis in mind, the long-term prospects for democracy may be better in developing countries like Brazil or India, which don't rely on one export commodity and have complex economies, than in countries like Venezuela, Nigeria, or Russia, which depend heavily on fossil fuel exports.

Economic change can bring about political change. Development can weaken the traditional land-holding political elites and bring about the emergence of a new middle class that has stronger desire to fight for political rights. It can also alter the way people think about politics, changing individuals' attitudes toward political authority. As countries grow wealthy, individuals grow less respectful towards traditional authority figures, and demand equal rights. However, economic development does not always bring about democracy, suggesting that we must continue to examine other domestic sources of regime change. As we shall see in the next section, the armed forces can play a key role.

The Role of the Military

Civic culture, class-conflict, and modernization theory all point toward the importance of long-term social and economic change as domestic sources of political change. However, other forces in a society may also work against democratization and in favor of maintaining a non-democratic regime. Suppose we had two countries that had identical civic cultures, similarly sized middle classes, equal levels of wealth, and economies that were identical in diversity. Yet, now suppose that these two countries differed in a key way: in one the armed forces were subordinate to civilian authorities, while in the other the armed forces refused to recognize civilian command and were decidedly anti-democratic. Which country would be more likely to democratize? This hypothetical scenario pushes us to consider the potentially critical role of the military.

One of the most common causes of regime change from democracy to non-democracy is a military coup, which occurs when elements in a country's armed forces overthrow a democratically elected civilian government and take control. "Coup" (pronounced "koo") is taken from the French term *coup d'état*, which means "a blow against the state." Coups have been historically frequent in Latin America, Africa, and parts of Asia, but they are not limited to the world's poorer countries. Between World War I and II, several military coups were attempted in European countries and succeeded in Spain, Greece, Portugal, and Latvia. As late as 1967, the military overthrew a democratic government in Greece and ruled for seven years.

military coup ■ when elements in a country's armed forces overthrow a democratically elected civilian government.

In truth, most military coups target non-democratic rulers rather than democratic regimes. For example, Colonel Muammar Qaddafi overthrew Libya's monarchy in 1969 and served as that country's personalistic ruler with the support of the military until 2011. In most cases, when the military overthrows a government, the state changes hands from one non-democratic ruler to another. Yet some coups end democratic regimes, as in Chile in 1973.

Coups against democratic regimes continue to occur. For example, in Thailand, the military overthrew democratically elected Prime Minister Thaksin Shinawatra in 2006. The military justified its actions by accusing Shinawatra of

Illustrating the military's self-perception as defender of Thai religious traditions, an officer offers a traditional salute to a monk in front of a prominent Buddhist temple in the capital city, Bangkok, just days before the 2006 military coup.

corruption, conflict of interest, abuse of power, nepotism, misuse of government funds, interfering with the system of checks and balances, and mistakes in pursuing Islamic guerrillas in Thailand's southern provinces. The Thai military set itself up as the defender of law and order and claimed that Shinawatra had "violated Thailand's ethics and moral integrity" and had destroyed the unity of the Thai nation.[8]

The Thai military's rationale for taking power sounds self-serving, yet this example illustrates a key factor in explaining regime change: whether a military traditionally perceives itself as subordinate to or independent of civilian authority. The question here for comparative analysis is, "What is the military's political identity?" Does that identity encourage the armed forces to intervene in civilian politics or does it constrain the military to remain on the political sidelines? Exploring the historical dynamic of civil–military relations helps us understand why military coups sometimes cause regime change from democracy to non-democracy and other times impede a regime change from non-democracy to democracy.

In some countries, militaries believe they are independent of any civilian authority—democratically elected or not. Military leaders sometimes claim to serve a higher power than the constitution, which in their view is just a piece of paper that organizes the institutions of the state. That higher power, they claim, is the nation—a cultural group based on collective identity.

Even though it is an abstract concept, most citizens tend to possess an image in their mind of their nation's identity—its land, people, and cultural practices. Such images do not change easily. In contrast, many countries frequently amend or even change their constitutions—and if chaos, corruption, and crime become commonplace, a constitution may not seem worth the paper it is written on. In such situations, powerful political actors will not fear the consequences of violating the highest law of the land.

The United States has a long-standing constitutional tradition of civilian control over the military, which impedes the military's direct intervention in politics. When personnel enlist in the U.S. military, they swear to defend the Constitution of the United States and to obey the orders of the president as commander-in-chief. In such a system, military officers tend not to believe that they have a legitimate right to replace civilian leaders, under any circumstances. And in other countries, the military is a relatively unimportant player in national politics, a fact that also helps preserve democracy. The survival of democracy in Costa Rica is a case in point, as this chapter's feature box helps explain.

However, in countries with weak traditions of civilian control over the military, leaders of the armed forces sometimes come to believe that they *must* intervene when—in their view—civilians have become incapable of ruling or (as was the case in Thailand, mentioned earlier) have brought shame to the nation. Military leaders tend to favor law and order and dislike the chaos of protests and radical change, and they sometimes project this desire for law and order into civilian politics, which they see as messy and disorderly.

Military leaders also see the armed forces' identity as selfless—for the good of all citizens—whereas they perceive politicians as corrupt, selfish, and particularistic, meaning they are interested in defending only narrow interests or identity groups. Thus, in military coups like those that occurred in Thailand, Chile, and elsewhere, coup leaders rationalize intervention by pointing to their self-professed role as "defenders of the nation." Such self-identity requires that constitutional traditions of civilian authority over the military be weak, which means that the military has historically enjoyed considerable political autonomy.

The military's identity helps explain many cases of collapse of democracy into non-democracy. However, as with the arguments presented above pertaining to the civic culture and the impact of economic change, military identity cannot explain every case. After all, even if the military remains subordinate to civilian authority, a civilian can still destroy democracy. This was precisely what happened in Germany in 1933—Hitler was a civilian, but his popularity, combined with the weakness of pro-democratic political forces, allowed him to destroy the democratic regime. In short, although military identity can be crucial, it may be wholly unrelated to regime change in many cases.

All the internal domestic elements that we have considered—culture, economics, and military identity—are potentially critical for understanding transitions from

HYPOTHESIS TESTING | Weak Landowning Elites and a Weak Military Can Sustain Democracy: The Case of Costa Rica

Several Latin American countries democratized during the second wave of regime change that followed in the wake of the Allied victory in World War II. However, during the Cold War, many of these democracies collapsed into dictatorship during the second reverse wave. Coups d'état destroyed democratic regimes in such countries as Brazil in 1964, Argentina in 1966, Uruguay in 1973, and as noted at the start of this chapter, Chile in the same year. In contrast, Costa Rica democratized in 1948, and its democracy has survived to the present day. Why did Costa Rica, which was vulnerable to the same international influences as its regional neighbors during the Cold War, not experience regime change to dictatorship when other similar countries did?

GATHER EVIDENCE

Costa Rica presents us with a good political science puzzle precisely because its democracy survived, even though it shares many attributes with other Latin American countries. Consider, for example, the similarities between Costa Rica and its immediate neighbors in Central America—El Salvador, Honduras, Nicaragua, Panama, and Guatemala, none of which experienced regime change to democracy until the 1990s. All countries in Central America are relatively poor compared to developed democracies like the United States or the UK, and all have economies that focused not on industry but on exporting agricultural products, such as coffee and bananas. None of these countries has a large middle class. Instead, a relatively small economic elite has dominated politics in each country since independence in the early 1800s. Given these internal political and economic conditions, we have little reason to expect democracy to emerge, much less survive.

All of these small, weak Central American countries were also all vulnerable to U.S. influence during the Cold War. During that period, U.S. foreign policy supported non-democratic rulers in the region. U.S. meddling or outright intervention sometimes

Democracy is so entrenched in Costa Rica that in May 2010 its citizens elected the country's first female president, Laura Chinchilla.

stymied countries' efforts to chart an independent political path, for example in Guatemala, where the U.S. government encouraged a military coup that overthrew a democratically elected president in 1954. We have noted that international influences were particularly important in the Cold War era, as well as during the later Third Wave of transitions to democracy. Yet, Costa Rica resisted the global pressures during the Cold War, which would have predicted a collapse of its democratic regime. What explains democracy's resilience in Costa Rica?

ASSESS THE HYPOTHESIS

Although Costa Rica shared many attributes with its neighbors, it also differed in two key ways. First, although Costa Rica had never experienced significant industrialization and consequently did not witness the emergence of a large middle class, its wealthy rural

(*Continued*)

landowners were politically relatively weak to begin with compared to rural elites in neighboring countries. Most importantly, instead of the typical pattern in which relatively few families controlled most of the good farmland, Costa Rica had a large number of family farms—relatively small operations owned by members of a single family. As a result, Costa Rica's large landholders had relatively less political influence than did their counterparts elsewhere.[9] Strong rural elites tend to prevent or delay the emergence of democracy; a weak landholding elite means democracy has a greater chance to emerge.[10]

Second, civil–military relations in Costa Rica were different from everywhere else in Latin America. Costa Rica not only had a strong tradition of civilian rule—which contrasts with the autonomy that militaries enjoyed in most other Latin American countries—after 1949, it didn't even have a military! That year, Costa Ricans rewrote their constitution, abolishing the country's armed forces (a national police force was established). This permanently and completely eliminated the military from politics,[11] which had the positive effect of removing a force that in many Latin American countries directly contributed to democracy's collapse.

In sum, Costa Rica differed from its neighbors on two key attributes. The combination of a weak rural elite and the absence of a military stabilized Costa Rican democracy over the long run, even during a period of history when international factors caused many other democracies to collapse. ◣

CRITICAL THINKING QUESTIONS

1. Why might rural landholding elites oppose the emergence of democracy?
2. If Costa Rica had had a military during the Cold War, would its democracy have survived? Why or why not? Consider the relative political importance of Costa Rica's landed elite in your answer.

democracy to non-democracy, or vice-versa. The table below summarizes the arguments in this section and provides illustrative examples. Although these domestic factors help us make sense of complex patterns of regime change, they do not always provide fully satisfying explanations. Other factors may be at work, particularly factors that are *external* to any country's politics. In the next section, we turn to the impact of international politics on countries' domestic politics.

INTERNATIONAL CAUSES OF REGIME CHANGE

Apart from domestic factors, international factors coming from outside any particular country are often critical causes of regime change. Such forces were especially relevant during waves of regime change to and from democracy since about 1945, and include the influence of four major global actors—the United States, the Soviet Union, the Catholic Church, and the European Union (EU)—as well as the impact of globalization, which is the spread of political and economic dynamics beyond the borders of any one particular country.

5.3 What are the international-level political sources of regime change?

globalization ■ the spread of political, economic, and cultural dynamics among governments, groups, and individuals beyond the borders of any one particular country.

U.S. Foreign Policy

Immediately after World War II , U.S. foreign policy interests encouraged democracy around the world, even imposing it upon several countries. The United States also gave massive amounts of economic and political aid to France and Greece,

👁—⎡Watch the **Video**
"Toppling Hussein"
at **mypoliscilab.com**

SUMMARY TABLE

Long-Term Factors Promoting Regime Change

Factor	Key Argument	Status	Hypothesized Impact	Illustrative Example
Civic Culture	*Civic engagement, political equality, solidarity*	High	Democratization	USA 19th century
		Low	No democratization	Saudi Arabia
Economic Factors				
Class Conflict	*Strong middle class.*	High	Democratization	UK
		Low	No democratization	North Korea
Modernization Theory	*Economic development fosters value change*	High	Democratization	Sweden
		Low	No democratization	Zimbabwe
Military Identity	*Military perceives itself as independent of civilian authority*	High	Democratic collapse	Chile 1973
		Low	Stable democracy	Costa Rica, 1949–present

where democracy appeared threatened by communism, and it oversaw regime change in the defeated Axis powers of Germany, Italy, and Japan. The Allied forces' defeat of fascism reverberated around the world, as non-democratic regimes in other regions also collapsed and democracy emerged, for example in Brazil in 1945 and Argentina in 1946.

However, as the Cold War developed, the United States frequently compromised its support for democracy in favor of military rulers and dictators who allied with the United States against the Soviet Union. Given this inconsistent support for democracy, anti-democratic forces gained strength and legitimacy in many countries, leading to the fall of democratic regimes in Brazil in 1964, Argentina in 1966, and Chile in 1973, to name a few. In this way, changes in U.S. foreign policy contributed to both the Second Wave of democratization and the reverse wave that followed.

By the 1970s and especially the 1980s, following the Vietnam War, U.S. foreign policy began to shift yet again, as the U.S. government began to redefine its national interest to support democracy and human rights. For example, in the 1970s and 1980s, Congress began conditioning U.S. foreign aid on recipient countries' human rights standards.[12] These policies continued under Republican presidential administrations of Reagan and Bush (1981–1992), due to those presidents' interest in contrasting the freedoms of U.S. citizens against the absolute lack of freedoms offered by the totalitarian government that ruled the Soviet Union.

During the Third Wave, American support for democracy meant that non-democratic rulers lost an important external ally. United States support for democracy—inconsistent as it was—contributed to regime change in the Third Wave because it both weakened non-democratic rulers and emboldened dictators' opponents, many of whom began to mobilize, organize, and lobby for democracy.

Soviet Foreign Policy

After the Allied victory over Nazi Germany in World War II, the Soviet Union occupied and established puppet regimes in several countries on its western frontier in Eastern Europe. It also provided overt and covert support to communist insurgencies around the world. At the time, the Soviet Union represented all the qualities of a non-democratic regime: the government prohibited contestation, popular participation was minimal, and the state exerted near-total control over the economy. Competition between the United States and the Soviet Union during this period never exploded into a "hot" war, but the Cold War was a dangerous time—and Soviet support for communist non-democratic regimes, coupled with U.S. support for anti-communist non-democratic regimes, made the Cold War era a hostile global environment for democracy.

By the 1980s, the Soviet Union's centrally controlled economy was in a tailspin. The country's leader at the time—Mikhail Gorbachev—attempted to reform the system from within, but he failed, and the regime collapsed in 1991. This meant that the world's most powerful non-democratic regime had failed. In the wake of Soviet collapse, five Eastern European communist regimes—Poland, Czechoslovakia, Bulgaria, Romania, and Hungary—all quickly transitioned to democracy. In addition, 15 Soviet provinces gained status as independent states, and several of these—including Latvia, Lithuania, and Estonia—adopted democracy.

With the collapse of the Soviet Union, after 1990 there was no global superpower advocating and attempting to spread a non-democratic form of government to other countries. Democracy appeared to be the only legitimate *and* viable regime left; fascism had lost all legitimacy after World War II, and communism followed in its wake 45 years later.

Changes in the Catholic Church

The Catholic Church is perhaps the only major global non-state actor that is hierarchically organized—with the pope at the top—that can reach into local communities in most regions of the world. In First and Second Wave democracies, the dominant form of religious identity was Protestant Christianity. In fact, democracy did not flourish early on in predominantly Catholic countries such as Poland, Spain, Chile, Mexico, or Brazil. However, all these and several other majority-Catholic countries democratized during the Third Wave.

Many predominantly Catholic countries remained non-democratic until the Third Wave at least partly because of the Church's historical indifference or even opposition to democracy. Yet in the 1960s, the Church adopted a firmly pro-democracy stand. Church leaders also nominated a cardinal from a non-democratic country—Poland—to be pope in 1978, signaling support for religious freedom against communist atheism and totalitarianism. That pope, John Paul II (1978–2005), actively campaigned for democracy during his tenure in his home country and around the world. The shift in Church doctrine was an important factor in advancing democracy in many Third Wave countries, because it meant that non-democratic rulers in predominantly Catholic countries lost one of their main allies, and because the change in doctrine gave ordinary Catholics in non-democratic regimes a religious seal of approval to lobby for political change.

The European Union

The final important actor on the international stage to push for democracy during the Third Wave was the European Union (EU). The EU is a supranational organization that distributes subsidies and benefits and controls or influences important elements of monetary, trade, agricultural, and other policies for its 27 member countries. What is relevant here about the EU is that it imposes strict membership qualifications: Countries that wish to join must adopt fully democratic rules. This pressure helped advance the Third Wave, especially in Eastern and Southern Europe. For example, since achieving status as an official EU candidate for membership in 1999, Turkey has implemented new human rights policies, abolished the death penalty, and granted additional rights to ethnic minorities. In short, because many countries have strong interests in joining the EU for its economic benefits, the EU has helped spread democracy.

Major global players do not always promote the spread of democracy; they sometimes actively seek to spread non-democracy or undermine democratic regimes. When major global actors are not promoting democracy, non-democracies are unlikely to democratize—and democracies are more likely to collapse into nondemocracy. This dynamic characterized the early decades of the Cold War between 1950–1975, which coincided with the second reverse wave. However, by the late 1980s, the world's most powerful actors—the Vatican, the EU, the United States, and the USSR—had either shifted policies toward the explicit promotion of democracy or had become more or less democratic themselves. The key point is that by the end of the Cold War in 1991, no major player in global affairs supported nondemocracy as part of its stated foreign policy. This change in the global political environment made it harder for dictators to maintain legitimacy and remain in power.

Globalization

Foreign policy actions of major global players are not the only way that international factors can impact the likelihood of regime change. Globalization—the spread of political, social, and economic dynamics beyond the borders of any single country—can also work in less direct ways. In some cases a powerful neighborhood effect exists, as countries in a particular geographic region tend to follow their neighbors in terms of adopting a regime type. Specifically, the probability that a randomly chosen country is a democracy is about 75 percent if more than half of its geographic neighbors are democracies—but only about 15 percent if more than half of its neighbors are non-democracies. The case of Chile illustrates this effect well: by 1989, all of its Latin American neighbors had transitioned to

neighborhood effect
■ when countries in a particular geographic region follow their neighbors in terms of adopting a regime type.

democracy, making Chile stand out as unusual and putting extra peer pressure on her military rulers to conform to the regional trend.

Second, a "global" effect also appears to be at work in recent waves of regime change: The overall level of democracy in the entire world—as measured by averaging the Freedom House score for all countries—influences whether any particular country will experience a regime change. At the global level, when non-democracy is the "thing to do," non-democratic rulers find remaining in office easier. Yet, when democracy comes into fashion, non-democratic rulers have a harder time retaining power. If the world happens to be experiencing a wave of democratization, then the remaining non-democratic regimes are more likely to democratize.

These findings help explain the Third Wave of democratization. Global political dynamics help by changing the balance of political power *within* countries. For example, during a wave of regime change to democracy, pro-democratic political parties, social movements, and interest groups can more easily observe and identify with political events in neighboring countries. And if a regime change occurs in a neighboring country, citizens may be emboldened to act, reasoning, "If those people—who look, sound, and think like us—can have a democracy, then so can we." Government leaders around the world also see political reward in resembling their neighbors—perhaps because governments of similar regime types are better able to communicate on a friendly basis with each other, are less likely to fight each other, and have more profitable trade and investment relations.

The interests of major global actors as well as the dynamics of neighborhood and global effects are all external to the domestic politics of a given country, but they all play an important role in driving regime change. The long-term internal factors identified in the previous section—the civic culture and economic arguments—were relatively more important in the first wave of regime change. In contrast, the international factors summarized in the table on the following page were more important during the Second and Third Waves.

SHORT-TERM CATALYSTS OF REGIME CHANGE

Several domestic and international forces drive regime change. These arguments offer predictions based on background conditions, such as "a wealthy country is more likely to democratize," or based on changes in the global political environment, such as whether major powers' foreign policies influence the likelihood of democratization in less-powerful countries.

However, hypotheses such as these do not necessarily explain all of the precise reasons that non-democracies evolve into democracy, or vice versa. In fact, the specific short-term catalysts for regime change tend to vary quite widely from country to country. Sometimes an acute economic crisis leads to regime collapse, as it did to Germany's democratic regime in 1933, but this is not always the case—the global economic crisis in 2008 did not immediately lead to the collapse of any democracy around the world. Likewise, the death of a longtime dictator can catalyze regime change to democracy, as in Spain in 1975 when General Francisco Franco died, but not in North Korea when Kim Il-Sung passed away in 1994.

5.4 What are the short-term causes of regime change?

👁 Watch the Video "August 1991: The Collapse of the Soviet Union" at **mypoliscilab.com**

> ▸ **SUMMARY TABLE**
>
> **Global Causes of Regime Change**
>
> | Factor | Key Argument | Status | Hypothesized Impact | Illustrative Example |
> |---|---|---|---|---|
> | Major Powers' Foreign Policies (US, USSR, Catholic Church, EU) | *Major global actors promote democracy* | Yes | Transitions to democracy | Eastern Europe ~1990 |
> | | | No | Transitions to non-democracy | Latin America during the Cold War |
> | Globalization | *Number of democratic regimes in the "neighborhood"* | High | Transitions to democracy | Latin America during the Third Wave |
> | | | Low | Transitions to non-democracy | Latin America during the Cold War |
> | | *Number of democratic regimes in the world* | High | Transitions to democracy | Third Wave of Democratization |
> | | | Low | Transitions to non-democracy | Second Reverse Wave during the Cold War |

Here's an analogy to illustrate the contrast between long- and medium-term factors versus those at work in the short term: suppose you wanted to explain why the Titanic sank. On the one hand, you might suggest that the Titanic sank because it hit an iceberg. On the other hand, you might argue that the ship was doomed before it even left port because its design was vulnerable to flooding.[13] Which explanation is more satisfying? The ship certainly would not have sunk without the iceberg, but it also might not have sunk had its design been better, even if it had hit the iceberg. Both explanations—the background conditions and the immediate cause—are important. Both explain the same outcome, but emphasize different factors.

In light of this analogy, consider the transitions to democracy in Argentina, Brazil, Chile, and Paraguay in the 1980s. On the one hand, all four of these regimes were under similar international pressures to democratize. Yet on the other hand, each regime collapsed because of a different short-term factor: Argentina's military was humiliated in a war with the UK over the Falkland Islands in 1983; Brazil's military regime grew divided over how to govern the country during an economic crisis and handed power back to civilians; Paraguay's long-term military ruler died without an obvious heir; and—as noted at the start of the chapter—Chile's dictator decided to obey the results of a plebiscite that denied him another term in office.

In any case of regime change, short-term factors are the iceberg that sinks the ship. Crises tend to expose a regime's flaws and delegitimize it in citizens' eyes. Because the regime has lost its leader, its war, or its way, crises provide catalysts that encourage fed-up citizens to mobilize against the government. In many countries, such popular protests prove critical to the regime's downfall. In particular, because non-democratic regimes do not have the safety valve of rotating leaders and regular elections, non-democratic regimes may be more brittle and susceptible to collapse in a crisis situation. In these Latin American cases, these short-term catalysts were all different, but led to the same outcome: a transition to democracy.

Such short-term events are always important, but because they can be so different, they are not subject to the more systematic comparative analysis we undertook for the domestic and international factors. Unlike domestic and international causes, short-term factors typically apply only to a particular case, not a whole pattern of regime change. Sometimes a dictator dies but another dictator assumes power, leaving the non-democratic regime in place. Likewise, an economic crisis may cause a fatal decline in regime legitimacy in one democracy but not in another. Because short-term factors vary so much from country to country, the key to answering this chapter's main question lies with the domestic and international background conditions. And now that we have a handle on the sources of regime change, in the next section consider what the future of regime change might look like.

THE FUTURE OF REGIME CHANGE

Given what we've discussed thus far, what does the future hold in terms of regime change around the world? Will the Third Wave of democratization continue and will more non-democracies and partly free countries transition to democracy—for example, in countries like Egypt or Tunisia? Or will we soon see a reverse Third Wave of regime change? There are grounds for optimism as well as pessimism. With the demise of the Soviet Union in 1991 and China's abandonment of communism as a totalitarian ideology, some are optimistic that democracy is now the only form of government around the world with broad legitimacy.[14] Recent events in the Middle East, where multitudes have demanded an end to non-democratic rule, have fueled this optimism. And to the extent that this view is correct, we have reason to expect more transitions to democracy in the future.

However, we also have reason to be pessimistic. In the late 2000s, several countries that had at least partially democratized have sunk back into non-democracy, such as the case of Thailand mentioned earlier, where the military overthrew a democratically elected prime minister. In July 2011 elections were held and a civilian government returned to power, but Thailand's future remains uncertain. Moreover, despite widespread protests and great hopes for deep and lasting change in the region, no Middle Eastern non-democracy has yet to truly transition to democracy.

In general, our crystal ball peering into the future remains cloudy. Although the number of "Free" democratic countries increased and the number of

5.5 What does the future hold in terms of regime change around the world?

Watch the **Video** "Venezuela's Constitutional Referendum" at **mypoliscilab.com**

"Not Free" non-democracies declined during the Third Wave, the number of "Partly Free" countries increased also during this period. Partly for this reason, some worry that contemporary global factors are inauspicious for the further spread of democracy,[15] and that countries that have never transitioned to democracy may get stuck in this "Partly Free" middle category, or even that countries that have made it into the middle category will revert to the fully "Not Free" group.[16]

Illiberal Democracies

illiberal democracies ■ regimes that combine elements of democracy, such as voting and elections, with non-democratic elements, such as restrictions on political contestation and individual rights.

Another term for "Partly Free" countries is illiberal democracies. Illiberal democracies are regimes that combine elements of democracy such as universal suffrage and regular elections with non-democratic elements such as restrictions on political contestation and a free press, and widespread violations of citizens' rights.[17] The dividing lines between democracy, illiberal democracy, and non-democracy can be hard to draw. This is because illiberal democracies *appear* democratic in some ways—especially since citizens sometimes willingly, even eagerly, elect their leaders, who then violate the democratic rules of the game. Even so, illiberal democracies are not, technically speaking, *non*-democracies.

Venezuela is sometimes cited as an example of a contemporary illiberal democracy.[18] Venezuela was one of the few Latin American countries to democratize during the Cold War—in 1958. Yet in the 1990s, Venezuela experienced considerable political and economic turmoil and its two main political parties lost popular legitimacy—so much so that the entire democratic regime collapsed. Venezuelan army colonel Hugo Chávez, who led a failed coup against a democratically elected president in 1992, won Venezuela's 1998 presidential election in a free and fair contest. He was reelected in 2000, and won another six-year term in 2006.

Soon after winning office, Chávez called a referendum to elect members of a constitutional convention. His allies won nearly all the seats, and they drafted a constitution that centralized power, weakened Venezuela's federal system, eliminated its Senate, and gave Chávez the power to pass decrees that have the force of law without legislative approval. In 2009, Chávez also gained voter approval of a plebiscite that abolished presidential term limits, giving him the ability to run for reelection indefinitely.[19] Observers worry that Chávez will never relinquish power. Venezuela has experienced a partial regime change from democracy to illiberal democracy because although its rules still allow for popular participation, Chávez has stacked the political deck to such an extent that the rules constrain political contestation.

The Venezuela case illustrates the paradox of illiberal democracies. Leaders in illiberal democracies win elections and may —at least temporarily—have considerable popular legitimacy. Moreover, illiberal democracies do not explicitly eliminate all the institutions of democracy. Instead, rulers govern within a formally democratic institutional framework. However, these rulers subtly and gradually change the institutions of government rather than engaging in overt and widespread political repression, as in fully non-democratic regimes. Such manipulations of the rules of the game weaken political contestation without explicitly eliminating it, limiting citizens' ability to vote leaders out of office, thereby undermining democratic accountability.

From Illiberal Democracy to "Not Free"?

The growth in the number of "partly free" illiberal democracies suggests that the future of regime change toward democracy remains uncertain. To assess the possibilities, we will focus on the impact of the international political climate as we did in the previous section, asking whether major political actors currently support, oppose, or are indifferent to democracy.[20]

During the Cold War, the Soviet Union actively supported communist non-democratic regimes while the United States often supported anti-communist non-democratic regimes. As the Cold War wound down in the 1980s, the Soviet Union collapsed and U.S. foreign policy shifted toward support for democracy. In today's world, no major global power actively encourages the spread of non-democracy. Instead, the world's major powers at least implicitly support democracy.

Protesters in Brussels—where the European Union is headquartered—call upon the EU to take a stronger stance in defense of democracy outside of its own borders during a crackdown on protests in Egypt in February 2011.

However, there are two reasons why the international climate today may provide only weak support for democracy, encouraging backsliding into illiberal democracy, or even into non-democracy. First, although in principle both the United States and the EU support democracy, both apply this principle inconsistently. For example, both Democratic and Republican U.S. presidents have long supported a repressive monarchy in Saudi Arabia, in order to protect U.S. strategic interests in the Middle East. European leaders are no less inconsistent—for example they demand that EU member states adhere to strict democratic principles, while they also coddle favor with dictators on other continents. In many cases, democratic global powers conclude that strategic interests in protecting a non-democratic ruler outweigh promoting democracy.

Second, the foreign policies of two other major global powers do not clearly support the spread of democracy, even if they do not actively promote the spread of non-democracy. The first major power is Russia, which has grown increasingly non-democratic since 2000, and which has sought to influence the politics of countries on or near its borders. Russia has little interest in promoting democracy; it is only concerned with achieving its foreign-policy interests. The second major global power that does not necessarily support the spread of democracy is China. China's rapid economic growth has extended the country's economic influence to every corner of the planet. Because its economy depends on exports and the imports of food and raw materials, China has strong interests in maintaining ties to friendly governments. Thus far, China has not sought to explicitly support non-democracy, but it has also used its economic influence to sustain dictators in Africa and Asia, for example.[21]

Overall, as the summary table below suggests, today's global political environment contains both pro- and anti-democratic elements, and as we have seen, these elements go a long way toward helping us answer this chapter's main question about why some countries experience regime change and others do not. The United States and the EU both support democracy, but both also apply this principle inconsistently, supporting democracy in some regions or countries, while propping up dictators elsewhere. Moreover, Russia and China are at best indifferent to democracy, favoring *any* government that supports their interests.

SUMMARY TABLE

The Future of Regime Change

Element at Work in Global Politics	Effect
No major global actor actively spreads non-democracy.	Tends to support democracy
US and EU foreign policy is inconsistent; sometimes support dictators.	May undermine democracy
Russian and Chinese foreign policy do not actively support democracy, sometimes support dictators.	May undermine democracy

CONCLUSION

Presidents and prime ministers are elected and then lose office; dictators eliminate their rivals to acquire power, but are then eliminated in a later coup d'état. In comparative politics we do not focus on why individual personalities come and go. Rather, we are interested in a more important political question: why states sometimes change political regimes, from democracy to non-democracy, or vice-versa. The world has experienced three "waves" of democratization, two of which were followed by "reverse waves" in which many democracies collapsed into dictatorship. What drives these changes in political regimes?

In this chapter, we explored two sorts of background conditions—domestic and international—that systematically drive waves of both democratization and the collapse of democracy. At the domestic level, the main causes of regime change lie with whether a country has a preexisting "civic" political culture or not, with the way economic development has reshaped the political interests and cultural identities of a country's citizens, and with civil–military relations. Cultural and economic factors appear more important in pre-1945 waves of regime change, while the military's attitude toward civilian institutions remains relevant in recent waves.

The domestic sources of regime change—culture, economics, and military identity—are often critical. However, these factors often do not fully explain transitions to or from democracy. In addition—particularly in the post-1945 era—we discovered that we must include important international factors such as the foreign-policy interests of major global powers and neighborhood and global effects. The domestic and international sources of regime change appear to work systematically; that is, if similar forces are at work in different countries, we expect similar outcomes—for example, transitions to democracy in countries subject to the same international influences.

The background domestic and international factors help us understand patterns of regime change. However, they never give us the complete story. We also noted that the catalyst of regime change—the event that finally causes a democracy to collapse or forces a dictator out of power—tends to be different in each and every case. Because these short-term causes of regime change vary so greatly from country to country, they are not subject to systematic comparative analysis, like the background domestic and international factors. Nonetheless, they are a critical part of the story.

This chapter's main question—what are the causes of regime change?—remains pertinent for understanding politics around the world today. Is the Third Wave likely to spread further, or are we likely to see a reverse Third Wave? Recent events in countries in the Middle East signal that the question is far from settled. In short, although the Third Wave has reinvigorated the global legitimacy of democracy, many parts of Africa, the Middle East, and Asia remain solidly non-democratic. What are the prospects for democracy in those regions?

The future of regime change around the world depends in the main on the relative weight we accord to domestic factors such as political culture or economic development, and international factors such as the global geopolitical context. If

✓—Study and Review
the Post-Test &
Chapter Exam
at mypoliscilab.com

the cultural identity context is associated with regime change, then what are the prospects for democracy in countries that lack a civic culture? Or, if we believe economic development paves the road toward democratization, which non-democratic regimes are, therefore, more likely to experience regime change? Finally, what impact might today's global political environment have on the prospects of regime change—in both democracies and non-democracies? ▲

KEY TERMS

democratization   120
civic culture   123
civic engagement   123
political equality   123
solidarity   124
modernization theory   127

resource curse   128
military coup   129
globalization   134
neighborhood effect   136
illliberal democracy   140

REVIEW QUESTIONS

1. Consider the non-democratic countries around the world today. What "background factors" help explain why some of these countries are not democracies?
2. Why do some rich dictatorships not become democracies?
3. What sort of "modernization" helps change a political culture to support democracy?
4. In a democracy, what aspect of military identity is most crucial to preventing regime change to non-democracy, and why?
5. What do current events imply about the future of 'illiberal democracy' in the world?

SUGGESTED READINGS

Collier, Ruth Berins. *Paths toward Democracy: The Working Class and Elites in Western Europe and South America*. New York: Cambridge University Press, 1999. Discusses the relative merit of the "class-conflict" argument across different "waves" of democratization.

Diskin, Abraham et al. 2005. "Why Democracies Collapse: The Reasons for Democratic Failure and Success." *International Political Science Review* 26, 3 (2005): 291–309. An empirical exploration of the reasons democratic regimes survive or collapse.

Inglehart, Ronald, and Christian Welzel. *Modernization, Cultural Change, and Democracy*. New York: Cambridge University Press, 2005. A prominent example of the "civic culture" argument applied to the whole world.

Kuran, Timur. "Now Out of Never: The Element of Surprise in the East European Revolutions of 1989." *World Politics* 44 (1991): 7–48. An exploration of how and why regime change can happen relatively rapidly in several countries almost simultaneously.

Przeworski, Adam, and Fernando Limongi. "Modernization: Theories and Facts," *World Politics* 49 (1997): 155–183. A famous critique of modernization theory, based on extensive empirical exploration of the evidence for and against.

Zakaria, Fareed. "Illiberal Democracy." *Foreign Affairs*. 76, 6 (1997): 22–43. The now-classic statement of the emergence of illiberal democracies.

NOTES

1. Shirley Christian, "Foes of Pinochet Win Referendum, Regime Concedes," *New York Times,* October 6, 1988, A1.

2. See for example, Adam Przeworski et al., *Democracy and Development* (New York: Cambridge University Press, 2000).

3. Samuel Huntington, *The Third Wave: Democratization in the Late 20th Century* (Norman: University of Oklahoma Press, 1991).

4. I base the periodization on Huntington. To calculate the number of democracies and number of countries, I used the cutoff of "6" on the POLITY IV scale, which ranges from −10 (least democratic) to 10 (most democratic). You can find these data at http://www.systemicpeace.org/polity/polity4.htm.

5. See Robert Putnam, *Making Democracy Work.* (Princeton, NJ: Princeton University Press, 1991).

6. See Sheri Berman, "Civic Culture and the Collapse of Weimar Germany," *World Politics*, 1997, vol 49 #3, 401–429.

7. See for example, Josef Joffe, "Why Tunisia Isn't a Tipping Point for the Arab World," *The New Republic Online,* January 18, 2011, accessed April 27, 2011, http://www.tnr.com/article/politics/81658/tunisia-revolution-riot-economy-democracy or Francis Fukuyama, "Political Order in Egypt," *The American Interest Online,* May/June 2011, accessed April 27, 2011, http://www.the-american-interest.com/article.cfm?piece=953

8. See the list of reasons in "What Thaksin Had Done Wrong," in *The Nation,* a Bangkok newspaper, accessed December 1, 2008, http://nationmultimedia.com/2006/11/22/headlines/headlines_30019578.php *The Nation* has been accused of anti-Thaksin bias.

9. Jeffrey M. Paige. *Coffee and Power: Revolution and the Rise of Democracy in Central America* (Cambridge, MA: Harvard University Press, 1997), 87.

10. See Daniel Ziblatt, "Does Landholding Inequality Block Democratization? A Test of the 'Bread and Democracy' Thesis and the Case of Prussia," *World Politics* 60, 4 (2008): 610–641.

11. John Peeler, "Elite Settlements and Democratic Consolidation: Colombia, Costa Rica, and Venezuela," in *Elites and Democratic Consolidation in Latin America and Southern Europe*, edited by John Higley and Richard Gunther (Cambridge: Cambridge University Press, 1992), 81–112.

12. See Kathryn Sikkink, *Mixed Signals: US Foreign Policy in Latin America.* (New York: Cornell University Press/Century Foundation, 2004).

13. There are countless theories about the Titanic's sinking. A recent book that advances this argument is Jennifer Hooper McCarty and Tim Foecke, *What Really Sank the Titanic* (Lebanon, IN: Citadel Press, 2008).

14. See Samuel Huntington, *The Third Wave.*

15. Larry Diamond, "Thinking about Hybrid Regimes." *Journal of Democracy* 13 (2002): 5–21.

16. See for example, Joshua Kurlantzick, "The Great Democracy Meltdown," *The New Republic*, May 19, 2011, http://www.tnr.com/print/article/world/magazine/88632/failing-democracy-venezuela-arab-spring.

17. Fareed Zakaria, "The Rise of Illiberal Democracy," *Foreign Affairs*, November/December 1997, http://www.foreignaffairs.org/19971101faessay3809/fareed-zakaria/the-rise-of-illiberal-democracy.html.

18. See for example, Peter Smith and Melissa Ziegler, "Liberal and Illiberal Democracy in Latin America," *Latin American Politics and Society* 50, 1 (2008): 31–57.

19. "Chavez Wins Chance of Fresh Term." BBC News online, February 16, 2009, accessed April 15, 2009, http://news.bbc.co.uk/2/hi/americas/7891856.stm.

20. See Steven Levitsky and Lucan Way, "Elections without Democracy: The Rise of Competitive Authoritarianism," *Journal of Democracy* 13, 2 (2002): 51–66.

21. See for example, David Zweig and Bi Jianhai, "China's Global Hunt for Energy." *Foreign Affairs*, September/October 2005.

Political Identity

A young Frenchwoman displays two facets of her political identity by wearing a headscarf in the colors of the flag of France while she participates in a protest against the government's decision to ban religious clothes and accessories in public schools.

> **?** When does identity become politicized?

⬛ Read and Listen
to Chapter 6
at mypoliscilab.com

✓• Study and Review
the Pre-Test & Flashcards
at mypoliscilab.com

In 2004, France's government passed a law banning the wearing of "conspicuous religious garments" in public primary and high schools.[1] Although the law applies to any religious garment and includes skullcaps that Orthodox Jewish boys wear, turbans that observant Sikh boys wear, and even large Christian crucifixes, the main target of the law was the headscarf of Muslim women.

French laws and legal institutions dictate a greater degree of separation of church and state than the U.S. Constitution. In France, a majority of citizens support laws that require French public schools to be "religion-free zones." Before the 1960s, French secularity laws attracted little attention. However, around that time, many Muslims began immigrating into France. Their interests at the time were largely economic—they were looking for work. Most came from Algeria and Morocco, former French colonies in North Africa. Today, estimates put the number of Muslims in France at about 4.7 million, out of a total population of about 65 million.[2] The religious identity of many of these immigrants clashes with the principles of French secularity.

Our politicized identities are a function of individual choices and our surrounding social contexts. Politicization depends on how strongly people feel about aspects of their identity—but our choices are also shaped by what's going on around us. When other peoples' actions restrict our personal choices, corresponding aspects of our identity are thrust into the political spotlight. Consider the young Frenchwoman pictured at the beginning of the chapter. Why is she participating in a protest march? She seems of college age, so she might be active in a campus women's group or she might be marching with others for minority rights. Or perhaps she's a strong French nationalist, as the colors of her headscarf imply, and she's celebrating France's 1998 World Cup victory.

Any of these identities—as a woman, struggling student, ethnic minority, or French nationalist—might shape how she thinks, feels, and acts politically. The fact is, this young woman is taking political action on the basis of her *religious* identity. Her picture was taken at a march to support the wearing of headscarves, which many Muslim women regard as part of *hijab*, a religious requirement for modesty in dress. Perhaps this Frenchwoman had always thought of Islam as a private and personal choice. However, when the French government forced the issue, barring her from wearing the headscarf, she was mobilized to action. In short, her individual choice to wear the headscarf, a part of her identity, became political.

The explanation for much political competition and conflict around the world lies with questions of political identity—perceptions of membership in different social groups. Yet *when does identity become politicized?* To understand the interplay of individual choice and social context in the politicization of identity, this chapter first explores the forms political identity can take—economic and noneconomic—and then critically assesses two approaches to explaining the politicization of identity: primordialism and constructivism.

FORMS OF POLITICAL IDENTITY

Everyone has some form of political identity, which is the way individuals categorize themselves and others, and how they understand the relationships of domination and oppression that exist between groups. The Frenchwoman in the chapter-opening example might categorize herself as a feminist, a Muslim, an Arab, an intellectual, or a soccer fan. Others might categorize her based on her dress and see only what they recognize from Hollywood portrayals: a religious radical. How does your own self-perception influence your views about politics? If you're religious or secular, how do your views about faith influence your politics? If you define yourself as a member of a racial or ethnic group, how does your membership in that community shape the way you engage in politics?

Regardless of how you answer those questions, have you ever wondered *why* you feel so strongly about a particular form of identity? After all, claiming to identify with a particular group does not necessarily imply that you will engage politically on behalf of that group. This point puts a finger on a broader comparative politics puzzle: the politicization of identity varies in intensity. Identity becomes politicized when large numbers of people mobilize to advance interests of or defend perceived threats to their identity group. Yet even in countries marked by considerable diversity, most groups typically live in peace. Ethnic or religious conflict, for example, is not a simple function of a diverse population living within a country's borders. Yet when instigated, such cultural conflicts can be particularly divisive and explosive. That is why it is important to know when and why identity sometimes becomes highly politicized.

Identity involves both our own perceptions of how we fit in, and others' perceptions of how we fit in. Its importance lies not simply with recognizing that you fit into this or that group, but in recognizing the political significance of your membership in or exclusion from certain social groups. This is because sharing membership in a group doesn't only give people a sense of meaning about how they fit into society; it also offers a sense that others share their political interests and their vision for how to pursue those interests in politics. A sense of shared identity can thus facilitate collective action, because it shapes what individuals want governments to do.

In this section, we discuss two ways of thinking about the sources of political identity. The first originates with the ideas of Karl Marx and suggests that one's economic position in society—for example, as a farm laborer, an industrial worker, or a financier—is the primary way in which people think about individual and collective political identity. The second approach, rooted in the ideas of German sociologist Max Weber, suggests that identity is primarily noneconomic in origin, formed primarily among groups of people who share an understanding of a common heritage based on religion, race or the related concept of ethnicity, language, territory, or family ties. The section concludes by contrasting Marx and Weber's view of the relationship between identity and political power.

6.1 What are the main forms of political identity?

political identity ■ the ways that individuals categorize themselves and others, and how they understand the power relationships of domination and oppression that exist between groups.

Explore the Comparative "Political Campaigns" at mypoliscilab.com

race ■ categorization of humans into large populations supposedly based on hereditable physical characteristics such as skin color, facial features and hair texture.

ethnicity ■ a group of people who share an understanding of a common heritage based on religion, language, territory, or family ties.

Karl Marx and Economic Identity

Karl Marx (1818–1883) was a scholar, journalist, and activist. Inspired by what he believed to be the start of a workers' revolution across Western Europe, together with Friedrich Engels, he wrote the *Communist Manifesto* in 1848. By 1849, those revolutions had fizzled out, but one could argue that the *Manifesto's* twenty-odd pages have had more impact on the intellectual and political history of the world than any other single work in the past 150 years, helping to inspire later revolutions in Russia, Cuba, and China.

Marx had such a powerful impact because he was one of the first to emphasize the way economic interests can shape political identity. He argued that an individual's political identity is rooted in his or her economic position in society—at the top, in the middle, or at the bottom. So, if asked why the woman in our opening example was protesting, Marx might explain that the real reason is because she is economically exploited.

In the *Communist Manifesto*, Marx explored the consequences of the Industrial Revolution of the early 1800s, which radically transformed the economies of Western Europe. Before that time, agriculture dominated economic production, and there were two main economic groups: a small number of elite landowners and a huge number of landless peasants. As industrialization advanced, two new economic groups emerged: the bourgeoisie and the proletariat. Members of the bourgeoisie are wealthy capitalists who invest in factories and the like. Members of the proletariat are the wage laborers who work in those factories.

bourgeoisie ■ an economic class of wealthy capitalists that emerged during the Industrial Revolution.

proletariat ■ an economic class of wage laborers who work in factories that emerged during the Industrial Revolution.

class-consciousness ■ individuals' self-awareness of the political implications of being a member of a particular economic class.

Marx understood that industrialization meant that landowners would grow relatively weaker, while both the bourgeoisie and the proletariat would grow stronger. As both these new economic groups grew, politics would increasingly turn into conflicts between the "haves" and the "have-nots"—the bourgeoisie versus the proletariat. What is critical for Marx is that industrialization not only increased the number of people in the proletariat, it also created a new form of political identity among that group: class-consciousness. Class-consciousness has two elements for workers:

1. Self-awareness that they are members of an economic group that the bourgeoisie exploits, and
2. Self-awareness that their class has particular economic interests.

Marx argued that workers' collective identity as an economic class would facilitate their ability to form trade unions and advance their interests—for better wages and working conditions, for example—against the bourgeoisie's political influence, which derived from their wealth.

Marx's notion of class-consciousness implies that economic status is the source of political identity. Marx was so sure of this connection that he believed industrialization would wipe out other forms of political identity such as nationalism, religion, and ethnicity, because he supposed that a factory worker in one country would have the same class-consciousness as a factory worker in another country. Indeed, Marx believed that nationalism and other forms of cultural identity were merely smokescreens that obscured powerful economic interests and that only served to impede workers' unifying their mobilization efforts.

Marx was wrong: industrialization and capitalism have not wiped out "noneconomic" forms of identity. In fact, two workers who perform the same job in the same factory often have very different political interests. Nonetheless, around the world, economic status still shapes individuals' political choices. For example, in the world's wealthier democracies, voters who make relatively less money are more likely to vote for political parties on the left of the political spectrum, such as socialist or social–democratic parties. In contrast, people who tend to make relatively more money are more likely to vote for parties on the right of the political spectrum, such as conservative or Christian Democratic parties.[3]

However, economic class provides an incomplete guide to understanding identity and its role in understanding politics: around the world, many relatively poor people vote for conservative parties, and many wealthier people vote for left-leaning parties. And in poorer countries where industrialization never advanced very far, economic status explains relatively little compared to other forms of political identity. These facts turn our attention to the discussion of noneconomic forms of political identity.

Max Weber and Cultural Identity

Marx's view that economics determines political identity is limited. For a broader conception of identity, we turn to German sociologist Max Weber (1864–1920). Weber noted that people have identities based on multiple factors: attachment to a geographic region or even a neighborhood; tribal, racial, or ethnic identities; religious or national identities; or combinations of these and others. These noneconomic forms of identity can serve as powerful engines of political mobilization. For example, individuals in an ethnic group may share communal attitudes, values, and knowledge. They may also recognize and understand the political significance of cultural symbols, which can include flags, forms of music, food or art, particular phrases or terms, a mode of dress or of wearing one's hair or beard, religious icons, local, regional or national festivals, or the deliberate use of a regional accent. Any of these characteristics might mark individuals as members of a particular ethnic group.

Although people who share a form of cultural identity may also share political interests in defending and promoting their group, Weber insisted that most forms of political identity are not rooted in economic interests. He noted that people from different economic classes could have the same political identity: both the haves and have-nots could belong to the same race or religion, or be equally patriotic. Given this, both rich and poor members of one racial or ethnic group might discriminate against both the rich and poor from another ethnic group. Weber also noted that money cannot buy membership in certain identity groups. For example, in a society where discrimination exists, members of an oppressed ethnic or racial group may have limited upward mobility no matter how wealthy they become. Thus, if Weber were asked about the woman in the opening example, he might point out that even if she were economically exploited, her economic situation did not motivate her to take political action. Instead, it was a feeling of resentment about religious discrimination.

Interests and Identity for Marx and Weber

Given their differing views, Marx and Weber conceived of the relationship between interests and identity differently. The table below summarizes these distinctions. Marx's argument is simple: political identity and underlying political interests are a function of economic status. He believed that the proletariat would organize and mobilize on its own behalf almost naturally, because class conflict was an inevitable product of the process of industrialization. Weber dismissed this notion, noting that economic classes are not communities in the usual sense of the word. Instead, noneconomic forms of identity—ethnicity, tribe, or religion for example—more naturally provide the basis of the communities in which people live their day-to-day lives. This view implies that mobilization along noneconomic lines would be easier than mobilization of economic classes, because noneconomic groups share both cultural orientations and lived experiences such as religious observance or family and community history, practices and traditions.

political cleavage

■ a deep and lasting salient dimension of political conflict and competition within a given society, such as religion, ethnicity, ideology, or other forms of identity.

Weber's insight explains why a view of identity that relies on economics only weakly predicts the nature of political conflict in most societies. A central concept here is the political cleavage—a deep and lasting salient source of political conflict based on identity that pits one group against another or several others. In some societies, an economic class cleavage emerges, pitting the relatively poor against the relatively well off. The UK has a distinct class cleavage, for example: the Labour Party tends to obtain support from working-class voters, while the Conservative Party tends to obtain support from wealthier voters.

However, other societies see the emergence of political cleavages based on noneconomic forms of identity—for example, pitting ethnic groups against one another or adherents of one religion against adherents of another. Thus, in India, most political competition results not from economic class differences but from a religious cleavage between Hindus and Muslims and from various ethnic cleavages that divide Hindus from each other.

Most countries are divided by several political cleavages, which helps us understand why political identity based on economic interests only weakly explains the

▶ SUMMARY TABLE

Political Interests and Identity: Marx vs. Weber

	What Defines Interests and Identity?	What Drives Mobilization?
Marx	Political identity and interests are a function of economic status.	Mobilization will occur along *economic class* lines, for example bourgeoisie versus proletariat.
Weber	Political identity and interests are a function of noneconomic group differences.	Mobilization will occur along *noneconomic* status group lines, for example, one ethnic group versus another.

main forms of political conflict around the world. And this brings us back to our main chapter question—why certain forms of identity become the basis for political mobilization and others do not. In the next sections, we analyze two ways to answer this question.

POLITICIZING IDENTITY: PRIMORDIALISM

In different countries and at different times, both Marx's economic approach and Weber's cultural approach may help us classify the existing forms of political identity. Yet, we still need a way to understand why political cleavages emerge around the world. What explains why certain forms of identity are politicized in one country but not another similar country, for example? We will consider the two main approaches to understanding the politicization of identity: primordialism, which assumes political identities are innate and largely unchanging, and constructivism, which assumes that individuals have some choice over their political identities, but that such choice is constrained by the social context. To foreshadow this discussion, we shall discover that primordialism is the way that most people intuitively think about their own identities, but constructivism is the approach taken in nearly all contemporary scholarship.

The word *primordial* means something ancient but fundamental for understanding contemporary reality. In political science, primordialism suggests that political identity is something you are either born with or that emerges unconsciously during childhood, given your family and community context. This view implies that you do not choose your identity, nor can you change it.[4]

Primordialism emphasizes kinship bonds—a connection to others formed by blood, marriage, or other family relations—as the fundamental building blocks of collective political identity. There are two ways to think of kinship bonds. First, they can be thought of as actual genetic links between people. The thinking here is that because individuals depend on their family to survive, people naturally develop the closest emotional and psychological bonds to their family members. Primordialism suggests that the survival instinct, rooted in biological blood ties, arouses group loyalties and provides the basis for the politicization of identity.

The glue that cements kinship bonds need not literally be based in biology. Kinship bonds can also be metaphorical, based in cultural and historical connections to an imaginary "extended family." Primordialism suggests that identity becomes politicized as a result of deep emotional and/or psychological attachments individuals feel toward members of a broader community. These communal connections give people a sense of their place in the world and teach people how to act appropriately toward others in their community, as well as toward outsiders. This version of primordialism suggests that a form of identity will be politicized to the degree that individuals view the visible manifestations of their community's culture—its language, religion, symbols, clothes, food, and other practices—as natural, timeless, and worth defending. According to this view, political identity is rooted in shared historical experience—and that once created, it is long-lasting, largely unchanging, and has the power to motivate political behavior.

6.2 What is the primordialist approach to understanding the politicization of identity?

primordialism ■ an approach to understanding identity which assumes that identities are something people are born with or that emerge through deep psychological processes in early childhood, given one's family and community context.

constructivism ■ an approach to understanding identity which assumes that political identities are malleable, even if they often appear to be primordial, and suggests that we think of identity as an evolving political process rather than as a fixed set of identity categories.

kinship bonds ■ a connection to others formed by blood, marriage, or other family relations.

◉ Watch the Video "Contesting Political Cultures in Britain" at **mypoliscilab.com**

Primordialism suggests that collective mobilization occurs when groups perceive a threat to the continued practice of their collective identity. They react just as they would if their family were threatened. Collective identities can also mobilize even when survival is not directly at stake, because individuals feel affection for and loyalty toward those who share common physical characteristics, language, religion, customs, or culture, while naturally feeling a sense of alienation, mistrust, and antagonism toward outsiders, strangers, and those who do not share their community's characteristics. Primordial attachments that can motivate political action can thus extend far beyond one's immediate relatives into an imaginary extended family—to one's clan, tribe, ethnic group, or nation.

Samuel Huntington and Global Conflict

In his 1993 article "The Clash of Civilizations," Harvard political scientist Samuel Huntington explored the political implications of the end of the Cold War.[5] He concluded that the collapse of the Soviet Union effectively ended ideological conflict between capitalist democracies and communist dictatorships. Many hoped that this development would herald the dawn of a peaceful era in global affairs, but Huntington poured cold water on that idea and suggested that conflict in the post–Cold War era would continue—only that it would be cultural and based on forms of political identity besides ideology.

Huntington argued that civilizations are the broadest cultural identities that exist, and that they are defined by language, history, religion, customs, and by individuals' subjective self-identification as members of one civilization and not another. These primordial differences are deeply held, "less mutable, and hence less easily compromised and resolved" than are ideological differences rooted in economic class. Huntington viewed religion as a particularly problematic source of civilizational conflict, because issues of faith are not subject to negotiation.

The explanation for politicization of these identities is straightforward: communities act in defense of their collective identity because doing so is in their very nature. People want to protect their community just like they want to protect their family. For example, as in the case of French Muslims, if the government passes a law that prohibits the wearing of certain clothes, primordialism predicts that members of the oppressed identity group would naturally rise in protest. This approach seems to explain why such passionate emotions erupt in cultural conflicts. Such clashes pivot on deep-rooted communal insecurities, anxieties, and fears. An outsider may not comprehend such powerful emotions, but such sentiments remain very real to those involved.

Huntington's argument is primordialist not simply because he insists that cultural characteristics will drive future conflicts but because he assumes that individuals are born with one set of characteristics or another; that such characteristics are immutable; and that groups with different cultural characteristics will inevitably clash. He believed that the Cold War's ideological battles had temporarily suppressed but never destroyed primordial cultural attachments. When the Cold War ended, these longstanding ethnic and religious animosities reemerged, and Huntington predicted that conflict would emerge between nations and different "civilizations."

Several events since the end of the Cold War are taken as evidence of primordialism's usefulness for explaining patterns of global conflict. For example, for many Americans, evidence of a clash of civilizations comes from the post–9/11 global War on Terror. Huntington predicted that conflict between Islamic and non-Islamic civilizations would intensify after the Cold War. He pointed to centuries of warfare between Christian and Muslim rulers, a reaction against European colonization of Islamic regions in the 1800s, and a resurgence of militant Islam in the late twentieth century. Given events such as 9/11 and the wars in Iraq and Afghanistan, many believe that Huntington's predictions were accurate.

Samuel Huntington's Critics

In the post–Cold War era in which religion, nationalism, and ethnicity rather than class conflict motivate much political violence, Huntington's primordialist answer to this chapter's main question—when does identity become politicized?—has had broad appeal. Yet, Huntington's argument that politicized identities are innate has inspired strong critiques. For some, his argument is a simple-minded and politically incorrect stereotype of Islam, even if his theory is meant to apply to all religions.[6] How might we test Huntington's primordialist hypothesis to explain the politicization of identity in the contemporary world?

For Huntington's theory to work, we should see evidence that civilizations actually exist and act. However, civilizations do not really exist. Thus, while members of Al-Qaeda may claim to speak for Islamic civilization, in reality they represent only a small radical fringe. In truth, the Muslim world is divided into many states, ethnicities, languages, and competing (often incompatible) visions of what Islam requires and prohibits. No single unifying identity mobilizes all Muslims everywhere, and no political entity speaks for, coordinates, and acts on behalf of all Muslims. The same holds true for Western civilization, or any other.

Second, there exist many examples of "clashes" that do not fit the logic of Huntington's argument. Two common forms of conflict in the contemporary world that Huntington's thesis cannot explain are international warfare between states of the same civilization, and civil wars within states. For example, international conflict in the Democratic Republic of Congo—among states of the sub-Saharan African civilization—has caused more deaths than any conflict in the world since World War II.[7] Moreover, in recent years, political conflict within states has become far more frequent and bloodier than either international terrorism or war between states of different civilizations. The list of countries that have experienced civil war in recent years—conflict between members of the same "civilization"—includes Somalia, Colombia, and Cote d'Ivoire. In each of these cases, it is far from clear that one "civilization" is at war with another.

Evaluating Primordialism

Huntington's clash of civilizations is possibly the best-known primordialist explanation of identity politicization in the contemporary world. To be fair, the fact that civilization is a slippery concept and that Huntington's argument cannot explain much of the political violence around the world does not mean such an approach is always wrong. Still, the argument falls short of answering this chapter's main question—*why does identity become politicized?*—for three key reasons.

First, primordialism cannot explain the emergence of collective identity. Contrary to the notion that identity is ancient and timeless, many forms of identity are, in fact, not that old. For example, the idea of nationalism only emerged about two centuries ago; many supposedly ancient groups such as "French people" or "German people" have only come to think of themselves as nations in the relatively recent past. To the extent that *any* form of identity emerged only relatively recently, primordialism offers no help in answering this chapter's main question, because it cannot explain what caused that form of identity to emerge in the first place.

Primordialism also cannot account for change in the meaning of different forms of identity, no matter how old. The political significance of ethnicity, religious affiliation, gender, or other forms of identity are not timeless, regardless of whether people believe they are. For example, Islamic religious identity only became a salient political identity in many countries in the late twentieth century, partly in reaction to the economic and military success of Israel. Similarly, even though India's Hindu religion is much older than Islam, Hindu radicalism grew only in recent decades, partly in response to the politicization of Islam in India and elsewhere. Likewise, only in recent decades have indigenous activists in Latin America found a way to successfully mobilize around ethnic identity, even though the existence of indigenous groups obviously predates the arrival of Christopher Columbus. The potential to mobilize a form of identity is not constant over time, even though a primordialist account implies that it is.

Finally, primordialism also ignores the possibility that individuals can and do choose—and sometimes change—their own identities. While it is true that individuals develop powerful emotional and psychological attachments to identity groups early in life, they may also adopt new and different forms of identity later on. For example, people can become more liberal or more conservative over time, or more religious or more secular.

These problems—the assumption that identities are timeless and always politically salient and that individuals have no capacity to choose their own identities—mean that a primordialist argument cannot explain most variation in the politicization of identity in the real world. Primordialism tends to over-predict conflict. For example, Africa has thousands of linguistic, tribal, and other ethnic groups, yet civil wars are actually quite rare: there has been only *one* instance of ethnic violence in Africa for every 2,000 cases that would be predicted based on the existence of cultural differences alone.[8] Primordialism cannot explain why such differences, which are very real to people in different ethnic groups, become politicized in some cases but not others—meaning that it cannot answer our chapter's main question.

As summarized in the table on the following page, primordialism offers an intuitive explanation for the sources of political identity: you're born with it. It then offers a simple explanation for the politicization of identity: being born into a group instinctively arouses group loyalties and provides a rationale for political mobilization when the group's interests or survival are threatened. However,

> **SUMMARY TABLE**
>
> ### Primordialism and Political Identity
>
> | Why It's Useful | Offers an intuitive explanation for the sources of political identity: you're born with it |
> | --- | --- |
> | | Offers a simple explanation for the politicization of identity: group membership instinctively arouses group loyalties |
> | Why It's Problematic | Cannot explain variation in the emergence or change in the politicization of identity |
> | | Cannot explain how or why individuals and groups change identities over time |

the approach leaves many key questions unanswered, and for this reason few scholars take it up. Identities are not always so easily politicized, and the political salience of a form of identity often changes over time. We thus require additional information to explain variation in when, where, and why identity becomes politicized, and why groups only sometimes enter into conflict. An alternative approach to understanding the politicization of identity—constructivism—may offer a more satisfying explanation.

POLITICIZING IDENTITY: CONSTRUCTIVISM

Unlike primordialism, constructivism assumes that the forms, meaning, and political salience of different forms of identity can change. Constructivism forces us to delve more deeply into the question of how identity becomes politicized, at both the individual and societal levels. In this section, we first consider the ways individuals actively choose and consciously attach political significance to particular forms of identity. We then consider how the social and political context shapes, constrains, and, thus, constructs those individual choices. Finally, we illustrate the logic of the constructivist approach to identity by exploring the evolution of the racial divide in Brazil and the politicization of nationalist identity in Europe.

6.3 What is the constructivist approach to understanding the politicization of identity?

👁 Watch the Video
"Youth in Iran"
at **mypoliscilab.com**

Identity and Individual Choice

The first way of thinking about how identity is constructed starts with individual choices—for example, the young woman in our opening example who has chosen to protest the French ban on wearing headscarves. Constructivism does not suggest that individuals are completely free to choose their identity. Obviously, biology constrains racial or ethnic identity choice, for example. Facial features or skin, hair, or even eye color tend to designate us as members of one group or another, whether we want to identify as a member of a particular group or not. Many individuals do not obviously fall into a clear racial or ethnic category, but depending on the context, people's looks or accents can limit the identities they can choose and may even push them more or less inevitably into certain groups. After all, an ethnically Norwegian woman cannot pass as a black Nigerian; a Japanese man cannot pass as a Pakistani woman.

Despite such constraints, individuals can and do choose to try out different identities—especially those that do not depend on visible attributes, such as religion. Consider national identity: when individuals migrate from one country to another, they may retain some attachment to their ancestral homeland, but they may also adopt all the visible elements of their adopted home, such as clothing, language, and food, and they may also develop a powerful emotional attachment to their new country. And even for racial or ethnic identity, many people have ancestors from more than one identity group—U.S. President Barack Obama is one notable example. In such situations, some people choose one identity over the other, but others develop affinities to multiple groups. Some choose to identify with one racial group in certain contexts (for instance, at work or school) and with a different group in others (for instance, at home or with friends).

In any case, the fact that people look a certain way hardly means they all attach political significance to their appearance—or that everyone who looks a certain way attaches the *same* political significance to their appearance. For example, it is extremely unlikely that every young French Muslim woman of Arab descent feels the same about the headscarf ban. Some refuse to take the headscarf off and engage in sustained protest; others might be upset about the ban but take the headscarf off; and others might not care at all. Because people can at least partly pick and choose aspects of their identity and can attribute political importance to their identity in different ways, constructivism asks us to consider what interests individuals might have in attaching political salience to a particular form of identity. This insistence on understanding why identities are politicized in a particular way—rather than assuming it will be politicized, as in the primordialist approach—forces us to consider the social context as well as individual choices.

Identity and the Social Context

The flip side of accepting that individuals can and do choose to highlight different aspects of their identities turns our attention to the second way of thinking about how identity is constructed, which focuses on the social context. Unlike primordialism, which assumes individuals attribute political importance to pre-existing forms of identity, constructivism suggests that individual choices or physical attributes only take on meaning as a result of the historical evolution of the political context, which shapes, enables, and/or constrains individuals' identity choices.

Two aspects of the social context are particularly important for explaining the politicization of identity. First, long-term social, economic, or technological change can politicize identity. For example, Marx correctly noted that industrialization creates an urban working class, whose members may come to understand the political implications of their economic status differently from their ancestors who had worked the land. Rapid economic development can also dramatically alter how people perceive the proper roles for men and women inside and outside the home, thereby changing the nature of gender identities. Migration by large numbers of people—due to environmental disaster, war, or economic development—can bring about competition for natural resources, which sometimes spurs the politicization of ethnic or religious differences, for example. And the spread of religions can politicize differences about morality and community ethics. For example, missionary activity by Christians and Muslims in Africa and elsewhere has contributed to the politicization of religious identities. Oftentimes, slow, long-term change in the social context shapes how individuals conceive of themselves and their community, which, in turn, influences the politicization of identity as whole.

Second, identity can become politicized because someone or some group had an interest in that outcome. That is, constructivism suggests that identity can be politicized as a result of competition for political power. To establish authority or enhance their legitimacy, leaders attempt to articulate an appealing image of the community and its goals. Some politicians attempt to gain followers by highlighting differences between their group and others—such as divides based on race, religion, or differing ideologies—while others attempt to articulate a vision that unifies everyone, for example by highlighting the commonalities that unite citizens of a particular nation. Constructivism highlights how efforts to acquire and hold onto power can politicize different forms of political identity.

Sometimes, such efforts can involve coercion. For example, for centuries, Spanish colonial authorities in Latin America rigorously repressed indigenous forms of ethnic identity, in order to eliminate the threat of separatist movements. Such repression often continued after Latin American countries gained independence in the early 1800s, and only in recent decades have activists managed to carve out political space to successfully reinvigorate indigenous political identity.

To this day, some governments attempt to restrict the expression of certain forms of identity. For example, by implementing a policy that restricted women and girls' ability to wear the headscarf as they please, the French government politicized religious identity, perhaps seeking to win votes of French citizens uncomfortable with the rapid growth of the country's Muslim immigrant population. The government attempted to legitimize its policy by tapping into a notion of French nationalism, suggesting that wearing headscarves violates centuries-old French secular traditions. The goal may be to change Muslims' attachments to religious identity and promote a version of French national identity. Yet, such efforts may backfire and push many Muslims to hold more tightly to their own religious traditions, pointing to France's national motto of "liberty, equality, and fraternity" to justify the maintenance of a diversity of cultural practices and political identities.

However, coercion is not necessary to politicize identity. Politicians can also gain or hold onto power by using evocative language, images, and cultural symbols to generate a sense of community and legitimize the use of power. For example, those who led independence movements in Asia or Africa against European colonialism sought to establish credibility as potential future rulers by fostering a sense of nationalism, even though the colony may have lacked any unifying cultural traditions. In fact, many former colonies—such as Nigeria or India—are noted more for their incredible cultural and religious diversity, not for traits that unite the population. The constructivist perspective pushes us to examine how efforts to acquire and consolidate political power can transform the social context and politicize different forms of identity. Both aspiring and established leaders attempt to use cultural symbols to mobilize followers, defend their group's interests, and compete with other groups, and in doing so, they highlight, reinvigorate, or attach new meanings to different forms of identity.

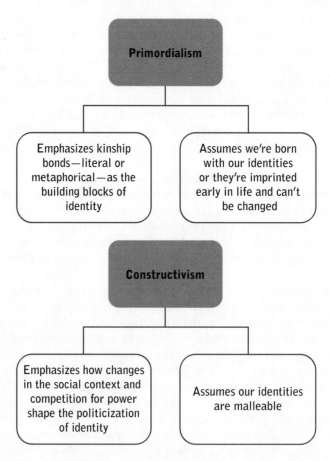

FIGURE 6.1

Understanding Primordialism and Constructivism

Primordialism and constructivism differ in their assumptions about where identities "come from" and in the degree to which we can assume they are timeless and unchanging versus whether politics and individual choice can interact to shape and change them.

Why are forms of identity politicized in different ways, depending on the social context? In contrast to primordialism, constructivism does not presuppose that people instinctively attach political significance to another person's physical or other visible attributes. Instead, it suggests that the evolving political and social context shapes the way people classify others into this or that group and shapes the political significance people attach to such group differences. Although constructivism allows for some degree of individual choice in the question of identity, it focuses attention on how the social context shapes and constrains those choices.

Constructivism and Racial and National Identity in Brazil

To understand how physical attributes can lack meaning outside their social context and how identity is constructed, let's explore the way Brazilians think about racial differences differently from Americans. About 54 percent of Brazilians have some African heritage, compared to about 13 percent of Americans.[9] The percentage differences, however, does not provide a sense of how people *think* about race in the two countries. In fact, it would be a mistake to assume that Brazilians think about race relations in the same way as Americans do. To illustrate, consider the men in the photo below.

Of the members of Brazil's national team in 2010, it is likely that most Americans and Brazilians would classify 7 (front row, holding the banner) and 8 as

Brazilians and Americans have very different ideas about racial identities. More Americans would classify 3, 2, and 10 as not white compared to Brazilians, for example.

not white, while identifying 4, 5 (front row center), 9, and 1 as white. However, what about 3, 2, or 10? When presented with pictures of men with similar facial features and skin tones, most Americans would tend to classify these men as "not white." However, most Brazilians respond differently, and include people with those kinds of features as "white." In general, Americans have a narrower definition of who is "white" and tend to apply a hard "color line" that divides people between races. In contrast, Brazilians accept a broader spectrum of "whiteness"—they are less willing to divide people into just two groups, black and white.[10]

Partly because Americans see a hard color line, while Brazilians do not, race has been politically salient in the United States—but not historically in Brazil. The civil rights movement in the 1960s is the most prominent example of how race has served as a source of political mobilization in the United States. Blacks felt politically excluded and organized to obtain equal rights. In Brazil, blacks comprise a much larger proportion of the population, but no large-scale political mobilization built along racial lines has ever emerged.[11]

A primordialist argument cannot explain why people in Brazil and the United States think so differently about race, or why race has historically been hotly politicized in the United States but much less so in Brazil. If racial divisions were primordial, white people would know that they were white, and black people would know that they were black—end of story. In the United States, although some people identify as biracial or multiracial, racial identification between blacks and whites has historically been largely an "either/or" question. This view aligns more closely to a primordialist view: races exist naturally; people are either one race or another; and people understand the political significance of racial differences. Yet, Brazilians do not recognize this same, rigid color line.

Why not? Both Brazil and the United States share a historical experience of slavery. As in the United States, millions of black Africans were brought to Brazil, to work on sugar and coffee plantations. This experience left black Brazilians in conditions of social, economic, and political exclusion. Yet, American blacks share this history, meaning that slavery cannot explain the different way that race is politicized in the two countries.

The key to explaining why racial identities were constructed differently in Brazil and the United States lies with a different aspect of the social context: the political interests of late nineteenth-century and early twentieth-century Brazilian leaders who wanted to consolidate political control over the country.[12] When Brazil gained independence in 1822, part of Portugal's royal family established itself as Brazil's rulers. Brazil's emperors Pedro I and his son Pedro II enjoyed widespread legitimacy and played key roles as symbols of Brazilian national unity. In 1888, Pedro II's daughter, Princess Isabel, decreed the abolition of slavery. This Brazilian Emancipation Proclamation angered the country's politically conservative, wealthy, white, land-owning and slave-owning elites. A year later, Brazil's military overthrew the monarchy and handed the reins of power to members of this powerful group.

The fact that blacks comprised a numerical majority of the population presented Brazil's new rulers with a political challenge. In the United States, after the Civil War, many states passed Jim Crow laws that segregated and discriminated against anyone who looked even a little bit black. Yet, because blacks in Brazil comprised a far larger proportion of the population than blacks in the United States, Brazil's white rulers hesitated to enact discriminatory and segregationist public policies. They believed that they might not be able to control a potential backlash against such policies.

In order to consolidate their hold on power without politicizing the racial divide, Brazil's rulers articulated an inclusive idea of Brazilian nationalism, one in which blacks were politically equal with whites. Brazil's rulers frequently described their country as a racial democracy, contrasting their country against the United States. To back up this claim, they adopted nondiscriminatory laws and policies—not because they were particularly enlightened or racially tolerant, but because of their interests in political stability, from which they would profit economically. The hope was that by adopting a different political strategy from the United States, Brazilians would adopt a more flexible view of race and that racial differences would become politically unimportant. This chapter's feature box illustrates how Brazilian leaders drew upon different public perceptions of who "counted" as a member of the national community to construct this inclusive form of political identity.

The efforts of Brazil's white political elites a century ago did not dramatically improve the lives of black Brazilians, most of whom remained on the bottom of the economic, social, and political ladder. Yet, it did have profound consequences for Brazilian culture and politics. As census and survey results illustrate, to this day Brazilians have greater flexibility in their identity choices. This flexibility had profound political consequences: the idea that Brazil was a racial democracy diminished the likelihood of black political mobilization. Despite doing little or nothing to alleviate black poverty, Brazilian government policy gave blacks few obvious targets of inequality against which to mobilize. After all, if Brazil was a racial democracy, then black political protest was unjustified. Because formal discrimination never existed, individuals who perceived racial injustice had a harder time convincing others that the social context was a sham. And, in fact, Brazil has experienced little mobilization along racial lines: to this day, Brazilian social movements and interest groups based on race remain relatively weak.[13]

To explain the relative depoliticization of racial identity in Brazil, constructivism highlights politicians' deliberate efforts to generate an inclusive form of nationalist political identity. This example illustrates a broader constructivist hypothesis, one you can use when comparing and contrasting the emergence and politicization of other forms of identity, such as ethnicity, economic class, or religion: political efforts to highlight clear lines between groups can politicize identity, but efforts to blur such lines of difference can also depoliticize identity. Let's reinforce this lesson by considering another illustration of how constructivism works, by turning our attention to the emergence of nationalist identity in Eastern Europe.

Collective Memory Influences the Construction of Political Identity:
HYPOTHESIS TESTING | Comparing the United States and Brazil

Social scientists often use the term "collective memory" to refer to the idea that successive generations in a society tend to attach the same meaning and significance to particular historical events. Collective memory can be reinforced by the kinds of memorials and public art that are erected in public spaces. For example, the National Mall in Washington, D.C., memorializes the role of key U.S. presidents in founding or guiding the country, reinforcing those presidents' heroic image in the mind of the millions who visit each year.

Paintings, photos, movies, and TV also continually produce a flow of images that reinforce—and sometimes challenge—established visions of a society's collective memory. For example, Americans today tend to "remember" events such as Kennedy's assassination, the moon landing, or 9/11 in particular

ways, because of the impact of shared TV, newspaper, and Internet images, even if they did not actually witness those events personally. Such visions cement bonds between members of a community about common experiences, values, and ideals.

How a society remembers key people and events can shape the collective memory. If certain people or groups are portrayed negatively, that image may stick in the collective memory as a stereotype. What a society chooses *not* to memorialize can also be important. If certain people or events are never memorialized at all, they may be effectively erased from the collective memory.

How did Brazil and the United States end up with such different conceptions of racial identity? Exploring how Brazil and the United States tend to "see" founding events in their respective collective

John Trumbull, *Signing of the Declaration of Independence* (1819). The images in this famous painting convey important signals about race, class, and gender—about what kinds of people were important in the formation of the American national community.

(*Continued*)

memories helps illustrate how political identity is constructed.

GATHER EVIDENCE

Who comes to mind when you're asked, "*Who made this country what it is*?" Schoolbooks you've read since kindergarten have shaped how you'll answer this question, by highlighting the legends of Paul Revere, George Washington, Ben Franklin, and other Founding Fathers. Trumbull's painting is a famous rendition of one of the founding moments of the United States of America: the signing of the *Declaration of Independence* in 1776.

This painting, which hangs in the Rotunda in the U.S. Capitol, offers a "textbook" representation of the key leaders of the American Revolution: it portrays them as a group of relatively well-off, respectable, middle-aged white men. The setting is formal and businesslike—a large meeting hall with tables, chairs, drapes, and tablecloths. Everyone is dressed in the contemporary equivalent of a suit and tie. The overall atmosphere is somewhat stuffy and exclusive—"members only." *Average* Americans— even average white and male Americans—are nowhere to be seen. By omission, the painting tells us who was *not* important to the American Founding: less-wealthy white men, all women, and all minorities. Contemporary children now learn a somewhat more inclusive story of American independence, but Americans have inherited this notion—visible not just in this painting but in textbooks, monuments, museums, and in the names of numerous cities, states, and towns around the whole country—that the only *really* key figures in the founding of the United States were relatively wealthy, older white men.

Now take a look at Debret's painting, which depicts the founding moment of Brazil's independence from Portugal in 1822. This painting portrays the coronation of Emperor Pedro I. The portrayals of the American and Brazilian founding moments are quite distinct. In contrast to Trumbull's painting, Brazil's founding moment is idealized as taking place in an informal environment: at the beach, with gentle ocean waves lapping onto shore, palm trees providing some shade, and mountains in the distance. Although Pedro is wearing his imperial robe and crown, he is acclaimed not by his peers—princes, dukes, and counts—but by common folk of several races. On

Jean-Baptiste Debret, *The Coronation of Dom Pedro I* (c. 1822). The contrast with the image of the American Founding Fathers is stark. This image conveys very different signals about what kinds of people were important in the formation of the Brazilian national community.

(*Continued*)

the left, we see a slave mother and her child, both of whom hold farm implements—and the mother even holds a rifle. Behind her, a black soldier presents his baby for the emperor to see, and an indigenous woman kneels with her three children. On the right of the painting we see several white Brazilians—including an oldster and a member of the armed forces, but all of them appear to be average people—note that of all the people whose feet are visible, only one wears shoes. Overall, the painting portrays the idea that Brazilians of all races and economic classes are included in the new nation.

ASSESS THE HYPOTHESIS

These two paintings cannot encompass the full range of sentiments artists have portrayed about the nature of the national community in the United States or Brazil. Nevertheless, they echo common images in the collective memory of the founding events in each country's history that are taught in schools in both countries to this day. These images carry significance for how individuals in successive generations tend to perceive who qualifies as a full member of the national community. Trumbull's image has entered Americans' collective memory; his painting projects the notion that a very narrow social group was responsible for forming the American polity. In contrast, the Brazilian image includes women and people of different races and economic classes, implying that Brazil's initial conception of its national community was more inclusive—even though, quite paradoxically, both countries relied on slavery. This sort of image, residing in Brazilians' collective memory, lies at the root of notion that Brazil embodies a "racial democracy." ◤

CRITICAL THINKING QUESTIONS

1. What other images come to mind when you think about American nationalism, and what political significance to those images carry?

2. What purpose do public monuments and memorials play in constructing national memory?

Constructivism and Nationalist Identity in Europe

In Brazil, national leaders made strenuous efforts to *de-emphasize* racial differences between whites and blacks, in an effort to promote political stability and social peace. Let's now consider an example of how political elites attempt to *emphasize* a particular form of identity. Nationalism can generate a sense of belonging to a large community in which everyone shares a cultural framework. One key way that political elites construct nationalist identity is by making education compulsory.[14] Suppose that a new country has just declared independence, but its citizens are mostly illiterate peasants who live in rural villages. These villagers may be isolated on cultural "islands" that speak different languages or dialects, wear different clothes, listen to different music, tell different tales, and worship God differently. Given this cultural fragmentation, a strong nationalist identity—an emotional identification with the newly independent country that unites all the villagers together—is unlikely to exist.

To make nationalism a meaningful form of political identity, people must be encouraged to think they have much in common with those outside their immediate community. One way to construct such an identity is by promoting mass literacy. Literacy in a single national language—which governments of states only began to encourage in the early 1800s—permits communication among a multitude of strangers and means that many more citizens can understand and pass on a single, unified version of a society's history.[15]

An effective way to use literacy to construct nationalist identity is through primary and secondary education. Before nationwide school systems developed, children were educated (if at all) at home or in religious institutions. As a result, they acquired their political identity by emulating the behavior, habits, and beliefs of their parents and local community leaders. Nationalism requires creating an emotional or psychological bond between large communities of strangers, something not easily learned by observing and imitating people in one's immediate surroundings.

Since the 1800s, with the rise of mass schooling, many governments have constructed a national identity by implementing a unified curriculum that injected nationalist ideas into subjects such as history, literature, geography, and music. When they attended school, children acquired a sense of patriotism by learning the significance of important national dates and symbols as well as key aspects of the national culture such as prideful songs, stories, or poems. These nationwide school curricula homogenized national populations by deemphasizing local or regional identities. Governments also set up national Ministries of Education that controlled teacher training to ensure that teachers uniformly implemented the nationalist curriculum across the entire country.[16]

Encouraging literacy and promoting widespread schooling served politicians' interests, because it cemented citizens' political identities in a particular way; citizens would only regard rulers as legitimate to the extent that those rulers governed according to principles of national culture that the rulers themselves had helped define.

The rise of nationalism as a form of political identity can, thus, be traced at least partly to changes in the way governments educated and socialized youth. For example, in the aftermath of World War I, governments in Hungary, Poland, Bulgaria, Romania, Latvia, Lithuania, and Estonia created centralized, standardized school curricula and teacher training institutes. The result was the emergence and persistence of strong nationalist identities in those countries. In contrast, nationalism remained weaker elsewhere in Eastern Europe—in Albania, Bosnia-Herzegovina and Macedonia, for example—where illiteracy persisted and governments failed to invest adequately in schools. As late as 1909, Albania had no teacher training school, and the Albanian language lacked a standardized written alphabet. Partly as a result, by 1940 only 20 percent of Albanians could read.[17]

Literacy, mass schooling, and centralized control over education help explain the relative strength or weakness of nationalism across countries. Mass education helped weaken local and regional identities and construct nationalist ones by giving authority and legitimacy to nationally trained bureaucrats and teachers, as opposed to parents or prominent local figures. Mass education also succeeded by shifting the tools of cultural socialization from informal oral traditions to government-sanctioned formal texts replete with nationalist cultural messages.

Once constructed, nationalism has tended to persist. As Huntington noted, the end of the Cold War allowed preexisting forms of political identity to reemerge. Thus, on the one hand, Huntington correctly predicted that nationalism would regain political salience in Eastern Europe after the end of the Cold War. Yet, on the other hand, as we have just explained, nationalism can hardly be considered primordial. After all, nationalist political identities in Eastern Europe did not even exist before the twentieth century.

In contrast to primordialism, constructivism does not assume that forms of political identity are timeless or natural, and does not assume that individuals and communities more or less naturally respond to perceived communal threats. Instead, as our examples of racial and nationalist identity demonstrate, constructivism starts by assessing a country's social context in order to explain the extent to which different forms of identity have become politicized or not. In particular, it looks to the impact of interests on the formation of identity. Such an approach offers better explanations than primordialism for why forms of identity such as race or nationalism become politicized in some places but not others.

Students and scholars can be forgiven for wanting to unpack the historical sources of political identity as they work with the constructivist framework. However, constructivism's clearest shortcoming is its inability to make sense of the way most people perceive their own identities. The fact is that most people think of their ethnic, racial, religious, national, or other identity as primordial, and they are uninterested in hearing that historical context shaped the identity choices available to them. In short, constructivism is better at explaining where different forms of identity around the world come from, but primordialism offers a more intuitive explanation of identity's capacity to move people to action. Few people critically assess their identity in order to know when and how to act in its defense; they accept that their identity constitutes an essential part of their being and must be defended, with blood if necessary.

One might reasonably wonder, if identity is so malleable, why do people fight and die to protect their group? Constructivism does offer an answer to this question: As the examples of race in Brazil and nationalism in Europe illustrate, behavior that appears rooted in one's identity—such as religiously inspired violence—is often linked to tangible interests, such as political competition for land, resources, or power. The politicization of identity is not always a product of interests, but the latter are often critical.

Constructivism recognizes that individuals can and do choose their identities. This means that the politicization of identity is not natural. However, it also acknowledges that for most people, identities feel natural, stable, and permanent—that is, primordial. Given this, just like primordialism, constructivism leaves key questions unanswered. The table on the following page highlights the key advantages and shortcomings of the constructivist approach to understanding political identity. In the end, it is extremely difficult to identify the precise processes by which identities are politicized across millions or even billions of people, and how such politicization is maintained from one generation to the next. Still, constructivism pushes us to think critically and ask how the social context shapes individuals' choices and to explore why some forms of identity not only become politicized, but remain so for long periods, while others remain politically irrelevant. Primordialism takes forms of identity and their political salience as given, but constructivism seeks to explain why forms of identity emerge and acquire political relevance. This focus on the origins and variation in the salience of different forms of identity is constructivism's main strength.

SUMMARY TABLE		
Constructivism and Political Identity		
Why It's Useful	Better able to explain cross-national variation in emergence and salience of political identity because it allows individuals to choose and consciously attach political significance to identity	
	Better able to explain cross-national variation in emergence and salience of political identity because it focuses on how the socio-political context shapes, constrains, and constructs individual choices.	
Why It's Problematic	Unable to make sense of the way most people perceive their own identities	
	Difficult to identify the precise mechanism by which identity becomes politically salient for millions of people and is transmitted from one generation to the next	

CONCLUSION

In the chapter-opening story, we considered the case of a young woman in a far-off country. Why is this one aspect of this Frenchwoman's identity—religion—highly politicized? The example illustrates a more general question: for any individual in any society, why are some forms of identity politicized and others not?

Karl Marx and Max Weber articulated different ways of categorizing forms of political identity and for thinking about the relationship between political identity and political power. For Marx, your economic status as rich or poor—an owner or a worker—fundamentally determines your political identity, and political power is always derived from economic power. Weber did not deny that economic status is important and did not deny the relationship between wealth and power, but he insisted that most salient forms of political identity are not rooted in economic interests, and he noted that sometimes money couldn't buy political influence. Instead, he suggested that most people believe that noneconomic forms of identity such as race, ethnicity or religion are more natural, and that as a result political mobilization along noneconomic lines would be easier than mobilization of economic classes.

Regardless of whether a particular form of political identity is rooted in economics or culture, comparative politics offers two broad ways of answering this chapter's main question—when does identity become politicized?—primordialism and constructivism. For both approaches, identity shapes people's political priorities—what they believe is worth defending or advancing in politics. However, primordialism takes both identity and its political salience as given, while constructivism assumes that political identities evolve even if they appear to be primordial and seeks to uncover the historical processes that shape the emergence and politicization of different forms of identity. In particular, constructivism emphasizes how political leaders attempt to use their control over the institutions of government to shape identity, in pursuit of their own interests.

Identity can take many forms, from economic class-consciousness to racial, ethnic, religious, sexual or ideological identities. Our discussion of primordialism revealed the limitations of assuming that identity is natural—such an approach cannot explain why identity is politicized in some contexts but not in others. As illustrated in our examples from Brazil and Europe, identities are not timeless and natural. Instead, their strength varies over time and from place to place. Brazil's rulers in the early twentieth century attempted to downplay the importance of race in an effort to ensure political stability. Discrimination was outlawed, and Brazil was portrayed as a "racial democracy," even if black Brazilians remained on the bottom of the economic ladder. As a result, to this day Brazilians perceive the salience of the black–white racial divide very differently from Americans, even though both countries share a historical experience of slavery. And in Europe, rulers sought to enhance the importance of national identity in an effort to unify their countries. An effective method to construct a national identity was through mandatory education in a single national language. Nationalism grew stronger where illiteracy was eradicated, while it remained relatively weak in countries that failed to invest in education.

√•—Study and Review the **Post-Test &** **Chapter Exam** at **mypoliscilab.com**

Although explaining the formation and politicization of identity remains difficult, comparative politics has developed tools for meeting this challenge. And given that questions of political identity drive many forms of contention and conflict in the contemporary world, you can understand why it is important to do so. Constructivism points us toward the importance of comparing and contrasting the historical context to explain why identities are politicized in different ways in different countries. As we move through subsequent chapters, we will continue to explore the interplay of institutions, identities, and interests in answering key questions in comparative politics. ◣

KEY TERMS

political identity   149
race   149
ethnicity   149
bourgeoisie   150
proletariat   150

class-consciousness   150
political cleavage   152
primordialism   153
constructivism   153
kinship bonds   153

REVIEW QUESTIONS

1. What differentiates Marx's from Weber's view of identity?
2. Give examples of political cleavages that divide countries into competing political groups around the world.
3. In what ways is identity politicized around the world today?
4. How does primordialism explain political conflict? What are the advantages and disadvantages of explaining interesting political phenomena through a primordialist lens?
5. How does constructivism explain political conflict? What are the advantages and disadvantages of explaining interesting political phenomena through a constructivist lens?

SUGGESTED READINGS

Anderson, Benedict. *Imagined Communities: Reflections on the Origin and Spread of Nationalism*. Rev. ed. London and New York: Verso, 1991. A classic constructivist account of the emergence of nationalist identity.

Brass, Paul. "Elite Groups, Symbol Manipulation and Ethnic Identity among the Muslims of South Asia: Primordialist and Instrumentalist Interpretations of Ethnic Identity." In Brass, *Ethnicity and Nationalism: Theory and Comparison* (1991): 69–89. Thousand Oaks, CA: SAGE. A critique of primordialism and defense of a constructivist approach for understanding ethnic conflict in India.

Cohen, Robin. "The Making of Ethnicity: A Modest Defense of Primordialism." In *People, Nation, and State: The Origins of Ethnicity and Nationalism,* edited by Edward Mortimer and Robert Fine, 3–11. London: I.B. Tauris, 1999. Argues in favor of primordialism.

Griffin, John Howard. New York: Houghton Mifflin, 1961. *Black Like Me.* A true story of a white American who takes medicine that turns his skin black in the late 1950s south. Illustrates the tension between individual choice and social context in the formation of identity.

Huntington, Samuel. *The Clash of Civilizations and the Remaking of World Order*. New York: Simon and Schuster, 1998. A prominent, thought-provoking, and controversial application of a primordialist approach to understanding the politicization of identity in the contemporary world.

NOTES

1. For news coverage of the law's passage, see for example "French Scarf Ban Comes into Force," accessed January 6, 2010, http://news.bbc.co.uk/2/hi/3619988.stm. A brief but useful study of the headscarf ban is "Veiled Meaning: The French Law Banning Religious Symbols in Public Schools," Brookings Institution US-France Analysis, March 2004, accessed January 6, 2010, http://www.brookings.edu/fp/cusf/analysis/vaisse20040229.pdf.

2. Pew Forum on Religion and Public Life, 2011: "The Future of the Global Muslim Population," January 2011, accessed April 29, 2011, http://features.pewforum.org/muslim-population-graphic/#/France.

3. See for example, Russell Dalton, "The Quantity and Quality of Party Systems: Party System Polarization, Its Measurement, and Its Consequences," *Comparative Political Studies* 41(7)(2008) 899–920.

4. The classic primordialist statement comes from Clifford Geertz, *The Interpretation of Cultures* (New York: Basic Books, 1973). See especially 259.

5. See *Foreign Affairs* 72 (3) (1993): 22–50.

6. For example, see Edward Said, "The Clash of Ignorance," *The Nation*, October 4, 2001, http://www.thenation.com/doc/20011022/said.

7. See "Congo War-Driven Crisis Kills 45,000 a Month: Study," accessed January 16, 2010, http://www.reuters.com/article/idUSL2280201220080122.

8. See James D. Fearon and David D. Laitin, "Explaining Interethnic Cooperation," *American Political Science Review* 90(4)(1996): 715–735.

9. Brazil, Instituto Brasileiro de Geografia e Estatística (2006), "Pesquisa Nacional por Amostra de Domicílio," accessed February 16, 2009, http://www.ibge.gov.br/home/estatistica/populacao/trabalhoerendimento/pnad2006/brasilpnad2006.pdf. United States Census Bureau, accessed April 30, 2011, http://quickfacts.census.gov/qfd/states/00000.html.

10. On this process of "whitening" in Brazil, see Thomas Skidmore, *Black into White: Race and Nationality in Brazilian Thought* (Durham, NC: Duke University Press, 1993), or Edward Telles, "Racial Ambiguity among the Brazilian Population." *Ethnic and Racial Studies* 25(3)(2002): 415–441.

11. Brazilian scholar Gilberto Freyre was the first to advance this argument in his 1933 book, *The Masters and the Slaves: A Study in the Development of Brazilian Civilization* (Berkeley: University of California Press). See also Michael Hanchard, *Orpheus and Power: The Movimento Negro of Rio de Janeiro and São Paulo, Brazil, 1945–1988* (Princeton, NJ: Princeton University Press, 1994).

12. See Anthony Marx, *Making Race and Nation: A Comparison of the United States, South Africa, and Brazil* (New York: Cambridge University Press, 1997).

13. See Marx, *Making Race and Nation*. However, in an interesting twist, recent Brazilian government policy has created "affirmative action" programs such as reserved spots at public universities for Brazilians with (self-declared) black ancestry.

14. Keith Darden and Anna Grzymala-Busse, "The Great Divide: Literacy, Nationalism, and the Communist Collapse," *World Politics* 59(2006): 83–115.

15. See Karl W. Deutsch (1953), *Nationalism and Social Communication* (Cambridge, MA: MIT Press, 1953), and Benedict Anderson, *Imagined Communities* (New York: Verso, 1991).

16. See Eugen Weber, *Peasants into Frenchmen: The Modernization of Rural France, 1880–1914* (Stanford, CA: Stanford University Press, 1976).

17. Darden and Grzymala-Busse, 96–97.

Religion and Politics

A woman in Baghdad carries a box of pamphlets explaining Iraq's 2005 draft constitution. Voters approved the document in a referendum, enshrining individual rights and strong regional autonomy, among other political institutions. Still, it remains an open question as to whether Iraq's volatile mix of religious groups can coexist under democracy.

? What is the relationship between religious identity and democracy?

[📖] Read and Listen
to Chapter 7
at mypoliscilab.com

[✓] Study and Review
the Pre-Test & Flashcards
at mypoliscilab.com

Since the 9/11 terrorist attacks, the U.S. government has engaged in warfare in Iraq and Afghanistan based in part on an assumption that if their non-democratic rulers could be forcibly removed, those countries could become democracies. That is, official U.S. government policy assumes Islam and democracy are compatible. On July 26, 2006, Iraq's first democratically elected prime minister, Nouri al-Maliki, spoke to a packed joint session of the U.S. Congress. In his speech, Maliki directly addressed the tension between religion and democracy in Iraq, saying,

> Our people aspire to liberty, democracy, human rights, and the rule of law. Those are not Western values; they are universal values for humanity. They are as much for me the pinnacle embodiment of my faith and religion as they are for all free spirits. . . . I know that some of you here question whether Iraq is part of the war on terror. Let me be very clear: this is a battle between true Islam, for which a person's liberty and rights constitute essential cornerstones, and terrorism, which wraps itself in a fake Islamic cloak, waging a war on Muslims and Islamic values. . . . Human rights are not an artificial construct reserved for the few. They are the divine entitlement for all. . . . It is on this unwavering belief that we are determined to build our nation, a land whose people are free, whose air is liberty, and where the rule of law is supreme.[1]

Iraq's future—and the path of U.S. policy in the Middle East and elsewhere—depends considerably on the extent to which Maliki and his successors put these words into practice. This chapter continues our investigation of the sources and consequences of collective political identity by exploring the relationship between religious identity and politics. We focus specifically on one of the toughest questions confronting comparative politics today: *what is the relationship between religious identity and democracy?*

Given its salience for global politics, this question is far from academic. Recall Samuel Huntington's argument that the most important civilizational fault line is not ethnic, linguistic, or national, but religious: the potential clash between Islamic civilization and the largely Christian Western civilization. Around the world, politicians have long mixed politics and religion, using religion as a mobilizational tool—sometimes to promote peaceful change, sometimes to promote violence against others who believe differently.

Certain religious identities may be more or less compatible with certain institutions of government. Religion, ethnicity, and nationalism are often linked—and religious beliefs also shape how individuals view gender relations. Religious identity powerfully shapes what many people think they want from participating in politics. In this way, religion also impacts the forms of collective political mobilization we observe in different countries, both peaceful and violent. For example, religion often motivates social movements or political parties, and religious disputes also frequently motivate civil wars.

Are some religions fundamentally incompatible with democracy? By examining contemporary real-world examples, we will reveal the historical and political factors that help explain why no primordial connection exists between either Christianity and democracy or Islam and non-democracy. Still, to further understand why most predominantly Christian countries are democracies while most predominantly Islamic countries are not, we will assess the argument that long-term economic development can alter the political significance of religious identity in any particular country—and whether such cultural change can support democratization.

RELIGION AND DEMOCRACY

Democracy poses a difficult problem for any religious tradition, whether Christian, Muslim, or other. Why? Because democracy requires majority rule and recognizes that the interests or preferences of the majority can change over time. Many people with strong religious beliefs regard the principles of their religion as timeless, unchanging, and—most importantly—morally binding, regardless of what everybody else might believe. People with strong religious beliefs the world over confront the possibility that a majority of their fellow citizens might vote for policies that contradict their moral principles.

When religious people believe that a policy or law violates their moral principles, they frequently get involved in social movements or interest groups to press for political change. Consider, for example, the prominence of churches in both the U.S. civil rights movement and the anti-abortion movement. In a democracy, the losers must accept the outcomes of the process and mobilize their energies toward winning the next election. Yet, sometimes, a group of people finds a policy so offensive to their religion that they reject the principle of majority rule and seek to overthrow the democratic system as a whole. Are some religions more likely to accept democracy unconditionally, while others are more likely to accept democracy with strings attached—that is, only if the outcomes of the democratic process do not violate certain nonnegotiable religious precepts?

People the world over differ as to how strictly they interpret their faith's principles. In other words, every religion has liberals and conservatives. Yet, democracy requires a certain degree of liberality: not just freedom of expression for everyone, but a "live and let live" attitude. Democracy by definition requires tolerance for a variety of beliefs that extremists within some religions may be unwilling to accept. But as this principle holds true for all religions, why do so many wonder whether Islam, in particular, and democracy are inherently incompatible? Just a few decades ago, many believed Catholicism did not support democracy. In fact, up through the 1980s, most of the predominantly Catholic countries in Latin America and Southern and Eastern Europe were non-democratic regimes. Given this, students in an earlier era might have read in their comparative politics textbook that *Catholicism* and democracy were incompatible. Such a claim sounds ludicrous today, so perhaps textbooks 30 years from now won't even contain a chapter on religion and politics—particularly if more Islamic countries adopt democracy.

7.1 What is the potential tension between any religious tradition and the principles of democracy?

✴ Explore the **Comparative "Civil Liberties"** at mypoliscilab.com

How compatible are different religions with democracy in the real world? Is there a clear relationship between a country's predominant religion and democracy? Consider the democracies first. Most democracies are in areas where Christianity dominates. Yet several non-Christian democracies exist, such as Japan, Israel, and India. Moreover, several predominantly Christian countries remain non- or only partially democratic, such as Russia and Belarus (which are predominantly Eastern Orthodox Christian); Venezuela and Colombia in Latin America; and most countries in sub-Saharan Africa.

In contrast, nearly all predominantly Muslim countries are non-democracies. Forty-six countries in the world have Muslim majority populations, and on average those countries rank worse than countries without a Muslim majority on Freedom House's democracy rankings. In fact, in 2011 Freedom House classified only two of the 46 majority-Muslim countries as "Free." Seventeen were classified as "Partly Free," and 27 were classified as "Not Free." Included in the list of Free and Partly Free majority-Muslim countries are Turkey, Senegal, Indonesia, Bangladesh, Mali, Sierra Leone, and Albania.[2]

The fact that not every predominantly Christian country is "Free" casts doubt on the idea of a necessary connection between Christianity and democracy. Likewise, the fact that some majority-Muslim states are "Partly Free" or "Free" refutes the idea that Islam and democracy are necessarily incompatible. Still, a clear picture does emerge: currently, countries where Christianity dominates tend to be democratic, while non-democracy dominates in Muslim-majority countries. What explains this pattern?

CHRISTIANITY AND DEMOCRACY

7.2 Does having a predominantly Christian religious tradition necessarily mean democracy will emerge?

Is there something primordial about Christianity that explains its connection with democracy? Or is there something in historical experience that points toward a constructivist interpretation of this pattern? Jesus never sought to set up a political or legal system, but he did provide some clues regarding his views about earthly political matters by saying, "My kingdom is not of this world" and by urging his followers to, "Render unto Caesar that which is Caesar's, and render unto God that which is God's" (Matthew 22:21). These biblical statements affirm the separation of church and state.

As a matter of historical fact, democracy did originate in Western Europe, a region powerfully shaped by Christianity. Many argue that this connection between Christianity and democracy in Europe is not coincidental. However, modern democracy took root under the Protestant version of Christianity as opposed to the Catholic or Orthodox versions, which are prevalent in southern and eastern Europe. This fact leads us to a different question: is there something (perhaps primordially) pro-democratic about Protestantism? In this next section, we concentrate on the historical connection between Protestantism and democracy, and then consider why a connection between Catholicism and democracy only emerged later.

Protestantism and Democracy

There are about 800 million Protestants in the world. Over the past century, Protestantism spread rapidly in Africa, Asia, and Latin America: in 1900, about 2 percent of Africans were Protestant, but by 2000 that number had grown to more than 27 percent. In Latin America, the figures for those same two years are 2.5 and 17 percent, while in Asia they are 0.5 and 5.5 percent.[3] Scholars have long perceived a connection between Protestantism and democracy—and the more Protestants a country has, the more likely Freedom House is to rate that country "Free."

What explains the apparent affinity between Protestantism and democracy? On the one hand, one could argue that democracy is primordially inscribed in the very DNA of Protestant Christianity. In the year 1517, Martin Luther nailed his "95 Theses" to the church door in Wittenberg, Germany, instigating a split within the Catholic Church that became known as the Protestant Reformation. Four years later, Luther defied an order from the pope to recant his heretical views. From that moment forward, Luther stopped trying to reform the Church from within and began a process of founding a new form of Christian faith. Protestantism ultimately came to differ from Catholicism in fundamental ways that have important implications for the relationship between religion and politics.

Protestant Reformation ■ a sixteenth-century division within Christianity that resulted in the formation of various Protestant Christian religious sects, which split off from the Catholic Church.

An important distinction between Protestantism and Catholicism for individual believers is that Protestants reject the idea that a priest must mediate between an individual and God. Instead, Protestants believe in the "priesthood of all believers"—that individuals can have a direct personal relationship with God and can acquire salvation only by personally accepting God's word. Given these beliefs, Protestants historically tend to favor the separation of Church and State, because they believe the individual conscience is inviolable—meaning that no religious *or* civil authority should coerce an individual to think or pray a certain way.

Protestantism also lets the formation of church communities and sects be relatively unregulated by a central religious authority, and—in contrast to Catholicism—it lacks a centralized mechanism for settling disagreements about religious doctrine. Therefore religious pluralism—a diversity of forms of worship— tended to emerge in societies where Protestantism took root early on, for example in the UK and the United States. Such diversity of religious views tends to prevent any single religious organization from dominating the state or society. In contrast, in predominantly Catholic countries such as Spain or Italy, the Church historically exerted a powerful influence over both state and society, which slowed the emergence of democracy.

religious pluralism ■ a diversity of forms of worship.

Where religious pluralism took root and to prevent one religious denomination from gaining recognition as the "official" government-sanctioned church, some Protestant sects began advocating freedom of religion for *all* denominations and the independence of all churches from state control. For example, growing religious pluralism in seventeenth-century Britain eventually forced the king and parliament to issue the "Act of Toleration" in 1689, which allowed freedom of worship not only to Anglicans but also to Methodists, Baptists, Quakers, and Congregationalists. (However, the Act continued to discriminate against Catholics and Unitarians, who were regarded as heretics.)

When the Puritans and representatives of other dissenting religious sects emigrated from Britain to the American colonies, many became vocal advocates for religious freedom. Their political activism helped establish the principle that voluntary associations could exist in civil society, outside of state control. Today, we call these forms of collective action nongovernmental organizations (NGOs), social movements, or interest groups. Although this considerably simplifies centuries of history, we can characterize the emergence and spread of Protestantism as one of voluntary religious organizations formed outside of centralized state control.

These key elements of Protestant faith, along with Protestant efforts to prevent government meddling in religious affairs, opened the door for the spread of the concept of separation of Church and State. This supports the notion that something in the historical experience of Protestantism is associated with the rise of democracy. Yet, despite the historical connection between Protestantism and democracy, being a Protestant does not automatically make one a friend of liberty. For example, many Protestant leaders in the early decades of the United States sought biblical justifications for slavery; numerous German Protestant leaders supported Hitler's Nazi regime; and leaders of the Dutch Reformed Church in South Africa preached a religious justification for apartheid, the political and legal system by which the white minority oppressed the black majority until the early 1990s. These examples suggest that there is no necessary "primordial" connection between Protestantism and democracy, although a general affinity between Protestantism and key democratic principles does exist.

If Protestantism were automatically associated with democracy, the dramatic growth of Protestant churches in Latin America, Asia, and Africa would be good news for the future of democracy in those regions. Yet, there is an important contrast between the early and more recent spread of Protestantism: Lutherans, Methodists, Congregationalists, and Presbyterians led Protestantism's early spread, while Evangelical and Pentecostal congregations are leading Protestantism's more recent growth spurt.

What implications might this difference have for any future connection between Protestantism and democracy? On the one hand, both newer and older Protestants hold to the conviction that salvation must come from within and cannot be compelled by the state. Yet, on the other hand, considerable differences exist between older Protestant denominations—which emphasize education and learning—and some newer congregations, which bestow authority and leadership based on revealed spiritual gifts rather than through study and knowledge. In earlier eras, the older Protestant denominations dominated in what were then (and are now) the world's wealthiest countries. More recently, Protestantism has spread more rapidly in poorer countries.

Democratization tends to follow modernization—in particular, when the expansion of educational opportunities and the breakdown of traditional social hierarchies encourage the spread of democratic values. Given the differences between older and some newer Protestant congregations, the recent spread of Protestantism might not support democracy as it did in earlier centuries. Some observers even suggest that new Protestant churches in Africa, Latin America, and elsewhere reproduce or reinforce existing non-democratic social hierarchies, thereby limiting the potential spread of democracy.[4]

In sum, a historical association does exist between the spread of Protestantism in Western Europe in earlier centuries and the spread of ideas that tend to support democracy. However, it is not clear that such a connection exists between Protestantism and support for pro-democratic ideas in the contemporary world. The apparent lack of such a connection outside of Western Europe undermines the idea of a "primordial" connection between Protestant Christianity and democracy. We can only make a clear connection between Protestantism and democracy under particular historical circumstances.

Catholicism and Democracy

The world contains approximately one billion Catholics, just less than half the total Christians worldwide. Three out of every four transitions to democracy since 1975 occurred in predominantly Catholic countries. A proportion this high suggests the association is more than coincidental: something about being predominantly Catholic appears to have predisposed certain countries toward democratization in recent decades. However, this strong relationship between Catholicism and recent democratization does not mean Catholicism and democracy are primordially related. Instead, global political events shape and construct this connection.

The relatively close connection between Catholicism and democracy today is quite a surprise in historical perspective, because up through the mid-twentieth century Catholicism and democracy did not mix well. In fact, the Catholic Church long opposed democracy on principle. For centuries the Catholic Church maintained its conviction that the state's primary purpose was to promote Catholicism as the "one true faith" and to restrict the spread of alternative forms of religious belief. Also, since opposition to religious authority is a form of political dissent, this meant that the Catholic Church opposed ideas such as freedom of expression and freedom of speech.

As the Protestant Reformation spread in Western Europe and the concept of individual rights began to gain traction in the 1700s, the Catholic Church confronted new threats. The American Revolution firmly established the concept of freedom of religion and the separation of Church and State. Similarly, during the French Revolution in the 1790s, violent outbursts against Catholic Church authority erupted, and anti-Church movements swept across Europe throughout the 1800s.

Even in the face of such developments, the Catholic Church refused to moderate its position. Instead, it adopted a defiant, conservative attitude. For example, in 1832, Pope Gregory XVI mocked freedom of conscience as "an absurd and erroneous opinion," and in 1864 Pope Pius IX sweepingly condemned religious

Pope John Paul II addressing a multitude in communist-controlled—that is, officially atheist—Poland, 1979. The pope was instrumental in encouraging Poles to demand freedom of worship.

freedom, the separation of Church and State, and "progress, liberalism, and recent civilization" in its entirety. Despite sounding outlandish today, the Church held tightly to these views.

Change in the Catholic Church's attitude toward democracy only emerged in the last decades of the twentieth century, following the 1965 Second Vatican Council, a meeting at which Church authorities from around the world sought to grapple with the political, social, and religious challenges of modernity. Church leaders reformulated many longstanding doctrines, and after the meeting, Pope Paul VI declared that religious liberty was a fundamental God-given human right and that states should not interfere with an individual's search for religious truth.

The Catholic Church's approval of freedom of conscience and religious toleration was part of a broader modernization of Catholic religious doctrine and practice. Once the Church undertook these changes, many of its leaders around the world—the cardinals, bishops, and priests who lead the Church in each country—began agitating for political reforms in non-democratic states—often to promote freedom of worship for Catholics. For example, Pope John Paul II, elected in 1978, was a native of Poland, which was ruled by a communist dictatorship at that time. He strongly advocated democracy—not just in Eastern Europe, but also around the entire world. John Paul II led the Catholic Church's important role in promoting the third wave of democratization.[5]

Second Vatican Council ■ 1965 meeting of Catholic authorities from around the world that reformulated longstanding Church doctrines.

Partly because of the Church's doctrinal changes since 1965, we now take it for granted that Catholicism favors democracy. Yet, because this policy shift came recently in the Church's long history, the connection between Catholicism and democracy is obviously not primordial. Instead, the Church reevaluated its longstanding opposition to key principles of democracy in the face of tremendous global political, economic, and social changes.

The connection between democracy and Christianity appears obvious today, but this connection is historically constructed. A primordialist hypothesis would suggest that there is something timeless and constant about Christianity that is associated with democracy. If this were true, then we should have seen consistent support for democracy across the centuries and in every region where Christianity dominated. However, although Europe was fully Christianized by the year 800, it took another thousand years for the idea of democracy to emerge and evolve. Moreover, democracy emerged first where Christianity had changed the most—in Protestant northern and western Europe, where historical processes such as the Reformation, the Renaissance, the Enlightenment, and the Industrial Revolution had the most impact—and not in the Catholic countries of southern and eastern Europe. In those regions, religious doctrine formally changed only in the late twentieth century.

In short, as the summary table below suggests, there is no necessary and natural association between Christianity and democracy. Instead, dramatic economic, social, intellectual, and political changes in certain countries transformed Christian religious doctrines, in different historical eras. These transformations, rather than religious doctrine itself, go a long way to explaining why democracy today is most

SUMMARY TABLE

Assessing the Relationship between Christianity and Democracy

	Affinity with Democracy	Tension with Democracy
Protestantism	Doctrine has historically supported religious pluralism, opposed an "official" government church, and favored separation of Church and State.	Church leaders do not always support democracy, as exemplified by Protestant support for slavery in the United States, the Nazi regime, and the racist regime in pre-1994 South Africa.
Catholicism	Post-1965, affirmed individuals' right to religious freedom. Pope John Paul II (1978–2005) promoted freedom of worship around the world, helping to spread the third wave of democratization.	Pre-1965: in predominantly Catholic countries, the Church frequently allied with governments to promote the "official" version of the faith, restricted alternatives, and opposed the idea of freedom of conscience.

often found in predominantly Christian countries. With this conclusion in mind, let's turn to the alleged incompatibility of Islam and democracy.

ISLAM AND DEMOCRACY

7.3 Does a Muslim religious culture necessarily offer little support for democracy?

Arab ■ an ethnic group defined by language and geographic location, in countries in North Africa and the Middle East.

👁 Watch the **Video** **"Iraq's Oil Curse"** at **mypoliscilab.com**

Islam is the world's second-largest religion, with approximately 1.3 billion adherents compared to Christianity's 2.1 billion and Hinduism's 900 million. Majority-Muslim states cover a wide swath of the world's territory, from Morocco in Northwest Africa to Indonesia in Southeast Asia. Although Islam originated in what is now Saudi Arabia, about 75 percent of the world's Muslims are not Arabs—an ethnic group defined by language and who predominate in countries in North Africa and the Middle East. In fact, the countries with the largest Muslim populations are all *outside* the Arab world: Indonesia (200 million), Pakistan (160 million), India (150 million), and Bangladesh (130 million).

Separation of Religion and the State under Islam

Democracy only emerged in predominantly Christian Europe after considerable political, social, economic, and especially religious change. This undermines the idea of a primordial connection between Christianity and democracy. Still, some suggest a primordial link exists between Islam and *non*-democracy.[6] If this is true, then perhaps Samuel Huntington's argument has some merit: the world is fated to witness an ongoing clash between the Islamic and Christian civilizations. Yet, as with Christianity, historical and political factors have shaped the

Country Populations with Large Percentages of Muslims

The darker the shading, the higher the proportion of Muslims in the population. Orange shading represents a Sunni majority, while green represents a Shiite majority.

contemporary correlation between Islam and non-democracy.[7] To the extent that this is the case, then further democratization in the Islamic world is theoretically possible, although not inevitable.

Muhammad, whom Muslims consider to be God's prophet, founded Islam almost 1,400 years ago. In contrast to Jesus's suggestion that one should, "Render unto Caesar things that are Caesar's," Muhammad's revelations in the Koran, which is Islam's holy book, do not suggest separating religion and politics. According to many Islamic scholars, in its ideal form, Islam does not recognize the separation of religion from the state. A primordialist argument like Huntington's suggests that the absence of such a separation dooms predominantly Islamic countries to non-democracy.

Yet, is the separation of Church and State a necessary precondition for democracy? Many believe so. However, several democratic constitutions (for example, those of the UK and Israel) contain no such provision. Some democratic constitutions (those of Denmark, Finland, and Greece) even directly support particular religions by financially subsidizing religious schools, social organizations, and places of worship. The fact that the constitutions of some democracies directly support particular faiths suggests that democracy and religion can be compatible. So if the separation of Church and State is not necessary for democracy to emerge, then democracy is possible under any dominant religious identity—including Islam.

One point must be made clear. Just as in every other religion, Muslims disagree over how to correctly interpret the meaning of their own religious texts. Islamic practice involves attention to an elaborate set of laws known as *Sharia*, which govern individuals' public and private lives. Multiple schools of Islamic law exist, as well as multiple interpretations of the same laws—some more conservative, some more liberal. As a result, substantial debate exists among Muslims around the world about whether Islamic doctrine precludes democracy.

Sharia ■ the body of Islamic religious law, which governs individuals' public and private lives.

In practice, Muslims have historically found reconciling faith and politics difficult. Like everywhere else, political rulers in the Islamic world make decisions based on expediency and necessity, often ignoring or downplaying religious requirements or interpreting doctrine to suit their immediate needs. Because rulers often sacrifice religious precepts for practical politics, many reform and revolutionary movements throughout Islamic history—like the 1979 Iranian revolution—were motivated by complaints that political leaders were paying insufficient attention to religion. The bottom line is that Islamic doctrine is more fluid and diverse than many casual observers realize. With this in mind, we cannot conclude that Islamic religious identity necessarily precludes democracy. Still, despite recent popular movements demanding democracy in several Middle Eastern Muslim societies, the strong overall correlation between non-democracy and Islam remains—and demands explanation.

The Status of Muslim Women

If religious doctrine does not automatically mandate non-democracy in Muslim societies, why the relative lack of democracy in the Islamic world? One alternative argument connects the relative weakness of democracy to the subordination of women in some Islamic countries.[8] Such discrimination can start early in life. For example, many Islamic societies have a higher proportion of men than women. Such sex-ratio imbalances—which occur in many non-Muslim countries, as well—can have many causes, including selective abortion, inferior nutrition in infancy, poor healthcare for infant girls, or even female infanticide. In some Islamic societies, women are also more likely to be illiterate than men, reflecting the lower social value placed on girls' education. Naturally, illiteracy greatly diminishes a woman's chances of having a successful professional life outside the home. Perhaps because of their treatment as girls and young women, compared with other similar but non-Muslim countries, women in Muslim societies are also less likely to hold government positions.[9]

This lifelong economic and/or cultural discrimination against girls and women can have profound political consequences. When men are entrenched in dominant positions in society, they tend to be more comfortable with social inequalities and political hierarchies than are women. Male social dominance can reflect deep-seated cultural values of respect for hierarchical authority—values that may support non-democratic rule. In this way, it is possible that longstanding practices of gender discrimination may account for the predominance of non-democracy in the Islamic world.

However, evidence suggests that female subordination is not driven directly by religious identity, because the treatment of women varies widely across Islamic societies—just as it does across predominantly Christian societies. In some Muslim countries, gender discrimination is far worse than anything Islamic law might mandate, and those countries tend to be non-democracies. Yet, in other Muslim-majority countries, women enjoy good educational, social, and economic opportunities—as they do for example in Turkey, Indonesia, and Malaysia, countries that Freedom House ranks either as "Free" (Indonesia) or "Partly Free" (Turkey and Malaysia). (It is also useful to remember that both the Hebrew and Christian Bibles suggest far greater female subordination than is practiced anywhere today.)

Given such variation, one cannot attribute the mistreatment of women to Islam itself, since women's rights and opportunities vary considerably across Muslim societies. Gender relations may be a function of political factors only indirectly related to religious doctrine, as considered in this chapter's feature box on India. And just as they have in Judeo-Christian culture, gender relations in Islamic cultures could change over time—which, in turn, implies that political change might follow.

civil law code ■ a set of laws that covers issues pertaining to private property rights and family law.

partition ■ the creation of two separate sovereign states out of a territory that initially comprised only one state, in order to separate antagonistic groups.

Islam and Politics in Arab Societies

Neither religious doctrine nor the treatment of women fully explains the connection between Islam and non-democracy in the contemporary world. Political scientists have offered a third potential explanation: *Arab* Islamic countries are far less likely to be democratic than *non-Arab* Islamic countries in sub-Saharan Africa,

In a Democracy Deeply Divided by Religious Disputes, Treating Everyone Equally Is the Best Way to Promote Domestic Stability and Peace:
HYPOTHESIS TESTING | The Case of India

With an estimated population of 1.1 billion, India is by far the world's largest democracy. The country is incredibly diverse in terms of political identities, including tribe, economic class, ethnicity, and religion. About 80 percent of Indians are Hindus, 14 percent are Muslim, 2.5 percent are Christian, and the rest comprise several other faiths. In a country of India's size, even minority populations are impressive—there are almost 150 million Muslims and 25 million Christians, for example. Only Pakistan and Indonesia have more Muslims.

A civil law code is the set of laws that covers private property (its acquisition, administration, transfer, and inheritance) and the family (for example, dowries, marriage, divorce, and child custody). India lacks a single, uniform civil code that applies to all citizens. Instead, Hindus and Muslim have separate civil codes. This means, for example, that while Muslim men can have more than one wife, polygamy is illegal for Hindus. Is equal treatment before the law a requirement for political stability and peace under democracy, or is having different laws apply to different groups a good idea?

GATHER EVIDENCE

For centuries, Muslims ruled almost the entire Indian subcontinent—meaning that they dominated the Hindus—until the British colonized the region in the mid-1700s. When the British finally left in 1947, they partitioned their former colony into the new countries of India and Pakistan. (Bangladesh later separated itself from Pakistan and became independent in 1971.) The idea behind partition—the creation of two separate sovereign states—was that separating Hindus from Muslims would diminish the likelihood of bloodshed. However, the process of partition was chaotic and violent: millions were forced from their homes, and perhaps 500,000 people died. The two countries have also fought two wars and numerous skirmishes since independence.

After partition, Pakistan established itself as an Islamic state, while India was founded as a predominantly Hindu yet secular democracy, with sizeable religious minorities. According to Samuel Huntington, the Hindu–Muslim divide represents a "Clash of Civilizations." This clash occurs not just between India and Pakistan, but also within India, where interfaith violence remains frequent. Hindus have attacked mosques and attempted to push Muslims out of certain regions, and Muslims have responded in kind. For example, soon after the 9/11 attacks in the United States, Islamic suicide terrorists attacked the Indian parliament building.

Even so, despite the frequency of religiously inspired violence, India has always posed a puzzle for students of comparative politics. On the one hand, except for a brief period of martial law, it has been fully democratic since independence. Yet, on the other hand, it lacks many of the characteristics typically associated with democracy, such as wealth, religious, or ethnic homogeneity, and Christian cultural roots.

Political institutions play a paradoxical role in moderating interreligious strife and maintaining Indian democracy. India's constitution states that the country is a "secular democratic republic" and mandates equal treatment and tolerance of all religions. The constitution also contains several anti-discrimination provisions, such as gender equality. Yet, India's civil law code appears to violate these principles. For example, because Hindus and Muslims have different civil codes and because Islamic law is based in *Sharia*, women's legal rights differ across the Indian Hindu and Muslim communities. "Equality before the law" may be written into India's constitution, but in practice it does not exist across all Indian religious groups.

(Continued)

Police presence is high in many areas of India where multiple ethnic groups live and work in close proximity. Here, Hindus and Muslims mingle in downtown New Delhi, India's capital.

Article 44 of India's 1947 constitution recommends adoption of a single civil code, but Indian politicians have ignored this requirement. Many Hindus believe the failure to enact a single civil code discriminates against them, because it affords Muslims "separate and unequal" treatment. Some also argue that a religiously based legal system violates the separation of Church and State. Many Hindus want to adopt a uniform civil code, while most Muslims oppose such a move.

ASSESS THE HYPOTHESIS

What are the potential costs and benefits of having separate civil codes? Consider what might happen if India's nearly 900 million Hindus voted to adopt a uniform civil code, forcing the country's 150 million Muslims to change their ways. One of India's major political parties has long advocated this policy: the Bharatiya Janata Party (BJP) or Indian People's Party, sometimes known in English as the Hindu Nationalist Party. The BJP advocates what it calls *Hindutva*, or "Hinduness," a form of political identity promoting Hindu religious nationalism. The BJP claims that advocating a uniform civil code fits key principles of democracy, such as equality before the law. However, the BJP also advocates pro-Hindu

positions such as a total ban on cow slaughter, which would have a significant impact on Muslims, who eat beef but not pork. In defending Hindu identity, many accuse the BJP of fomenting inter-religious conflict, and, in particular, of promoting anti–Muslim bias.

Why has the BJP failed in its effort to implement a uniform civil code? The main reason is that it has controlled India's government only briefly, in 1996 and then again from 1998 through 2004. Instead, for most of India's history since independence, the Indian National Congress party (INC) has governed. The INC has long pursued a policy of coexistence with the Muslim minority. In return, Muslims have tended to support INC governments. The BJP calls such efforts appeasement—a treasonous sacrifice of Hindu religious beliefs and political interests.

India's electoral system partly explains why the INC feels that it needs Muslims' support. India uses plurality rule with district magnitude of one. Although Muslims form only about 14 percent of India's population, that is still a sizeable bloc of votes—and Muslims frequently comprise a much larger proportion of the vote in certain electoral districts; meaning that Hindus cannot afford to ignore them if they want to win parliamentary seats in those districts.

The INC sees the Muslim minority as a valuable ally because it is far more politically unified than the Hindu community, which is deeply divided by caste. High-caste Hindus are reluctant to support candidates from lower castes, and vice-versa. Lower-caste Hindus see high-caste Hindus as arrogant snobs, while high-caste Hindus disdain lower-caste Hindus as not worthy of their vote. This means that in many Indian states, multiple parties nominate candidates who happen to be Hindu, each seeking to attract votes from different castes of Hindu voters. This tends to fragment the Hindu vote, giving a significant advantage to the unified Muslim community. Under the plurality system, the candidate who obtains the most votes in a constituency wins the seat. Given this, the INC has powerful incentives to "buy off" Muslim

(Continued)

leaders with promises to continue to ignore the Indian constitution's call for a unified civil code, along with other sorts of political payoffs—something the BJP would never do. The electoral system and political self-interest pushes the INC (and several other parties) to trade Muslim electoral support for Muslim self-governance in legal affairs—possibly preventing a massive civil war from erupting across India. In the end, having separate civil codes appear to reduce—but not eliminate—the incidence of violence across India, and preserve its fragile democracy. ▶

CRITICAL THINKING QUESTIONS

1. How does having a separate civil code for Muslims in India promote civil peace?
2. Would letting different religious communities establish their own civil codes strengthen or weaken democracy in the United States? Why or why not?

southeastern Europe, or Asia.[10] Table 7.1 lists Muslim-majority countries, divided by whether the population is Arab or not.

In 2011, according to Freedom House, 86 percent of all Arabs live in a "Not Free" society, but only 21 percent of non-Arab Muslims do. In fact, non-Arab Muslim societies are about 20 times more likely to have held competitive elections than Arab countries.[11] This implies that the observed connection between Islam and non-democracy worldwide is largely shaped by the resilience of non-democracy in Arab cultures. What aspects of Arab culture or politics could account for this connection? Since both Arab and non-Arab Muslim societies share religious identity, something besides religion must account for the variation in the quality of democracy between Arab and non-Arab Islamic societies. Let us consider two explanations: oil and geopolitics.

Oil: The Resource Curse   Some observers suggest that an abundance of oil explains the persistence of non-democracy in the Arab world.[12] Political scientists have labeled this argument the resource curse, which hypothesizes that any country possessing sizeable deposits of petroleum or other exportable natural resources is unlikely to distribute the resulting wealth to the majority of people, to develop a diversified modern economy, or to become a democracy.[13] In oil-rich non-democracies, rulers have strong interests in keeping a lid on political participation and contestation, in order to maintain control over the vast wealth that oil production generates. This argument suggests that political interests—specifically, dictators' interests in staying in power—rather than religious identity explain the persistence of non-democracy in Arab societies.

This argument has great appeal, but unfortunately it does not hold up to scrutiny.[14] First, although many Arab states have lots of oil—including Saudi Arabia, Libya, Algeria, Iraq, and Kuwait—others have none or very little, including Syria, Jordan, Morocco, and Egypt. Since none of these latter countries are yet democracies, we cannot say that oil directly causes the persistence of non-democracy across the entire Arab world. And, in any case, four of the top ten oil producers in the world—the United States, Canada, Mexico, and Norway—*are* democracies,

resource curse ■ hypothesizes that any country whose economic growth relies on one valuable natural resource is unlikely to result in an equitable distribution of wealth, which in turn creates problematic political consequences.

TABLE 7.1

Countries with Muslim Majorities

Arab Countries	Population	Non-Arab Countries	Population
Algeria	32,531,853	Afghanistan	29,928,987
Bahrain	688,345	Albania	3,563,112
Egypt	77,505,756	Azerbaijan	7,911,974
Iraq	26,074,906	Bangladesh	144,319,628
Jordan	5,759,732	Brunei	372,361
Kuwait	2,335,648	Burkina Faso	13,925,313
Lebanon	3,826,018	Chad	9,826,419
Libya	5,765,563	Comoros	671,247
Mauritania	3,086,859	Djibouti	476,703
Morocco	32,725,847	Eritrea	4,561,599
Oman	3,001,583	Gambia, The	1,593,256
Qatar	863,051	Guinea	9,467,866
Saudi Arabia	26,417,599	Indonesia	241,973,879
Syria	18,448,752	Iran	68,017,860
Tunisia	10,074,951	Kyrgyzstan	5,146,281
United Arab Emirates	2,563,212	Malaysia	23,953,136
		Maldives	349,106
Yemen	20,727,063	Mali	12,291,529
		Niger	11,665,937
		Nigeria	128,771,988
		Pakistan	162,419,946
		Senegal	11,126,832
		Sierra Leone	6,017,643
		Somalia	8,591,629
		Sudan	40,187,486
		Tajikistan	7,163,506
		Turkey	69,660,559
		Turkmenistan	4,952,081
		Uzbekistan	26,851,195

Note: Population figures are 2005 estimates.

Source: Pew Forum on Religion and Public Life, "Muslim Population by Country," http://features.pewforum.org/muslim-population/, Accessed December 8, 2011.

suggesting that great resource wealth does not automatically curse a country to a perpetual status as a non-democracy.

Oil and Geopolitics   A more promising explanation connects international factors to the persistence of non-democracy in the Arab world. In particular, Western democracies' need for stable access to oil and a desire to prevent another Arab–Israeli war may help explain the persistence of non-democracy in both oil-rich and oil-poor countries in the region. This view suggests that the United States and other wealthy democracies prefer the stability of non-democratic rule in the Arab world to the unpredictability of democracy, in order to ensure continued access to petroleum and to maintain peace between Israel, Egypt, Syria, and Jordan.

To promote regional stability, the United States and its allies provide non-democratic rulers billions of dollars in economic and military aid every year. However, the Arab–Israeli conflict and the U.S. invasions of Iraq and Afghanistan have generated strong anti-Western sentiment around the region. To deflect criticism about their relationship with the United States and other Western countries, Arab rulers attempt to generate nationalist support by stirring up animosity against the United States and Israel, and also argue that allowing democracy would only bring chaos and violence to the region.

According to this argument, it is not religious identity but rather international geopolitical dynamics that has sustained non-democracy in some Islamic countries. This argument has the advantage of explaining both the prevalence of non-democracy in the Arab world as well as the political liberalization of some non-Arab Muslim countries, where oil and the Israeli conflict are not at issue. However, the protests that rocked the Arab Middle East in 2010–2011 may undermine the logic of this hypothesis. The multitudes of ordinary Arabs who took to the streets did not shout anti-American or anti-Israel slogans—they blamed their own rulers for their countries' problems with corruption and weak economic growth. And the United States and other powerful oil-dependent countries did not—as one would expect if this argument were true—automatically support Arab rulers who sought to crack down on dissent. Because the situation in the region is rapidly changing, scholars and students will continue to debate the sources of resistance to democracy in the Arab world—but geopolitics has and will likely continue to play an important role.

Religious identity cannot explain the connection between Islam and non-democracy in the world today. Provisional alternative explanations for the prevalence of non-democracy in Muslim societies include cultural practices that enforce female subordination, the preponderance of non-democracy in the Arab world compared to non-Arab Muslim societies, and oil wealth. Geopolitics also offers a promising explanation for the prevalence of non-democracy across the Middle East, but recent events may have undermined this connection.

In any case, the summary table on the following page highlights the implication that—as with Christianity—several historical and political factors have shaped or "constructed" the relationship between Islam and democracy—in different ways,

SUMMARY TABLE

Assessing the Relationship between Islam and Democracy

Reason Islam and Democracy May Be in Tension	Logical Flaw with this Argument
Without no clear separation of religion and politics, respect for freedom of conscience may be difficult if not impossible in Muslim societies.	Formal separation of Church and State is not a prerequisite for democracy, an example such as the UK confirms.
Lack of equal gender rights in many Muslim societies reinforces non-democratic values, particularly among men.	The extent of gender discrimination varies widely across the Muslim world, meaning it cannot be automatically linked to religious doctrine.
Arab societies are far more unlikely to be democratic than non-Arab Muslim societies.	Implies that the lack of democracy in the Arab world cannot be a function of Islamic religious doctrine per se.
■ *The resource curse: oil gives some Arab rulers powerful incentives to crack down on dissent, in order to remain in power.*	Implies religion is not the reason non-democracy dominates in the Arab world. In any case, some Arab states have no oil but are still non-democratic—and some democracies have lots of oil.
■ *Geopolitics: the United States and other wealthy countries subsidize non-democracy in the Arab world to maintain stable access to oil and prevent a regional war.*	Contradicting the hypothesis' implications, recent unrest in the Middle East demonstrates that many in the region do not blame the United States or Israel for their problems and reveals that the United States will not automatically support its allies in the region.

depending on the context. The notion that a "primordial" connection exists between Islam and non-democracy is unsustainable: some Islamic societies are moving or have moved towards democracy, while others remain solidly non-democratic.

MODERNIZATION, SECULARIZATION, AND DEMOCRACY

7.4 Is there a relationship between economic modernization, secularization, and democratization?

Thus far, we have learned that there is no primordial connection between either Christianity and democracy or Islam and non-democracy. Democracy took centuries to evolve in predominantly Christian countries and was never a predetermined outcome. Moreover—especially given recent popular protests against Middle Eastern dictatorships—the fact that democracy is rare but not unknown in the Islamic world today suggests that changes in the economic, social, or geopolitical context could potentially bring about regime change. To further explore this possibility, let us return to the argument connecting economic modernization and democratization.

Elsewhere, we considered a potential direct connection between economic modernization and the emergence of democracy. In this section, we consider the potential connection between economic modernization and secularization—a gradual decline in the societal importance of religion—and in turn, a possible relationship between secularization and democratization. Debate has persisted for more than 200 years about whether economic modernization leads to a decline of religion. The argument has spurred intense debate, partly because it tends to offend religious people who live in economically wealthy countries.

secularization ■ a gradual decline in the societal importance of religion.

A global comparative assessment of the relationship between secularization and democracy suggests that perhaps the answer to this chapter's question should not focus on whether any particular religion supports democracy or not, but whether any intensely religious society could support a democratic regime. Perhaps we should focus on whether—if economic modernization causes secularization—secular countries are more likely to be democracies. This question applies to all countries, regardless of their dominant religious identity. That is, maybe we associate Christianity and democracy because predominantly Christian countries were the first to modernize and, thus, to experience a decline in religiosity. In turn, perhaps we associate non-democracy with the Islamic world because of the lack of economic modernization in many predominantly Muslim societies. Let us consider the evidence.

Evidence of Secularization

The importance of religion has diminished over time across most wealthy democracies. Table 7.2 provides a key piece of evidence—a broad decline in the percentage of people who affirm a belief in God. Americans tend to diverge from the pattern.

TABLE 7.2

Belief in God, 1947–2001 (Percent)

Country	1947	1968	Late 1990s	Change
Sweden	80	60	46	−34
Netherlands	80	79	58	−22
Australia	95	—	75	−20
Norway	84	73	65	−19
Denmark	80	—	62	−18
UK	—	77	61	−16
Greece	—	96	84	−12
Germany	—	81	69	−12
Finland	83	83	72	−11
France	66	73	56	−10
Switzerland	—	84	77	−7
Austria	—	85	83	−2
USA	94	98	94	0

Source: Data taken from Inglehart and Norris, *Sacred and Secular*. New York: Cambridge University Press, 2004, p. 90.

value emphasis on personal survival ■ people who value personal survival emphasize the importance of nuclear family, childrearing, and hard work; worry a great deal about having enough money; and wish for greater government involvement in the economy.

value emphasis on personal well-being ■ people who focus on personal well-being place higher value on individual freedom, leisure time, and being happy; work as a source of personal satisfaction; and value freedom of expression and the ability to participate in politics.

traditional values ■ people who value traditional forms of political authority such as kings, tribal chiefs, and religious leaders tend to be more religious and nationalistic, express respect for hierarchical authority relations, and express a belief in a clear difference between good and evil.

secular–rational values ■ people who hold secular–rational values tend to not be religious; are skeptical of authority figures in general; and are reluctant to affirm a simple difference between good and evil.

Yet—as Figure 7.1 shows—even Americans have become somewhat more secular over time: Participation in organized religious activities more than once a week declined from about 35 percent of the population in 1970 to about 24 percent in 2006; in that same time period, the proportion of people who say they "never" participate in organized religious activities increased from 10 percent to about 20 percent of the population. In general, evidence points toward a decline in religiosity in wealthy democracies, no matter how religiosity is measured.[15]

How does the evidence of secularization in the world's wealthy democracies stack up against the rest of the world? To answer this question, we can explore the World Values Surveys (WVS), a set of public-opinion surveys taken in many countries around the world every few years since the 1970s. As befits the name, the WVS explores the evolution of citizens' political values, which reflect their political interests and identities.

To describe cross-national variation in political values, the WVS takes peoples' responses to its surveys (tens of thousands from around the world) and boils them down to just two dimensions: (1) whether people's values tend to focus on personal "survival" or personal "well-being," and (2) whether people value "traditional" or "secular–rational" forms of political authority. Statistical analysis can then place a person on a "world values map" along these two dimensions.[16] Similar statistical procedures can also be used to place the average person from a given country on the same map, and then to compare the average individual response in one country against average responses in other countries.

To understand these two dimensions, consider Figure 7.2. People who indicate a concern for survival tend to respond to certain survey questions in a way that

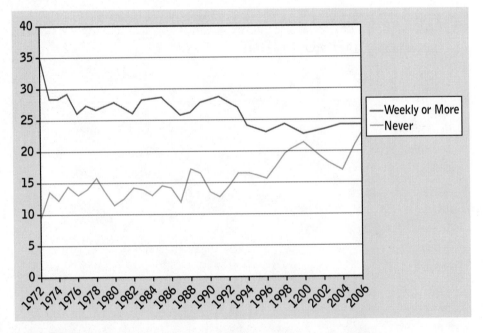

FIGURE 7.1

Religious Participation in the United States (Percent), 1972–2006

Americans have grown somewhat more secular and less religious over time.

Source: General Social Survey. Data obtained from http://www.thearda.com/quickStats/qs_105_t.asp, May 1, 2009. Question: "How often do you attend religious services?"

Nuclear family
Childrearing
Hard work is important
Need money
More government involvement in the economy

Individual freedom
Leisure time
Work is source of personal satisfaction
Being happy is important
Freedom of expression

Emphasis on Survival

Emphasis on Well-being

FIGURE 7.2

Survival versus Well-being

Responses to questions on the World Values Surveys can be boiled down to one of two dimensions. This figure reveals the different ways people respond to questions abut "survival" versus "well-being."

places a high value on the nuclear family, childrearing, and hard work. Also, they worry a great deal about having enough money, and tend to express a desire for greater government involvement in the economy. In contrast, people who express concern for personal well-being place relatively higher value on quality-of-life issues such as individual freedom, leisure time, and "being happy." Such individuals value work as a source of personal satisfaction, not because it puts food on the table, and value freedom of expression and the ability to participate in politics.

The World Values Surveys also measure a second dimension, represented in Figure 7.3: the degree to which individuals value traditional or secular–rational

Respect for Secular–Rational
Forms of Authority

Not likely to be religious
Associated with nonpartisan bureaucracies and elected officials

Respect for Traditional
Forms of authority

Likely to be religious, with a belief in clear good and evil
Associated with nationalism and clear forms of hierarchical authority
such as kings, tribal chiefs, and religious leaders

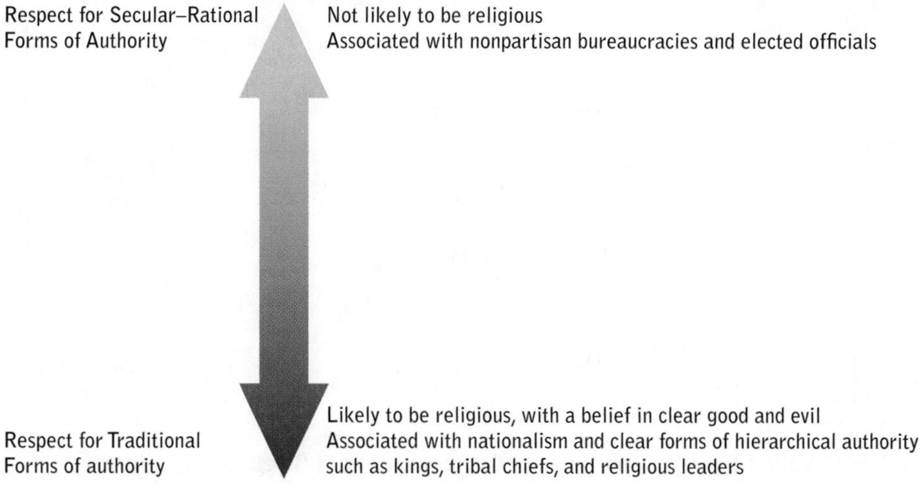

FIGURE 7.3

Secular-Rational Forms of Authority versus Traditional Forms of Authority

Responses to questions on the World Values Surveys can be boiled down to one of two dimensions. This figure reveals the different ways people respond on the second dimension, respect for "traditional" or "secular–rational" forms of political authority.

forms of political authority. Religiosity, nationalism, respect for hierarchical authority relations, and a belief in a clear difference between good and evil are all associated with respect for traditional forms of authority such as kings, tribal chiefs, and religious leaders. In contrast, people who are not religious tend to be more skeptical of authority figures. Also, those who support secular–rational forms of authority are reluctant to affirm a simple difference between good and evil, and are more likely to accept independent judges, nonpartisan bureaucracies, or elected officials—forms of authority present in democracies.

How do citizens' values around the world compare against each other? Figure 7.4 lays several key countries on the dimensions of Figures 7.2 and 7.3. In general, average responses to questions on the World Values Survey in the world's wealthier countries tend to fall to the upper-right quadrant, while people in poorer countries tend to fall in the lower-left quadrant. This lends some support to modernization theory: secularization tends to be associated with country wealth, but not with a country's predominant religious identity. For example, although almost all predominantly Muslim countries fall in the lower-left quadrant, many non-Muslim societies can also be found there.

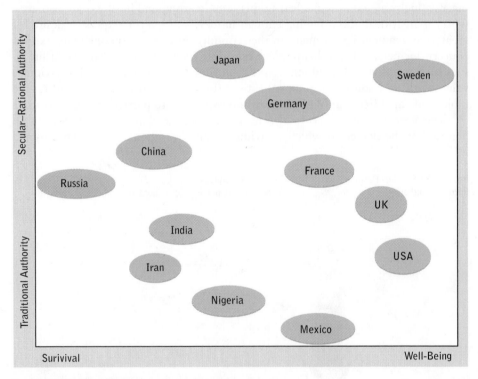

FIGURE 7.4

World Values Surveys: Approximate Country Locations Given Average Survey Responses, as of 2008

Approximate location of most citizens of several countries on the WVS' two dimensions, given their responses to the survey questions.

Source: "The WVS Cultural Map of the World." http://www.worldvaluessurvey.org/wvs/articles/folder_published/article_base_54, Accessed December 8, 2011

A Prada store in Istanbul. The Italian luxury fashion label opened its first store in Turkey in 2009. Prada bags and accessories are viewed worldwide as symbols of wealth and high status—"lifestyle" images associated with economic modernization and secularization.

Connecting Modernization, Secularization, and Democratization

How exactly might modernization drive secularization, and how might secularization, therefore, drive democratization? Let us start with the alleged connection between modernization and secularization. For economic development to drive secularization, it must be relatively equitable: far greater support for secular–rational forms of authority has emerged in wealthy countries with relatively low levels of economic inequality, such as Japan or Sweden, than in wealthy countries with relatively higher levels of economic inequality, such as the United States.

A low level of economic inequality in a rich country means that the country has few truly poor people. In contrast, high inequality means that although the country has plenty of wealthy people and even a large middle class, a sizable group of truly impoverished people remains—people who tend to retain survival values and a faith in traditional forms of authority relations to a relatively greater degree. Secularization follows economic modernization only if by modernization we mean "growth with equity." To have a secularizing effect, economic development must reach as many in society as possible, and leave few behind.

The WVS provides a global picture of differences in political values around the world and offers some evidence connecting modernization with secularization. Can we now connect the dots from secularization to democratization? Why are the countries in the upper-right of Figure 7.4 all democracies? Modernization theory suggests that democracy is more likely to emerge over the long run in countries where cultural values favor secular–rational forms of political authority and personal well-being. We most likely see this tendency because people in wealthier countries in the upper-right quadrant worry less about day-to-day survival and have more resources and time to devote to politics. As people gradually grow less concerned about survival, they grow more concerned about individual well-being in a broader sense—and, thus, many come to hold political values that motivate participation in emancipative social movements that seek to attain, sustain, or extend democratic freedoms.[17]

In contrast, people in countries in the lower-left quadrant of Figure 7.4 remain worried about putting food on the table. To them, democratic freedoms may be a luxury. Moreover, they tend to place relatively less value on concepts associated with democracy, such as political liberty and individual equality, while remaining attached to hierarchical forms of political authority.

The WVS suggests that over time, poor countries will move up and to the right on Figure 7.4 as their economies develop. Yet, since the WVS started in the 1970s, few countries have moved solidly into the upper-right quadrant. This is because historically, very few countries have been able to combine growth with equity without massive government intervention in the economy. The challenge facing the world's poor countries—whether predominantly Islamic, Christian, or something else—is not just figuring out how to grow, but figuring out how to spread the wealth around as widely as possible without leaving masses of people in misery.

To the extent that most poor countries today have experienced economic development at all, it has been relatively unequal. Even countries with oil or other natural resources do not seem able to escape this pattern—in many cases, economic inequality is worse in countries that have abundant natural wealth. Regardless, the fact that tremendous inequality accompanies economic development in the contemporary world suggests that secularization is unlikely to occur in most countries today, whether the predominant religious identity in those countries is Muslim, Christian, or other. In fact, scholars point to increasing religiosity in the contemporary developing world, not secularization.[18] Only time will tell what these trends in religion hold for the future of democracy.

As discussed elsewhere and as Figure 7.5 suggests, a "direct" route from economic modernization to democratization may exist: certain kinds of economic growth can expand educational opportunities, generate urbanization, and break down traditional social hierarchies, transforming individuals' values and increasing their support for democratic principles. However, Figure 7.5 illustrates another possible causal pathway, which we've discussed here: economic modernization could lead to secularization, which, in turn, could promote democratization.

These two arguments are similar, and debate continues over the precise way in which modernization may (or may not) generate support for democracy. Evidence from the World Values Surveys does support the argument that modernization is associated with secularization: religiosity and support for traditional values remain strong in the world's poorer countries, while secular–rational values have gained ground in the world's wealthier societies. However, recent research has suggested that secularization only follows from a particular *kind* of modernization—growth with equity—which in turn means that only this kind of economic modernization will be associated with the value change that aids democratization.

The twist on modernization theory presented in this chapter helps explain why Freedom House scores connect Christian religious identity with democracy and Islamic religious identity with non-democracy: most wealthy countries in the

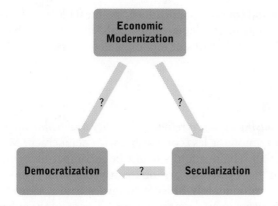

FIGURE 7.5

Economic Modernization, Secularization, and Democratization

Economic development is hypothesized to promote democratization. However, the causal connection may not be direct, as we considered in Chapter 6. Instead, economic modernization may transform religious identity by leading to secularization—a gradual decline in overall societal religiosity—which may in turn generate support for democracy.

world are predominantly Christian, and most wealthy countries are democracies. They are not democracies because they are wealthy, but because a certain path of economic development has transformed religious identity in such a way as to support democracy. In contrast, most Muslim countries are relatively poor. Economic development has not yet transformed cultural values to the point where such values might lend support to democracy.

Modernization theory also rejects the primordialist argument connecting religious identity to political regime type. As the summary table below hints, it suggests that the degree to which cultural values in predominantly Christian countries support democracy results from the way those countries developed economically. This argument is constructivist in the sense that it suggests that long-term paths of economic development shape the relative *intensity* of faith in a given country, whatever the basis for that faith, and that changes in the relative intensity of religious faith can have important political consequences. Constructivism suggests that social context

SUMMARY TABLE

Connecting Modernization, Secularization, and Democratization

Evidence of Secularization?	Widespread among wealthy democracies, but nonexistent among less-wealthy developing economies.
Reasons for secularization	Economic development tends to change cultural values to be more supportive of democracy only if modernization is accompanied by "growth with equity."
Future of secularization?	Secularization may not occur—and thus cultural values in many religious and non-democratic societies may not gradually evolve—because few developing societies have experienced "growth with equity" in recent decades.

powerfully shapes and constrains individuals' political identity. Likewise, a change in social context can potentially change individuals' identities. At base, modernization theory suggests that certain paths of economic development can change how people view the world.

CONCLUSION

What is the relationship between religious identity and democracy? Are some forms of religious identity more or less compatible with democracy? We first considered the potential that all religious faiths might be incompatible with democracy, but then noted that in the real world, predominantly Christian countries tend to be democracies, while predominantly Muslim countries tend not to be. Yet, most reject primordialist arguments to explain this pattern. The connection between Christianity and democracy took centuries to develop, implying that the connection only took root because of changes in Christianity itself. This suggests a constructivist explanation: the rise of Protestantism and recent changes in Catholic Church doctrine have shaped the contemporary association between Christianity and democracy.

As for the connection between Islam and non-democracy, again our analysis rejects a simple primordial connection between religious identity and political practice. As Iraqi President Maliki implied in his speech to American lawmakers, Islam and democracy are not necessarily incompatible. Like Christianity, Islamic doctrines vary around the world and include liberal as well as extremist views. Alternative explanations for why majority-Muslim states tend to be non-democratic include cultural practices that subordinate women, the resource curse, and the geopolitical situation in the contemporary Middle East.

For both Christian and Muslim countries, the relationship between religious identity and democracy or non-democracy is a function of historical and contemporary political factors, not religious identity per se. The impact of economic modernization on citizens' values around the world provides additional support for this conclusion, by suggesting that it is the intensity of religious beliefs, rather than the nature of those beliefs (Christian, Muslim or other) that might aid democracy's emergence. The greater the support for secular–rational rather than traditional forms of political authority, the likelier democracy is to emerge, regardless of a society's religious tradition. A particular form of economic modernization—growth with equity—appears to be the primary engine driving such value change.

Many countries in the world have yet to experience much sustained economic growth, much less growth with equity. Without growth with equity, modernization will have minimal impact on cultural change, and support for traditional forms of authority—whether religiously inspired or not—will remain fairly strong. Secularization has not advanced much in most low-income countries. In fact, the salience of religion seems to be *increasing* in many poor countries around the world, whether Hindu, Muslim, or Christian.

Growing religious fervor in Latin America, Africa, and Asia and across much of the Muslim world poses an important challenge to secularization theory. Perhaps the clash between the "West and the Rest" is really between the increasingly secular wealthy "West" and the increasingly religious poor "Rest," not between Christian and Muslim civilizations. If so, any clash is not simply cultural—between secular and religious—but also economic, between haves and have-nots. Given the argument in this chapter, these global divisions might be avoided if poor countries can achieve growth with equity.

Issues of faith are by definition not resolved by recourse to logical reasoning, and the role of religion in politics around the world has obvious relevance in the post–9/11 world. American leaders have expressed their belief that democracy can take root in the Middle East. Suppose that the Arab–Israeli conflict were resolved, and that scientists discovered a miraculously cheap replacement for oil. Such developments are obviously unlikely, but the thought experiment is useful nonetheless: The arguments in this chapter suggest that if Arab Middle Eastern countries could develop relatively equitable societies, they could emulate other Islamic states such as Turkey, Indonesia, or Mali and begin the process of democratization. Is such a large-scale political transformation outside the realm of plausibility? And what would the world be like if it were? These questions demand further exploration. ▶

✔●—Study and Review the Post-Test & Chapter Exam at mypoliscilab.com

KEY TERMS

Protestant Reformation   177
religious pluralism   177
Second Vatican Council   180
Arab   182
Sharia   183
civil law code   184
partition   184

resource curse   187
secularization   191
value emphasis on personal survival   192
value emphasis on personal
   well-being   192
traditional values   192
secular–rational values   192

REVIEW QUESTIONS

1. Under what conditions can a strong religious identity *promote* democracy?
2. What arguments tend to support the association between Christianity and democracy, and what arguments tend to refute that association?
3. What arguments tend to support the association between Islam and democracy, and what arguments tend to refute that association?
4. On Figure 7.4, Americans' values on the vertical "secular/traditional" axis are closer to citizens of India or Iran than to citizens of Japan or other Western European countries. Why does the United States appear to confound the predictions of secularization theory?
5. What is the connection between economic modernization, secularization, and democratization?

SUGGESTED READINGS

Ghalioun, Burhan. "The Persistence of Arab Authoritarianism." *Journal of Democracy* 15, 4 (2004): 126–132. Also focuses on explaining non-democracy's prevalence in Arab countries, focusing on the geopolitical context and the consequences of economic modernization.

Jamal, Amaney, and Mark Tessler, "Attitudes in the Arab World." *Journal of Democracy* 19, 1 (2008): 97–110. Provides information about what citizens of Arab countries think about democracy and non-democracy.

Keddie, Nikki. "A Woman's Place: Democratization in the Middle East." *Current History* 103, 669 (2004): 25-30. Explores the ways in which women are pushing for democratic reforms in Islamic countries.

Traub, James. "Islamic Democrats?" *New York Times Magazine,* April 29, 2007, 44–49. Explores the evolving role of the Islamic Brotherhood, a formerly radical movement, as part of the legal opposition to Egypt's secular yet dictatorial regime.

Zakaria, Fareed. "Islam, Democracy, and Constitutional Liberalism." *Political Science Quarterly* 119, 1 (2004): 1-20. Explores various reasons for the connection between non-democracy and Islam in the Arab world.

NOTES

1. You can find the full text of Maliki's speech on the website Real Clear Politics, at http://www.realclearpolitics.com/articles/2006/07/iraq_will_be_a_graveyard_for_terrorists.html.
2. See Freedom House, "Table of Independent Countries," accessed May 6, 2011, http://www.freedomhouse.org/template.cfm?page=549&year=2010.
3. Figures cited in Robert D. Woodberry and Timothy S. Shah, "The Pioneering Protestants," *Journal of Democracy* 15(2)(2004): 47–61.
4. See Woodberry and Shah, "The Pioneering Protestants."
5. See also Daniel Philpott, "The Catholic Wave," *Journal of Democracy* 15(2)(2004): 32–46.
6. Huntington's *Clash of Civilizations* is frequently cited as one example of such an argument. See also Sanford Lakoff, "The Reality of Muslim Exceptionalism," *Journal of Democracy* 15(4)(2004): 133–139.
7. Such opinions can be found in the political press (for example, see Edward Said, "The Clash of Ignorance," *The Nation,* October 22, 2001), in research reports for the policy community (for example, see David Smock, "Islam and Democracy," published by the United States Institute for Peace in September 2002 and available online at http://www.usip.org), and in academic research (for example, see John Esposito and John Voll, *Islam and Democracy* (Oxford: Oxford University Press, 1996), or Vali Nasr, "The Rise of 'Muslim Democracy,'" *Journal of Democracy* 16(2)(2005): 13–27.
8. See for example, M. Steven Fish, "Islam and Authoritarianism," *World Politics* 55(1) (2002): 4–37.
9. See the sources cited in Fish, "Islam and Authoritarianism."
10. See Alfred Stepan and Graeme Robertson, "An 'Arab' More than 'Muslim' Electoral Gap." *Journal of Democracy* 14(3)(2003): 30–44.
11. See Stepan and Robertson, "An 'Arab' More than 'Muslim' Electoral Gap."
12. See for example, Michael L. Ross, "Does Oil Hinder Democracy?" *World Politics* 53 (2001): 325–361.
13. See for example, Terry Lynn Karl, *The Paradox of Plenty: Oil Booms and Petro-States* (Berkeley: University of California Press, 1997), or Michael Ross, "The Political Economy of the Resource Curse," *World Politics* 51(2)(1999): 297–322.
14. See for example, Stephen Haber and Victor Menaldo, "Do Natural Resources Fuel Authoritarianism?" Stanford Center for International Development, Working Paper 351.
15. See Pippa Norris and Ronald Inglehart, "God, Guns and Gays: The Supply and Demand for Religion in the U.S. and Western Europe," *Public Policy Research* 12(4)(2006): 224–233.
16. See Ronald Inglehart and Christian Welzel, *Modernization, Cultural Change and Democracy* (New York : Cambridge University Press, 2005).
17. Christian Welzel and Ronald Inglehart, "Emancipative Values and Democracy: Response to Hadenius and Teorell," *Studies in Comparative International Development* 41(3)(2006): 74–94.
18. See for example, Todd Johnson and Sun Young Chung, "Tracking Global Christianity's Statistical Centre of Gravity, AD 33–AD 2100," *International Review of Mission* 93(369)(2004): 166–181.

Gender and Politics

With a mosque in the background, a few hundred Afghan women protest against a law legalizing rape in marriage.
About three times as many men organized a vocal counter-protest nearby, threatening the women with violence.

? How do attitudes about gender influence politics?

Read and Listen to **Chapter 8** at **mypoliscilab.com**

Study and Review the **Pre-Test & Flashcards** at **mypoliscilab.com**

In 2009, the parliament of Afghanistan made it legal for a husband to withhold food from his wife if she refused his sexual demands.[1] The law also required a wife to get her husband's permission to work outside the home and granted guardianship of children in cases of divorce exclusively to fathers or grandfathers. Political leaders in the United States and other countries that had sent troops to fight the Taliban—which had enacted similar laws before being overthrown in 2001—objected strenuously to this effort to legally subjugate women. Yet, despite international condemnation—and even though it contradicted Afghanistan's own constitution—parliament approved the new law. This fact speaks volumes about both the way many Afghan men think about women and family relations and about the inability of Afghan women to determine their own fates. Indeed, when several hundred women tried to protest the new law, as the chapter opening photo illustrates, a much larger crowd of angry, stone-throwing men confronted them and called them whores.

Until recent decades, political scientists paid little attention to the political implications of episodes like the one above, dismissing issues of family law and relationships between men and women as purely private matters bound by centuries-old traditions. When political science emerged as an academic discipline in the late 1800s, relatively few women participated in politics, and fewer still conducted political research. When men proclaimed new discoveries about *human* political behavior, they were really only writing about *male* political behavior—and not just because most government officials were male, but also because they considered women and women's interests and opinions irrelevant, or inconsequential.

Yet, just as more women have entered politics around the world, more women have also become political scientists—earning about 40 percent of all doctorates awarded each year by the 2000s. New generations of scholars (male and female) have demonstrated the myriad ways public policy shapes what many consider to be private practices, and in doing so they have raised a host of important questions about gender and politics. For example, many have sought to explain the extensive cross-national variation in women's legal rights in cases of divorce, job discrimination, property inheritance, or rape. Others scholars examine why some governments pass reform laws in support of maternity leave, child care, availability of birth control, or abortion, while others do not. Still other scholars explore the persistence and change in informal cultural practices such as honor killings of women suspected of adultery, selective abortion favoring male babies, and female genital cutting.[2]

These issues may affect more women personally and directly than men, but research on gender is not the same as research on "women's issues." Contemporary research has incorporated issues of gender into key questions of comparative politics such as the likelihood of war and peace, the emergence and survival of democracy, and the prospect of social protest or civil conflict. Issues of gender also impact us all at a personal level, because each of us has an interest in laws that govern what we can or cannot do with our own bodies. Because most policymakers around the world are men, it is worth asking both why men sometimes work with women to change these policies and practices, relinquishing centuries of political, economic, and/or social advantage, and also whether increasing the number of women in politics will bring about more change.

In this chapter, we focus on one particular question: *how do attitudes about gender influence politics?* As with religion, we first define what we mean by the term "gender" in terms of primordial and constructivist identities. We then consider the impact of economic modernization on political values about gender equality around the world, in particular how socioeconomic change has reconstructed women's political interests in the wealthy, established democracies. We then turn to consider the impact of women's increased presence in legislatures on change in public policy. And lastly, we connect institutions of the state to change in gender-related policies.

DEFINING "GENDER"

In recent decades, scholars have developed a concept of gender that distinguishes the social and cultural characteristics associated with femininity and masculinity from the biological features we associate with sex differences, such as male and female reproductive organs, chromosomes, and hormones. When we talk about gender as a category, we ponder questions such as, "What does it mean to 'be a man' or 'act like a woman' in different societies?"

Answers to questions like these are not obvious, because the meanings of masculinity and femininity have changed with time and continue to differ both within as well as across societies. Consider the fact that military commanders accept that the meaning of gender is socially constructed. They know that human evolution has not resulted in anything resembling a perfect fighting machine, even among the most aggressive and physically powerful males. Boot camp is jarring and intense because it is designed to overcome and counteract primordial human instincts to flee imminent physical harm. To develop an effective fighting force, military leaders accept the constructivist hypothesis that "warriors are made, not born," through a process of socialization that trains individuals to withstand the stresses of battle. In the distant past, such socialization frequently involved getting men powerfully drunk or symbolically transforming them into animals to give them courage. Today, to "construct" warriors out of average, everyday men and women, military training tears down soldiers' individuality and uses incentives such as pride, glory, camaraderie, and hope for promotion, as well as disincentives such as humiliation, demotion, and dishonorable discharge.

Some may argue that political identities as masculine or feminine are primordially rooted in biological differences between men and women, but this argument is fraught with difficulties. To illustrate just one problem with this view, assume for a moment that all women have a maternal instinct that psychologically predisposes them to be more caring and giving than men. If this were true, would women be politically more liberal or more conservative than men? On the one hand, being caring and giving implies that women should be more liberal than men—they should favor increased spending on welfare policies, especially if funds

8.1 What is "gender"?

gender ■ a concept used to distinguish the social and cultural characteristics associated with femininity and masculinity from the biological features associated with sex, such as male or female reproductive organs.

✴ Explore the **Comparative "Identity"** at **mypoliscilab.com** are directed toward children or education. On the other hand, being caring and giving also implies that women should be more conservative than men, because they have greater concern for family rather than career and should defend "traditional family values." Genetic primordialism implies that biology is destiny—yet it is not obvious that political interests and identities are a function of whether or not you have a Y chromosome.

There are two ways to build on a constructivist understanding of gender. First, we can think of gender much as Max Weber categorized status groups—as two socially constructed "categories" of political identity that define people as typically "masculine" or "feminine," based on different societies' predominant values, norms, and practices. Second, we can think of gender as a "process"—as the ways that men and women engage in politics to either preserve or change gender relations, and the impact that the political context has on their efforts.

Gender as a Category

gender as a category ■ a form of socially constructed political identity that considers variation in the social meaning of masculinity and femininity around the world.

The idea of gender as a category recognizes that both women and men possess gender identities—as masculine or feminine, or somewhere in between. Research on gender categories seeks to understand how people in different societies define socially acceptable versus transgressive male and female behavior, and how variations on the spectrum of femininity and masculinity translate into matters of political significance. For example, 50 years ago, women who went to college with the goal of finding a career rather than a husband—and who upon graduation moved into an apartment on their own—were regarded as having "low morals" and were socially suspect. Today, public opinion about what constitutes a normal life course for young women differs dramatically. The category of "female" and all that it stands for has changed in marked ways in recent decades. The same can be said for the gender category of "male," although masculine identity has not changed as dramatically as has feminine. Thinking about gender this way helps us categorize continuity and change in the cultural traits commonly associated with male and female biological characteristics.

Gender as a Process

gender as a political process ■ individual involvement in political institutions to either preserve or change gender relations, or ways that existing social context and political institutions shape one's relative ability to preserve and/or change gender relations.

We can also think of gender as a political process, not just a political category. In order to understand gender as a process, we turn our attention away from *what* has changed or stayed the same about concepts of gender to the question of *why* and *how* they have changed. Why do people engage in politics, and how does women's involvement change the political environment? There are two ways to understand gender as a political process. Let us focus on the ways that people—especially women—either preserve or change ideas about gender and gender relations. For example, activists—whether liberal or conservative—can join social movements, lobby the government, or engage in party politics to alter conventional understandings of gender as a category, or to directly shape public policy. Indeed, by entering politics and engaging in what traditionally has been a "man's game," women have changed the meaning of acceptable "feminine" behavior.

This way of thinking about gender as a process focuses on the ways people engage in politics to shape and reshape gender relations.[3]

Thinking about gender as a process also requires that we consider how entrenched interests and existing public policies shape different degrees of male domination and female subordination. Legal systems often keep women in subordinate positions; political institutions sometimes exclude women's issues from the agenda; and powerful interest groups —especially those organized around religious principles—may seek to shape what people think are legitimate relations between genders.

For example, marriage and divorce laws around the world have historically entrenched men's political domination. This is not merely the case in Afghanistan. For example, Chile only legalized divorce in 2004 and still requires a three-year waiting period if one party objects. In many countries, until recently, marriage laws explicitly named the man as the head of the household and often prohibited women from working outside the home, testifying in court, or enrolling children in school without the husband's permission. Laws regarding adultery, divorce, and child custody have traditionally reinforced men's freedom and women's submission.[4] Without a separate income or the means for self-sufficiency, women's ability to mobilize on their own behalf is severely curtailed. Political institutions and social practices can directly shape men's and women's relative political, social and economic rights and opportunities.

Thinking about gender pushes us to separate socially acceptable "meanings" of masculinity and femininity from men's and women's biological features. The table below summarizes these two ways political scientists explore the concept of gender. Some scholars draw attention to the political implications of the ways people think about femininity and masculinity around the world. Others seek to illuminate how people mobilize to change those understandings—and how state institutions and political actors shape and constrain the possibilities for change. In the next two

SUMMARY TABLE

Understanding Gender

Gender as a Category	The images people in different societies have of what is considered to be socially-acceptable versus transgressive "male" and "female" behavior.	Example: in contrast to 50 years ago, in wealthy democracies, most people now accept that women will gain as much education as men, work outside the home, and become engaged in politics.
Gender as a Process	How people engage in politics to challenge existing conceptions of gender roles; and how political institutions and public policies shape different degrees of male domination and female subordination.	Examples: (1) more women run for office, challenging the notion that only men are "fit" to govern; (2) around the world, marriage and divorce laws have historically advantaged men over women.

sections, we consider variation in attitudes about gender around the world, and then turn our attention to how women are working to reshape gender relations and how the political context impacts those efforts.

ATTITUDES ABOUT GENDER AROUND THE WORLD

8.2 How does socioeconomic modernization change attitudes about gender relations?

In the previous section, we touched upon gender as a category and as a process. In the next two sections, we explore the ways gender as a category differs around the world. To the extent that gender relations are constructed rather than primordial, we should be able to connect variation in the social context to differences in the ways people think about socially acceptable male and female roles. Specifically, in this section we connect patterns of socioeconomic modernization to cross-national differences in attitudes about gender: In wealthier societies, both men and women tend to have more liberal attitudes about gender roles. These attitudes, in turn, may indicate variation in mass support for democracy.

Modernization and Attitudes about Gender

The process of modernization—industrialization, economic growth, and the spread of educational opportunities and mass communication technology to more segments of the population—can bring about change in citizens' political and cultural values. This process can help explain variation across countries in attitudes about gender-related questions. Figure 8.1 highlights a few of these differences. When comparing responses to the World Values Surveys, countries where citizens hold "traditional" values fall towards the bottom-left, while countries where citizens hold "modern" values fall towards the upper-right.

In relatively poorer societies, citizens retain values that discourage women from entering the workforce, encourage them to focus on childbearing and childrearing, and frown on divorce, abortion, homosexuality, and principles of gender equality. In contrast, people in wealthier societies express stronger support for abortion and divorce, are less likely to oppose homosexuality, are more likely to support women's equality, and reject the notion that women "need to have children" to be personally fulfilled. To put a point on it, both men and women in wealthier societies tend to have more liberal attitudes about gender roles and sexuality.

These are general tendencies—many people in wealthy societies remain quite conservative, and many people in poorer societies have liberal attitudes on these issues. Still, the pattern is clear: in countries where average public opinion falls in the upper-right quadrant of Figure 8.1, both women's and men's lives differ radically from just a few decades ago, due to greater educational opportunities for women and the incorporation of greater numbers of women into the labor force, which work to change attitudes about family dynamics and sexual mores. Such aspects of modernization transform individuals' political values and cultural beliefs, giving greater weight to freedom, self-expression, and gender equality. In contrast, traditional views of women and gender roles prevail in poorer societies.

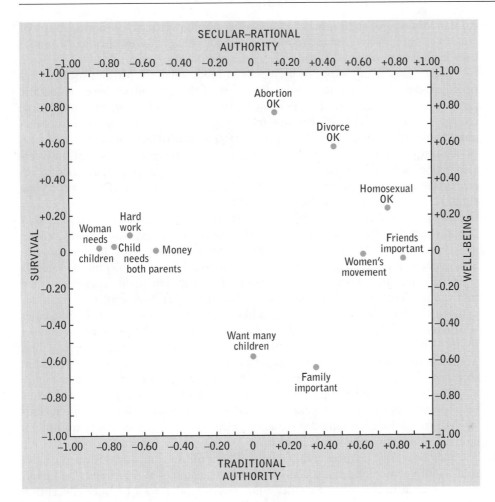

FIGURE 8.1

Gender-related World Values Surveys Questions

Responses to World Values Surveys questions on gender-related issues. Note the relative placement of the answers given the "survival vs. well-being" and "traditional vs secular–rational authority" axes of the figure.

Source: Ronald Inglehart, *Modernization and Postmodernization* (Princeton, NJ: Princeton University Press, 1997).

Attitudes about Gender, Attitudes about Democracy

Differences in attitudes about gender equality may impact whether citizens tend to support democracy or not. Let us focus for a moment on a subset of countries that fall in the lower-left quadrant of Figure 8.1, where the social context has traditionally kept women subordinate: the majority-Muslim countries. Although Freedom House classified about 45 percent of the world's countries as "Free" in 2011, only about 5 percent of majorty-Muslim countries were similarly rated. Given this, you might be surprised to learn that citizens of Western democracies and non-democratic Islamic societies actually agree on many of the key principles of democracy. For example, similar proportions of citizens in both groups of countries agree with statements on the World Values Survey such as "Democracy has many problems, but it is the best form of government."[5]

The finding is paradoxical: if citizens in predominantly Muslim societies express pro-democratic attitudes, why do so few of these countries have democratic governments—particularly given recent widespread popular demands for regime change in the Middle East? Perhaps the explanation has to do with factors discussed in earlier chapters such as geopolitics, a lack of economic development, or the resource curse. However, we also considered the possibility that only certain "civic" attitudes support democratic institutions. Specifically, democracy requires that citizens steadfastly uphold the value of political equality—that everyone should have equal rights and be held equal before the law.

Table 8.1 indicates that although most people in Islamic countries *say* that they support democracy, a greater proportion of citizens in established democracies include gender equality as essential to the definition of democracy. In contrast, citizens of predominantly Muslim societies remain on average less tolerant of women's rights, divorce, and abortion. Overall, support for gender equality is closely linked to a country's actual level of democracy. Of course, men and women in wealthier democracies have not always held such liberal attitudes about women and gender relations—attitudes have changed rapidly only in the last half-century or so as a result of both socioeconomic modernization and women's struggles for equality. Yet, such attitudes have not yet changed as dramatically in predominantly Muslim societies, along with other countries that fall in the lower-left quadrant of Figure 8.1. These findings suggest that although no "clash of civilizations" exists in terms of popular support for democracy, attitudes about gender equality and sexuality do differ in longstanding democracies, compared to societies where traditional cultural values continue to predominate.

Socioeconomic change tends to undermine traditional attitudes toward gender roles, family structures, and socially acceptable meanings of masculinity and femininity. And attitudes toward gender equality are related to a broader conception of political equality—a principle essential to the definition of democracy. People

TABLE 8.1

A "Sexual" Clash of Civilizations?

Approval of Political and Social Values in Western and Islamic Societies

	Western Societies	Islamic Societies
Democratic performance	68%	68%
Democratic ideals	86%	87%
Gender equality	82%	55%
Divorce	60%	35%
Abortion	48%	25%

Source: Ronald Inglehart and Pippa Norris, "The Real Clash of Civilizations," *Foreign Policy* (March/April 2003): 67–74.

SUMMARY TABLE

The Impact of Modernization on Attitudes about Gender and Democracy

Socioeconomic Modernization	Expected Change in Attitudes about Gender	Resulting Support for Principle of Equality for All
Limited	Limited	Limited
Extensive	Extensive	Widespread

in majority-Muslim societies overwhelmingly express support for democracy, but, just as in other countries that fall in the lower-left quadrant of Figure 8.2, it remains an open question as to whether their more traditional attitudes about gender support democracy or not. In the next section, we turn our attention to the impact of socioeconomic change on attitudes in the wealthy democracies.

GENDER GAPS IN ESTABLISHED DEMOCRACIES

In the previous section, we related patterns of socioeconomic development to variation in attitudes around the world about gender equality. Men and women in relatively wealthier societies tend to be more liberal on such questions, suggesting that—when combined with direct mobilization by activists—modernization tends to "reconstruct" gender relations. In this section, we explore a related phenomenon, the fact that although both men and women become more liberal on matters related to gender as a function of socioeconomic change, women grow even more liberal than men. Specifically, the World Values Surveys reveal a rising gap between men and women's political preferences in many of the world's wealthiest democracies. This implies that the process of modernization has a stronger impact on women's perceptions of their political interests.

8.3 Why do women's attitudes change more than men's as a result of socioeconomic change?

The "Traditional" versus the "Modern" Gender Gap

Fifty years ago, a traditional gender gap in political attitudes existed, in which women were more likely to vote for conservative political parties than were men. Table 8.2 illustrates the strength of this difference as of the early 1970s. Even after the social transformations and political turmoil of the 1960s, women remained more likely to vote for conservative parties in most wealthy established democracies. The United States is an exception—but only because the traditional gender gap had vanished by that time.

If liberal attitudes spread with socioeconomic change, why did women in wealthy democracies remain more conservative than men up through the 1970s? Explanations for women's traditional conservatism emphasize their religiosity and different labor force participation. Up through the 1970s, women were more likely to be religiously observant and to stay home and raise children rather than to work outside the home. Women's political attitudes tended to follow their social roles, which focused

traditional gender gap ■ a situation in a country in which women are more likely to be conservative and vote for conservative political parties than are men.

> ▶ **TABLE 8.2**
>
> ### The "Traditional" Gender Gap
>
> **Percent of Voters Supporting Parties of the Left, 1970s**
>
> | Country | Men | Women | Gap |
> |---|---|---|---|
> | Italy | 44 | 30 | -14 |
> | Germany | 60 | 47 | -13 |
> | United Kingdom | 50 | 41 | -9 |
> | Belgium | 40 | 36 | -6 |
> | France | 54 | 49 | -5 |
> | Netherlands | 47 | 45 | -2 |
> | United States | 32 | 37 | +5 |
>
> Source: Ronald Inglehart, *The Silent Revolution* (Princeton, NJ: Princeton University Press, 1977), 228.

on church and family. In contrast, men worked outside the home, which frequently exposed them to union politics and other left-leaning political options, and they also tended to be less religiously observant.

In recent decades, women's traditional conservatism has vanished in most of the world's wealthy democracies. In its place, a **modern gender gap** in political attitudes has emerged, in which women are now likely to be more liberal than are men—a reversal of the trends revealed in Table 8.2. In contrast, the traditional gender gap persists in less-developed countries, where women tend to remain more conservative than do men. The correlation between country wealth and the emergence of a modern gender gap is far from perfect, but a pattern is evident.[6]

modern gender gap ■ a situation in a country in which women are more likely to be more liberal and vote for more liberal parties than are men.

Shaping the Modern Gender Gap

What caused women's attitudes in wealthier democracies to become more politically liberal than men? Given the correlation between country wealth and the modern gender gap, consider the impact of modernization—in particular, women's increased labor force participation and access to education. To illustrate, consider the following questions: did both your grandmothers graduate from college? Did your mother? It is far more likely that your mother graduated from college than did both of your grandmothers. And even if both grandmothers graduated from college, did they work full-time after college, while also raising children? Did your mother? Again, it is also far more likely that your mother attended college and then worked full-time than did your grandmothers, and it is even more likely today that young women will attend college and then work full-time. The same is true in other wealthy democracies, to greater or lesser degrees.

Socioeconomic change has dramatically transformed gender categories—the socially acceptable roles for men and women. Such changes have altered the "private sphere" of family roles as well as the "public sphere" of women's participation in politics. For example, going to college and entering the

---

SUMMARY TABLE

The Traditional versus the Modern Gender Gap

Traditional Gender Gap: women are more politically conservative than men.	**Reason:** women are more likely to have less education, to work at home, and to be more religious.
Modern Gender Gap: women are more politically liberal than men.	**Reason:** economic change opens job and educational opportunities for women, which changes their attitudes—more than men's—toward an array of public policies.

---

workforce altered many women's perspectives about an array of public policies, relative to what their mothers or grandmothers may have thought. As a result, in recent decades, many women have organized and engaged in lobbying efforts to change public policies about job and pay discrimination, parental leave, healthcare, childcare, and primary education.

An increase in women's education and work opportunities has changed men's and women's perspectives on proper gender roles. What most people in wealthy democracies consider acceptable gender roles today differs dramatically from what they accepted as normal 50 years ago. In contrast, as in Afghanistan, where economic change has advanced relatively little, what counts as a socially acceptable role for a woman has changed much less. Even though many women lobby for political change in places like Afghanistan, their efforts encounter resistance not only among men, but also among women who retain more traditional conceptions of gender roles.

The argument builds on what we've learned in previous chapters: *economic change can generate social and political change.* Modernization has transformed men's and women's actual gender roles, and it has reshaped their attitudes about gender and gender-related policies—yet it has changed women's attitudes more than men's. Over just two generations, women in wealthy democracies have gone from being more conservative to being more liberal than men, especially on issues related to gender and the family. Changes in the socioeconomic context can powerfully reshape people's attitudes—but as we will see in the next two sections, women's engagement in politics as well as political institutions also shape and constrain the possibilities for change in gender relations.

WOMEN SHAPING GENDER RELATIONS

In the previous two sections, we explored "gender as a category," focusing on how variation in socioeconomic context constructs gender as a salient form of political identity in different ways around the world. Yet, gender may be thought of not just as a "category" but also as "process." In this section, we focus on the impact of women's increasing presence in legislatures around the world.

The previous section suggested that the cultural and socioeconomic context shapes men and women's attitudes about gender-related practices and policies.

8.4 How has women's growing participation in politics changed gender-related policies?

Logically, to the extent that men and women have different political attitudes, then variation in the number of women engaged in politics should impact cross-national variation in gender-related policies. After all, if women are more liberal than men but have no political rights, then policy will remain a function of men's interests alone. And in a country in which women were more liberal than men and their interests totally dominated politics, men's interests would be irrelevant. This contrast suggests that to explain cross-national variation in gender-related policies, we need to know three things: (1) the degree to which both men and women's attitudes are "traditional" or "modern"; (2) the level of the "political gender gap"; and (3) the extent to which women are involved in politics.

Scholars have recently begun exploring the degree to which the number of women in politics influences policy outcomes. Table 8.3 provides information on the percentage of female legislators in several countries around the world. Many of the countries with the highest proportion have passed what are called gender quota laws, which set aside a certain proportion of candidacies or legislative seats for women.[7] For example, Rwanda passed a quota law after civil war and genocide in the early 1990s, because women represented almost 70 percent of the remaining population and women's groups were among the most important surviving civil-society organizations. Their influence and importance to Rwandan society at that time helped advance gender-equity changes to Rwanda's new constitution, including the quota law.[8]

gender quota laws ■ rules that require that a certain proportion of candidates for office or legislative seats be reserved for women.

> **TABLE 8.3**

Percent of Women Legislators, Selected Countries (2011)

Rank	Country	Percent of Women	Rank	Country	Percent of Women
1	Rwanda	56%	67	Turkmenistan	17%
2	Sweden	47%	68	United States	17%
3	South Africa	45%	70	Azerbaijan	16%
4	Cuba	43%	71	North Korea	16%
5	Iceland	43%	80	Zambia	15%
6	Finland	40%	85	Sierra Leone	13%
7	Norway	40%	92	Japan	11%
8	Belgium	39%	96	Mali	10%
9	Netherlands	39%	101	Turkey	9%
10	Mozambique	39%	104	Hungary	9%
29	Afghanistan	28%	108	Brazil	9%
32	Mexico	26%	126	Bahrain	3%
37	Iraq	25%	131	Oman	0%
56	Israel	19%	134	Saudi Arabia	0%

Source: Inter-Parliamentary Union, "Women in National Parliaments," accessed July 19, 2011, http://www.ipu.org/wmn-e/classif.htm.

Rwandan President Paul Kagame (center) attends a conference in May 2010 on the role of women in his country's parliament—the only national legislature in the world where women outnumber men.

Many factors affect whether a country's policies favor gender equality or not, including relative wealth, religious history, and the quality of democracy. Nevertheless, the number of women in elected positions is particularly influential, for several reasons. First, given the modern gender gap in wealthy societies, female legislators tend to be more liberal than their male counterparts. This turns out to be the case even *within* political parties, meaning not only that liberal or left-wing parties tend to elect more women legislators than do conservative or right-wing parties, but that women in both liberal and conservative parties tend to be more liberal than the average male member of that party.[9]

Second, women legislators tend to have different policy priorities from men. In particular, they are more likely to see themselves specifically as representatives of women and women's interests, while men are unlikely to see themselves as representatives of only men.[10] Women around the world also tend to focus more on issues related to women's rights, children, and family-law policy, and express less interest in budget, tax, and business issues.[11]

Finally, the presence of greater numbers of women in political leadership positions tends to change the perceptions of women and discourse about women. A lack of women in positions of power tends to perpetuate gender stereotypes—for example, that men are calm, calculating, and rational, while women are emotional, weak, and incapable of leadership. As more women assume positions of power, fewer politicians and voters assume that politics is a man's game, and both voters and male politicians' assumptions about how to speak about and to women begins to change.

Gender Quota Laws are the Only Way to Dramatically Increase the Number of Female Legislators: Comparing Costa

HYPOTHESIS TESTING | Rica and South Africa

South Africa and Costa Rica have distinct cultural histories. Costa Rica gained independence from Spain in the early 1800s, while South Africa gained independence from the UK in 1948. Costa Rica has been a democracy since that year, while in South Africa, the African National Congress (ANC) movement engaged in violent struggle to end a white supremacist non-democratic regime that ruled from 1948 to 1994. Neither South Africa nor Costa Rica is among the most developed countries in the world—per capita income in both countries is about $10,000 per year. Yet despite their status as middle-income countries with traditionally conservative cultures—in which one would not expect the most progressive gender relations—the proportion of women in the parliaments of Costa Rica and South Africa are among the highest in the world's democracies—39 percent and 45 percent, respectively. Do gender quotas explain these comparatively high figures?

GATHER EVIDENCE

The Inter-Parliamentary Union, a Swiss organization founded in 1889 to foster understanding of how legislatures around the world operate, has counted the proportion of women in every legislature in the world every year since 1945. That year, only about 3 percent of all legislators worldwide were women. This figure reached 11 percent by 1975, but did not increase again through 1995.[12] Given the slow increase in the number of women in politics, many scholars and policymakers called for a more effective method to reach gender balance in political institutions. As noted, the solution many countries have adopted is a gender quota—national legislation requiring that a certain proportion of legislators be women. Today, about 19 percent of all legislators worldwide are women—an increase of about 50 percent in fewer than 20 years.[13] Gender quota laws were uncommon prior to 1980, but by 2010, about

50 countries adopted some sort of gender quota.[14] Can countries substantially and rapidly increase the number of women in politics without a gender quota law?

ASSESS THE HYPOTHESIS

To explore this question, let's consider two countries with similar proportions of female legislators: Costa Rica and South Africa. In the former, women mobilized to enact a quota law starting in the late 1980s, as part of a broader effort to pass equal rights legislation. The legislature adopted a gender quota law in 1996, which required that women comprise 40 percent of all candidates for office. The law originally did not require parties to ensure that women would win 40 percent of the *seats*, however—only that they filled 40 percent of the slots on the ballots. This meant that parties often put women in races they could not win.

Women activists argued that this result violated the spirit of the law, and eventually Costa Rica's Supreme Court agreed, requiring that women be placed in 40 percent of the "electable" positions—based on the number of seats the party had won at the last election. As of 2011, women must comprise 50 percent of all electable positions. As a consequence of these reforms, the proportion of women in Costa Rica's parliament increased from 14 percent in 1994 to 39 percent in 2006. The efforts of women activists clearly paid off in Costa Rica, as the quota law now mandates full gender equality. Costa Rica's current president is also a woman.

The story in South Africa is different. Before democratization in 1994, just 3 percent of South Africa's legislators were women—yet just 15 years later, almost half were. However, South Africa reveals that quota laws are not the only way to increase the number of women in politics, as it has no such legal requirement on the books. Instead, the dominant political party, the ANC, has adopted a *voluntary* and internal quota—as if the Democratic

(Continued)

Party in the United States were to decide that 50 percent of all its elected officials had to be women. During the ANC's struggle for equal rights for citizens of all races, its Women's League actively lobbied ANC leader and future South African president Nelson Mandela to increase women's presence within the party.[15]

South Africa's President Jacob Zuma (right front) receives congratulations after being sworn into office in 2009. Zuma is surrounded by legislators from his party, the African National Congress—almost half of whom are women.

The ANC Women's League faced fierce resistance from many male politicians, but it eventually succeeded in pushing the party to adopt a rule requiring that one-third of all its candidates for office be women. This internal regulation was first implemented in 1994, causing an immediate increase in the proportion of women in parliament, from 3 percent to 27 percent. In 2009, the ANC adopted a voluntary gender parity rule, meaning women would have to comprise half of all its candidates. This resulted in 49 percent of ANC elected representatives being women. Since the ANC dominates South Africa's parliament, the overall proportion of female legislators climbed to 45 percent. South Africa clearly shows that a quota law is not the only way to enhance the proportion of women in legislatures. Women can be brought into legislatures either through a quota law or through voluntary quotas that political parties adopt. ◤

CRITICAL THINKING QUESTIONS

1. Why is a quota law not necessary to generate a higher overall proportion of female legislators?
2. What else do you think help explains why more women are getting involved in politics around the world?

If female legislators tend to be more liberal on average and have somewhat different political values and interests than are their male colleagues, and if a relatively greater presence of women in the halls of power tends to demolish stereotypes about feminine weakness, does the number of female legislators influence the likely success of issues that women prioritize? Table 8.3 showed that women rarely comprise a legislative majority. Although scholars cannot identify a "magic number" of female legislators that guarantees change in gender-related policies, scholarship has confirmed that electing more women increases the likelihood that the legislature will pass more policies that women want.[16] The table on the following page summarizes the reasons why democracies with higher proportions of female legislators tend to pass more laws that benefit women, children, and families.

In terms of our chapter question, *how do attitudes about gender influence politics,* this section explored the first way of thinking about gender as a "process"—how female legislators act differently from their male counterparts. Attitudes about gender matter because women often bring different issues to the table when they engage in politics. In particular, they draw greater attention to how public policies and political institutions discriminate against women and

Then-Speaker of the House Nancy Pelosi (D-CA) discusses the healthcare reform bill, in March 2010. Pelosi was the first woman to lead a major US political party, and the first woman to hold the office of Speaker.

women's interests. As a result, as more and more women win elective office, policies begin to change. Of course, legislative activism is not the only way that women can mobilize to change gender relations or reshape established cultural understandings of gender. However, it is an important and obvious manifestation of this first way of thinking about gender as a process. Let us now explore the limits of explanations based on political attitudes, and consider how entrenched (male) political interests can shape and constrain gender relations—regardless of attitudes.

SUMMARY TABLE

How Having More Women in Office Shapes Gender-Related Policies

1. Female legislators tend to be more liberal than are men.

2. Women have different policy priorities than do men.

3. Having women in office changes stereotypical perceptions of women and the way men talk about women.

4. Democracies with more female legislators pass more laws benefiting women, children, and families.

POLITICS SHAPES GENDER ROLES

In this section, we consider the second way of thinking about gender as a process—the way the political context favors or harms gender equality, regardless of women's attitudes or level of participation. Consider the implications of modernization theory: to the extent that socioeconomic change reshapes citizens' attitudes, policy change should follow as more women enter the workforce, take advantage of educational opportunities, marry later, and have fewer children. Such societal transformations should generate political pressure—primarily but not exclusively from women—for policy change in areas related to family life, gender equality, and sexual relations.

8.5 What other factors shape gender-related policies?

In addition, if modernization changes political attitudes, then countries at similar levels of development should have similar policies, while countries at different levels of development should have different policies. Yet, in the real world, countries with similar levels of development often have very different policies. This is because cross-national variation in attitudes does not always predict cross-national variation in policy. In many cases, the key factors shaping public policy—about gender or anything else—are politicians' interests in obtaining or maintaining power, and their need to form alliances with powerful interest groups or political parties to accomplish that goal. This way of exploring gender as a process considers how the interests of the (usually male) politicians who dominate politics influence the formal institutions and informal practices that shape gender relations.

While the first way of thinking about gender as a process suggested that individuals can shape and reshape gender relations, this second approach focuses on how a country's political system shapes the degree of gender inequality, regardless of what women want. Even in a democracy—where women can vote and freely express their opinions—public opinion never perfectly translates into policy, because powerful interest groups may overwhelm the influence of citizens' attitudes. As a result, some societal interests may dominate while others may go unrepresented in the policy process, because some can invest more resources to get their way. In terms of gender-related policies, this suggests that in democracies, powerful political interests can stymie women's efforts to bring about change.

The gap between citizens' attitudes and public policy might be even larger in non-democratic regimes, where rulers can sometimes ignore public opinion entirely. And just as in many democracies, men tend to dominate politics in non-democratic systems. If men dominate politics and no one holds the government accountable, women's interests could go completely unrepresented. In sum, in both democratic and non-democratic systems the politics of gender may have little to do with attitudes or women's engagement in politics. To better understand this notion of "gender as a process," in what follows we explore two examples of countries that vary little in terms of gender-related attitudes but a great deal in terms of gender-related policies.

Similar Societies, Different Outcomes: Tunisia, Morocco, and Algeria

Our first example illustrates the potential disconnect between political attitudes, the number of women in politics, and gender-related policies by examining variations in family law in three similar North African countries: Tunisia, Morocco, and Algeria.[17] The differences in family laws in these three countries highlight the importance—particularly in non-democratic societies—of paying attention to the interests of those who hold power and their political allies.

Tunisia, Morocco, and Algeria share many characteristics: they are geographic neighbors on the Mediterranean coast in an area of North Africa known as Maghreb; they are all former French colonies; and they gained independence around the same time. Moreover, they share a religious and cultural history in which Islamic law has traditionally afforded greater legal rights to men than to women. Finally, none has any experience with democracy. (However, the situation may soon change in Tunisia and Morocco.) Despite these similarities, in recent decades, each country took a different path in terms of enacting a family law code—a set of laws governing marriage, divorce, inheritance of property, responsibility for children, and other related legal matters.

family law code ■ a set of laws governing marriage, divorce, inheritance of family property, responsibility for children, and other related matters.

Almost immediately after winning independence from France in 1956, Tunisia's new government sharply broke with existing traditional Islamic law. A new family law code prohibited polygamy, abolished a husband's unilateral right to divorce his wife at will without a court proceeding, permitted women as well as men to file for divorce, increased mothers' child-custody rights in cases of divorce, and expanded women's inheritance rights. In short, Tunisia rapidly and radically liberalized women's formal legal rights, simultaneously weakening husbands' and male tribal leaders' longstanding informal cultural authority.

Morocco passed a family law code that same year. Yet, in contrast to Tunisia, Morocco's system reinforced conservative Islamic law and reaffirmed traditional male domination and female subordination. Finally, Algeria, which gained independence from France in 1962, failed to pass any major laws pertaining to the family for 22 years, until its government finally adopted a conservative legal code in 1984 that also reaffirmed support for traditional Islamic law and traditional gender roles.

These three cases provide substantial variation in family law outcomes: an immediate liberalization in Tunisia, an immediate conservative retrenchment in Morocco, and a two-decade delay before a conservative outcome in Algeria. Neither variation in cultural attitudes nor variation in the number of women in politics can explain these divergent outcomes. Instead, two factors related to the way that ruling elites sought to hold onto political power are crucial: (1) the relative cohesiveness of the ruling elite that took power in each country upon independence; and (2) the degree to which this elite depended on traditional tribal kinship groups to retain power. Table 8.4 illustrates the way that these two factors relate to each other.

In Morocco, the postcolonial political elite was cohesive and closely allied with the traditional tribes, whose leaders were all men. Most tribal leaders wanted to maintain the existing system, in which they dominated local politics. Following independence, Morocco's rulers thus immediately enacted a family-law code that pleased their conservative supporters.

In contrast, post-independence Tunisian political elites were cohesive, but in contrast to Morocco's leaders, they did not depend on the country's conservative tribes. In fact, Tunisia's post-colonial leaders sought to undermine tribal leaders' power, because they believed the traditional kinship groups threatened their own power. Tunisia's new rulers, therefore, enacted a radical reform of family law that

TABLE 8.4		
Explaining Policy Variation in Three Maghreb countries		
	Relative Cohesiveness of Ruling Elite	
Dependence on Traditional Kin Groups	High	Low
High	Morocco (*No Reform*)	Algeria (*Delayed Reform*)
Low	Tunisia (*Radical Reform*)	

expanded women's rights, in order to weaken tribal leaders and reorient citizens' political loyalties away from kin groups and toward the nation-state.

Finally, in Algeria, a political split within the ruling elite at the time of independence explains the long delay. Violent battles between reformists and conservatives continued long after independence, but eventually the conservatives gained a decisive victory. Like Morocco's rulers, Algeria's conservative leaders relied on religious traditionalists for support. Consequently, only after consolidating their hold on power in the early 1980s could Algeria's leaders enact a family law code to their liking.

Although the World Values Survey did not exist when these three countries gained independence, all indications are that in the late 1950s or early 1960s, most people—men as well as women—in these three countries held similarly conservative values about gender equality. Yet, the variation in outcomes illustrates the difficulty of connecting cultural values to public policies, especially in non-democratic societies. The degree of cohesiveness of the post-independence ruling authorities and their dependence on powerful political actors—the traditional tribal leaders— shaped variation in family law policies, even though cultural values were similar. The logic of this conclusion echoes the ideas discussed in earlier chapters about the formation of nationalist and ethnic identities: just as in those stories, in North Africa, the strategies and relative success of the ruling elite in consolidating power proved critical to explaining different policy outcomes.

Similar Societies, Different Outcomes: Wealthy Democracies

Let us now consider a second example of how politics shapes relations between men and women independently of attitudes: variation in the nature and extent of government policies that affect families in wealthy Western European democracies.[18] These countries share several attributes: they are among the world's richest; they are democracies and have been for some time; and they share a cultural history of Western Christianity. And as noted earlier in this chapter, individual responses to World Values Surveys questions about family and gender relations tend to be relatively similar across these countries.

Despite these similarities, politicians in different European countries—who in earlier eras were, of course, nearly all men—responded very differently to the question of whether public policy should encourage women to focus on having and raising children or to pursue education and a long-term career. As any working parent can tell you, balancing family and work is a constant struggle—and public policies can make this task easier or harder. Should government policy support the "single male breadwinner" model that embodies traditional gender roles by encouraging women to stay home and have children, or should it support women who choose to work outside the home, but who also want to have a family?

Numerous policies influence the degree to which gender roles in wealthy societies conform to the traditional view or not. For example, in some countries government policy supports both single parents and dual-income families by mandating long, paid parental leaves and providing government-funded childcare and early childhood education. Sweden, for example, provides universal, all-day public childcare. By way of contrast, by omission, the Netherlands encourages traditional gender roles by leaving daycare and preschool responsibilities largely to families, compelling many women to stay home if they have children. To illustrate these differences, Table 8.5 presents comparative data on government-mandated maternity leave policies.

To the extent that governments guarantee extensive maternity leave at full pay, women who bear children suffer less of a penalty over the course of their careers in terms of salary and professional advancement. The availability of

TABLE 8.5		
Guaranteed Maternity Leave Policies, Wealthy Democracies		
	Duration of Leave	**Percent of Wage Replaced**
United States	12 weeks	0%
Germany	14 weeks	100%
Japan	14 weeks	60%
Belgium	15 weeks	75-80%
Austria	16 weeks	100%
France	16 weeks	100%
Netherlands	16 weeks	100%
United Kingdom	18 weeks	100%
Italy	20 weeks	80%
Finland	42 weeks	70%
Australia	52 weeks	0%
Canada	52 weeks	55%
Denmark	52 weeks	60%
Norway	52 weeks	80%
Sweden	52 weeks	80%

Source: The Clearinghouse on International Developments in Child, Youth and Family Policies at Columbia University, Table 1.11, accessed March 2, 2009, http://www.childpolicyintl.org/familyleavetables/Table%201.11%20Maternity%20&%20Parental%20Leaves.pdf.

subsidized daycare and preschool education also influences whether a woman will even return to the labor force at all after bearing a child. Variation in female labor force participation is a function of many factors, including individuals' personal preferences, family circumstances, and even whether government-mandated school schedules and after-school programs facilitate full-time work outside the home (in some countries the school day ends long before the normal work day ends). Table 8.6 provides information on labor-force participation among women with young children; scholars have noted that variation on this outcome is heavily influenced by government support for parental leave and childcare.[19]

Government policies can shape the persistence or evolution of traditional gender roles in which women and children depend on a man as the single breadwinner. For example, the likelihood that a single mother will end up in poverty varies as a function of the extent of government support for childcare. In the United States, the wage gap between men and women—the difference between what a man and a woman earn for doing the same exact job—is almost entirely a function of whether a woman has children: childless women earn just about as much as their male counterparts, while women who have children earn less than 75 percent of what an otherwise-similar man does.[20] Given this, in the United States—but to a lesser extent elsewhere, partly due to variation in government support for working parents—a "nuclear" family in which both parents work suffers a wage penalty—meaning that the men, women, *and* children in such families pay a financial price over the long run.

wage gap ■ the difference between what a man and a woman earn for doing the same job.

TABLE 8.6

Labor Force Participation (Percent) of Women with Children Aged 3–5 (2002)

Australia	45.0
Italy	51.7
UK	56.9
Germany	58.1
USA	60.0
France	63.2
Belgium	67.4
Canada	68.1
Netherlands	68.2
Austria	70.3
Finland	74.7
Denmark	77.5
Sweden	82.5

Source: Kimberly Morgan. *Working Mothers and the Welfare State* (Stanford, CA: Stanford University Press, 2006), 11.

At the start of this chapter, we asked how attitudes about gender explain variation in political outcomes. How can we explain such clear-cut variation in family policies across these fairly similar countries? Political attitudes by themselves cannot provide an answer: for example, citizens' responses to the World Values Surveys in the Netherlands and Denmark are similar, but as Table 8.5 indicates, their policies differ a great deal.

If variation in attitudes cannot explain cross-national variation in policy, the relative strength of organized interests in society can help. With this in mind, some scholars have suggested that the relative size and mobilization capacity of leftist parties and labor unions promotes welfare state policies. Others, however, have concluded that this hypothesis lacks support. For example, government funding of childcare is far more extensive in France than in Norway, where leftist parties have traditionally been stronger.

Likewise—and perhaps surprisingly—variation in the size and strength of feminist movements does not explain cross-national variation in government policies related to gender and the family. In fact, sometimes the expected relationship runs backwards: both Germany and the Netherlands have prominent feminist movements, but government policies in those two countries tend to strengthen traditional gender roles. In contrast, public policy in France strongly supports gender equality, even though the feminist movement there is comparatively weak and fragmented.

Similar to the policy variation across the three Maghreb countries, to explain variation across Europe in gender- and family-related policies we must focus on the relative capacity of tradition-minded interests to wield political power. In Western Europe, the relative extent of support for policies related to gender and the family is rooted in the historical strength or weakness of religious institutions and religiously inspired conservative political parties. In particular, church influence has powerfully shaped attitudes about the appropriate relationship between the state and the family.

The Protestant Reformation, the French Revolution, and other battles to eliminate religion's political influence in the eighteenth and nineteenth centuries challenged the political power of national churches—whether Protestant, as in the Nordic countries for example, or Catholic, as in Southern Europe. The intensity of such conflicts over religion energized mass mobilization over the proper balance of church–state relations. In some countries, strong Christian Democratic parties formed in response, to defend the role of religion in society. In others, religious influence was permanently weakened, and party competition never focused on religious questions.

As the table on the following page illustrates, the outcome of these conflicts shaped how future generations of politicians would address questions of government involvement in family affairs. For example, in France, Sweden, Finland, Denmark, and Norway secularism largely won out. Religious institutions' political influence waned, and the state assumed responsibility for family and child welfare. Secularism also encouraged changes in the way the law treated gender as a category, undermining male "breadwinners'" privileged position and institutionalizing gender-neutral policies regarding access to social welfare benefits.

In contrast, a more conservative vision of gender roles persisted in such countries as Germany, the Netherlands, Spain, Italy, and Austria, where organized

SUMMARY TABLE

Explaining Policy Variation in Wealthy Democracies

Impact of Conflict over Religion in 18th/19th Centuries	Strength of Religious Institutions/ Conservative Political Parties	Support for Gender-Related Policies	Examples
Church became weaker; no strong religiously oriented political party formed.	Low	Higher	France, Sweden, Finland, Denmark, Norway
Church remained influential; strong religiously oriented political party formed.	High	Lower	Germany, Netherlands, Spain, Italy, Austria

religion continued to play an influential political role, particularly through religiously inspired conservative Christian Democratic political parties. In these countries, religious institutions retained a key role in the delivery of primary and secondary education and social services.

In sum, variation in policy outcomes is not always a function of citizens' values, even in democratic societies. France and Germany differ little in terms of economic wealth, meaning that variation in modernization cannot explain variation in family policy. And just as the three Maghreb countries all share Islam, all the European countries share a Christian historical background, meaning the cultural context offers little guide in terms of explaining policy variation.

As with the North African cases, in Europe we can explain variation in gender-related policies as a function of variation in the relative political influence of conservative religious interests. Where citizens successfully challenged the power of religious institutions, the secular state expanded its responsibility for children's education and family welfare, and instituted policies that support working mothers and that tended to challenge traditional gender roles. Elsewhere, public policy tends discourage mothers from working while their children are young.

If modernization changed men's and women's political attitudes, then countries with similar levels of economic development should have similar policies, while countries at different levels of development should have different policies. Yet, things do not always work out this way in the real world. Often, similar countries have different policies, partly because attitudes alone do not neatly predict policies. In both non-democracies as well as democracies, entrenched interests can derail the influence of attitude change and stymie popular efforts to transform politics. To understand how gender works as a process, we also need to consider how powerful interest groups can shape gender-related policies, regardless of what men and women want. In this section we explored two examples that illustrate this dynamic, from the Maghreb region of North Africa and from Western Europe. In both cases, the ability of traditional social forces to remain politically relevant over time has powerfully shaped the degree of change in gender-related policies, independently of citizens' political attitudes.

CONCLUSION

Around the world, governments extend their reach into the private sphere, shaping relations between men and women and parents and children, determining what one can and cannot do with one's own body. In recent decades political scientists have increasingly focused attention on the politics of gender-related issues. Some concentrate on persistent informal discriminatory practices against women; others seek to explain variation in outcomes on gender-related public policies. Research on gender is not the same as research on women—scholars have brought issues of gender and politics into research on key comparative politics questions such as the influence of religion in politics, the likelihood of civil conflict, and regime change. Yet, because most politicians today are still men, a key question facing comparative politics remains explaining variation in gender-related policies and practices.

In this chapter, we considered the question, *how do attitudes about gender influence politics?* Mass attitudes can offer substantial insight into variation in support or opposition for change in cultural practices and public policies. While there is no question that men and women differ genetically, biological primordialism cannot help us explain why men and women's political attitudes vary so much around the world. Given this, we explored how gender can be thought of as a social category—much like Max Weber's "status groups"—a socially constructed form of political identity that encompasses the salient values, norms, and practices that people in different societies regard as typically "masculine" and/or "feminine." Research focuses on how conventional notions of gender identity vary across countries, and change over time. We focused on a key factor that shapes and reshapes gender as a category: socioeconomic modernization. The emergence of a wealthy, diverse, and complex economy tends to change both men and women's attitudes about gender as a category—but it has a greater impact on women, whose political values tend to grow more liberal than do men's.

We then considered two aspects of gender as a process—the way that politics shapes real world relationships of domination and subordination between men and women. First, we showed that legislatures with more women tend to enact more policies that women advocate, partly because female legislators tend to have more liberal political attitudes than do their male colleagues. Given this, as women enter politics in greater numbers, we are likely to see more pronounced policy change, particularly in areas that women consider important.

Second, we explored two examples that illustrate how the political context shapes gender relations. We discovered that under both democracy and non-democracy, variation in gender-related policies sometimes has little to do with either political attitudes or the number of women in politics. The three Maghreb countries are similar—most importantly in that attitudes about gender issues tend to be conservative and very few women play a prominent role in politics. Even so, gender-related policy outcomes vary a great deal. Likewise, the Western European cases are also relatively similar—in this case attitudes tilt toward liberal, and comparatively more women are involved in politics. Yet, once again, neither numbers nor attitudes explain why some countries adopt liberal gender-related policies, while others retain conservative ones.

Instead, we highlighted how the relative strength of ruling elites and powerful interests in society—tribal leaders in the Maghreb, Church authorities in Europe—play a key role in determining variation in gender-related outcomes. Attitudes reveal popular sentiment, but they do not always directly shape gender relations. As with any policy, gender relations may evolve as a consequence of power struggles between different political groups. Whether the society is generally very liberal or extremely conservative, the result of these struggles may have profound effects. ◣

✓●—⌐Study and **Review**
the **Post-Test &**
Chapter Exam
at **mypoliscilab.com**

KEY TERMS

gender   203
gender as a category   204
gender as a political process   204
traditional gender gap   209

modern gender gap   210
gender quota laws   212
family law code   218
wage gap   221

REVIEW QUESTIONS

1. Describe the between the different ways we might discuss the idea of gender, first as a category and then as a process.
2. How does modernization influence the role of women in society?
3. Do you think support for egalitarian gender ideals could eventually emerge in Muslim societies? If so, how?
4. What explains the shift from the "traditional" to the "modern" gender gap in wealthy democracies?
5. What best explains variation in the extent of government support for parental leave and childcare in wealthy democracies?

SUGGESTED READINGS

Baldez, Lisa. *Why Women Protest: Women's Movements in Chile*. New York: Cambridge University Press, 2002. Focuses on explaining the conditions under which women will mobilize, comparing conservative and liberal efforts.

Blaydes, Lisa, and Drew Linzer. "The Political Economy of Women's Support for Fundamentalist Islam." *World Politics*. 60, 4 (2008): 576–609. Uses surveys to analyze why women offer support for gender inequalities in some Islamic societies.

Htun, Mala. "Is Gender Like Ethnicity? The Political Representation of Identity Groups." *Perspectives on Politics* 2, 3 (September 2004): 439-458. Explains how and why gender differs from other forms of political identity such as race, ethnicity, or religion.

Ross, Michael. "Oil, Islam and Women." *American Political Science Review* 102, 1 (2008): 107–123. Explores the connection between the "resource curse," religion, and attitudes towards gender equality.

Weldon, S. Laurel. "Inclusion, Solidarity and Social Movements: The Global Movement on Gender Violence." *Perspectives on Politics* 4 (2006): 55–74. Explores the rise of contemporary global social movement networks to mobilize for greater legal protections against rape and other forms of sexual violence.

NOTES

1. See Human Rights Watch, accessed April 7, 2010, http://www.hrw.org/en/news/2009/08/13/afghanistan-law-curbing-women-s-rights-takes-effect.
2. Because research on gender in comparative politics thus far has focused largely on *women* and the political process, this chapter also focuses on women. Few comparative studies on attitudes toward homosexuality exist, for example.
3. See also Joni Lovenduski, "Gendering Research in Political Science," *Annual Review of Political Science* 1 (1998): 333–356, 339.
4. See for example, Mala Htun, *Sex and the State: Abortion, Divorce, and the Family under Latin American Dictatorships and Democracies* (New York: Cambridge University Press, 2003).
5. Ronald Inglehart and Pippa Norris, "The True Clash of Civilizations," *Foreign Policy* (March/April 2003): 67–74.
6. Ronald Inglehart and Pippa Norris, "The Developmental Theory of the Gender Gap: Women's and Men's Voting Behavior in Global Perspective," *International Political Science Review* 21(4)(2000): 441–463.
7. Other countries require that political parties *nominate* a certain proportion of women but do not require a set number in the legislature. For information on gender-quota laws, see http://www.quotaproject.org.
8. See Elizabeth Rowley, "Rwanda: Women Hold Up Half the Parliament," In *Women in Parliament: Beyond the Numbers*, ed. Julie Ballington and Azza Karam, rev. ed. (Stockholm: International IDEA, 2011), 154–163, accessed July 18, 2011, http://static2.idea.int/publications/wip2/upload/Rwanda.pdf.
9. See for example, Mark Jones, "Legislator Gender and Legislator Policy Priorities in the Argentine Chamber of Deputies and the US House of Representatives," *Policy Studies Journal* 25(4)(1994): 613–629.
10. See for example, B. Reingold, "Concepts of representation among female and male legislators," *Legislative Studies Quarterly* 17(1992): 509–537.
11. See for example, Leslie Schwindt-Bayer, "Still Supermadres? Gender and the Policy Priorities of Latin American Legislators," *American Journal of Political Science* 50(3)(2006): 570–585.
12. Inter-Parliamentary Union, accessed January 26, 2009, http://www.ipu.org/wmn-e/history.htm.
13. Inter-Parliamentary Union, accessed December 10, 2010, http://www.ipu.org/wmn-e/world.htm.
14. See Mona Lena Krook, "Reforming Representation: The Diffusion of Candidate Gender Quotas Worldwide," *Politics and Gender* 2(3)(2006): 303–327 or Drude Dahlerup and Lenita Freidenvall, "Quotas as a 'Fast Track' to Equal Political Representation for Women. Why Scandinavia is No Longer the Model," *International Feminist Journal of Politics* 7(1)(2005): 26–48 (2005).
15. G. Geisler, "'Parliament Is Another Terrain of Struggle': Women, Men and Politics in South Africa," *Journal of Modern African Studies* 38(4)(2000): 605–630.
16. See for example, Jane Jaquette, "Women in Power: From Tokenism to Critical Mass," *Foreign Policy* (March 1997): 23–37; Sarah Childs and Mona Lee Krook, "Should

Feminists Give up on 'Critical Mass?' A Contingent Yes," *Politics and Gender* 2(4) (2006): 522–530.

17. This section relies on Mounira Charrad, *States and Women's Rights: The Making of Post-Colonial Tunisia, Algeria and Morocco* (Berkeley: University of California Press, 2001).

18. This section relies on Kimberly Morgan, *Working Mothers and the Welfare State: Religion and the Politics of Work-Family Policies in Western Europe and the United States* ((Stanford, CA: Stanford University Press, 2006).

19. See for example, Gøsta Esping-Andersen, "The Household Economy," in *Social Foundations of Postindustrial Economies* (New York: Oxford University Press, 1999): 47-72 or Mary Daly, "A Fine Balance: Women's Labour Market Participation in International Comparison," *Welfare and Work in the Open Economy,* vol. II (Oxford: Oxford University Press, 2000): 467-510.

20. You can see the wage gap by different professions in the United States at http://www.nytimes.com/interactive/2009/03/01/business/20090301_WageGap.html?scp=5&sq=wage%20gap&st=cse. Research on the subject includes Jane Waldfogel, "The Effect of Children on Women's Wages," *American Sociological Review* 62(1997): 209–217.

Collective Action

University students confront riot police during a protest in Caracas, May 27, 2007. Police used water cannon and tear gas to disperse students, who mobilized against President Hugo Chávez's decision to force RCTV off the air.

? Why do people participate collectively in politics?

First elected in 1998, Venezuela's president Hugo Chávez has enjoyed substantial popularity and support—yet he has also endured considerable controversy. In May 2007, Chávez decided not to renew the broadcast license for RCTV, a television station that often criticized his policies. (A similar situation would be if President Barack Obama tried to shut down *Fox News* via the U.S. Federal Communications Commission.) Protests erupted in response—but they came from an unexpected quarter: university students. During Chávez's first nine years in power, student opposition to his government was inconsequential. Yet, after deciding to strip RCTV of its broadcast license, huge protests erupted at both public and private universities across Venezuela.

Students—many of whom came from middle-class backgrounds—had no beef with Chávez's economic policies, which tend to favor the poor. Instead, they took to the streets to protest against Chávez's efforts to restrict freedom of speech and assembly. Many of the students had never protested anything in their lives, but they soon faced police repression—tear gas, arrests, and beatings. Despite their efforts, RCTV still lost its broadcast license. Yet, later that year, when Chávez asked voters to give him additional political powers, students again took to the streets. This time, their mobilization proved successful, as Chávez's referendum went down in defeat—his first loss at the polls.

In 2010, when Chávez proposed to completely shut down RCTV—stripping away not only its broadcast license but also its cable TV license—students again mobilized. That year, they also broadened their movement's appeal, complaining that Chávez had failed to fulfill promises to end crime and corruption and to redistribute Venezuela's wealth. Students used social media to organize protests—for example, several anti-Chávez Facebook pages have hundreds of thousands of fans, in a country of only 27 million people. In response, Chávez called student protesters "terrorists."

Student protest organizers in Venezuela faced a difficult challenge: how to get their classmates—all of whom have many other things on their minds, including studying, partying, and paying for school—to participate in antigovernment protests that often become confrontational and frequently turn violent. Whether an activist or not, most people do not relish the possibility of having to confront riot police. Protest organizers in Venezuela, thus, faced a problem that all political leaders and would-be political leaders inevitably must face: how to get people to pay attention, get engaged, and become active advocates for a particular cause.

In this chapter, we explore a key question about engagement in politics: *why do people participate collectively in politics?* The answer to this question will help explain why people often voluntarily participate when the benefits are unclear and the costs potentially severe—as in the case of Venezuelan college students. The answer also requires that we explore resolutions to the collective action problem—the tension between individual and collective interests. The state can resolve the problem of political order by threatening to use coercion to keep people in line. This chapter, however, focuses largely on the ways individuals and organizations attempt to mobilize people on the basis of their interests, identities, or both, without the use

Read and Listen to Chapter 9 at mypoliscilab.com

Study and Review the Pre-Test & Flashcards at mypoliscilab.com of coercion. We consider the ways that leaders seek to mobilize followers in general terms, and then explore the most common forms of collective political mobilization around the world: social movements, interest groups, and political parties.

RESOLVING COLLECTIVE ACTION PROBLEMS

9.1 How do individuals coordinate their separate interests to mobilize collectively?

Political identity provides individuals with a notion of how they fit into a larger group. Identifying with a group allows people to strengthen and defend their own interests, preferences, and values. Yet while shared identities and interests may generate feelings of group solidarity, a collective action problem remains: it takes a potent combination of interests and opportunities to get people to work together toward a common goal.

free ride ■ to reap the benefits that collective action provides after other people have put in the time, energy, or money to generate collective mobilization.

Collective action problems exist when individuals have incentives to free ride off of others' efforts—to reap the benefits that collective action provides after others have invested the time, energy, or money to mobilize in the first place. For any individual, working toward a group goal entails some sort of cost—in lost time, money, energy, or pleasure they could have gained from doing something else. Because everyone faces a similar conflict between free-riding and joining the group, collective action may not occur at all.

Explore the Comparative "Interest Aggregation and Political Parties" at mypoliscilab.com

For example, perhaps you have listened to National Public Radio (NPR)—maybe *Car Talk* or one of the news programs. Every so often, NPR interrupts its regular programming with pledge drives, when the hosts request donations from listeners. Everyone who has listened to NPR finds these appeals incredibly annoying—but the stations would go silent without the money. The problem is that every listener would rather free ride by not sending money and continuing to enjoy the programming free of charge.

Incentives to free ride pervade politics, especially when there is some risk to participating in collective action—as when, for example, organizers face the threat of violence if they try to unionize a workplace. In comparative politics, we study situations where collective action problems arise—where achieving group mobilization hinges on resolving the conflict between what the group might gain from cooperation and the private incentives to stay on the sidelines.

Politics is never an individual effort—it requires collective action. Yet, because of the tension between individual and collective incentives, even if all members of a group have exactly the same political interests, generating and sustaining any collective activity remains difficult. Still, it happens everywhere: people volunteer their time for groups and causes, march in rallies, sit in protest, and even pick up weapons in revolutionary movements. In terms of time and energy, these are all costly activities and they can become dangerous. Given the evidence of participation, does the idea of a collective action "problem" make a mountain out of a molehill? Perhaps collective action is not such a "problem" after all.

How do individuals unite to overcome their separate interests and free-riding? When and why do we see this happen? In this section we first discuss the three ways to resolve collective action problems: coercing, appealing, and enticing. Then we consider the role of leadership, and we conclude by considering the interplay of interests and identities in motivating and sustaining collective action.[1]

Coercing

Coercion involves the use of force or the threat of force. In such cases, people must participate whether they want to or not. States can coerce collective action by imposing taxation, jury duty, or military service. In civil society, unionization is sometimes coercive. For example, many workplaces are known as "union shops." A union shop is a labor agreement in which the employer has agreed to hire only union members. So, for example, in the entertainment industry, the Screen Actors Guild (SAG)—a union that represents more than 120,000 TV, stage, and movie performers—prohibits any member from working in a production that does not pay a certain wage and provide certain working conditions. The SAG provides health insurance and pension plans, defends actors' labor rights, keeps tabs on unauthorized use of recordings of performances, and distributes royalty payments. If you want a career in Hollywood, you eventually join the SAG—whether you want to pay the dues or not. If you don't, you won't work—because most studios will hire only SAG members as performers.

Apart from unions, most civil society organizations such as social movements, interest groups, and political parties typically do not compel participation. Instead, individuals volunteer—or organizations offer something to encourage participation. Coercion does offer an explanation for this chapter's main question: sometimes we see collective action because people have no choice but to participate. However, if coercion is not an option and if incentives to free ride exist, how do people and organizations get individuals to volunteer?

Appealing

One way to mobilize collective action without coercion is by appealing to people. Appealing involves calling for volunteers to spend their time, money, or other resources working toward a collective goal without offering anything specific in return. Such appeals depend on the emotional or psychological satisfaction that many people gain by working with like-minded individuals toward a collective goal, rather than on the promise of receiving a personal reward or payoff for participating.

Sometimes, appeals can succeed fantastically. For example, Barack Obama's 2008 run for the presidency brought in more than $500 million in contributions from more than 3 million people, and about 1.5 million individuals volunteered in some way for his campaign.[2] In any election, a few volunteers may hope to land a job if their candidate wins, but many more get involved because they simply like the candidate's personal appeal or what he or she stands for politically.

Volunteerism with no expectation of getting anything in return is by no means limited to political campaigns—and certainly not limited to Americans. For example, *Médecins Sans Frontiéres,* a French non-governmental organization (NGO) known as Doctors Without Borders in the United States, has attracted tens of thousands of medical-professional volunteers since its founding in 1971 to work in crisis regions around the world where people are in desperate need of medical attention.[3] It bases its appeal on strict neutrality in political conflicts, emphasizing the rights of all victims of violence to medical care. This appeal has proven so successful that several other NGOs have adopted the "Without Borders" motto, such as Engineers Without Borders, which sends volunteers to work on infrastructure projects in developing areas,[4] and Reporters Without Borders, which focuses on issues of freedom of the press and publishes a widely cited "Worldwide Press Freedom Index."[5]

Attempting to mobilize collective action often involves appealing to people's emotions or moral sensibilities. When such efforts succeed, participants may be unable to articulate a concrete reason why they have engaged in collective action; they may say that it just "feels right." Appeals work best when the costs to involvement are relatively low in terms of time, money, or threats to personal safety.

Enticing

A cynic might doubt that appeals alone can resolve collective action problems. True, if strong emotions and altruism were the key ingredients for mobilizing political activism, we would see a lot more political activism than we do. In fact, a very small proportion of any country's population voluntarily engages in extensive political activism, and very few people will engage in full-time activism without compensation. Given this, groups frequently provide enticements to encourage individuals to join. Such enticements come in the form of private goods, which are things that only one or a few people can consume, and that others are excluded from consuming. For example, unions are interested in protecting wages for their members, but they are less interested in protecting wages for nonmembers. People who are not dues-paying members do not benefit from the union's lobbying activities or wage negotiations: the benefits of union membership are private goods available only to members.

private goods ■ goods that only one person or a few people can consume.

In contrast, a public good is something that everyone can consume, and no one can be excluded from consuming. For example, an environmental NGO such as Brazil's *SOS Mata Atlântica* (SOS Atlantic Forest) may seek members to lobby Brazil's government to preserve old-growth forest, which in turn protects water supplies, promotes cleaner air, and preserves areas as parkland. A clean environment is a public good: everyone in Brazil benefits from clean air and water if *SOS Mata Atlântica*'s lobbying efforts succeed, it won't be just the people who donated money to the organization or who volunteered their time.

public goods ■ goods that everyone can consume, whether they helped produce them or not.

To generate collective action, organizations often entice participation by offering private goods—even if that group seeks to provide a public good like clean air or civil rights. Anyone can click a Facebook petition to support this or that cause—but organizations often offer individuals who donate money or time the opportunity to shape the lobbying campaign itself. They will also offer individuals different levels of private goods, to encourage or reward people to give even more time, money, or effort. Someone who sends $50 to an environmental group might get a canvas tote bag; someone who gives $5,000 might get a dinner invitation and a chance to meet a celebrity; but someone who donates $500,000 might receive an invitation to sit on the organization's board of directors.

Appealing to volunteers is costless. However, enticing individuals with private goods imposes demands on an organization, both in terms of money and in terms of political compromises: it has to pay for and mail out all those "Save the Rainforest" tote bags and may have to cede some control over shaping the appeal of a social-action campaign to its most prominent donors. In any case, in the absence of coercion, organizations seeking to engage in collective action typically combine appeals and enticements, depending on the availability of resources.

Political Leadership

In addition to providing enticements, mobilizing people requires organizations to articulate a coherent message that resonates with individuals' sentiments and feelings. Organizations need to appeal and entice—yet these mobilization efforts do not appear out of thin air. Who gets the ball rolling? Who articulates the messages that strike chords in people's hearts and minds?

Initiating collective mobilization requires political leadership. Some people lead by example; they set a standard to which we aspire, for whatever reason. Others are charismatic; we don't know why or how—they just are. Examples of people whose leadership enabled them to catalyze the growth of the movement they came to lead include Nelson Mandela, Mahatma Gandhi, and Martin Luther King Jr., as well as Adolf Hitler and Ayatollah Khomeini. As the examples indicate, leaders come from all sides of the political spectrum.

Political leaders are, in some senses, like business entrepreneurs: they must be willing to take risks and invest their time and resources to mobilize other people in pursuit of a set of goals. They must also feel intensely about a particular issue and hope that their enthusiasm motivates others to participate. A business entrepreneur seeks to exploit a perceived lack of supply in the market for a certain product. To fill supply, he or she invents something new, and then seeks to create demand for that product by marketing it. Political leaders act similarly. They look to motivate collective action by marketing an idea rather than a product—by developing new political appeals that resonate with peoples' interests and/or identities, or by finding a new way to reinvigorate an old issue. They use existing or emerging forms of collective identity to generate a sense of solidarity—a collective sense that many people think, feel, or believe similarly about a political issue. This sense of group cohesion and purpose may bring in volunteers and financial support, and thus provide the basis for broader group mobilization.

Why do people participate in politics? The collective action problem highlights the fact that individuals always face certain costs and uncertain benefits when considering whether to engage in collective political mobilization. These costs can range from lost time to the danger of physical harm or even death. Given the certainty of costs and the uncertainty of concrete benefits, individuals have strong incentives to free ride off the efforts of others. The table on the following page summarizes the main ways to overcome these incentives.

The logic of collective action helps us understand why a small number of business owners in a particular industry are likely to coordinate their lobbying activities, even though those same people may compete with each other for market share. In a sector with relatively few owners—say the oil industry—each has sizeable resources to bring to bear, and they all share concrete interests and stand to profit from collaborating. They may, thus, come to an understanding about what lobbying activities to undertake as a group, rather than trying to influence politics as individual firms.

SUMMARY TABLE	
Ways to Resolve Collective Action Problems	
Ways to Resolve Collective Action Problems	**Example**
Coercing: people participate because they have no choice.	Union shop—the union can force you to join before you can start working.
Appealing: organizations call for volunteers without offering anything concrete in return except emotional or psychological satisfaction.	Youth volunteerism for political campaigns.
Enticing: organizations attract participants by offering private goods in exchange for participation.	Donors will acquire greater influence in the organization the more money they give.
Leadership: leaders articulate coherent messages and use organizational skills and charisma to attract followers.	Nelson Mandela, Adolf Hitler, Martin Luther King, Ayatollah Khomeini.

The same logic explains why it is relatively hard to mobilize large masses of people either for or against some diffuse policy or issue. Take antiwar protests, for example. In contrast to business owners, who are all trying to improve their bottom line, people who oppose the use of force as an instrument of foreign policy do so for a variety of reasons. Antiwar protestors also do not directly and personally benefit from halting the use of military force overseas, and they may fear getting arrested in a protest. Consequently, would-be protesters may not even be able to agree on goals, much less strategy or tactics. In the end, even though a large majority of citizens may oppose a particular war, sustained and purposeful collective antiwar mobilization may not occur.

The collective action problem provides insight into abstract questions, but it is not helpful at predicting specific instances of group mobilization. Indeed, because we all have incentives to free ride off the efforts of others—if only because there are countless demands on our time—the collective action problem presents an extremely pessimistic view of politics, implying that relatively little mobilization should ever occur, except when groups consist of few members who have resources and who share concrete goals. Yet mobilization does occur. People get off their couches and get involved. To understand how individuals resolve collective action problems, we need to look at the ways that (1) political leaders create abstract appeals and provide concrete enticements to engage people and (2) the political context shapes the likelihood of sustained mobilization.

In the next three sections, we move from the abstract to the concrete, and explore the main ways that people around the world actually do participate in politics: through social movements, interest groups, and political parties. Social movements are the least institutionalized form of sustained collective action and best reflect the role of political identity in generating political participation. By way of contrast, interest groups—as the name implies—best reflect the role of concrete political interests in mobilizing people into politics. And finally, parties combine identities and interests in society to directly engage the institutions of the state.

SOCIAL MOVEMENTS

Social movements are defined as organized, sustained, and collective efforts that make claims on behalf of members of a group. Social movements exist to challenge the power of government authorities or other groups in civil society, to contest the legitimacy of established ideas or practices, and to foment institutional change.[6] Such groups address broad or narrow issues, vary from liberal to conservative, and mobilize at the local, national, or even at the transnational level. Social movements are often referred to as "grass roots" forms of political mobilization, because they are the main vehicles for ordinary people's engagement in politics. Examples include groups favoring environmental protection or minority rights, or opposing globalization or abortion. In this section, we first explore the characteristics of social movements, focusing on how they differ from other forms of collective action. We then explore the factors that facilitate or hinder social movement formation. Finally, we discuss a dilemma all successful social movements confront: how to maintain their status as grassroots "outsiders" after learning how to play ball with political "insiders."

9.2 What are social movements and how do they form?

social movements ■ organized, sustained, and collective efforts that make claims on behalf of members of a group; challenge the power of government authorities or other groups in civil society; contest the legitimacy of established ideas or practices; or advance new ideas or practices.

Watch the **Video** "The Zapatista Rebellion" at **mypoliscilab.com**

Characteristics of Social Movements

Social movements differ from other forms of collective action such as interest groups and political parties in three ways: the nature of their appeals, their organizational characteristics, and where they concentrate their activities. First, relative to other forms of collective action, social movements attempt to attract followers by making broad, abstract appeals and are less likely to offer concrete enticements. Many of the world's most prominent social movements—such as the civil rights movement in the United States, the anti-apartheid movement in South Africa, or indigenous movements in Latin America—are based on appeals to individuals' perceived political identities.

To be sure, these movements want to achieve concrete political change, and interests certainly motivate collective action, as well. However, even when social movements form around interests, the goals may remain relatively abstract. For example, pro-democracy movements around the world demand concrete political change but base their appeals on abstract principles such as political equality and a demand for individual political freedoms. In short, relative to interest groups, social movements' appeals are broad rather than narrow and are often more likely to resonate with individuals' political identities rather than with narrower and more concrete political interests.

Second, compared to interest groups and parties, social movements have relatively informal organizations, and tend to have less hierarchical and more fluid structures.

This does not mean that social movements are strictly spontaneous, such as riots or street protests. Even though they may not be as highly institutionalized as an interest group or political party, social movements can and do often endure, whereas riots and protests are typically ephemeral.

Third, compared to interest groups and political parties, social movements tend to concentrate their activities to the sphere of civil society rather than in the formal institutions of the state. Some social movements even distance themselves from the government and engage in "consciousness-raising" or educational activities designed to change the way people think about an issue rather than directly lobbying the government to change a policy.

For example, thousands of Christian "base communities" emerged in Latin America in the latter part of the twentieth century—small informal groups of usually poor people who joined together to study the Bible. Leaders of base communities encouraged participants to question the established political and economic order—activities that Catholic Church leaders did not necessarily condone. The primary goal of Christian base communities was to change the way people think about politics generally and not necessarily to change any particular public policy. In contrast, the goals of parties and interest groups require engagement with the institutions and personnel of the state.

Still, in many cases, social movements end up confronting or pressuring the state in order to advance their goals. Social movements' relative informality and

People who have long faced oppression might be unlikely to mobilize. Yet in 1986, Ecuador's indigenous peoples joined together to form the *Confederación de Nacionalidades Indígenas del Ecuador* (Confederation of Indigenous Nationalities of Ecuador, CONAIE). In this photo, from 2010, indigenous people protest against a proposed law that would reduce local communities' control over water and land rights.

focus on grassroots mobilization in civil society provide them with advantages that parties and interest groups lack. Fluidity means greater flexibility of goals and tactics, compared to parties or interest groups. Parties must always seek votes—or else they'll go out of business—while interest groups must constantly "represent" their members' interests, since members provide their funding. And informality means that social movements can take a long-term view and focus on defining or redefining the terms of political discourse rather than concentrating exclusively on changing policy or institutions in the short term. However, informality also carries several disadvantages. Social movements often lack institutional and organizational resources relative to parties and interest groups, and they may struggle for funding. This poses a challenge in terms of their ability to sustain mobilization over the long term.

How Social Movements Form

Why do movements appear in some times and places and not others? No consensus answer to this question exists, because social movements form around so many different identities and the interests. Indeed, the number of social movements appears limited only by the imaginations of individuals who seek to press a collective claim in the public sphere. Still, to get a handle on the question of how social movements form, let us consider the role of leadership, and the broader political context.[7]

To explain the success or failure of social movement mobilization, we must first pay particular attention to the role of leadership. To understand why average people do or do not find leaders' efforts appealing, we can consider leaders' personal qualities and decision-making skills, the ways they try to construct or reconstruct collective political identities to develop successful appeals, and the resources they use to entice people to participate.[8] As you might imagine, explaining why some leaders are better than others and why some ideas catch on and others flop is very difficult. To explain social movement emergence it is important to connect the process of collective identity formation to leaders' resources, capabilities, and goals.

We must also consider the nature of the larger political context, which provides both opportunities and constraints for social movement formation. Scholars call this the political opportunity structure—the way a country's political system shapes, promotes, checks, or absorbs the challenges it confronts from organized civil society. The political opportunity structure can be thought of as the relative degree of openness or closure of a polity to new forms of contentious politics. It provides the incentives and disincentives for collective mobilization, because it affects individuals' and leaders' beliefs about the likelihood of success.[9]

A key element of the political opportunity structure is the degree to which existing organizations already "cover all the bases" in terms of contentious issues, interests, and identities in a given society. For example, if there are many civil rights movements already active in a democratic society, it's less likely that a new one that repeats the appeals of existing movements will successfully mobilize. In contrast, if a political leader attempts to organize a pro-democracy movement in a non-democratic society where no such movement exists, that leader might have a better chance of success.

political opportunity structure ■ the way a country's political system shapes, promotes, checks, or absorbs the challenges it confronts from organized civil society.

mestizo ■ in Latin America, a person of mixed white and native ancestry.

HYPOTHESIS TESTING | Political Context Shapes Social Movement Mobilization: Comparing Indigenous Movements in Bolivia and Peru

Bolivia and Peru—South American neighbors—are very similar: for centuries, the Inca Empire—the largest and most powerful political entity in the western hemisphere before the arrival of Columbus—ruled over the future territory of both countries. Around 1530, Spanish conquistadores arrived, defeated the Incas, and established colonies. Both countries achieved independence from Spain about 300 years later. Economically, both are now middle-income countries, but with tremendous economic inequalities. Geographically, both countries have extensive mountainous areas, as well as vast tropical forest regions in the Amazon basin. Politically, since the Spanish era a white and/or mestizo—mixed white and native ancestry—elite, which comprises a small fraction of the total population, has tended to dominate both countries. Finally, both countries have sizeable indigenous populations. However, somewhat puzzlingly, Bolivia has seen considerable indigenous ethnic social movement mobilization in recent years, while Peru has not. Given their similarities, *what aspect of the political context explains the different mobilization outcomes?*

GATHER EVIDENCE

Consider Table 9.1. Based only on the proportion of the national population that identifies as indigenous, we might most expect mobilization along ethnic lines in Bolivia, and least expect it in Mexico. Yet all of these countries *except* Peru have seen indigenous ethnic social movement mobilization in the last 25 years. This outcome is puzzling: despite a sizeable indigenous population, no influential indigenous movement has formed in Peru. Princeton University political scientist Deborah Yashar suggests that indigenous communities in all five countries share political interests, which implies that the key factor explaining variation in indigenous mobilization in Latin America is not interests but the political context—specifically whether would-be social

movements have space in the political arena to get their message out and attract adherents.[10]

TABLE 9.1 Estimates of Indigenous Population in Latin America

Country	Percent of Total Population
Bolivia	60–70
Guatemala	45–60
Peru	38–40
Ecuador	30–38
Mexico	12–14

Source: Deborah Yashar, "Contesting Citizenship in Latin America: The Rise of Indigenous Movements and the Post-liberal Challenge" (New York: Cambridge University Press, 2005), 21.

Let's consider the similarity of interests first. Indigenous peoples in both Bolivia and Peru had similar goals as of the 1980s, as a consequence of political and economic reforms governments in both countries undertook that challenged indigenous communities' autonomy. For example, reforms in Bolivia eliminated indigenous communities' rights to communal land-holding, reduced health-care and education spending in indigenous communities, and eliminated decades-old forms of communal representation that indigenous people enjoyed within government agencies. These reforms generated discontent because they threatened land security and thus food security, undercut social and communal resources, and eliminated the means through which indigenous communities could seek redress for grievances.

Indigenous communities' interests in Peru do not differ fundamentally. As in Bolivia, the Peruvian government undertook reforms that undercut indigenous communities' autonomy, welfare, and ability to seek redress, thereby providing motive for collective mobilization. For example, in Peru, 60 percent of communal

(Continued)

agricultural cooperatives were eliminated and redistributed as individual parcels of land in the early 1980s, threatening indigenous communities' longstanding practices.[11] In short, indigenous communities had good reason to mobilize in both countries—but if similar identities and interests were sufficient for collective action, we would've seen the emergence of indigenous social movements in Peru. To understand why mobilization occurred in Bolivia but not Peru, we must turn to the political context.

ASSESS THE HYPOTHESIS

Given the hardships caused by the economic reforms, the end of military rule and emergence of democracy in Bolivia in 1982 provided new opportunities for indigenous mobilization. Around that time in Bolivia, the Unique Confederation of Bolivian Rural Laborers (*Confederación Sindical Única de Trabajadores Campesinos de Bolivia*, CSUTCB)—an agricultural workers' movement that emphasizes indigenous identity—emerged in highland communities in the western part of the country. Around the same time, the Confederation of Bolivian Indigenous Peoples (*Confederación de Pueblos Indígenas de Bolivia, CIDOB*) began organizing in the lowlands to the east.

Evo Morales, president of Bolivia since 2006. His facial features and ability to participate authentically in indigenous rituals and festivals indicate something key about his political identity: he is the first Bolivian president to come from the country's indigenous majority.

Both movements gained increasing prominence in Bolivian national politics following democratization. For example, CIDOB led a series of marches from the eastern lowlands up to the national capital in the highlands to demand indigenous land rights. The politicization and mobilization of indigenous ethnicity helped propel Evo Morales, a candidate with strong indigenous facial features, to victory in the country's 2005 presidential election. Interests, capacity, and opportunity all combined in Bolivia, resulting in successful indigenous social-movement mobilization.

The difference between Bolivia and Peru results from the lack of opportunity, which was a function of the latter country's devastating civil war in the 1980s. Peru did experience widespread political

(*Continued*)

mobilization in the countryside—by guerrilla groups the Tupac Amaru Revolutionary Movement (MRTA) and the *Sendero Luminoso* (Shining Path). Despite its name, the MRTA had no commitment to advancing indigenous identity. Instead, both the MRTA and Sendero were Marxist movements that deliberately sought to mobilize rural communities on economic class lines, downplaying the political relevance of indigenous identity. Sendero guerrillas even murdered indigenous activists who opposed its presence in their communities, deliberately destroying potential opportunities for indigenous mobilization.

During the war, indigenous communities in Peru were caught between guerrillas and government military forces, which also brutally repressed suspected guerrilla sympathizers. In this situation, indigenous people hesitated to self-identify as Indians. In short, no opportunities for mobilization existed in Peru: incipient indigenous movements were squeezed between already mobilized Marxist guerrillas and the repressive force of the state. The Peruvian civil war is the key factor that

prevented indigenous mobilization. Even though the war ended in the 1990s, the destruction of potential mobilization networks has endured, meaning no indigenous movement has emerged. No such devastation occurred in Bolivia, giving activists greater opportunities to mobilize. In sum, although both Bolivia and Peru share key attributes—the presence of a sizable indigenous population with strong interests in mobilizing—it is the differences in political context that explain why we have seen extensive indigenous mobilization in Bolivia, but not in Peru. ▶

CRITICAL THINKING QUESTIONS

1. How did the constriction of political opportunities in Peru shape the possibility of indigenous mobilization?
2. Could better leadership have made a difference for indigenous mobilization in Peru, or is the quality of leadership secondary to the political context?

Of course, the chances of success also depend on a second key element of the political opportunity structure, whether the state allows mobilization or seeks to repress it. A civil rights movement might be easier to form in a democracy, while a pro-democracy movement might face surveillance and police repression in a non-democratic state. Under democracy, a free press can spread the word about emergent movements, but in non-democratic societies, such freedoms may not exist, and the government may tightly control the media. Where the state seeks to control society, political leaders and followers mobilize against the state at their own peril. So, even though social movements tend to be informal organizations, state institutions and policies wield powerful influence as to their likely success.

The Dilemma of Formalization

Thus far, we have explored conditions that encourage or inhibit the emergence of social movements. Let us assume that a social movement has successfully mobilized. Now it confronts a tricky problem. Like interest groups but in contrast to political parties, success may spell social movements' doom because it eliminates the group's very reason for existence. At the very least, success may take the wind out of a movement's sails if it cannot quickly redefine itself.

Growth and success can also hasten social movements' institutionalization. As movements grow, they face ever-stronger incentives to create a formal organization, with clear membership rules and a more hierarchical leadership structure. Moreover, when a social movement successfully forces a new issue onto the agenda, entrenched interest groups and political parties inevitably take note. Often, political parties will attempt to absorb the issues that social movements have raised. In Western Europe, for example, in response to social movement pressure on environmental or women's issues, many political parties altered their election platforms and adapted their organizations to portray themselves as leading policy change.[12] Social movements may begin their struggle as "outsiders," but successful mobilization to bring pressure on governments may mean their incorporation, displacement, or even replacement by organizations in the formal realm of politics.

Social movements, thus, face a challenge of whether and to what extent they should institutionalize, enter formal politics, or become more like an interest group or a political party. Doing so may entail "selling out"—potentially sacrificing their credibility as true outsiders who represent the interests of average people. For example, the political parties known as "Greens" in Western Europe started out as environmentalist social movements. After deciding to enter electoral and legislative politics, they have moderated some of their more radical positions. Social movements face a tension between success and cooptation: on the one hand, agreeing to enter the formal realm of politics may appear to "sell out" the group's principles. Yet on the other hand, cooptation may be a necessary—and even proper—price to pay for political success.

Social movements—which tend to articulate broad and abstract appeals, have relatively informal organizations and concentrate their activities in civil society rather than in the state—play a key role in strengthening the connection between civil society and institutional politics. Factors specific to each group—particularly leaders' capacity to mobilize followers—as well as the receptiveness of the political context to new forms of mobilization help explain why social movements form in some places but not in others. In the end, in democratic states the struggle to exercise rights and to present new political demands inevitably involves the sphere of formal politics, in which social movements lose their preeminent role, and parties and more formally organized interest groups gain importance. And so it is to this topic—interest groups—that we turn next.

INTEREST GROUPS

9.3 What are interest groups and why do they form?

Interest groups—sometimes also called lobbies or pressure groups—differ from both social movements and political parties. Interest groups are defined as organized groups of citizens who seek to ensure that the state enacts particular policies. In this section, we will look more closely at the differences between interest groups, social movements, and political parties. We will then explore the reasons why interest groups form, again dividing these reasons into internal and external factors.

interest groups ■ organized groups of citizens who seek to ensure that the state enacts particular policies.

👁 Watch the **Video** **"Banking Interests and Regulatory Reform"** at **mypoliscilab.com**

✴ Explore the Comparative **"Interest Groups"** at **mypoliscilab.com**

Characteristics of Interest Groups

The definition of an interest group applies at least in part to social movements and parties as well, but interest groups are distinct from social movements in that they tend to focus their mobilization efforts on obtaining concrete benefits for their supporters. They also tend to be relatively more formally organized, with a professional rather than activist membership. Moreover, they concentrate their energies on influencing the formal sphere of institutional politics, by lobbying legislators and bureaucrats or engaging in lawsuits, rather than focusing on grassroots mobilization in civil society.

Interest groups also differ from political parties in three ways. First, they tend to focus on a single issue or a narrow set of issues, whereas parties must present and campaign on a platform that covers more political terrain. Second, interest groups do not present candidates for elections. Third, because they do not need to win votes like parties do, interest groups do not require as extensive a formal organization or membership base. Instead, they often rely on a relatively narrow base of supporters who provide labor and/or funding. Of course, the more members an interest group has, the more likely that it will gain credibility and attract attention to its cause.

Examples of interest groups include employees' associations, such as the United Auto Workers in the United States, the Mexican *Sindicato Nacional de Trabajadores de la Educación* (National Education Workers' Union, SNTE) or the French *Confédération Générale du Travail* (General Labor Confederation, CGT). They also include employers' associations or business groups such as the Chamber of Commerce in the United States or the Canadian Manufacturers and Exporters Association, and professional associations such as the Nigerian Medical Association or the Jordanian Bar Association. Many other kinds of interest groups exist to advocate on behalf of the specific policy goals of various social or demographic groups such as the Ukrainian Association of Retired Persons, the National Association of Women Organizations in Uganda, or the Korean Veterans' Association; or on behalf of people who share specific interests such as the National Rifle Association in the United States or the Royal Society for the Prevention of Cruelty to Animals in the UK.

The lines between social movements and interest groups may not always be clear. Are networks of environmental NGOs such as Friends of the Earth International a social movement or an interest group? Similarly, are ethnic minority rights groups such as CONAIE in Ecuador social movements, or interest groups? Perhaps the answer is "both." Both organizations engage in mobilization based on broad appeals and organize followers at the grassroots level. They also engage in protests, marches, and other relatively informal forms of mobilization. However, like many other organizations that focus on a wide range of issues important to people around the world, both groups also directly engage in lobbying efforts at the local and national level in an effort to directly change laws or public policies.

How Interest Groups Form

What influences interest group formation? Unlike social movements, which tend to focus their appeals around questions of identity or abstract political goals, the most important factor that prompts interest group formation is the existence of a group of people who share a common, concrete political interest. Interest groups focus on representing, defending, or advancing specific interests, which are typically tied to advancing, repealing, or changing particular policies, government programs, or laws. Relatively less relevant here are the abstract ideological or identity-based reasons for why people support social movements. Consider financial services, energy, or insurance corporations. In any country, the major players in these sectors of the economy have a clear interest at stake: the bottom line for their shareholders. Given this, these corporations have powerful incentives to devote resources toward mobilizing on their own behalf to protect their profitability and defend against government policies that they believe would hurt their performance.

The political opportunity structure also influences patterns of interest group formation. Interest group mobilization tends to follow one of two patterns. Under pluralism, interest groups mobilize and organize societal interests freely, in a decentralized fashion. A pluralist pattern of interest group formation can only thrive in a democracy, because it requires that the political opportunity structure be wide open. Thus, when we see a pluralist pattern, we know that the state plays relatively little role in fostering or impeding interest group formation. In a sense, under pluralism there is a "free market" in interest group formation: the cleverest political entrepreneurs, or the most efficient interest groups, will come to represent societal interests in the formal realm of politics.[13] The United States is cited as the clearest example of interest group pluralism.

pluralism ■
a pattern of interest group mobilization in which societal interests organize freely in an unregulated fashion.

Most other democracies do not have such "free markets" in interest group formation. Instead, they exhibit a pattern of interest group mobilization known as corporatism. Corporatism is a pattern of interest group mobilization in which the state plays an active role in organizing groups and mediating between them. The idea is that because different groups in society all perform necessary functions, each should have institutionalized channels of representation in the state. In theory, such institutionalized representation levels the political playing field and promotes social peace.[14]

Neither corporatism nor pluralism perfectly describes any country; most countries lean toward one or the other pattern, while embodying elements of both. The key distinction between pluralist and corporatist patterns of interest group organization is the extent to which the state shapes, promotes, or impedes the emergence and persistence of interest groups. In the pluralist pattern, interest groups form from within civil society, from the "bottom-up." In contrast, in the corporatist pattern the state influences interest group formation from the "top-down."

Under corporatism, the government centrally organizes societal interests, especially business and labor associations. This means the state actively promotes some interest groups, while preventing others from forming. For example, a corporatist system of interest groups may allow only "official" labor unions recognized by the government, and prohibit independent unions from organizing workers. In exchange for government recognition, official unions gain a direct voice in determining policies, but they will be expected to compromise; they cannot hold to radical positions on wages or benefits. Government-sanctioned business owners associations, for their part, will also be expected to work with union representatives to resolve disputes, and cannot try to "break" unions or hire nonunion workers.

Illustrating Corporatism: The Case of Sweden

To illustrate how corporatism works, let us explore a prominent example. In a pluralist system, business and labor lobbies must jockey for position and fight for influence. In contrast, in a corporatist system, the state guarantees that both sides will have input and influence. In Sweden, state corporatist institutions have promoted cooperation between workers and employers. By law, government administrative boards must consult with both business leaders and labor unions to formulate and pass policies. Representatives of both sides are guaranteed membership on these boards, and both remain heavily involved in administration of any policy that is enacted.

This system not only guarantees all major actors a seat at the negotiating table but also guarantees each some degree of influence over policy. For most of the twentieth century, the Swedish government coordinated all labor negotiations, something highly unlikely in a pluralist state. This high level of coordination facilitates nationwide agreement on wages, working conditions, and labor practices, with relatively few strikes or other forms of labor strife. The state's role as coordinator of these negotiations pushes both business owners and labor unions to concede when necessary. Corporatism requires something of a cooperative spirit, while pluralism implies greater competition between groups for political access and influence.

Corporatism may seem like a fairer system compared to pluralism. Under pluralism, for example, an interest group is not guaranteed a seat at the bargaining table, much less any influence over policy. However, corporatist institutions tend to crystallize the existing set of interest groups over time and discriminate against the formation of new groups. When economic circumstances change, corporatism makes it harder to enact political change. In Sweden, dramatic economic changes due to globalization, deindustrialization, and the rise of the service economy over the past 30 years have put increasing strain on this cooperative spirit—so much so that by the early 1990s, labor negotiations proved increasingly difficult to coordinate at the national level. In recent years, Sweden has significantly decentralized wage negotiations, dramatically altering its corporatist institutions.[15] Interest group organization in Sweden still does not resemble the American pluralist model, but it has become somewhat more flexible.

Pluralism and corporatism reflect ideas about how societies should be organized. Advocates of corporatism believe that the state can and should help unorganized interests in society resolve their collective action problems and that the state can play a more-or-less neutral role in mediating between competing societal interests. Proponents criticize pluralism as ignoring the fact that not all interests in a society can organize and compete freely; some groups, they say, such as those representing big business, simply have a greater ability to organize and influence the policy process because they have more resources or they already control the agenda.

Proponents of pluralism disagree, arguing that corporatism is simply "Big Brother" with a smiling face, and that the state has no business determining which groups should gain representation and which should not. Supporters of pluralism hold that the state should play as little a role as possible in organizing societal interests, and that, in any case, history knows many examples of supposed underdogs succeeding against great odds. Advocates of pluralism are optimistic about the possibility that unrepresented societal interests can resolve their collective action problems, organize, and elbow their way into the arena of politics. In contrast, advocates of corporatism take a more pessimistic view about the possibility for weaker groups overcoming the obstacles and successfully mobilizing.

Interest groups are more formalized than social movements, and they pursue narrower and more specific political interests than either parties or social

SUMMARY TABLE	
Explaining Interest Group Formation	
Group-Specific Factors	**Political Context**
The existence of a common, concrete political interest, typically tied to particular laws or regulations	The pluralist or corporatist nature of state-society relations: if pluralist, groups form from the bottom-up in society. If corporatist, groups form from the top-down, with state guidance.

movements. However, the most important factor shaping the opportunity structure for interest group formation is the degree to which the state actively resolves collective action problems in society, regardless of whether other factors promote or hinder group formation. Let us now explore the ways in which the final key form of collective political action—political parties—differ from both social movements and interest groups.

POLITICAL PARTIES

9.4 What are political parties and where do they come from?

political party ■ a group of people who have organized to attain and hold political power.

◉ **Watch** the **Video** "The Problem of Party Discipline" at mypoliscilab.com

✳ **Explore** the Comparative "Political Parties" at mypoliscilab.com

party in public office ■ made up of (1) party members whom voters elected to the executive or legislative branches of government or (2) party members appointed to high-level bureaucratic posts, for example, in the cabinet.

party in the electorate ■ comprised of a party's supporters in the electorate—its "card-carrying" members and its local- or regional-level party organizations, but not its national-level organization.

Political parties, the third and last form of sustained collective action we will study, are the main organizations that act on behalf of citizens and their interests within the institutions of the state. A political party is a group of people who have organized to attain and hold political power. Note that parties can exist in both democratic and non-democratic settings. Parties differ from interest groups and social movements because even though both of the latter try to influence policy, neither tries to take political power. In their pursuit of political power, parties recruit and socialize potential leaders, nominate candidates, mobilize the electorate, represent different social groups, aggregate political interests, structure political issues under consideration, and form and sustain governments. Parties can also inject energy into the process of collective mobilization. To the degree that parties succeed at forming a coherent notion of what they stand for, they can also promote a particular form of political identity.

In this section, we will first develop the definition of political party by describing three elements common to all parties. We then turn to the patterns of competition between parties in party "systems." Finally, as we have done with social movements and interest groups, we consider the factors that help explain the emergence of parties and party systems.

Characteristics of Political Parties

All parties by definition organize to seek and hold onto government power. Parties can accomplish this goal in a variety of ways, but all parties establish a presence in three interrelated ways: (1) through the party in public office; (2) through the party in the electorate; and (3) through the party organization.[16] Social movements and interest groups both have the latter two elements, but only parties have members in public office. The relative importance of each of these three elements tells us something important about who holds power within a political party, and how those people attempt to capture and use government power.

The party in public office is made up of (1) party members elected to the executive or legislative branches of government or (2) party members appointed to high-level bureaucratic posts, for example, in the cabinet. The primary interest of politicians who comprise the party in public office is—not surprisingly—staying in office.

The party in the electorate is comprised of a party's core supporters among voters—its "card-carrying" members and its local- or regional-level party organizations, but not its national-level organization. More often than not, members of the party in the electorate are motivated by ideology and policy commitments to a greater extent than members of the party in public office, who must grapple with pragmatic concerns of winning elections and governing. Many parties, especially socialist, communist, and other "workers'" parties on the left of the political spectrum, rely on an extensive base of supporters who provide funding, spread the party's message, and help get out the vote on election day. Other parties—such as both large American parties as well as many conservative parties around the world—have never depended on a large, formal membership base for their existence.

Finally, the party organization is the party's central office or national headquarters, and the party's professional staff. The motivations of members of the party organization tend to fall somewhere in between the pragmatic concerns of members of the party in public office and the ideological or policy commitments of members of the party on the ground. On the one hand, people who work for the party organization face no direct electoral incentives and may adhere more tightly to ideological principles than members of the party in public office. Yet, on the other hand, a party organization cannot afford to completely ignore electoral concerns. If the party organization ignores what its supporters want, the party in public office will lose votes and as a result, the party organization will lose its financing.

party organization ■ a party's central office or national headquarters, and the party's professional staff.

Some parties have relatively small professional staffs. This reduces the influence of the party organization relative to the party in public office. For example, both major American parties have comparatively few permanent personnel who work directly for the party organization. In contrast, other parties—especially those with large and widespread membership bases—have large staffs. For example, the German Social Democrats had more than 1,200 full-time employees in the 1990s.[17]

All parties have the three core elements described above, but the relative importance of each element can vary considerably from party to party. Elite parties are dominated by the party in public office and have weak organizations and relatively few active members in the electorate. Such parties seek and obtain power based on their leaders' personal fame, arising, for example, due to their success in business or their family's longstanding prominence. These parties also frequently rely on their leader's personal wealth—or their connection to wealthy people—to finance the party's activities. Elite parties—such as Italy's *Il Popolo della Libertá* (People of Freedom), founded and led by billionaire businessman Silvio Berlusconi—typically invest relatively little energy and money in building a wide base of activists in the electorate or in developing a strong party organization, because the leader wishes to remain free to change policy positions as he or she sees fit and wants to avoid, as much as possible, being held hostage to the interests of their most active and vocal supporters.

elite party ■ a political party dominated by leaders who hold office in government rather than the party in the electorate or the party organization.

In mass parties, by contrast, the members in the electorate and the party organization are relatively more important and play a more active role in determining the party's policy commitments and ideological profile. Mass parties rely relatively less on leaders' personal prominence and wealth and more on members' willingness to commit time, energy, and money, and they tend to seek to adhere closer to ideological appeals than elite parties. In many countries, mass parties formed as extensions of labor unions. Prominent examples include socialist and communist parties of Western Europe that formed in the late nineteenth and early twentieth centuries, such as the Labour Party in the UK or the German Social Democratic Party.

mass party ■ a political party in which the party in the electorate and the party organization are relatively important, playing an active role in deciding the party's policy commitments or ideological profile.

The lines between elite and mass parties are often unclear; these two terms are meant to distinguish parties from one another in general terms. Moreover, even in mass parties, the importance of the party on the ground has declined in long-standing democracies in recent decades, due to the growing importance of television and the Internet and because most democracies now either prohibit private campaign contributions or provide public funding to all parties, based on their relative success in the last election. Both factors have reduced parties' need to have a large permanent membership base to mobilize support.

Party Systems

party system ■ the typical pattern of political competition and cooperation between parties within a state.

Political parties emerge and evolve in competition with other parties, in what we call a party system. A party system is defined as the typical pattern of political competition and cooperation between parties within a state. We are interested in comparing patterns of party competition for two reasons: because they tell us whether a country qualifies as a democracy or not and because they tell us about government stability and the nature of interest representation in a given country.

The two key elements of party systems are (1) the number of parties and (2) their relative size.[18] However, when we compare party systems we are not really interested in the *total* number of parties that can legally run candidates. Rather, we are interested in the main competitors—the parties that can credibly compete to hold at least a portion of government power. So although a party system might have twenty or thirty officially registered parties, perhaps only three or four of those may really matter. Given these two key elements for comparing across countries, political scientists identify four types of party systems, as in the table below.

SUMMARY TABLE

Patterns of Party System Competition

Type of Party System	Main Pattern of Competition	Examples
Non-Democratic One Party	Participation without contestation	China, North Korea, Cuba
One Party	Participation with limited contestation	Japan (1950–2009)
Two Party	Participation with contestation largely limited to the two largest parties	USA, UK (until 2010)
Multiparty	Participation with contestation between more than two parties	Mexico, India

Italy's charismatic former Prime Minister Silvio Berlusconi makes his last campaign speech in April 2008. Berlusconi was elected prime minister for the first time in 1994, just three months after founding his party. Berlusconi rose to fame due to his charisma and business acumen, not due to the hard work of grassroots supporters and a large party organization.

Patterns of party system competition tell us, first, about the extent to which a country qualifies as a democracy. Democracy requires more than one competitive party because at least one alternative group must be willing and able to assume power should the voters remove the incumbent party. Thus, one-party systems in which the government actually prohibits contestation are non-democratic. For many years, debate existed as to whether Japan should be classified as a democracy or not because one party, the Liberal Democrats (LDP), almost always won. The government did not prohibit contestation, and, in fact, in 2009, another party finally beat the LDP. This means that one-party systems can be democratic even if a single party retains power for considerable time—just so long as contestation is permitted and elections remain free and fair. As the Japanese case illustrates, even long-ruling parties can lose their dominance, no matter how much they manipulate the rules in their own favor.

Patterns of party competition also reveal how countries address the tradeoff between limited and effective government. In every democracy, these two ideals exist in tension with each other. Majority rule appears to promote effective government, while empowering minorities might promote limited government. Party systems reflect this tradeoff in different ways: one-party systems embody effective government by concentrating power in a single party. Two-party systems tend to give one party temporary control over government, but also check that party's influence because both major parties tend to alternate in power.

Multiparty systems most clearly embody limited government. In such systems a single party rarely controls a majority of legislative seats. As a result, even the largest parties must usually share power with other parties. Under such conditions, coalition governments—governments that comprise several parties that hold at least one of the cabinet ministries—often arise. Coalitions tend to disperse political power by forcing parties that represent diverse societal interests and identities to work together to control government. Because no single party holds a majority, multiparty systems might also be chaotic, polarized, and even prone to deadlock. Although most democracies around the world have multiparty systems, highly fragmented party systems may sacrifice effective government in the name of enhancing representativeness.

coalition governments ■ a government comprising several parties that hold at least one cabinet portfolio. These are frequent in multiparty systems.

Origins of Parties and Party Systems

Why does the number of parties in party systems around the world vary so much—from single-party dominance in Japan to highly fragmented multipartism in India, for example? Where do the parties in a party system come from? As with social movements and interest groups, political leaders who want to create a political party confront a collective action problem. To get votes, they must convince people that their idea—and not some other idea—about how to use government power is worthwhile. To do so, they must appeal or entice people to collectively follow them and pursue power.

We cannot predict precisely how many or what kinds of parties will come to populate a party system, or how those parties will evolve over time. However, research suggests that as with social movements or interest groups, the political context in a given society—in particular the political institutions and salient existing forms of political identity—shape party formation and, thus, patterns of party system competition.

Institutions and Party Emergence   A country's formal political institutions shape the opportunities politicians face when they are contemplating forming a party. In particular, electoral rules can increase or reduce party system fragmentation. Plurality and majority electoral rules enhance the likelihood of majority control of the legislature. The reason they have this effect is because in some countries such electoral institutions reward larger parties and punish smaller parties in terms of the way votes are translated into seats. As a result, these electoral institutions tend to reduce the number of viable political parties to two or three. In contrast, proportional representation rules tend to disperse political power more and result in coalition government because they do not punish smaller parties as much as alternative electoral institutions. Proportional electoral systems, thus, tend to have relatively more viable political parties.

For example, in an electoral system like Israel's, where the whole country is a single electoral constituency, a party needs only about 3 percent of the national vote to win a seat in parliament. The institutional context in Israel gives politicians the opportunity to carve out a small electoral niche. Because of this, we expect many parties to form. In contrast, in the UK, a party needs a plurality to win the seat in any parliamentary constituency—typically, about 35 percent or more of the votes. This context offers fewer opportunities to carve out an electoral niche, making it harder for newcomers to gain entrance to the party system.

A second political institution that impacts party system formation is federalism. Federalism can counteract the effects of the electoral system by offering space for politicians to promote regional autonomy in their electoral campaigns. Given this, it tends to increase opportunities for regional political parties to form, which, in turn, tends to increase the overall level of party system fragmentation. India and Nigeria, for example, have numerous region-based political parties and highly fragmented party systems. Although not every federal system has a great number of regional parties, to explain why a country has few or many parties, a good place to look is at the relative opportunities that the electoral system, federalism, and other political institutions offer. The more spaces the institutional context provides for entrants to gain a toehold, the more parties we are likely to see in the system.[19]

Identities and Party Emergence   Institutions are a good place to start, but they do not tell the whole story. To understand the number and nature of parties in a party system, we also have to take into account the relationship between the number of salient dimensions of political identity that divide citizens of a society from one another and the relative degree of fragmentation of the party system. Dimensions of identity that have supported party formation include class, race, ethnicity, religion, region, and language. The relationship between identity and the party system is the following: the more homogenous the society, the fewer parties we expect to form. The more diverse the society, the more parties we expect. In homogenous societies there are fewer dimensions of political identity around which to organize and mobilize partisan support. In contrast, the more heterogeneous the society, the more opportunities politicians have to encourage voters to follow an identity-based political party.

Exploration of the way political identities shape party formation started with a question about the relative importance of economic class identity. Class identity emerged as a result of conflict between workers and owners during the Industrial Revolution in the nineteenth and early twentieth centuries. In every country in the world, workers outnumber owners—yet working-class parties—socialists and communists, for example—rarely win majorities of votes in democratic elections. The question is the following: why don't more workers vote their economic interests—to tax the rich, for example, or legislate higher wages?[20] The answer is that other forms of political identity dilute the salience of economic class, reducing the likelihood that working-class people will vote for parties that claim to represent the interests of the working-class. Most workers—even those with the bluest of blue-collars—simply do not see themselves as "just" workers. They may regard their economic class as politically relevant, but they may also believe that other forms of identity—such as religion, ethnicity, or region—are more important. These other forms of political identity tend to diminish the salience of economic class identity and offer opportunities to mobilize and form political parties on alternative bases.[21]

One can, thus, imagine a hypothetical country that has just transitioned to democracy from a military dictatorship that had prohibited political parties. To determine what sorts of parties might emerge, we would need to know the relative salience of various forms of political identity—race, class, ethnicity, language, religion, or region, for example. To win elections, would-be political leaders may attempt to articulate political appeals promoting those forms of identity, promising to advance and/or defend their group's particular policy interests in government, and attempting to tie a group's political fate to a specific political party.

When seeking to understand why a party system has a certain number of parties, we must consider institutions, interests, and identity all together. The table below illustrates the different degrees of party system fragmentation that might result from different combinations of institutions, interests, and identities, juxtaposing the effects of a relatively "closed" or "open" institutional context against the relative number of salient interest- or identity-based political cleavages in a society. In relatively homogenous societies and where the institutional context tends to offer few opportunities for leaders to form political parties, we should see the fewest parties.

The UK is a good example of such a system: historically, economic class has been the dominant form of political identity, and over the last 90 years only two parties have held the prime minister's office. In contrast, where there are many cleavages and the institutions offer many opportunities to enter the political arena, we may see considerable party system fragmentation. For example, the Indian parliament, the Lok Sabha, has 543 seats. In 2009, 38 parties won at least one seat,

SUMMARY TABLE

Sources of Party-System Fragmentation

Number of Salient Political Interests and Identities	Institutional Context	
	Closed	Open
Few	Lowest	Medium
Many	Medium	Highest

and ten parties won at least ten seats each. Many of these parties are based on particular ethnic or religious forms of political identity found in relatively small parts of the country. In sum, the table on the previous page suggests the degree of party system fragmentation is partly a function of the relative diversity of political identities and partly a function of whether the institutional context gives politicians many or few opportunities to carve out a political niche.

Unlike social movements, parties are more formalized forms of collective action. And in contrast to interest groups, parties typically pursue broad political interests. Moreover, unlike both social movements and interest groups, they act on behalf of citizens' interests by seeking to acquire and hold power within the institutions of the state. Parties will differ in the extent to which elites—leaders elected to public office—dominate such efforts, or—as in mass parties—whether supporters in the electorate and/or those who work for the party organization have influence, as well. The key factors shaping the number and size of the parties that seek to represent citizens' interests are the political institutions and the number of salient forms of political identity. A focus on parties and party systems helps us understand whether the country is a democracy or not, who gets representation in the political system, and how the country addresses the tradeoff between limited and effective government.

CONCLUSION

Why do some people engage in peaceful forms of collective action, whether in a social movement, an interest group, or a political party? This chapter considered the question of why people participate in such activities. The collective action problem teaches us that a group of individuals will not necessarily mobilize, even if they share preferences, identities, or political interests—because they always face costs in terms of time, money, or effort. Given certain costs and uncertain benefits, people have strong incentives to free ride off the efforts of others—hoping that someone else will get involved, succeed, and provide the collective benefit.

Several factors are related to the likelihood that a group will successfully mobilize, in particular leaders' ability to craft appeals that evoke an emotional response and their capacity to entice people by promising specific benefits. To get people involved in a spontaneous protest, appealing to people's sense of indignation about a political issue may suffice. But to sustain collective action—whether in a social movement that seeks to build off the momentum from that protest, in an interest group, or in a political party—leaders must both provide inspiration to work toward abstract goals and also entice people with the promise of providing something specific in return for people agreeing to get involved.

The broader political context is also key to understanding sustained collective action. States possess enormous capacity to shape individuals' decisions to get involved. A non-democratic state can hinder mobilization of social movements and interest groups and may limit the number of political parties to one. Under democracy, a pluralist state may impose relatively few barriers to the formation of

✓•—Study and Review
the **Post-Test &**
Chapter Exam
at mypoliscilab.com

social movements and interest groups. In contrast, a corporatist state may take the initiative to organize collective action in particular ways, in order to institutionalize representation of relatively weak groups and to promote social peace.

The political context also includes additional factors that offer or foreclose opportunities for political mobilization: the existence of rival organizations and/or potential allies; the impact of political institutions such as electoral rules and federalism; and the number and relative salience of different forms of political identity. This means that successfully resolving collective action problems—whether for a social movement, an interest group or a political party—depends on crafting appeals and providing incentives that will work best given the broader political environment. This context delimits the opportunities and constraints for collective mobilization, meaning that efforts at collective mobilization are both shaped by politics, and seek to shape and reshape it. Our next chapter continues this analysis of the relationship between institutions, identities, interests, and collective action by considering various explanations for civil wars. ▰

KEY TERMS

free ride   230
private goods   232
public goods   232
social movements   235
political opportunity structure   237
mestizo   238
interest groups   242
pluralism   243
corporatism   244

political party   246
party in public office   246
party in the electorate   246
party organization   247
elite party   247
mass party   247
party system   248
coalition governments   250

REVIEW QUESTIONS

1. What are the main ways to resolve collective action problems?
2. How do would-be social movement leaders attempt to mobilize followers?
3. What are the main differences between pluralist and corporatist forms of interest group organization?
4. What is the main difference between an "elite" party and a "mass" party?
5. What are the key factors that explain why certain countries have many political parties vying for power, while other countries have relatively few?

SUGGESTED READINGS

Cox, Gary W. *Making Votes Count: Strategic Coordination in the World's Electoral Systems* (New York: Cambridge University Press, 1997). Classic reference for understanding the relationship between electoral institutions and party systems.

Dahl, Robert A. *Who Governs?* (New Haven, CT: Yale University Press, 1961). A classic description of pluralist interest-group mobilization.

Kitschelt, Herbert. "Party Systems." In Carles Boix and Susan Stokes (eds), *The Oxford Handbook of Comparative Politics*. (Oxford: Oxford University Press, 2007). Useful, brief summary of the different ways that party systems are organized.

Olson, Mancur. *The Logic of Collective Action*. Cambridge, MA: Harvard University Press, 2006 [1965]. The original and classic statement about why generating collective action is politically problematic.

Tilly, Charles. *Social Movements, 1768–2004* (Boulder, CO: Paradigm Publishers, 2004). A history of social movement mobilization in different contexts around the world.

NOTES

1. See Mancur Olson, *The Logic of Collective Action: Public Goods and the Theory of Groups* (Cambridge, MA: Harvard University Press, 2006 [1965]).

2. See David Talbot, "The E-Campaign: Rallying Volunteers and Voters," accessed April 15, 2010, http://www.america.gov/st/democracy-english/2009/March/20090309105245ebyessedo0.9717371.html, and John Berman, "Obama Supporters without a Cause," *Good Morning America*, accessed April 15, 2010, http://abcnews.go.com/GMA/Weekend/story?id=6258425.

3. See Medecins sans Frontieres http://www.msf.org/.

4. See Engineers Without Borders—International, http://ewb-international.org.

5. See Reporters Without Borders, http://en.rsf.org/.

6. Sidney Tarrow, *Power in Movement: Social Movements and Contentious Politics*, 3rd ed. (New York: Cambridge University Press, 2011); and Charles Tilly, *Social Movements, 1768–2004* (Boulder, CO: Paradigm Publishers, 2004).

7. See for example, Doug McAdam, Sidney Tarrow, and Charles Tilly, *The Dynamics of Contention* (New York: Cambridge University Press, 2001).

8. See for example, Jeff Goodwin and James Jasper, eds., *Rethinking Social Movements: Structure, Meaning and Emotion* (Lanham, MD: Rowman and Littlefield, 2003).

9. See Tarrow, *Power in Movement*.

10. Deborah Yashar, *Contesting Citizenship in Latin America: The Rise of Indigenous Movements and the Postliberal Challenge* (New York: Cambridge University Press, 2005).

11. Yashar, 236.

12. For example, see the different sections in the UK Labour Party's website on women (http://www.labour.org.uk/women/) and the environment (http://www.labour.org.uk/environment/).

13. On pluralism, see Robert A. Dahl, *Who Governs?* (New Haven, CT: Yale University Press, 1961); or Charles Lindblom, *Politics and Markets: The World's Political-Economic Systems* (New York: Basic Books, 1977).

14. A recent review of developments in European corporatism is Wolfgang Streeck and Lane Kenworthy, "Theories and Practices of Neo-Corporatism," in *The Handbook of Political Sociology*, ed. Thomas Janoski et al. (New York: Cambridge University Press, 2005), 441–460.

15. Sources: Arthur Gould, *Capitalist Welfare Systems: A Comparison of Japan, Britain, and Sweden* (New York: AB Longman & Co., 1993); and Torben Iversen et al., eds., *Unions, Employers, and Central Banks: Macroeconomic Coordination and Institutional Change in Social Market Economies* (New York: Cambridge University Press, 2000).

16. See Richard Katz, "Party Organizations and Finance," in *Comparing Democracies: Elections and Voting in Global Perspective*, ed. Lawrence LeDuc et al. (Thousand Oaks, CA: Sage Publications, 1996), 107–133.

17. See Gerard Braunthal, *The German Social Democrats since 1969* (Boulder, CO: Westview Press, 1994), 58.

18. See for example, Herbert Kitschelt, "Party Systems," in *The Oxford Handbook of Comparative Politics*, ed. Carles Boix and Susan Stokes (Oxford: Oxford University Press, 2007): 522-554.

19. The definitive statement of this argument is Gary W. Cox, *Making Votes Count: Strategic Coordination in the World's Electoral Systems* (New York: Cambridge University Press, 1997).

20. This example is derived from Adam Przeworski and John Sprague, *Paper Stones: A History of Electoral Socialism* (Chicago: University of Chicago Press, 1986).

21. The classic statement of this argument comes from Seymour M. Lipset and Stein Rokkan, "Cleavage Structures, Party Systems and Voter Alignments," in *Party Systems and Voter Alignments*, ed. Seymour M. Lipset and Stein Rokkan (New York: The Free Press, 1967): 1-64.

Political Violence

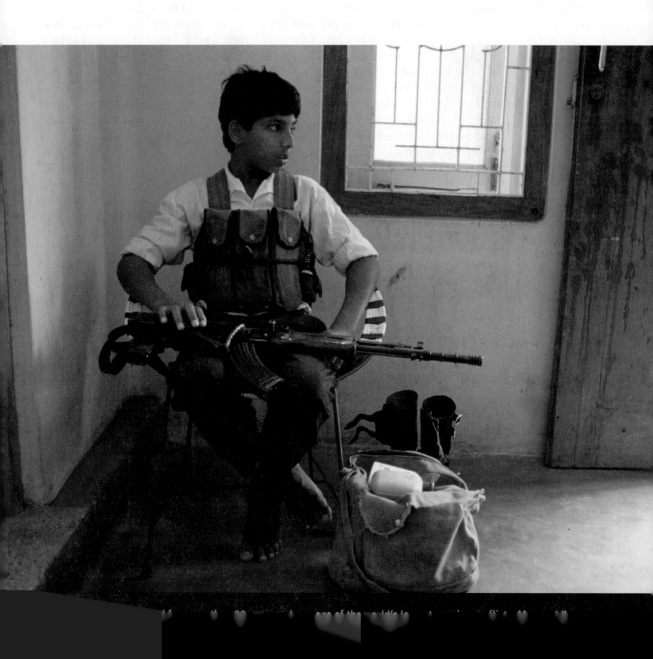

? What causes political violence?

Read and Listen
to Chapter 10
at mypoliscilab.com

Study and Review
the Pre-Test & Flashcards
at mypoliscilab.com

May 2009 saw an end to one of the world's longest civil wars, when Sri Lanka's government finally defeated a rebel army known as the Liberation Tigers of Tamil Eelam (LTTE)—the Tamil Tigers. Sri Lanka—an island off the southern coast of India, with a population of about 20 million—gained independence from Britain in 1948. Ethnic Tamils—who are mostly Hindu—were on the political defensive right from the start, because they comprise only about 15 percent of the population. About 75 percent of Sri Lanka's people are ethnic Sinhalese, and they are mostly Buddhist.

The Tamil Tigers took up arms in 1983, seeking to secede from Sri Lanka and set up an independent Tamil state. Yet, given the imbalance of forces—the Tamils were vastly outnumbered, were virtually surrounded, and had the sea at their backs—it is puzzling why they took up arms in the first place, and how they managed to sustain armed conflict for decades.

Many countries confront ethnic tensions, but only some of these erupt into civil war. The question is why we see violence in some places and not in others. In this chapter, we explore the question, *what causes political violence?* Like peaceful collective action, in the case of collective political violence the potential benefit to mobilization often remains unclear. Yet, unlike peaceful mobilization, the potential cost of collective violence is obvious: death. In the face of potentially mortal danger, it is not obvious why people would take up arms against the established authority of their own state. In this chapter we first define collective violence and then explore the opportunities and interests that create the conditions for civil conflict to emerge.

DEFINING POLITICAL VIOLENCE

10.1 What is political violence?

political violence ■ the use of force by states or non-state actors to achieve political goals.

interstate warfare ■ the use of violence by states against other states to achieve political goals.

Watch the Video
"The Litvinenko Affair"
at mypoliscilab.com

The daily news brings so many reports of bloodshed around the world that it is hard to isolate and understand what causes the violence. Political violence is defined as the use of force by states or non-state actors to achieve political goals. Historically, political violence has predominantly occurred *between* states. In interstate warfare, states use violence to achieve political goals, which include the subordination or even conquest of another state. For example, in World War II, Germany and Japan initiated hostilities against other states in order to expand territory and resources under their control. You might study interstate violence in greater depth in an International Relations course. However, in this course and in this text, we focus on political violence that occurs *within* states—even if such violence is transnational in nature in that other states or non-state actors are somehow involved.

Governments often perpetrate political violence upon their own citizens in order to consolidate power—by repressing, imprisoning, or even murdering individuals or entire groups. In some senses, violence committed by states is easy to understand because states claim a legitimate use of force to maintain law and order. Powerful incentives exist for governments to claim that their use of force is always legitimate. Particularly in non-democratic regimes, rulers wield violence as a means to maintaining power, even if they mask their true goals by claiming only to use violence in the name of law and order. In short, governments everywhere have both interests and readily available opportunities to employ violence for political ends.

We also often see headlines filled with news of insurgent groups that seek to weaken state authority with riots, bombings, or assassinations. In contrast to violence perpetuated *by* state rulers, outbreaks of sustained collective political violence that *target* the state present us with a puzzle. If the state were always so fearsome and coercive, few individuals would have the courage or resources to take up arms against it—simply because they would anticipate being crushed. There is a collective action problem behind the question, *what causes political violence?* Why, under certain conditions, do individuals overcome their fear and resolve this collective action problem? Scholars tend to divide the explanations of political violence into "opportunities" and "interests." For political violence to emerge and persist, individuals must have opportunities to organize and mobilize collectively and the interest in doing so. In this chapter, we explore the domestic and transnational sources of four key sorts of political violence: civil war, revolution, genocide, and terrorism.

CIVIL WARS

A civil war is defined as armed combat within the boundaries of a sovereign state between parties that are subject to common authority at the start of hostilities.[1] Usually, one of the parties in a civil war is the state. In contrast to international wars, civil wars occur within the borders of a single country, rather than between two or more sovereign states. And although foreign meddling is often part of a civil war, civil wars are really about "states and societies that are at war with themselves." Unlike assassinations, coups d'état, rioting, or looting that do not last long, civil wars last for a sustained period of time—at least a year—and accumulate a certain number of casualties—at least a thousand deaths.[2]

Departing from the historical trend, since World War II, most large-scale political violence has not taken place between states, but rather within them. By one estimate, between 1945 and 2000, more than 125 civil wars in 73 countries have killed almost 20 million people and displaced almost 70 million more from their homes.[3] These numbers—as well the fact that such conflicts are prominently highlighted in the news—give an impression that civil wars are common. However, despite this massive death toll and despite widespread poverty and repression of ethnic or religious minorities around the world, civil wars are actually rare. For example, for every 1,000 potential conflicts between ethnic, racial, or religious groups, only one violent conflict actually erupts.[4] Still, the fact that civil wars only break out in certain places and at certain times raises a good question: why? To explain civil war, we turn to both opportunities and interests.

Opportunities for Civil War

The best predictor of whether a country will experience civil war is state weakness. In a weak state, the central government may claim authority over the entire territory, but it cannot police the streets, enforce the laws, or deliver public services such as

10.2 What causes the outbreak of a civil war?

civil war ■ armed combat within the boundaries of a sovereign state between parties that are subject to common authority at the start of hostilities.

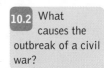 Explore the Comparative "Violence and Civil Wars" at mypoliscilab.com

health care or education. Law and order exist in strong states, while state weakness facilitates violence and lawlessness. This means that in a strong state, there are few opportunities for would-be insurgents to organize and sustain collective violence, while a weak state offers greater opportunities to organize, mobilize, and obtain supplies and weapons. Let us consider the factors associated with state weakness in more detail.

Colonial Legacies   States that gained independence from European colonial powers in the second half of the twentieth century tend to be weaker and more vulnerable to civil war. The reason lies in the flimsy political institutions that Europeans implemented, solely to achieve their goals: to extract valuable natural resources, co-opt local elites, and repress local opposition. When the colony gained independence, colonial institutions retained little legitimacy—and little of the sort of effectiveness that enhances legitimate rule, such as provision of public services for all citizens and an ability to foster economic development.

Many former colonies have never managed to overcome this legacy. Instead, their leaders are often caught in a vicious circle: reforms designed to overcome the colonial legacy only work over the long term—if they work at all. And most rulers are reluctant to risk fundamental political reforms, especially if their hold on power is tenuous. Because European powers established stability in their colonies through a combination of repression and the corruption of local elites, leaders of newly independent states are often drawn into the same dynamic to maintain themselves in office. This perpetuates the cycle and leaves the state with ineffective and illegitimate institutions. It follows that when leaders have weak authority and little legitimacy, an opportunity exists for competition over who should control the state—and such competition often leads to violence.

Consider the case of the Democratic Republic of Congo (DRC, a separate country from its neighbor known simply as the Congo). Belgium colonized the DRC in 1885 and set up institutions and economic infrastructure with one purpose in mind: to profit from extraction of valuable natural resources in the region, such as gold, rubber, and copper, and from the export of cash crops, such as cotton and palm oil. The Belgians built bridges and railways—not to help grow the local economy, but only to increase the ability to export raw materials and send profits back home. The local people were brutally exploited, forced to work for the Belgian authorities under threat of punishment.

When the DRC gained independence in 1960, it had few educated and experienced administrators capable of leading, uniting, and maintaining the territorial integrity of their diverse country, which is larger than Mexico in terms of land area. State institutions were ineffective and universally regarded as illegitimate. Given the situation, a violent separatist movement immediately emerged in the country's southern province. A strong central government only managed to consolidate authority in the middle 1960s, led by the corrupt and brutal Mobutu Sese Seko. Mobutu concentrated power in his own hands and made no effort to create enduring and legitimate political institutions. When he was finally forced from power in 1997, the DRC again collapsed into civil war. Since that year, violence in the DRC and neighboring countries has caused more than 5 million deaths—the bloodiest conflict in the world since World War II.

The DRC is an ongoing tragedy. Its weak state—partly a result of its colonial legacy—has provided ongoing opportunities for insurgent groups to form. However, civil war in the DRC has not occurred in isolation. The actions and attitudes of other states have fostered violence within the DRC, turning our attention to the international context as a source of opportunities for civil war.

The International Context The attitudes and actions of foreign countries—particularly dominant global powers like the United States and the EU—can exacerbate state weakness and create opportunities for insurgents to contest control over the state in three ways. First, insurgents can gain support from foreign governments, which may have several reasons to support or oppose political violence in a neighboring country. In the case of the DRC, the governments of Rwanda and Uganda backed rebel leader Laurent Kabila against Mobutu in what is known as the First Congo War, in 1996. This weakened Mobutu and catapulted Kabila to power in 1997. However, just a year later, Kabila's Rwandan and Ugandan allies turned against him. They created, financed, and armed a new rebel group in Congo's eastern provinces, sparking what became known as the Second Congo War. In the absence of foreign state meddling, the DRC might not have experienced such extensive violence over the last 20 years.

The international context can also include external support from non-state actors, especially expatriate communities that fund insurgents. For example, to maintain their military capacity against the government of Sri Lanka for so long, the LTTE counted on support from expatriate Tamils, particularly those living in the UK, Switzerland, Canada, and Australia. Tamil expatriates raised funds and purchased weapons, which were smuggled onto the island. In the absence of such support, it is doubtful that the civil war would have lasted so long.

Finally, the international context can shape opportunities for civil war through a spillover effect, which occurs when violence in one state spills over into neighboring states, because neighbor states are weak and cannot control their own borders. If you live in a bad neighborhood, your chances of becoming a crime victim are higher than if you live in a good neighborhood. The same holds for civil conflict. Central Africa is a particularly bad neighborhood, where several countries—Burundi, Rwanda, Uganda, Kenya, Sudan, and the DRC—have all experienced civil war.

spillover effect ■ when violence in one state spills over into neighboring states, because neighboring states are weak and cannot control their own borders.

Apart from whether neighboring governments or expatriate communities take sides, when civil war breaks out in one state, the flow of arms, money, and troops in one state often provides opportunities for insurgencies in other states. Let us now turn from the international to the domestic context to consider two additional ways that state weakness contributes to civil war: poverty and geography.

Poverty When we see a civil war on TV or read about it in the news, the conflict always seems to be in a poor country. Modern-day civil wars rarely occur in rich countries like Japan or Norway—and perhaps for this reason, poverty and inequality are among the most popular explanations for such conflicts. Scholars have confirmed that civil wars occur more often in relatively poorer states, particularly where the economy is stagnant.

The connection between poverty, state weakness, and civil war lies with the limited economic opportunities available to young men. In poor countries where young men have few opportunities to earn an honest living, joining an insurgent group offers the prospect of a steady paycheck—even though the job comes with great danger. As a result, where poverty is endemic, rebel leaders can build an army on the cheap, because more able-bodied men need a job. In a poor and weak state, governments may lack the resources to dissuade men from joining the insurgents.

However, if poverty were the most important cause of civil war, we would see more conflict than we do. Poverty, poor economic performance, and inequality certainly give people reasons to gripe about government, but they provide at best only a partial explanation for conflict.[5] Even in the DRC, one of the world's poorest countries, it is not clear that economic grievances can explain the violence. Civil war has never engulfed the entire country—combat is concentrated in particular regions—which implies that not everyone who is poor has felt compelled to take up arms against the government. The bottom line is that civil wars are only rarely initiated by groups of poor people who seek to change the economic structure of their society. This brings us to the final opportunity that contributes to civil war: natural geography.

Geography   Compared to the effect of poverty, geography is a more important source of state weakness contributing to civil war. In some countries, nature creates opportunities for rebels to mobilize and sustain conflict. Specifically, civil war is much more likely in countries with (1) rough terrain—mountains or dense forests, and (2) highly dispersed populations. Rough terrain and a dispersed population tend to weaken states' capacity to control their borders, provide public order, prevent smuggling, and deliver services to citizens. These same factors give insurgents a military advantage over the state's security forces, as they will have lots of opportunities to hide and to obtain supplies and support far from the central government's military bases.

In the DRC, both rough terrain and a dispersed population contribute to state weakness by giving insurgents opportunities to survive attacks by government forces. Of the population of 70 million, two-thirds are spread around rural areas that the government has difficulty controlling. The DRC is crisscrossed by rivers, and drenched by torrential rains, and much of it is covered with forest. To this day, the country has very few decent paved roads, and its railway system is limited and decrepit. Such geographic isolation gives insurgents the opportunity to mobilize outside of the reach of the state's authority.

The table on the following page summarizes the hypotheses that explain civil war as a function of "opportunities." Each hypothesis focuses on the central point: state weakness gives insurgents the opportunity to strengthen their position. In contrast, strong states are more likely to nip an insurgency in the bud. Having considered "opportunities," let us now turn our attention to how "interests" contribute to civil war.

Interests and Civil War

To answer the question *"what causes civil war?"* we have focused on opportunities. Yet without motivation, opportunities may not result in actual combat. What motivates individuals to participate in civil conflict? We shall explore four hypotheses; some interests offer better explanations than do others.

Cultural Grievances When you see news about a civil war, the most frequent explanation focuses on cultural grievances—the idea that discrimination, exclusion, or oppression provide the spark. The "ancient hatreds" explanation makes for good media copy, because it seems so logical. However, scholars have discovered that we can only relate cultural grievances to civil war under specific conditions.

SUMMARY TABLE

Civil War: Aspects of State Weakness

Opportunity	Example	Hypothesis
State is an ex-colony.	Sri Lanka, DRC	The state is relatively ineffective and illegitimate, giving people the opportunity to mobilize collectively to engage in political violence.
International: other states support insurgents.	DRC	States are weakened and civil war is more likely when insurgents' allies control nearby states.
International: expatriates support insurgents.	Sri Lanka	States are weakened and civil war is more likely when expatriates support insurgents.
International: spillover effects.	DRC	Opportunities to mobilize are greater when violence already exists in neighboring states.
Poverty & stagnant economy.	Sri Lanka, DRC	Rebel recruitment is easier because men have few job opportunities.
Geography: has rough terrain.	DRC	Opportunities are greater because insurgents can hide and the state lacks resources to eliminate them.
Geography: has a dispersed population.	DRC	Opportunities occur because the state must expend greater resources to control the countryside.

The logic here is like the story of Goldilocks and the Three Bears: on the one hand, in culturally homogenous countries—Japan, for example—cultural grievances are minimal or nonexistent and cannot spark a civil war. On the other hand, in extremely diverse countries where the largest ethnic group comprises only a tiny percentage of the population—Tanzania or Papua New Guinea, for example—civil war is also unlikely.[6] This is because in extremely diverse societies, no single ethnic, linguistic, or religious group can dominate, forcing all groups to come to an accommodation. Also, in highly fragmented societies, disgruntled minorities may never be able to recruit enough troops to achieve their goals through violence.[7]

Like Goldilocks's porridge, certain conditions may be "just right" for causing civil war. Specifically, we are more likely to see violence when the largest ethnic or religious group comprises between 50 and 90 percent of the population. Groups this large typically believe they should dominate politically. Not surprisingly, the efforts of dominant groups to assert themselves make minority ethnic groups feel politically insecure. Such situations sometimes lead to cultural polarization, defined as intergroup hatred fostered by cultural exclusion or repression. When cultural polarization occurs, civil war grows more likely because both the majority and minority come to think that peaceful solutions are impossible.

cultural polarization ■ intergroup hatred fostered by cultural exclusion or repression.

The Tamil and Sinhalese ethnic groups in Sri Lanka illustrate this dynamic. The majority Sinhalese led the independence struggle against the British in 1948 and dominated government thereafter. In 1956, they declared Sinhalese the country's official language, making it difficult for Tamil speakers to obtain government jobs. This and other discriminatory laws hardened the Tamils' sense of oppression. The concentration of the Tamil population in the northern and eastern part of the island gave would-be insurgents greater opportunities to organize a rebellion.

In cases like Sri Lanka, cultural grievances provide a useful albeit incomplete explanation for civil war. The problem is the same as with poverty: there are many more cases of cultural polarization than there are cases of civil war. In some cases, minority groups silently endure discrimination or even brutal oppression, believing that resistance is futile. We notice their resentment when grievances lead to warfare, but there are many cases of grievances that pile up decade after decade, with no conflict.

It remains unclear why aggrieved groups sometimes grudgingly tolerate oppression. And even when violence does break out, it is often unclear which grievance transformed cultural polarization into cultural warfare. Grievances certainly motivate political conflict, but their existence does not explain why political violence emerges in some places and not others. To understand why civil war occurs, we need to look beyond cultural grievances and consider the material interests of individuals and groups.

Greed Some insurgent leaders use the rhetoric of cultural grievances to mask shadier motivations—they may claim grievances exist, in order to stir up their followers and legitimize the use of violence. Yet in many civil wars—even those that seem obviously motivated by religious or ethnic hatreds—the stated motives for political violence are irrelevant. Instead, motivations for violence often come from greed—an interest in accumulating wealth by trafficking in drugs, gold, diamonds, or other valuable commodities through organized violence.

This argument supposes civil wars are often waged for profit rather than for lofty goals, such as self-determination or protection of minority rights. Insurgent groups can resemble the mafia or street gangs, which operate outside the law in pursuit of profits from illegal commerce. The plausibility of greed as an explanation for civil war depends crucially on the extent to which a country contains lootable resources. Movies like Leonardo DiCaprio's *Blood Diamond* and Nicholas Cage's *Lord of War*—as well as rapper Kanye West's song "Diamonds from Sierra Leone"—have focused attention on how the presence of valuable natural resources can fuel warfare—and these Hollywood treatments, unfortunately, reflect the actual facts on the ground.

The ongoing violence in the DRC illustrates the connection between lootable resources and civil war. In the mid-1990s, civil war erupted between Mobutu's government and Kabila's rebel forces. Kabila promised that he would end Mobutu's corruption and bring democracy to the DRC. However, he never followed through on any of his promises and, instead, began centralizing power and accumulating wealth—that is, governing just like Mobutu. Kabila's betrayal of his promises and his allies left him with a host of enemies, and he was assassinated in 2001. Since that year, the DRC's central government has been unable to regain control over the eastern part of the country—the region that Kabila and his ethnic group call home.

The people who live in the eastern DRC know that rebel leaders and troops are fighting only for themselves—for control of valuable deposits of gold, diamonds, and critical cell phone and video-game console ingredients such as tungsten.[8] Given the profitability of illegally trading minerals for arms, food, and other supplies, elements of Congo's national army also engage in plunder, collaborating with rebels to mine the country's wealth and splitting the profits.[9] The war in the DRC has many causes, but greed is clearly an important element.

Not every country rich in potentially lootable resources has experienced civil war. For example, Botswana—one of the world's largest producers of diamonds—has been peaceful since independence. How can we explain the difference between Botswana and the DRC? Critically, it is the combination of lootable resources and a weak state that leads to civil war. For every Congo in the world—resource-rich and conflict-ridden—there is a Botswana—resource-rich but peaceful. The key difference between the DRC and Botswana is not resource wealth, but the relative strength of the state. Botswana's state is relatively effective and legitimate and has been since its independence in 1966; the DRC has one of the weakest states on earth. The presence of natural resources can lead to civil war, but only where the state is weak. If lootable resources are available but the state is strong and can defend itself, insurgencies are unlikely to succeed.

Many civil wars are not caused by poverty or by cultural oppression. Instead, the relative profitability of looting a country's natural wealth is important. Where few opportunities for illegal profit exist, civil conflict is unlikely. But when lootable resources exist and the state is weak, civil war is more likely. Still, greed and state weakness do not completely explain civil war. Another factor that casts light on a dark side of politics is also critical—coercive pressures to join insurgent movements.

Pressure to Join   Another important explanation for civil war focuses on how insurgents encourage individuals to join their group. Tactics can run the gamut from relatively benign peer pressure to outright kidnapping. At the peer pressure end of the spectrum, individuals will have a stronger interest in joining a rebellion if members of their own community are already active in the movement and if their community supports the movement. Like street gangs or mafias, insurgent militias do not typically recruit troops based on their résumés or educational qualifications. Insurgencies are more likely to succeed if they emerge from communities characterized by networks of individuals who share values and beliefs. Such communities are also more likely to support insurgents with food, clothing, and shelter against the forces of the state.

coercive recruitment ■ where individuals are forced to take up arms to sustain an insurgent army in a civil war.

Still, even in a tight community, peer pressure may be insufficient to mobilize enough volunteers. In many cases it is a mistake to assume that individuals have "volunteered" to fight against the state; instead, coercive recruitment—where individuals are forced to take up arms—often sustains insurgent armies. In such cases, an individual's only "interest" in joining the fight is in not getting shot for *not* joining.[10] Even if recruits are not actually forced to "enlist" at gunpoint, they may fear that not joining would endanger their families or property. In other cases, insurgents use systematic abduction to obtain new troops. Members of rebel armies—many of whom were kidnapped earlier themselves—simply kidnap new "recruits" at gunpoint, and tell them that if they do not participate in the violence, they will be killed. Fear is a powerful motivator; it can push people to do things they would not otherwise do.

Consider the Tamil Tigers. In July 1983, Sinhalese mobs rioted, causing hundreds of Tamil deaths and destroying thousands of Tamil houses and businesses. This mob violence—known as "Black July" in the Tamil community—provided the LTTE with a useful recruitment tool. Nonetheless, the LTTE never exclusively relied on volunteers. It forcibly recruited thousands of adults and children, despite acknowledging that such practices undermined its support within the Tamil community. Every family in an area controlled by the LTTE was required to "volunteer" one person to serve in the rebel army—and larger families were required to provide two or more. To avoid forced recruitment, many Tamils would leave an area that came under LTTE control. To discourage such efforts, LTTE leaders would arrest up to ten relatives of anyone who dodged their draft and use those family members for hazardous duty on the front lines.[11]

Coercive recruitment suggests that in many civil wars, most combatants do not volunteer to join the fight out of self-interest—except to avoid being killed by the people supposedly fighting on their behalf. If rebel leaders sanction coercive recruitment, then all other supposed causes of civil war—cultural grievances, a call for social justice, or just plain greed—may be completely irrelevant. Still, in some cases of civil war, we cannot point to grievances, greed, or coercive recruitment as causes. This suggests that, in some cases, individuals have their own, personal interests in volunteering to fight.

Individual Psychology   Some people's only "interest" in joining an insurgency is in not getting shot by the insurgents themselves. Others might be motivated by the prospect of a steady job, or profiting from the gold or diamond trade, rather than by loftier goals of social justice. A focus on greed and coercion suggests that civil wars are often caused by leaders' selfish drive for power and followers' desire for income or fear for their personal safety. Nevertheless, some people do volunteer to participate in civil war for selfless motives, expecting little in return except the opportunity to participate in an effort to change their society. Most people run from physical danger; what differentiates those who run from those who face danger with a gun in their hands and with little prospect of personal gain?

Wars are fought for a mixture of motivations, some good and some bad. Most wars combine elements of both. Leaders always claim a higher purpose, but ideology is rarely the root cause of civil war.[12] Even so, we cannot discount the possibility that individual psychology and emotions influence why some people fight: some people volunteer simply because they feel that they need to or even must participate, even at great risk to themselves and even without the expectation of clear future benefits. Without joining up, such people feel they would not be true to themselves and their beliefs. The factors we've just discussed—cultural grievances, ideology, or other interests—may influence individual psychology. For example, a person deeply attached to his or her ethnic group or religion may react more strongly to perceived slights to the community than would someone whose attachment is relatively superficial. However, it remains unclear why some people who react strongly risk their lives by fighting, while others do not.

An illustration of the importance of individual psychology comes from the civil war in El Salvador. In the 1970s and 1980s, many Salvadoran peasants— poor farmers, most of whom rented land from rich landowners—joined an insurgency that sought to change long-standing political and economic inequalities. The government of El Salvador brutally repressed this insurgency, but individuals continued to join and the violence grew more intense. Political scientist Elisabeth Jean Wood argues that many individuals joined the insurgents to express moral outrage at existing social, political, and economic relations and to derive emotional pleasure by defying resented authorities.[13] In this view, participation in an insurgency is driven by a desire to assert one's dignity in response to a lifetime of humiliation.

Although insurgent leaders may claim that ideology justifies violence, leaders always claim lofty goals, and claim that the ends justify the means. For the typically poor individuals who serve as troops on the front lines in an insurgency, the motivation to participate may be simpler and less intellectual—it just "feels right." This sort of emotional pride derived from participation may not be important for most people, or in most cases of civil war, but it is possible that individual psychology explains why some people join up—and it's possible that such individuals may not be able to articulate a "reason" for their participation.

peasants ■ poor farmers who typically rent land from wealthy landowners.

SUMMARY TABLE		
Interests and Civil War		
Interest	**Examples**	**Logic of Hypothesis**
Cultural grievances	DRC, Bosnia, Sri Lanka	Conflict results when an identity group feels its interests or survival is threatened.
Greed	DRC	Conflict results because banditry is more lucrative than a regular job or because of the availability of "lootable" natural resources.
Social pressures	Sri Lanka	Conflict results if insurgents successfully use peer pressure and/or coercion to recruit troops.
Individual psychology	El Salvador	Conflict results if enough individuals feel they *must* participate, even at great personal cost and with little expectation of future benefits.

The table above summarizes the hypotheses relating interests to civil war. Each focuses on the idea that while opportunities set the stage, individuals need a motivation to pick up a gun and risk their lives in a violent political conflict.

The question of what causes civil war has no simple answer. To explain why we see civil war in some places and times but not others, we need to explore both opportunities and interests. In terms of opportunities, the key explanations of civil war lie with the sources of state weakness: colonial history, level of economic development, the international context, and natural geography. In terms of interests, cultural grievances predict conflict relatively poorly, because there are far more groups with grievances than there are civil wars. Instead, greed is a strong motivator, in the context of a weak state—the availability of wealth through corruption, extortion, or control over natural resources. Finally, although it is true that individual psychology may motivate some individuals to take up arms in a battle against state authority, scholars are increasingly drawing attention to the fact that social pressures or even coercion provide the motivation for individuals to take up arms.

REVOLUTIONS

10.3 When does a civil war become a revolution?

Revolutions are defined as armed conflict within a sovereign state between insurgents and the state, in which (1) both the insurgents and the state claim the allegiance of a significant proportion of the population; (2) authority over the state is forcibly transferred from the state to the insurgents, and (3) the insurgents subsequently bring about wholesale political change.[14] According to this definition, both civil wars and revolutions entail sustained violence within a state. However, civil wars occur with some frequency, while revolutions are rare. How can we tell the difference?

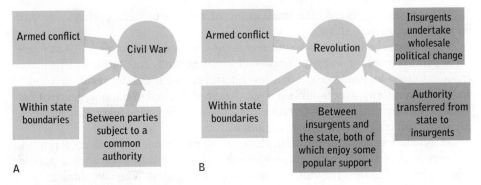

A   B

FIGURE 10.1

Civil Wars versus Revolutions: The Core Differences

All revolutions start out as civil wars. However, revolutions are different because combat is specifically targeted at the state (in some civil wars, two insurgent groups fight each other), and because the insurgents win and impose wholesale political change.

The simplest—and most important—distinction is the fact that a revolution is a civil war in which the insurgents win, and gain control of the state. In many civil wars, the insurgents lose, or a stalemate results. Yet, in a revolution, insurgents articulate a political grievance that resonates with a significant proportion of the population. And after winning on the battlefield and gaining control of the state, they follow through on their promises to remake society by implementing dramatic political, cultural and economic changes.

Because revolutions combine insurgent victory and popular support for dramatic political changes, examples are historically rare: scholars debate about whether a particular example qualifies as a revolution or not but almost always include France (1789), Russia (1917), China (1949), Cuba (1959), and Nicaragua (1979).

Note that the first element of the definition of revolution *is* the definition of civil war. This means that all revolutions are civil wars—but not all civil wars end up as revolutions. Revolutions differ from civil wars in two ways. First, it is not always the case in a civil war that both the state and the rebels enjoy widespread support. For example, a conflict between an unpopular dictator and an equally unpopular warlord who wants to declare himself president can become extremely bloody but is not a revolution. To qualify as a revolution, each party in a civil war must enjoy considerable popular support.

Second, not all civil wars result in a forcible transfer of authority over the state from one side in the conflict to another. Many civil wars end in defeat for the insurgents, in a stalemate, or in compromise. All of those outcomes leave the incumbent rulers at least partially in control of government after hostilities cease. To qualify as a revolution, a civil war must involve a clean break with the past in terms of who holds power. When the government loses a civil war, the insurgents and their supporters call their victory a revolution; the losers call the outcome a national tragedy.

This definition also distinguishes revolutions from other forms of political violence. Military coups d'état are not revolutions. Many coups are violent, but most involve relatively little armed combat, and few involve mass popular mobilization.

revolutions ■ armed conflict within a sovereign state between insurgents and the state, in which both the insurgents and the state claim the allegiance of a significant proportion of the population; authority over the state is forcibly transferred from the state to the insurgents, and the insurgents subsequently bring about wholesale political change.

Most coups are instigated by a small group of military officers, perhaps egged on by wealthy economic elites.

Separatist rebellions are also not revolutions, even if they succeed. For example, the separatist rebellion in East Timor—which successfully fought for independence from Indonesia in 2002—was not a revolution because it did not result in a forced transfer of authority over Indonesia, even though it resulted in the emergence of East Timor—formerly an Indonesian province—as a sovereign state. Separatist rebellions are successful civil wars, but not revolutions.

A revolution requires all three elements of the definition: collective political violence within a state between parties subject to that state's authority; popular support for and against the violence; and insurgent victory. When we think of revolutions that have changed different societies over the last two centuries, the second and third elements of the definition become critically important. To understand why, let us consider the causes and consequences of revolutions.

State Weakness

Because all revolutions are civil wars, explaining why revolutions occur is similar to explaining why civil wars occur. As with civil wars, we can divide the causes of revolutions into opportunities and interests. However, some of the factors that cause civil wars are relatively more important—and others relatively less important—for explaining revolutions.

Like civil wars, the most important reason why we see revolutions is state weakness. This should be no surprise—after all, in a revolution, the government fails to use the power of the state to defeat the insurgents. When the state is weak, insurgent groups have more opportunities to mobilize, spread word of their movement's goals, and successfully engage the forces of the state.

Colonial legacies are relatively unimportant causes of revolution. However, other elements of state weakness that cause civil war can also lead to revolution. First, the international context is critical. In particular, defeat in an international war leaves governments vulnerable to a revolutionary civil war. For example, Japan invaded and occupied large portions of China between 1931 and 1945. China's humiliating defeat left its armed forces demoralized and its governing Nationalist Party poorly equipped to reassert authority over China's territory after Japan's defeat in World War II. Nationalist military incompetence and low morale gave communist rebels—who had started their insurgency in the 1920s—greater opportunities to mobilize, and contributed to their revolutionary victory over the Nationalists in 1949.

Poverty and economic stagnation also contribute to revolutions, as the case of China also demonstrates. It is important to remember that until the 1990s, China was an extremely poor country. In 1945, the country was even poorer—and its economy had been shattered by years of war. Poverty and war left China's government with little tax revenue. The inability of the Nationalist government to provide services and put the economy to rights contributed to popular dissatisfaction,

Japanese army troops march as conquerors through Shanghai, China. Japan's defeat of China in the 1930s indicates the political weakness of China's state at the time—an essential opportunity for revolution to occur.

facilitating communist efforts to mobilize support and recruit troops from among the population.

Geography can also play an important role in many revolutions. As in many civil wars, revolutionaries can "head for the hills" to escape the clutches of government forces. In China, communist leaders led their troops on what is known as the "Long March," a tactical retreat that lasted for more than a year and traversed at least 6,000 miles (the equivalent of walking from New York to Los Angeles and back again) through rough terrain to escape from Nationalist forces. Like American revolutionary troops at Valley Forge, Pennsylvania, the Long March became legendary as a mark of the toughness of communist forces. Communist troops' perseverance during this difficult period helped them later recruit soldiers to their cause.

State weakness is not the only important explanation. We must also return to the definition of revolution and understand how widespread popular support for the insurgents contributes to a revolutionary outcome.

Widespread Popular Grievances

As in civil wars, interests are also important explanations for revolutions. Two sorts of interests that help explain civil wars are relatively less important explanations of revolution: greed and coercion. This is not to say that revolutionary armies never engage in plunder or looting, or that revolutionary armies never traffic in drugs, weapons, or valuable commodities. It is also not true that social pressures or outright coercion are absent from rebel army recruitment patterns. Nevertheless, it is important to remember that revolutions are successful insurgencies—they are civil wars that result in the defeat of the government. With that in mind, recall the second element of revolution's definition: both sides must enjoy considerable popular support. The key to a successful insurgency lies with the fact that those who wish to defeat the state must take care not to alienate average people by forcibly recruiting children, raping, or stealing. To succeed, a rebel army must cultivate citizens' support by combining appeals about what is just and right with appeals to people's concrete material interests.

For example, the Chinese Communist Party did not simply lecture peasants and workers about the supposed evils of capitalism and the wonders of communism. Such ideological appeals often fall on deaf ears among average citizens. Instead, the communists focused on two simpler ideas, both of which found a receptive audience. First, they appealed to the patriotism of their fellow-citizens, accusing the Nationalist Party of treason by failing to resist the Japanese invasion. Because during World War II the nationalists had in fact chosen to concentrate on fighting the communists rather than the Japanese, many Chinese concluded that the nationalists were more interested in fomenting chaos at home than they were in ridding China of a hated invader. The communists hit a raw nerve—Chinese people's sense of wounded nationalist pride. Patriotism proved a useful recruitment tool.[15]

Second, the communists appealed to the material interests of China's hundreds of millions of peasants, by engaging in massive land redistribution. As communist forces advanced, they would confiscate wealthy landlords' property and distribute it among the area's peasants. The communists also lowered peasants' taxes and increased taxes on the wealthy. Confiscating landlords' property and raising taxes on the rich fit with communist ideology—but it also fit the material interests of China's poor. Communist leaders knew peasants would not willingly support the insurgency unless they made it clear that they were fighting for peasants' interests.[16] This approach generated the widespread popular support that proved necessary for the revolution to succeed.

There is no simple explanation for why a revolution succeeds or fails. However—as in civil war—both opportunities and interests are important. In particular, state weakness—typically a result of loss in an international war—provides a key opportunity for insurgents to mobilize against the state. Interests also prove important. However, in the case of revolution, both greed and coercion by insurgent leaders appear less important. Instead, to build popular support, insurgent leaders appeal to widely held popular grievances—whether cultural or economic. Only with widespread popular support can a revolution succeed—and when the insurgents win, a wholesale transfer of power occurs, bringing about deep and long-lasting political change. Let us now turn to the political consequences of revolution.

Consequences of Revolution

Dictionaries define revolutions as events that bring about drastic and radical change. And indeed, all of the revolutions listed previously have been followed by wholesale political, social, and economic transformations. Revolutions are relatively rare in world history because they combine total victory by insurgent forces—a difficult accomplishment, even against a weakened state—with popular support for the insurgents. This combination helps explain why, after their victory, insurgents often implement such radical policy changes.

Rebels who defeat a government are not interested in compromise—they are interested in making sure that their enemies are completely forced from power. To do so, they typically remove every last appointee of the previous government from state bureaucracies—including the national ministries, the armed forces, local government offices, even the post office—and replace them with their own supporters. In a revolution, the insurgents win and completely take over control of the state. The losers and their collaborators are sent to prison, forced into exile, or simply killed.

The more extensive the transfer of political power from one ruling group to another in the aftermath of political violence, the greater the likelihood of truly revolutionary social and economic change. When a new government wins an election in a democracy, it is unlikely to implement such dramatic changes, even if it wanted to. Too many checks and balances are in place, and there is always the next election to worry about. Because change is risky, new democratic governments leave most policies in place, tweak some others, and perhaps attempt a few major reforms. Moreover, most bureaucrats and government officials keep their jobs, and officers are not purged from the armed forces because their loyalties are suspect. In contrast, in the aftermath of a revolution the victors do not waste time on small-scale changes. Instead, they implement radical change—partly because they can, having swept out the old government from top to bottom, and partly because they promised their supporters that they would do so.

For example, after defeating the nationalists, the Chinese communists made sure that only loyal party officials occupied government positions. To consolidate their hold on power, they completely remade China's political institutions. Prior to World War II, political power in China was highly decentralized, as large landowners held tremendous authority at the local level. The communists destroyed landowners' influence by redistributing land and by centralizing political power in the hands of top party officials in Beijing. Finally, although today the Party has all but abandoned the communist ideology that motivated many of its leaders and followers in the 1930s and 1940s, in the years immediately after the 1949 Revolution, the Party implemented communist-inspired policies such as centralized economic planning and sought to eliminate traditional Chinese cultural hierarchies that had existed for hundreds if not thousands of years.

Revolutions are a subtype of civil war in which the winning side not only takes control of the state but implements radical change, such as bringing previously excluded groups of people into power, redistributing economic wealth, and creating new political institutions. Revolutions are so rare because insurgents do not always win, and because many insurgent leaders are warlords or military leaders more interested in power and its trappings than in carefully cultivating popular support.

HYPOTHESIS TESTING | The Iranian Revolution Constitutes a Case of "Real" Revolution

In 1979, Iranians forced their king, Shah Mohammad Reza Pahlavi, to abdicate his throne and depart his country to exile. Much like the overthrow of Egypt's President Hosni Mubarak in 2011, the shah had ruled for decades and was regarded as the fulcrum of the country's entire political system. Before 1979, few observers would have guessed that the shah would be out of power within a year. Indeed, most believed that he was safely in control, as he had been since 1941. Often, when a leader is forced from power, observers call the outcome "revolutionary." But this term loses meaning if we apply it to every instance in which a dictator is tossed from office. Given the guidelines this chapter establishes, how would you go about confirming or disconfirming the

hypothesis, *the Iranian revolution constitutes a case of 'real' revolution?*

GATHER EVIDENCE

Let's explore both sides of this case. On the one hand, the evidence seems clear that the overthrow of the shah differs from other well-known cases of revolution. First, no one believed that the Iranian state was particularly weak: the shah had powerful and modern police and military forces, and the country had not just lost an international war, as had Russia in 1917 or China in 1949. Second, the shah's overthrow was not nearly as violent as the toppling of the pre-revolutionary Russian and Chinese cases. Considerable violence was directed at the shah's government, but an all-out civil war did not precede the shah's overthrow.[17] On the basis of these two pieces of evidence, we might conclude that the shah's overthrow was just that—one case among many of a dictator being tossed from office.

ASSESS THE HYPOTHESIS

However, if we test the hypothesis further, other facts lead to a different conclusion. First, as in other cases of revolution, the shah's regime confronted *widespread popular opposition*. Opposition emerged because by the 1970s Iran's economy was stagnating and because the shah's regime had grown increasingly repressive. Opposition also emerged because the shah had sought to undermine the authority of Iran's Islamic clergy, which had historically controlled educational, legal, and social welfare activities. Religious Iranians increasingly viewed the shah as anti-Islamic. In short, opposition to the shah intensified among secular and religious Iranians, for different reasons: secular Iranians wanted a democratic regime, while religious Iranians wanted to impose Islamic law.

Public opposition to the shah exploded in summer 1978, following government repression of protests against the visit of U.S. President Jimmy Carter. The success of the protests exposed the shah's weakness,

Iranians clamoring to glimpse Ayatollah Khomeini, the leader of the Iranian Revolution, crowd into a building under construction in Teheran, 1979.

(*Continued*)

and by November the shah's regime was crumbling, as elements of the police and army refused to fire on protesters. By December, literally millions were taking to the streets to demand the shah's ouster, in a country of approximately 40 million people. Demonstrators seized government buildings, shut down businesses, and assassinated government officials. On January 16, 1979, the shah left Iran for exile, abdicating his throne. In less than a year, sustained and widespread popular opposition had ended the shah's nearly 40-year reign.

A second factor also convinces many that the overthrow of the shah is not merely a coup d'état but a real revolution. A revolution must also entail a *clean break with the past*, in terms of who holds power. After the shah left, it was not clear who would govern Iran—or how. Iranians favoring democracy quickly found themselves opposed by Iranians who wanted theocracy. The outcome—an Islamic Republic, with religious authorities dominant—looks inevitable only in retrospect, but religious leaders did not fully consolidate authority until 1983.

Consolidation of the Iranian Revolution involved removing all elements of the shah's regime from government and imposing the new form of government, in which religious authorities dominated. Islamic leaders used overwhelming approval of a popular referendum in March 1980 in support of a religious form of government to consolidate control. Religious leaders banned all secular political parties, purged the military of thousands of pro-shah officers, fired thousands of university professors deemed too secular, and engaged in systematic harassment and imprisonment of opponents of the new regime. At least 500,000 Iranians, including members of the royal court, military officers, wealthy businessmen, secular political leaders, and former high-ranking government officials, all went into exile. Many

who refused or were unable to leave were killed, and even more were jailed.[18] No one also knows how many died opposing the new Islamic regime; Amnesty International estimates that the new government executed about 3,000 people in 1980 alone.[19]

The new regime also ensured a clean break with the past by having the government take over much of Iran's economy—especially its valuable oil industry. These moves eliminated foreign companies' influence and provided Iran's religious leaders with billions of dollars to distribute to supporters. Anti-American nationalist fervor also helped the religious authorities: in November 1979 university students invaded and occupied the U.S. embassy in Teheran, holding 52 Americans hostage for over a year. This event galvanized anti-American sentiment, which religious leaders manipulated in their favor.

The overthrow of the shah does not fit precisely within this chapter's definition, and yet political scientists have come to agree that this case *does* constitute a revolution.[20] Iran's revolution puzzled Western scholars principally because no observers at the time thought the shah's government was weak and because armed insurgents played such a minor role. However, the events of 1979 fit our definition in other respects: the Iranian Revolution was truly a popular uprising against a hated regime, and involved a wholesale transfer of power from one group to another. ◢

CRITICAL THINKING QUESTIONS

1. What factors make the Iranian Revolution "less similar" to other revolutions?
2. What factors make the Iranian Revolution "more similar" to other well-known cases of revolution?

TERRORISM

10.4 When do insurgents resort to terrorism?

guerilla wars ■ wars in which small groups of insurgents use irregular military tactics, such as sabotage and ambushes, to engage the state's military forces.

terrorism ■ threatened or actual use of violence for political purposes by non-state actors, directed particularly against civilian targets.

◉ Watch the Video "Bin Laden Killed in Pakistan" at **mypoliscilab.com**

Some civil wars are fought like conventional wars, with troops engaging each other on the battlefield. Others are fought as guerilla wars, in which small groups of insurgents use irregular military tactics such as sabotage and ambushes to engage a state's military forces. Since the attacks of 9/11, Americans have become increasingly aware of the use of another form of political violence, terrorism, which is the threatened or actual use of violence for political purposes by non-state actors, particularly against civilian targets.[21] States sometimes use coercion to terrorize citizens, and they sometimes sponsor militias or insurgent groups in other states. However, the definition of terrorism focuses on the actions and goals of non-state actors.

Terrorism occurs when non-state actors target civilians for political purposes. Avoiding military targets is a political tactic. Terrorists believe that attacking civilians is more likely to achieve their goals, instead of a conventional attack on the state's military forces. This distinguishes terrorism from civil war, in which non-state actors attack the state's military capabilities. Terrorists use violence not to overthrow the state directly, but to undermine state strength—to chip away at the appearance that the state is legitimate and effective.

Terrorism is frequently transnational in nature. Many terrorist organizations such as al-Qaeda find safe havens in weak states such as Afghanistan, Somalia, or Yemen in order to plan and train for attacks they will undertake in other states. For example, the terrorist organization Lashkar-e-Taiba, based largely in Pakistan, coordinated a series of brazen attacks in downtown Mumbai, the largest city in India, in November 2008, killing 166 and wounding more than 300 civilians.[22] Lashkar seeks to establish an Islamic state in South Asia, particularly over Muslim-majority areas ruled by India, which is dominated by Hindus. To achieve this goal, it attempts to stoke fear among the Indian population, so that India's government relinquishes control over the areas Lashkar contests.

Terrorists—whether operating transnationally or purely domestically—rarely achieve their long-term political goals. However, terrorism has dramatically reshaped many countries' security policies. In particular, terrorism impacts democratic states more than non-democratic states, because both domestic and foreign terrorists force democracies to reconsider how best to address the tradeoff embodied by Madison's Dilemma between limited and effective government. To prevent terrorist attacks, many democracies have ramped up their security policies—something we all see and experience when we go to the airport. This potentially weakens the freedoms that are central to democratic governance. Terrorism has never destroyed democracy, but it has forced citizens in democratic states to reevaluate their willingness to trade off national security and individual liberties.

suicide terrorism ■ acts of violence perpetrated against either combatants or non-combatants by individuals who are aware that they are unlikely to survive.

No explanation exists for why insurgents resort to terrorism. However, we do have a good explanation for the incidence of suicide terrorism, the use of violence for political purposes against civilian targets by individuals who are aware that they are unlikely to survive. Despite the prominence of shattering events like 9/11, relatively few groups employ suicide terrorism. Indeed, multiple suicide attacks occur in only one of every ten civil wars.[23] Still, because of the prominence of terrorist groups that employ suicide terrorism such as Lashkar-e-Taiba, al-Qaeda and

Hamas, in the remainder of this section we explore the conditions under which insurgents likely to employ such a tactic. As with other forms of political violence, explaining suicide terrorism requires considering opportunities and interests.

Hard Targets

Civil wars are likelier in poor countries with weak states and rough terrain. The absence of state authority gives insurgents opportunities to hide, build up their organizations, and win support. In a sense, civil wars are more likely against "soft targets"—weak and vulnerable states. However, the conditions that create opportunities for civil war are unlikely to give insurgents reason to use suicide terrorism. Instead, insurgents tend to employ suicide terrorism only against "hard targets"— wealthier, stronger states with accessible terrain. The reason is straightforward: other military tactics have proven ineffective.[24] Suicide terrorism is a weapon of last resort, used when other opportunities do not exist.

Consider the Israel–Palestine conflict. Because Israel is a relatively flat, wealthy country and has a strong military, standard insurgent tactics fail. There are no remote places to hide, and the state has resources to pursue and destroy insurgent groups. As a consequence, to attack Israeli territory, Palestinian groups turned to suicide terrorism. In response, Israel built a massive wall around its territory, in a largely successful effort to fence out suicide bombers. Note that when Palestinian groups attack Israelis troops or settlers in the West Bank—outside that massive wall—they rarely employ suicide bombing, precisely because they can hit and run and escape back to their own communities. Where insurgents have opportunities to survive military assaults and to build up support outside the reach of state authority, they are unlikely to ask their fighters to undertake one-way missions. Only when they have exhausted other tactics are they likely to turn to suicide terrorism.

Even when attacking a hard target, not all insurgent groups will resort to suicide terrorism. Only some kinds of insurgent groups employ this tactic—those that combine religious warfare with the provision of welfare to its supporters.

Religious "Warfare and Welfare"

Particular interests also drive suicide terrorism, which explains why insurgent groups employ it relatively rarely, even against hard targets. Suicide terrorists are not typically poor or less educated than average. In fact, many are highly educated and have good jobs. And for this reason, suicide terrorism is not associated with economic grievances—that is, we are not likely to see suicide terrorism in poor and unequal societies.

Suicide terrorism is, however, associated with one particular sort of cultural grievance: religious conflict. Suicide attackers are deeply and fervently committed to a cause, and are willing to die for it—but only if the victims come from another religion. This helps explain why suicide terrorism is rare: less than 20 percent of civil wars pit rebels of one religion against armies of a state dominated by a different religion. In separatist conflicts or civil wars driven by nonreligious disputes, we almost never see suicide attacks.

An Israeli tank patrols along the wall separating Israel from Gaza. Israel presents a "hard target," leaving Palestinian insurgents with few opportunities to engage in traditional military tactics.

Not all religious conflicts see suicide attacks, and suicide attacks are not exclusively associated with conflict between Muslims and other religions. In fact, 25 percent of all documented suicide attacks between 1946 and 2003 occurred in Sri Lanka alone, committed by the Tamil Tigers.[25] Variation even exists in the use of suicide attacks by Islamic insurgent groups: for example, in the Israel–Palestine conflict, Hamas and Hezbollah employ suicide attacks frequently, while Fatah does not. These two facts raise the questions of why we see suicide attacks in some religious conflicts but not in others, and why some religious insurgent groups use suicide attacks more often than others to promote their goals.

To explain such variation, scholars have determined that organizations that combine "warfare and welfare" are much more likely to sponsor suicide missions, rather than groups that simply engage in warfare. Some insurgent groups offer cash to an attacker's family after a successful detonation. Others provide communal health care or education, while simultaneously conducting warfare. For example, even before winning political control of the Gaza Strip in an election, Hamas provided welfare benefits to many Palestinians to offset the likelihood that many Palestinians object to using members of their community as suicide attackers. Groups that sponsor suicide bombings always confront the possibility that a bomber will get cold feet, or that a would-be attacker's friends, family, or neighbors will inform authorities in time to prevent the bombing, in the hope of receiving a reward. Of 189 Palestinian attacks attempted in Israel between 2000 and 2003, 77 were prevented.[26]

Suicide terrorism is a tactic used in both civil and international wars. It is used nearly exclusively in interreligious conflicts against "hard targets"—that is, against relatively wealthy countries with strong states and tends to be sponsored by insurgent groups that engage in "warfare and welfare." This information is useful in that it helps identify the conditions under which suicide terrorism is more or less likely to occur as part of civil conflict.

GENOCIDE

Victims of political violence sometimes claim that aggressors are guilty of genocide, a deliberate and coordinated effort to eliminate all members of a particular ethnic, religious, or national group through mass murder. Genocide differs from combatant or civilian deaths in international or civil war—no matter how severe—because it deliberately and systematically targets every man, woman, and child in a particular group. And it differs from terrorism in that it is systematic rather than random in targeting civilians for murder. Genocide also differs from episodes of mass murder that rulers sometimes commit for ideological reasons.[27]

Since the United Nations codified the definition of genocide in 1948, numerous groups have claimed status as genocide victims. The UN discourages using the term loosely because of high demand for international intervention to prevent genocide. Partly as a result, relatively few widely accepted cases exist. Those that are generally accepted as meriting the label include Turkey's murder of up to 1.5 million Armenians (1915–1920); the murder of millions of Jews, Gypsies, and other minorities during the Holocaust; Serbian "ethnic cleansing" of Bosnian Muslims in the early 1990s; the ongoing violence against residents of the Darfur region in Sudan; and Hutu efforts to exterminate the Tutsi tribe in Rwanda in 1994.

In Rwanda, upwards of one million Tutsis were murdered at the urging of the Hutu-led government. Rwanda had been a Belgian colony in the late nineteenth and early twentieth centuries. The Belgian administrators had favored the Tutsis over the Hutus, giving Tutsis privileged access to the few benefits the colonial administration provided. The Tutsis were a minority of Rwanda's population, but they retained political power after the country gained its independence in 1962. However, a Hutu-led rebellion overthrew the Tutsi government, leading to a period of civil war in the early 1990s. The UN intervened in 1993, and the Hutu president agreed to a cease-fire and a power-sharing deal. However, hardline Hutu leaders refused to comply. Later that year, unknown attackers shot down the Hutu president's airplane, and his death gave Hutu hardliners an excuse to encourage members of their tribe to murder Tutsis.

What explains why genocide occurs? As with the other sorts of political violence we have explored in this chapter, let us turn to opportunities and interests at both the domestic and international levels, using the case of Rwanda to illustrate the logic.

Ethnic War and Absent International Response

Most cases of genocide occur under a narrow set of conditions. First, ethnic divisions must exist. In Rwanda, Hutus and Tutsis recognized differences between their ethnic groups, although prior to the genocide, neither group held a particularly deep hatred for the other. In fact, Rwanda was an ethnically integrated society: Hutus and Tutsis lived and worked together, frequently intermarried, and speak

10.5 Why does genocide sometimes occur during warfare?

genocide ■ a coordinated plan seeking to eliminate all members of particular ethnic, religious, or national groups, through mass murder.

◉ Watch the Video "Western Arm Sales and the Rwandan Genocide" at mypoliscilab.com the same language. Ethnic divisions exist in many countries—even many countries that have been wracked by civil war—but, fortunately, genocide is very rare. Therefore, ethnic divisions themselves are insufficient to explain why people switch from seeing members of another ethnic group as friends, neighbors, and colleagues to seeing then as enemies who must be exterminated.

A second factor, ongoing civil war, creates the conditions for ethnic differences to degenerate into genocide. In the midst of war, law and order evaporate, while fear and uncertainty contribute to the escalation of violence. Those who participate in killing pressure others to kill; conformity is rewarded while refusal to participate is punished, often with death. In Rwanda, fear drove violence: people killed to protect themselves—from an advancing enemy army, as well as from their former friends!

A third opportunity that opens the door to genocide focuses on the international context: an inability or unwillingness of the international community to step in. In cases like the Holocaust, it is doubtful that the United States and its allies could have prevented the murder of millions. In more recent cases, the question is of both ability and willingness to intervene. Political and diplomatic obstacles often get in the way of timely intervention. For example, in Rwanda, the international community did little to stop the genocide—and, in some ways, doing nothing encouraged more violence. The UN largely withdrew its peacekeepers from the scene after they were briefly attacked; the government of France even supplied Hutu forces with weapons and denied that genocide was occurring. The U.S. government did nothing until most of the killing had stopped.

In terms of opportunities that make genocide more likely, ethnic divisions in the context of an ongoing war must be present, and the international community must be either unable or unwilling to step in. However, a particular political interest must also be at work: explicit and coercive pressure from the existing government.

Government Pressure

Even given a context of ongoing civil war, not all ethnic conflicts lead to genocide. This brings us to the final factor necessary to explain genocide: coercive pressures—not from one's neighbors—but from government leaders.[28] Genocide is not random murder motivated by bloodlust; it is deliberate, methodical and organized mass murder.

Given its systematic and organized nature, some scholars suggest that genocide is driven by strategic political calculations. It is typically ordered by a small group of leaders for a specific purpose, usually the quest to acquire, consolidate, or retain political power. In Rwanda, extremist Hutu leaders deliberately fomented violence against Tutsis; Tutsis as a group only became Hutu enemies after Hutu leaders labeled them as such. Hutu leaders used their control over TV and radio to mobilize support and disseminate propaganda that encouraged Hutus to commit acts of violence against Tutsis, and they used military and paramilitary forces to enforce compliance with their goals. When Hutu leaders who controlled the government ordered mass murder of Tutsis, killing became lawful—and failure to kill became akin to treason.

Political leaders do not organize genocide at the urging of the societies they rule. In fact, instigators and perpetrators do not even need active mass support to carry out genocide. Fear of speaking out, compliance with authority, and passivity or even indifference to suffering is as important as the active support and participation in mass

SUMMARY TABLE

Causes of Political Violence: Comparisons and Contrasts

Form of Political Violence	Definition	Opportunities	Interests	Examples Discussed
Civil war	Armed combat within the boundaries of a sovereign state between parties subject to common authority at the start of hostilities	A weak state, due to: ■ Colonial legacies ■ International environment ■ Poverty ■ Geography	■ Grievances ■ Greed ■ Pressure to join ■ Individual psychology	Sri Lanka, DRC
Revolution	Armed combat within the boundaries of a sovereign state between parties subject to common authority at the start of hostilities, in which each party claims the allegiance of a significant proportion of the state's population and which results in an insurgent victory	A weak state, due to: ■ International environment ■ Poverty ■ Geography	■ Grievances with wide popular support ■ Individual psychology	China
Suicide terrorism	Acts of violence perpetrated against either combatants or non-combatants by people who are aware that they are unlikely to survive	■ Strong states: "hard targets"	■ Specifically religious conflict ■ Insurgent groups that combine "warfare and welfare"	Israel–Palestine
Genocide	A deliberate and coordinated effort to eliminate all members of a particular ethnic, religious or national group through mass murder.	■ Ethnic divisions ■ Ongoing warfare ■ Permissive international environment	■ Leadership that sees mass murder as politically useful	Rwanda

murder. Perpetrators of genocide do not kill just for the pleasure of seeing their enemies die; they see genocide as a means to a political end. In short, genocide as a form of political violence is only likely in the context of an ongoing ethnic civil war in which the international community turns the other cheek, and in which political leaders have concluded that mass murder is a viable tactic for achieving their goals.

CONCLUSION

What causes political violence? In this chapter, we have mostly focused on violence that occurs within rather than between states, although the international context has loomed large as an explanation for when political conflict turns bloody. As with peaceful forms of political mobilization, a collective action problem underlies this question: individuals face costly risks and uncertain benefits when they decide to take up arms against the existing political order. Given the uncertainty and the dangers, most people refrain from engaging in armed combat against the state. Thus, political violence occurs infrequently, despite its prominence in the media.

To understand civil wars, revolutions, terrorism, and genocide, one must examine the opportunities open to political actors and the interests they pursue (see the table on the previous page). State weakness is the open door that may encourage civil war and revolution, but a strong state tends to be the target of suicide terrorism. As for genocide, the key opportunities include the existence of an ongoing ethnic conflict and an international community that ignores ongoing slaughter.

In terms of interests, civil conflicts tend to erupt when weak states cannot satisfy conflicting interests of different groups. Yet, because there are more ethnic and cultural grievances than cases of violence, the mere existence of political polarization cannot explain why we see violence in some places but not others. Instead, greed and coercion play critical roles in mobilizing and perpetuating civil conflict, although in some cases individuals do derive an emotional or psychological benefit from participating in insurgency. Such emotional benefits are particularly important when explaining revolutions and suicide terrorism. This is because revolutions require rebel armies to eschew coercive recruitment and cultivate a wide base of popular support, while suicide terrorism occurs in religious conflicts and when insurgent groups attempt to generate popular support by distributing social-welfare benefits.

Finally, the most extreme form of political violence, genocide, is utilized when political leaders need to rationalize horrendous violence on primordial grounds, but in truth simply use mass murder as politically expedient—a means to an end. These are just some of the opportunities and interests that explain political violence. ▲

✓•–Study and Review the Post-Test & Chapter Exam at mypoliscilab.com

KEY TERMS

REVIEW QUESTIONS

1. What are the most important causes of civil wars?
2. What is the difference between civil war and revolution?
3. What is the key to understanding why revolutions occur?
4. Under what conditions are we likely to see suicide terrorism?
5. What factors increase the likelihood of genocide?

SUGGESTED READINGS

Brass, Paul. "Elite Groups, Symbol Manipulation and Ethnic Identity among the Muslims of South Asia: Primordialist and Instrumentalist Interpretations of Ethnic Identity." In *Ethnicity and Nationalism: Theory and Comparison*, edited by Paul Brass, 69–89. New Delhi: Sage Publications, 1991. A simple constructivist explanation of how elite competition can shape mass beliefs and behavior.

Cohen, Robin. "The Making of Ethnicity: A Modest Defense of Primordialism." In *People, Nation and State*, edited by Edward Mortimer and Robert Fine, 3–11. London: I. B. Tauris, 1999. A brief argument defending the use of primordialism to explain the sources of ethnic conflict.

Elbadawi, Ibrahim, and Nicholas Sambanis. "How Much War Will We See? Explaining the Prevalence of Civil War." *The Journal of Conflict Resolution* 46, 3(2002): 307–334. A heavily empirical study of when wars start and how long they last, identifying ethnic diversity and democracy as key causes of civil conflict.

Humphreys, Macartan. "Natural Resources, Conflict, and Conflict Resolution: Uncovering the Mechanisms." *Journal of Conflict Resolution* 49(4)(2005): 508–537. Seeks out the precise way in which natural resources contribute to the onset of civil wars.

Wood, Elisabeth Jean. "The Emotional Benefits of Insurgency in El Salvador." In *Passionate Politics*, edited by Jeff Goodwin, James Jasper, and Francesca Polleta, 267–280. University of Chicago Press, 2001. Useful case study that attempts to unpack the puzzle of civil war in the absence of clear "opportunities" or "interests."

NOTES

1. See Stathis Kalyvas, *The Logic of Violence in Civil War* (New York: Cambridge University Press, 2006), 17.
2. See for example, the "Correlates of War" Project, http://correlatesofwar.org/.
3. See James Fearon and David Laitin, "Explaining Interethnic Cooperation," *American Political Science Review* 90(4)(1996): 715–735; and Nicholas Sambanis, "Using Case Studies to Expand Economic Models of Civil War," *Perspectives on Politics* 2(2)(2004): 259–279.
4. Fearon and Laitin, "Explaining," 717.
5. See for example, Paul Collier, Anke Hoeffler, and Nicholas Sambanis, "The Collier-Hoeffler Model of Civil War Onset and the Case Study Project Research Design," in *Understanding Civil War: Evidence and Analysis*, ed. Paul Collier and Nocholas Sambanis (Washington, DC: World Bank Publications, 2005), chapter 1.
6. See James Fearon and David Laitin, "Ethnicity, Insurgency, and Civil War," *American Political Science Review* 97(1)(February 2003): 75–90.
7. Collier, Hoeffler, and Sambanis, "The Collier-Hoeffler Model."
8. See for example Adam Hochschild, "Blood and Treasure," *Mother Jones*, March/April 2010, accessed December 15, 2011, http://motherjones.com/politics/2010/02/congo-gold-adam-hochschild.

9. Elizabeth Dias, "First Blood Diamonds, now Blood Computers?" *Time,* July 24, 2009, accessed December 15, 2011, http://www.time.com/time/world/article/0,8599,1912594,00.html?xid=rss-topstories.

10. See Macartan Humphreys and Jeremy Weinstein, "Handling and Manhandling Civilians in Civil War," *American Political Science Review* 100(3)(2006): 429–447; or Stathis Kalyvas and Matthew Kocher, "How 'Free' Is Free-Riding in Civil Wars? Violence, Insurgency and the Collective Action Problem," *World Politics* 59(2007): 177–216.

11. Human Rights Watch, "Trapped and Mistreated. LTTE Abuses against Civilians in the Vanni. Forced Recruitment of Adults and Children as Soldiers," 2008, accessed June 17, 2010, http://www.hrw.org/en/reports/2008/12/15/trapped-and-mistreated-0.

12. Mary Anderson, *Do No Harm: How Aid Can Support Peace—or War* (Boulder, CO: Lynne Rienner, 1999), 9.

13. Elisabeth Jean Wood "The Emotional Benefits of Insurgency in El Salvador," in *Passionate Politics*, ed. Jeff Goodwin, James Jasper, and Francesca Polleta (Chicago: University of Chicago Press, 2001), 267–280.

14. See Charles Tilly, *European Revolutions, 1492–1992* (Oxford, UK: Blackwell, 1993), 87.

15. See Eric Wolf, *Peasant Wars of the Twentieth Century* (New York: Harper and Row, 1969), 64.

16. See Theda Skocpol, *States and Social Revolutions* (New York, Cambridge University Press, 1979), 252–253.

17. Nikki Keddie, *Modern Iran: Roots and Results of Revolution* (New Haven: Yale University Press, 2003), 221–222.

18. Shaul Bakhash, *The Reign of the Ayatollahs* (New York: Basic Books, 1984), 4.

19. Quoted in Bakhash, 111.

20. See Theda Skocpol, "Rentier State and Shi'a Islam in the Iranian Revolution," *Theory and Society* 11(3)(1982): 265–283.

21. Gary LaFree and Gary Ackerman, "The Empirical Study of Terrorism: Social and Legal Research," *Annual Reviews of Law and Social Sciences* 5 (2009):347–374, 348.

22. Dean Nelson, "Mumbai Terrorist Attack Gunman Kasab Sentenced to Death," *Telegraph On-Line*, 2010 , accessed March 11, 2011, http://www.telegraph.co.uk/news/worldnews/asia/india/7685920/Mumbai-terrorist-attack-gunman-Kasab-sentenced-to-death.html.

23. See for example, Alan Krueger, *What Makes a Terrorist?* "Economics and the Roots of Terrorism" (Princeton, NJ: Princeton University Press, 2007), or Eli Berman and David Laitin, "Hard Targets: Theory and Evidence on Suicide Attacks" (working paper #11740, National Bureau of Economic Research, 2005).

24. See Krueger, *What Makes a Terrorist?*

25. See Eli Berman and David Laitin, "Religion, Terrorism and Public Goods: Testing the Club Model" (working paper #13725, National Bureau of Economic Research, 2008).

26. See Berman and Laitin (2005).

27. Benjamin Valentino explores the differences between genocide and mass killing in *Final Solutions: Mass Killing and Genocide in the Twentieth Century* (Ithaca, NY: Cornell University Press, 2004).

28. Scott Strauss, *The Order of Genocide: Race, Power and War in Rwanda* (Ithaca, NY: Cornell University Press, 2006).

Political Economy of Development

A protester outside Ireland's government buildings makes his opinion clear after learning of a series of tax increases and

> **?** How do states promote economic development?

Read and Listen to **Chapter 11** at mypoliscilab.com

Study and Review the **Pre-Test & Flashcards** at mypoliscilab.com

In September 2008, a profound economic crisis shook Ireland, similar to the one that hobbled the U.S. economy. The Irish housing market collapsed, investment levels dropped, and unemployment soared. Analysts attributed the deep recession to the bursting of an economic "bubble"—a period during which speculators, investors, and consumers buy and sell products at prices that exceed their true value. Some blamed the bubble on buyers' reckless investment decisions, while others blamed a lack of government oversight of those same risky and complex investments.

In the years preceding the 2008 crisis, Ireland's economy grew by leaps and bounds. Ireland had combined high growth rates with low government intervention in the economy. The Irish government believed such an approach was the best way to attract investment and create jobs. Many observers assumed Ireland's growth would endure, and they dubbed it the "Celtic Tiger"—a reference and comparison to the high-growth "Asian Tiger" economies of East Asia.

In contrast to Ireland's economic collapse, China's economy continues to grow by leaps and bounds—and it does so by combining high growth rates with heavy government intervention in the economy. This means that Chinese politicians rather than individual entrepreneurs have the most influence in determining the direction and success of the country's economy. Countries wishing to avoid Ireland's dismal situation and instead emulate China's economic boom have drawn a clear lesson: politicians *should* meddle in the market.

political economy ■ the study of the relationship between economics and politics.

Both the Irish recession and China's rapid growth are examples of the inextricable link between markets and governments. Political economy, the study of the relationship between economics and politics, focuses on the impact of government intervention on both individuals' ability to buy and sell as they please, as well as the country's overall rate of economic growth. Political economy concerns day-to-day issues of policymaking and governance, such as the ways in which politicians respond to economic crises; what economic policies governments attempt to implement; and how governments seek to pay for those policies—usually through taxation. Those who study political economy also consider important questions of political philosophy, such as the tension between individual freedom of choice and communal goals, such as equality of economic opportunity.

economic development ■ sustained increase in the standard of living of a country's population, resulting from changes and improvements in education, infrastructure, and technology.

Political economy is integral to political science because so much of politics is about how and why people mobilize to advance their economic interests, and how government policies favor some people, while imposing economic burdens on others. Economic development is sustained increase in the standard of living of a country's population, resulting from changes and improvements in wealth, education, infrastructure, and technology—the kind of change China has experienced since the 1980s. In this chapter, we focus on one of the most important questions of political economy: *how do states promote economic development?* The answer to this question is the Holy Grail for students of political economy, because a definitive answer could improve the lives of billions of people around the world.

Ireland and China represent very different economic paths. Because we cannot predict the future, we do not know whether China will come to regret the heavy hand of government in the economy over the long run—or whether Ireland will recover and regain its economic footing. Which approach best promotes long-term, sustained growth? Consider three key ways we can compare and contrast China and Ireland: the timing of state formation, democracy versus non-democracy, and experience with colonization.

Both Ireland and China have had to overcome a historical legacy of colonialism. Ireland only gained independence from the UK in 1922 and remained quite poor up through the 1960s. China was exploited and partially occupied by foreign powers from the 1800s through World War II, and its state remained extremely weak until 1949, due to a violent civil war. Only in the last 30 years has China managed to grow out of poverty.

Today, Ireland is a democracy, and has based its recent growth on free market principles—an economic system in which private individuals and firms (rather than the government) own and have rights to make all decisions about buying and selling property and goods such as land, financial assets such as stocks and bonds, and productive industries. In contrast, China is a non-democratic interventionist state, in which the central government allocates resources, makes investment decisions, and owns many of the country's productive industries and resources.

Variation on all states' experience with these three factors—democracy or non-democracy, the degree of state intervention in the economy, and experiences with colonialism—helps explain diverging patterns of economic development. Before delving into these three factors, let us first explore the fundamental question of political economy: why all states intervene in the market.

free market principles ■ an economic system in which individuals and firms, rather than the government, have rights to make all decisions about buying and selling private property such as land, stock, commodities, or productive industries.

interventionist state ■ an economic system in which the central government allocates resources, makes investment decisions, and owns many of the country's productive industries and/or resources.

STATES AND MARKETS

If asked what kind of state best promotes economic development, many Americans might respond by arguing that the state has no business promoting economic growth—and if only the government would get its sticky paws out of the economy, the United States would grow by leaps and bounds, creating good jobs and generating a better standard of living for everyone. Unfortunately, a complete separation of market and state is unrealistic because politics and economics influence each other at every level, from individual shopping decisions to international financial flows.

In theory, an economic market is a system of choice: individuals and firms choose how to produce the goods that consumers seek to purchase. Ideally, markets function

11.1 What is the relationship between states and markets?

economic market ■ mechanism of choice as to how firms produce goods and how consumers consume goods.

◉ Watch the **Video** "Environment and Economic Growth in China" at **mypoliscilab.com**

> **SUMMARY TABLE**
>
> ### Main Factors Influencing Paths of Economic Development
>
> Democracy versus Non-Democracy
>
> Degree of State Intervention in the Economy
>
> Colonial Legacies

as self-sufficient and decentralized mechanisms of coordinating supply and demand. Yet, by their nature, markets operate in tension with states, which exert centralized, sovereign authority over a territory and its population. Politics and markets clash because all states extend their coercive authority into the economic sphere, constraining individuals' freedom of choice in the process. Governments intervene in economic markets for a simple reason: states would cease to exist without a revenue source, and no state in world history has successfully maintained sovereignty by asking for voluntary contributions. States need tax revenue to provide their essential service: providing law and order.

What All States Take: Taxes

States intervene in the economy because they need taxes to survive. Yet, from the perspective of the state's rulers, tax collection is a massive collective action problem. This is because every citizen has incentives to free ride off everyone else—each expects that it is someone else's responsibility to pay for public services. How do governments solve this collective action problem? In many countries, authorities try to develop citizens' emotional attachments to the state by promoting patriotism and nationalism. Most governments also attempt to enhance state legitimacy by appealing to citizens' interests, providing economic assistance to specific groups, as the U.S. government does through Social Security payments, Medicare health insurance, or farm subsidies, for example.

People who receive government assistance tend to support those programs. Yet, even highly successful appeals to citizens' emotions and interests do not always overcome the free-rider problem: states would never receive enough voluntary tax contributions to survive. Instead, they must coerce citizens to pay. While this infringes on individual liberty, most people pay their taxes because of what the state provides in return: an escape from the anarchy that Hobbes described as a "state of nature." Moreover, economists agree that states can provide a crucial service that an unregulated free market cannot: protection against market failures.

What Some States Give: Protection against Market Failures

market failure ■ the failure of an economic market to produce or distribute needed or wanted goods or services.

Why do all states meddle in the market to some extent? States intervene to prevent market failures, which occur when an economy fails to produce or distribute necessary goods or services. In the late 2000s, the U.S. government intervened to prevent a complete collapse of the country's (and perhaps the world's) financial system. The government spent hundreds of billions of dollars to prop up a number of large banks that were in danger of going out of business, fearing that if those financial institutions collapsed, the rest of the system would fail as well, endangering not just the fat cats on Wall Street but the life savings of every average American. In crises like these, economists agree that the only solutions are political, not economic, and state intervention is warranted. Let us explore different sorts of market failures in order to understand why states frequently intervene in markets.

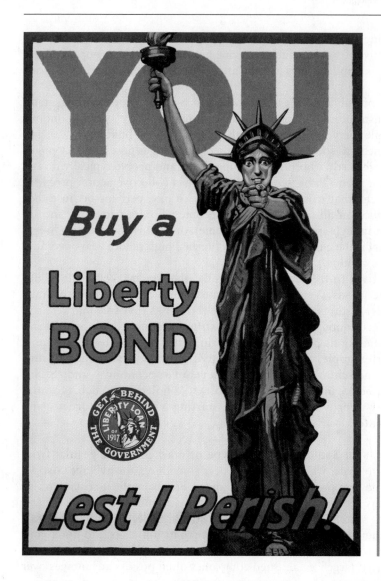

Even in the midst of total war, patriotic posters fail to help governments raise sufficient resources. The state must use coercion to raise taxes to avoid the free-rider problem.

Public Goods   The key reason states compel contributions is because the most important services they supply are public goods. Recall that public goods are things that by their very nature no one can be excluded from consuming—they are available to all citizens, not just to specific groups. For example, clean air is a public good: no matter how heavily you breathe, no one else will suffocate. Other common examples include transportation systems—roads, bridges, highways, railways, subways, and airports—public schools and hospitals, national parks, libraries, and national defense systems. Once a public good is created, nobody can be

private goods ■
goods that only one
person or a few people
can consume.

excluded from using it. Yet, most things people use or consume are not public goods but rather private goods, which only one person or a select group of people can consume. For example, apples are private goods: if you eat an apple, no one else can.

The provision of public goods tends to benefit a society: for example, states that invest in infrastructure and public education tend to have better economic outcomes. Yet, while everyone might agree that clean air, well-built highways, and good schools are useful to society, the provision of these items poses a tricky political problem: they are costly to produce and maintain, and people typically do not volunteer to pay for them. Public-goods provision is a collective action problem: most individuals deny that it is their responsibility to pay, perhaps because they do not use the services at all (as is the case of people who drive to work and see no reason to invest in high-speed rail, for example), or because they are no longer using the service (as is the case of people who finished high school years ago and/ or who do not have children).

Because incentives to free ride are so strong, the free market tends to underproduce public goods. Yet, precisely because public goods tend to make everyone better off, if states step in to provide the things that free markets can or will not, then economic intervention is justified. Around the world, states that invest in public-goods provision tend to do better on long-term economic development. For example, China has invested its taxpayers' money in new roads, highways, and schools in its effort to develop its economy—and this investment seems to be paying off nicely. In contrast, a failed state such as Somalia lacks the ability to provide public goods, starting with law and order—and its economy stagnates.

**increasing returns to
scale** ■ an economic
principle that states
that when a firm
produces a product,
the average cost of
producing each unit
of the product de-
creases as the scale of
production increases,
which can result in
monopoly.

monopoly ■
a situation in which
a single firm controls
the production,
distribution, or sale
of a particular good,
forcing all others out
of business and
preventing new
competitors from
emerging.

Increasing Returns to Scale A second type of market failure results from increasing returns to scale: when a firm produces something, the average cost per unit decreases as the firm produces more and more. For example, it costs your local electric company a tremendous amount of money to build a power plant and to set up the utility system that produces and distributes electricity. However, it costs the electric company next to nothing, relative to its initial cost, to hook your house up once the system has been built. The economic implication of increasing returns to scale is that larger, established companies often possess advantages over smaller, newer companies. Once the electric company has set up its distribution network, an entrepreneur would be hard-pressed to set up a competing power plant and distribution network, given the high start-up costs and likely market penetration of the existing electric company. The established company could even drive the new company out of business by temporarily discounting its prices at an unprofitable rate.

Increasing returns to scale are linked to market failures because they often lead to a monopoly, a situation in which a single firm controls the production, distribution, or sale of a particular product, which forces all others out of business and prevents new competitors from entering the market. A monopoly is a market failure, because in the absence of competition, one firm can set prices for its product above what a competitive free market would allow. Under these circumstances, members of a society are limited in their access to that product or service—and when this occurs, the monopolistic firm profits, but consumers lose.

Monopolies are inefficient because prices are not determined by supply and demand, and for this reason, politicians justify government regulation over particular markets. For example, Microsoft was forced to settle a lawsuit in the United States about whether its practice of inserting and giving away the web browser Internet Explorer created a monopoly that destroyed competition in that segment of the software industry; a similar suit resulted in $1.5 billion in fines from the European Union. Most governments around the world regulate monopolistic practices in some circumstances, because of the potentially negative political consequences—for consumers as well as the government—that result when private sector companies inflate prices beyond what a competitive market would bear.

Externality A third form of market failure is called an externality. An externality is something that an individual or organization does that affects the welfare of others, whether on purpose or not. A common example of an externality is pollution. For example, British Petroleum (BP) invests a great deal of money sinking oil wells into the ocean floor under the Gulf of Mexico, in the hope of profiting by finding large supplies of petroleum. However, if an oil spill occurs—as in summer 2010, when a BP oil platform caught fire and sank, releasing hundreds of thousands of barrels of crude oil into the Gulf—the pollution imposes costs on nearby individuals, businesses, and property owners—expenses that the polluter may not have to pay.

For example, those who wish to sell their homes face lower property values due to the presence of the pollution and likely recurrence of future pollution, and those who face health problems from the effects of pollution must pay for additional medical care. In this example, BP is the source of the externality; all else equal, if it had never built that oil well, the people in the region would not have incurred those additional costs. Because the disaster was so massive and damaging, individuals and the government sued to force BP to clean up and provide compensation. However, in many cases responsibility for an externality is unclear.

The BP oil spill generates the impression that all externalities are bad, but this is not true. Some externalities impose unforeseen costs, but others generate unforeseen benefits. For example, that BP oil well generates jobs and income for the same people affected by the pollution. Economic activities can produce both positive and negative externalities, depending on who is affected, how, and to what extent. The point is that private economic decisions (to drill for oil, for example) may be optimal or suboptimal from a public point of view, depending on the total costs and benefits of both the positive and negative externalities. When positive externalities occur, everybody is happy. But if the negative externalities outweigh the positive, we have

externality ∎
an action that affects the welfare of others, whether on purpose or not.

BP's *Deepwater Horizon* oil well on fire in June 2010. This accident caused negative externalities for millions of Americans who live on or near the Gulf of Mexico.

a market failure: society is made worse off, and the private sector will not willingly pay society for those losses.

Governments step in to rectify market failures that arise from negative externalities. For example, in the absence of government regulation and environmental laws, it is not clear that BP would have to pay for damage caused by its oil rig explosion. As with regulation of monopolies, negative externalities provide politicians with a rationale to regulate industries, levy taxes, allocate investment, and redistribute resources.

When the free market fails—whether in the form of failure to provide public goods, the consequences of increasing returns to scale, or the impact of externalities—neither individuals nor society as a whole can invest resources efficiently to provide a stable, positive rate of return. Markets are almost always inefficient in some way—for some individuals, all of society, or both. Ideally, by preventing market failures, governments improve everyone's lives. Yet, generating public goods that improve literally everyone's lives in a society is complicated. After all, we cannot assume governments have everyone's best interests in mind. Instead, governments may be corrupt, under the influence of narrow interests, or just incompetent. This tension between what states can do in the market and what

> **SUMMARY TABLE**
>
> ### Why Do States Intervene? To Prevent Market Failures
>
> | Type of Market Failure | Definition | Example |
> |---|---|---|
> | Public goods | Things that by their very nature no one can be excluded from consuming | Clean air |
> | Monopoly | A situation in which a single firm controls the production, distribution, or sale of a particular product, forcing all others out of business and preventing new competitors from entering the market | Microsoft's alleged privileging of web browser Internet Explorer |
> | Externalities | Something that an individual or organization does that affects the welfare of others, whether on purpose or not | Unexpected explosion of BP oil rig, causing pollution |

they actually do returns us to this chapter's main question: are some states better or worse at fostering the political conditions that generate economic growth? To answer this question, let's return to the comparison of the Ireland and China, and consider the question of whether democracy or non-democracy is better for development.

DEMOCRACY VERSUS NON-DEMOCRACY

All states intervene in the market, to prevent market failures. The question is, do some types of states promote development better than others? Do some kinds of states actually impede economic development? In this section and the next, we consider which types of state institutions best foster economic development. The discussion focuses on the impact of two aspects of state institutions: whether the state is a democracy or not, and whether the state takes a relatively free-market approach to the economy—as in Ireland or the United States, for example—or a more interventionist approach, as in China.

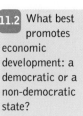

11.2 What best promotes economic development: a democratic or a non-democratic state?

👁 Watch the **Video**
"China's New Rich"
at **mypoliscilab.com**

command economy

■ an economy in which the central government controls and coordinates virtually all economic activity.

Figure 11.1 charts democratic and non-democratic states according to their level of intervention in the economy. On the horizontal axis, we have the degree to which a country is democratic or not, while on the vertical axis, we consider the extent to which the state intervenes in the economy. Free-market systems see relatively limited government intervention in the economy. At the other end of the vertical axis, command economies are highly interventionist states in which the government controls and coordinates virtually all economic activity. Placement of any country on this figure will be imprecise. However, we can put Ireland in the upper-right corner as a free-market democracy and place China towards the lower-left as a non-democracy where the government intervenes relatively heavily.

Note the placement of Ireland and Germany: Both are democracies like the United States, but Ireland is slightly more laissez faire than the United States, while Germany intervenes in its economy relatively more. Of the non-democracies, Singapore takes the same hands-off approach as Ireland, while South Korea's government—like Germany's—takes a more interventionist approach. North Korea, a totalitarian non-democracy, most closely resembles a command economy and has almost no free market whatsoever.

In the rest of this section, we focus on the question, "Is democracy or non-democracy the best way to promote rapid and efficient economic development?" Given the rapid growth of countries like Singapore, South Korea (which was a non-democracy until 1987), and now China, many observers believe that non-democracies are better than democracies at solving market failures and promoting economic growth. Let us consider why this might be the case, and then assess the evidence.

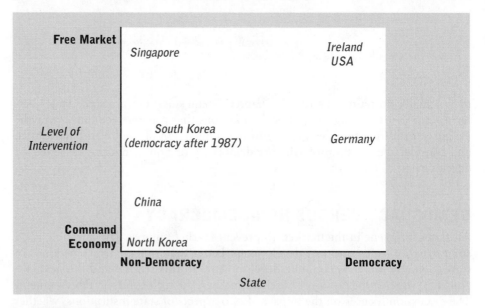

FIGURE 11.1

Levels of State Intervention under Democracy and Non-Democracy

This figure shows where democratic and non-democratic countries are situated on the spectrum of market and command economies. Notice the positions of China and Ireland. Consider where other countries might fall.

Scholars have long suggested that a tradeoff may exist between democracy and development, in that more democracy means less development.[1] The logic is as follows: under democracy, individuals have the right to demand resources from the state. In addition, interest groups and political parties have one overriding goal: to protect and advance the private interests of their supporters—even at the expense of the "public interest," the entirety of society. Elected leaders know that if they fail to respond to citizens' demands, they might lose their jobs. Yet, to the extent that governments respond to the louder and better-organized special-interest groups for increased spending on particular programs rather than to overall public opinion, taxes must also rise, potentially crowding out money for investment in the private sector.

In contrast, non-democratic governments are more insulated from the demands of political parties, interest groups, and lobbies. In theory, this means that non-democratic governments can make decisions to invest in public goods more efficiently, with no "crowding out" of the private sector. Insulation from organized interests for government assistance should—in theory—result in better economic growth. Given this, some have suggested that democracy hinders economic growth.

While this argument makes sense in theory, it suffers from two key flaws. First, non-democratic rulers are not always public-minded benevolent dictators who seek to provide public goods to everyone in society. In fact, the very insulation of these dictators from the general public gives them greater leeway to engage in corruption or make inefficient economic decisions that line their own pockets and those of their cronies, at the expense of everyone else. They also do not fear the political consequences that might come at the next election under a democracy. This insight turns the argument in favor of non-democracy on its head and suggests that the possibility of accountability makes democracy a better environment for economic development because it forces elected leaders to take economic efficiency into their political calculations.

Second, democracies protect individual property rights more than do non-democratic states. When people fear that their government may strip them of their possessions at any time, there's little incentive to work more or invest in the first place, so insecure property rights will hinder economic development. In a democracy, the separation of powers, an independent judiciary, and politicians' concern over reelection necessarily limits politicians' ability to radically alter the structure of property relations. In contrast, dictators are more likely to believe they can expropriate income or property without losing their grip on power.[2] Economists know that entrepreneurs and investors desire predictability—which is greater under democracy, where the policies may change but the fundamental rules of the game generally do not. Dictators may not only change policies, they may also change the rules of the game, with no accountability.

So which system is better—democracy or non-democracy—for promoting economic growth? We've offered arguments that could go either way—and empirical research is similarly inconclusive.[3] It is true that most wealthy countries are democracies, and most poor countries are not. Unfortunately, this is not evidence that democracy causes better economic growth. The causal connection may very well run in the opposite direction: perhaps economic growth causes democracy. There is no convincing evidence that either democracy or non-democracy is superior to the other in terms of promoting economic growth.

The debate about the merits of democracy and non-democracy has wide-ranging real-world implications. It figures, for example, in political discussions within the World Bank, the International Monetary Fund, the United Nations, and other international organizations about how best to lift developing nations out of poverty. In the 1970s and 1980s, many analysts in such organizations suggested that although non-democracies in Latin America, Africa, Asia, and elsewhere—such as Singapore or South Korea—violated human rights, at least they grew their economies. After all, the argument went, one cannot enjoy the rights and privileges of a democracy if one cannot eat. The implication was that poor countries could only afford the "luxury" of democracy after they had experienced sustained economic development, justifying World Bank, IMF, and U.S. policies that overlooked citizens' rights in numerous non-democratic regimes around the world.

Despite the recent rapid growth of China and slowdown in the United States, scholars have never found clear empirical evidence that democracy undermines or slows development and that non-democracy speeds it. Given this, the argument for tolerating dictators loses validity, because there is no evidence that governments have to sacrifice citizens' rights for the economy to grow. The lack of clear empirical findings in this debate provides democracy with powerful moral support: non-democracy provides citizens with no economic advantage, but it certainly offers political and social disadvantages. Democracies perform much better than non-democracies on indicators of human welfare, such as individual liberties,

SUMMARY TABLE

Economic Development: Democracy or Non-Democracy?

Hypothesis	Arguments for	Arguments against
Democracy impedes development.	Leaders must respond to special-interest pressures for spending, raising taxes and spending on economically unproductive activities.	Property rights broadly considered are better-protected under democracy, where rule of law exists.
Non-democracy impedes development.	Leaders are insulated from special-interest pressures for spending, thus more efficient managers of the economy.	Leaders are rarely purely public-minded; they are often corrupt, wasteful, and inefficient managers of the economy.

access to a legal system, and protection against random jailing or torture—all of which are public goods. Economic growth is not the only important public good; civil liberties and human rights are—or at least they ought to be.

We began this section by considering the different ways democracies and non-democracies promote economic growth. On the one hand, there might be a tradeoff between democracy and development. If elected leaders have to respond to organized special interests to keep their jobs, perhaps democracies hinder economic growth. Yet, on the other hand, perhaps non-democratic rulers' very insulation explains why no empirical evidence supports the hypothesized tradeoff between democracy and development. Many non-democratic rulers are corrupt, believing that control of the forces of repression lets them rule as they please.

The answer to this section's question—neither democracy nor dictatorship—is not very satisfying. However, this ambiguity does lead to one important conclusion—that there is no economic justification for supporting non-democracy. Like all politicians, dictators desire to hold on to power, and non-democratic leaders often attempt to justify their rule as a more efficient means of leading their citizens toward economic prosperity. Yet, we now know that such a claim does not hold water.

DEGREES OF STATE INTERVENTION

In response to this chapter's question, *how do states promote economic development?* thus far we have considered the impact of the distinction between democracy and non-democracy. In addition, political economists consider the state's level of intervention in the economy. Not all democracies model themselves after Ireland or the United States in supporting free markets. As Figure 11.1 revealed, some democratic states—such as Germany or South Korea, for example—are far more interventionist. Likewise, not all non-democracies are command economies like North Korea. China's state is now less interventionist than it once was, but other non-democracies—such as Singapore, for example—enact free-market principles even more than does the Unites States. Where along the vertical axis in Figure 11.1 offers the best recipe for long-term growth?

A state's position along the vertical axis of Figure 11.1 refers to its ability to influence or control individuals' and groups' economic decisions. At the top of the axis are states that deliberately take a laissez-faire approach to economic intervention and have a relatively "free" market, in which individuals and groups can acquire capital, invest, and buy and sell with minimal government interference. In contrast, at the bottom of the vertical axis, the state controls all economic decisions entirely: the central government allocates all economic resources, makes all investment decisions, and owns most of the country's productive industries and/or resources, leaving little room for the free market economy. Let us consider arguments for different degrees of state intervention in the economy—the light hand of a free market economy, the heavy intervention of a command economy, or a middle ground of social democracies or state-led development.

11.3 What best promotes economic development: a free market, or an interventionist state?

Watch the Video **"David Cameron on Corporate Social Responsibility"** at **mypoliscilab.com**

Explore the Comparative **"Development"** at **mypoliscilab.com**

Free Markets versus Command Economies

Advocates of the free market have long trumpeted the benefits of limited government intervention in the economy. In classical political thought, liberalism emphasizes individual political and economic freedom of choice—equality of opportunity. Consequently, economic liberalism is an approach that favors minimal state involvement in the economy as the best recipe for growth. Economic liberals promote laissez-faire economic policies, such as minimal government regulation of the economy, low tax rates, low government expenditures, and low tariffs and other barriers to imports as the best ways to both protect private property and encourage productive investment. This approach suggests that states should only provide the minimum necessary public goods for the market to flourish. In short, economic liberalism favors individual freedom of choice. The United States is the world's most prominent example of economic liberalism in action; other examples include Ireland and Singapore.

Despite the ideology of minimal government, even economically liberal states see extensive government involvement in regulating the market and establishing rules and legal procedures for investment and economic production. For example, the U.S. government sets interest rates, controls the money supply, imposes trade barriers, grants subsidies to producers of certain goods, and enacts countless rules and regulations governing every aspect of the economy. Moreover, the U.S. government does not simply let the chips fall where they may during severe economic crises. A truly non-interventionist government would let companies that make mistakes go out of business. However, after the collapse of several major investment banks in 2008, the U.S. government under Republican President George W. Bush initiated a program to bail out several Wall Street financial corporations with taxpayer money. Even free-market economies see considerable government intervention. Even so, many countries' governments intervene far more extensively in the market. Let us now consider the argument in favor of a heavily interventionist state.

At the extreme, such systems are command economies. In command economies, the market does not determine supply, demand, or prices—the government does. Communism and socialism are examples of political ideologies that advocate heavy state intervention to reduce economic inequalities, and they, thus, advocate an approach towards the "command economy" end of the vertical axis in Figure 11.1. The Soviet Union (until its collapse around 1990), China before the 1980s, contemporary North Korea, and Cuba are examples of command economies.

Although few truly command economies exist today, many states remain heavily interventionist, owning important companies or controlling entire industries. The government of China, for example, owns at least 143,000 corporations, which account for about 20 percent of all Chinese corporate assets.[4] Many of these companies are quite small, but some are among China's largest businesses—including China Mobile, the world's largest cell-phone company by number of subscribers; Baoshan Steel, the third-largest iron and steel company in the world and the largest in China; and PetroChina, an energy conglomerate that in 2010 was the most valuable corporation in the world, in terms of stock price.[5] The Chinese government also owns businesses that employ millions of people in such industries as shipbuilding, electronics, avionics, power generation, vehicle manufacturing, transportation,

economic liberalism
■ an ideology that favors minimal state involvement in the economy as the best recipe for growth.

mining, forestry and pharmaceuticals, among others. These industries provide jobs, goods, and services—and in theory, the government uses the profits from such enterprises to improve the lives of everyone in society.

Many states also intervene in the economy by setting below-market prices on certain goods—such as food and gasoline—to protect consumers. For example, in Venezuela—one of the world's largest exporters of oil—the government subsidizes the price of gasoline to keep voters happy. A gallon of gas costs just five cents, far below the actual cost. Other governments attempt to manipulate the value of the national currency for political purposes. In China, a key way the government intervenes in the economy is by artificially undervaluing its currency relative to other countries' currencies. This makes it cheaper for people in other countries to buy Chinese exports—and, thus, helps Chinese firms build market share around the world. Like many other countries, China also restricts many kinds of imports, to make them more expensive relative to domestically produced goods.

Advocates of an interventionist state argue that minimal state involvement in the economy is insufficient to jump-start or maintain economic growth. They also claim that the consequences of market failures often fall most heavily on the unlucky or unfortunate, meaning that free-market capitalism tends to generate economic inequalities for which there is no free-market solution. For example, many argue that without a bailout from other European governments, the Irish economy would have collapsed completely, hurting those without a financial safety net—the unemployed and poor—the most. The debate over the bailout neatly illustrates the question—one that governments and citizens around the world confront—of how best to resolve market failures. Proponents of state intervention—contrary to proponents of economic liberalism—hold that sacrificing some individual economic freedom is necessary to provide public goods and support the welfare of everyone in society.

The views we have considered—a free market and an interventionist state—are two ends of a wide spectrum. Some governments can clearly be classified as tending towards the "free-market" or "interventionist" end of the spectrum. However, many states take a third path, one that adopts elements of both the free market and state intervention. Let us now consider whether this middle ground can promote long-term development.

Social Democracies and State-Led Development

Contemporary debate about what amount of intervention is best to promote economic development sometimes sounds like the story of Goldilocks and the Three Bears: a state that intervenes too little and provides no public goods is a failed state, but a state that intervenes too much may stifle economic activity. Many argue that a middle ground between minimum and maximum state intervention is the best recipe for eliminating poverty and promoting growth. There are two approaches to this middle path: social democracy and state-led development.

Germany is an example of the first approach. On the one hand, Germany has some of the world's largest and most competitive private corporations. However, it is also an example of social democracy, a political ideology with roots in the late 1800s that tries to balance capitalist markets and private property with a greater

social democracy ■
a political ideology practiced widely across contemporary European states that tries to balance capitalist markets and private property with some degree of state intervention in the economy to ameliorate problems of economic inequality.

degree of state intervention in the economy than liberalism recommends, in an effort to ameliorate the economic inequalities that the free market tends to create.

Social democracy has been put into practice in several Western European states. In contrast to communism, social democracy advocates reforming rather than destroying capitalism by creating generous public pension systems and unemployment benefits, free or heavily subsidized public health care systems, and subsidized public education all the way through graduate school. Such efforts to redistribute wealth, encourage social mobility, and protect the relatively poor through social welfare expenditures mean higher tax rates.

state-led development ■ a strategy to promote economic growth that includes such policies as government coordination of private-sector investment, forced savings, and preferential treatment to certain industries regarded as essential for national economic development.

The second middle-ground approach is the path taken more recently by poor countries that seek to develop their economies as rapidly as possible, such as Japan, South Korea, and China. This path is state-led development, in which the government coordinates private sector investments, encourages individuals to save rather than spend their income, and gives preferential treatment to certain industries regarded as essential for national economic development. State-led development strategies are less concerned than social democracy with questions of inequality and redistribution—for example, Japan, South Korea, and China do not have particularly large "welfare state" policies that protect the economic and social well-being of the poor—and focus most on growing the economy.

Countries that have adopted state-led development are not command economies, but they do enact considerable state intervention in the market—much more than Ireland, the United States, Singapore, or other free-market economies. To be sure, individual private enterprise has been thriving in China, especially in manufacturing and exporting industries. Since the 1980s, China has pulled back from communism's command economy. Its government in effect admitted that communism had failed and that a dose of free-market capitalism would help grow the economy. However, in no sense can we say that China now has a "free market" economy like Ireland. In comparative perspective, China's government remains far above average in terms of state intervention in the economy.

Identifying precisely where a state falls on the vertical axis of Figure 11.1 is difficult. However, comparing states on a continuum of more or relatively less state intervention in the economy allows us to consider what sort of state best promotes economic development. Where along the vertical axis of Figure 11.1 is best? The relative advantages of the free market versus intervention have driven centuries of debate. In recent years, many observers have concluded that the rapid success of countries such as South Korea and China provides evidence that a relatively strong interventionist state is best, rather than a free-market liberal state.[6] Should states do more than minimally setting the conditions for a free market to flourish? Can state intervention in the economy quickly solve market failures and generate rapid economic development? Let us see what the evidence says.

Earlier we noted that democracy appears no better than non-democracy at promoting economic development. Yet, what degree of state intervention is best? Can a state be too interventionist—or not interventionist enough? Let's see whether empirical evidence supports prescribing a strong state or a weak state, or something in between. Take a look at Table 11.1, which shows the level of per capita income

TABLE 11.1

Richest and Poorest Countries in Terms of Yearly Per Capita Income and Overall Tax Burden, 2008

Richest Countries	Per Capita Income	Taxes as a Percent of GDP	Poorest Countries	Per Capita Income	Taxes as a Percent of GDP
Luxembourg	72,039	36.4	Uganda	1,077	12.6
Norway	49,416	43.6	Burkina Faso	1,072	11.5
Singapore	45,553	13.0	Mali	1,043	15.3
United States	42,809	28.2	Haiti	1,038	9.4
Ireland	39,433	34.0	Nepal	1,020	10.9
Netherlands	38,048	39.5	Guinea	975	8.2
Switzerland	37,788	30.1	Madagascar	974	10.7
Iceland	36,113	40.4	Rwanda	949	14.1
Canada	36,102	33.4	Ethiopia	802	11.6
Austria	35,866	43.4	Mozambique	774	13.4
Australia	35,624	30.5	Togo	767	15.5
UK	34,204	39.0	Malawi	744	20.7
Denmark	34,005	50.0	Timor-Leste	740	10.0
Sweden	33,769	49.7	Sierra Leone	723	10.5
Germany	33,668	40.6	Central African Rep.	685	7.7
Belgium	33,544	46.8	Niger	631	11.0
Finland	33,377	43.6	Guinea-Bissau	496	11.5
Bahrain	32,233	2.4	Liberia	358	13.2
Japan	31,464	27.4	Burundi	354	17.4
Eq. Guinea	31,309	1.7	Dem. Rep. Congo	290	13.2

Source: World Bank, World Development Indicators, accessed July 1, 2010, http://data.worldbank.org/data-catalog

Gross Domestic Product (GDP) ■ a measure of a country's total economic output.

in the world's 20 richest and 20 poorest countries in 2008, and also shows the proportion of Gross Domestic Product (GDP), a measure of a country's total economic output, that each government takes as tax revenue.

If you were to place all the wealthiest countries from Table 11.1 on the vertical axis of Figure 11.1, you would find that the degree of state intervention in the economy—measured by the proportion of GDP taken as taxes—varies considerably. Bahrain and Equatorial Guinea both have populations of less than one million and sit upon immense supplies of oil, so it is no surprise that they are wealthy but tax their citizens very little. As for the rest, the tax burden ranges from 13 percent of GDP in the bastion of free-market economic liberalism of Singapore, all the way up to 50 percent in Denmark, a social democracy. This means that the world's wealthiest countries can be placed at various points along the upper half of the vertical axis in Figure 11.1. As for the poorest countries on the right-hand side of Table 11.1, here we see more consistency in terms of the tax burden: all the world's poorest countries are "low tax" states.

According to the ideology of economic liberalism, the lower the tax rate, the better the environment for business and investors to profit. However, in global perspective, this is not the case. Instead, most of the wealthiest countries in the world have relatively high overall tax rates—higher even than the United States. This relationship between high taxes and high wealth—which contradicts the ideology of free-market economic liberalism—holds up when one considers all the countries in the world: in general, the higher the tax rate, the wealthier the country. Figure 11.2 reveals this relationship, with data from the Heritage Foundation, a free-market think tank.

The horizontal axis is the Heritage Foundation's "Economic Freedom" score for 176 countries; higher scores represent a free market economy like Ireland, while lower scores represent heavy intervention, like North Korea. The vertical axis maps the proportion of taxes as GDP in each of those countries. The cloud of points seems to slope upward, indicating that even the Heritage Foundation regards higher-tax economies as more competitive. In fact, the average proportion of taxes as GDP in the top half of the competitiveness ranking is 26.1 percent, while in the bottom half of the ranking it is 18.4 percent—taxes are higher in "more competitive" economies.

Taxes apparently do not stifle economic growth. Why not? The reason is that many of the world's poorest states are also among the world's weakest states. Weak states are ineffective and illegitimate—they fail to provide public goods such as political stability and law and order, which means they fail to create the conditions necessary for economic growth. These states do not have the capacity to extract higher taxes, even if they wanted to.

Not all of the world's poorest states are weak states: some relatively poor states—such as Zimbabwe, North Korea, and Cuba—are among the world's strongest in terms of effectiveness—but only in the sense of having overwhelming coercive control over society and the economy. In these countries, governments deliberately crush most if not all private sector initiative. None of the world's wealthiest states today have the degrees of political control over the economy that these three countries do—not even China.

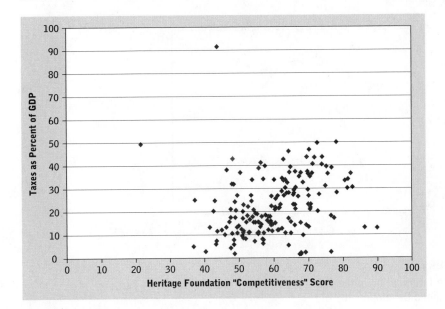

FIGURE 11.2

Size of the State and Economic Competitiveness

The Heritage Foundation ranks countries based on their economic competitiveness. Placing the ranking alongside a country's proportion of GDP taken in taxes paradoxically indicates that higher taxes are associated with economic competitiveness.

Source: Heritage Foundation, "2011 Index Raw Data" (Microsoft Excel Spreadsheet), accessed July 12, 2011, http://www.heritage.org/index/download.

The fact that both extremely weak and extremely strong states seem unlikely to foster economic growth returns us to Goldilocks: what level of state intervention is "just right"? As Figure 11.2 suggests, most wealthy societies are not "minimal government" states that tax very little. Yet extremely heavy state intervention also does not seem to be a great recipe for long-term growth. Most of the wealthiest countries in the world are high-tax social democracies like Germany—states that combine market capitalism with a strong dose of government intervention. In turn, the countries least likely to see sustained economic growth over the long-term have states that are too weak or too strong. Figure 11.3 illustrates the potential relationship between state intervention in the economy and the prospects for long-term economic development.

When the state is too weak or too strong, the prospects for development are low. Governments in the weakest states underinvest in public goods, corruption is rampant, and politics is often highly unstable. All of these conditions hinder productive long-term investment. Meanwhile, governments in the strongest states not only impose high taxes but also expropriate wealth and property, often arbitrarily—again, conditions that are not likely to foster long-term economic development. Just like Goldilocks, the degree of state intervention in the economy that is "just right" falls somewhere in the middle, at the peak of the inverted-U-shaped curve. However, the degree of state intervention that leads to success can vary

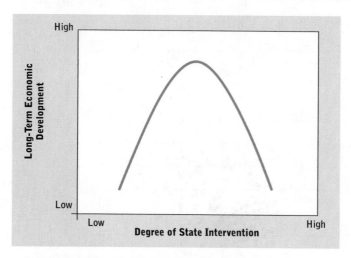

FIGURE 11.3

State Intervention in the Economy and the Prospects for Long-Term Economic Development

This figure suggests that the optimal level of state intervention is neither too high nor too low. Consider where countries such as the United States, Ireland, China, or Germany might fall along the curve.

considerably—from economically liberal free-market states to fairly interventionist social democracies or countries that have adopted state-led development policies.

All states intervene in the market to some extent—and differences in the degree of state intervention underlie variation in long-term economic performance across countries and over time. What we've discovered in this section is that governments can intervene too little—as in weak states such as Somalia or the Democratic Republic of the Congo (DRC)—or they can intervene too much, as in North Korea or Cuba. Too little or too much intervention destroys the conditions necessary for sustained long-term economic development. However, along the vertical axis from "free market" to "interventionist" in Figure 11.1, there appears to be no single institutional recipe that will eliminate poverty and promote development. States can succeed by adopting free-market principles like the United States, Ireland, or Singapore, or they can succeed by taking a more interventionist approach, like Germany, South Korea, or China. This finding may be somewhat unsatisfying, but it also warns against the uncritical acceptance and application of any particular "one size fits all" economic ideology.

COLONIAL LEGACIES

11.4 How do colonial legacies influence economic development?

Thus far, we have considered two political factors that might be associated with economic development: the difference between democracy and non-democracy, and the degree of state intervention in the economy. To answer this chapter's main question about the sources of economic development, however, we must turn to our final factor: colonial legacies. Modern states first emerged in Western Europe,

◉—▭Watch the Video
"Zimbabwe's
Economic Crisis"
at mypoliscilab.com

SUMMARY TABLE

Assessing the Degree of State Intervention in the Economy

Level of Intervention		Emphasis	Examples
Free market		Equality of opportunity: Maximizing individual freedom and minimizing government involvement	Ireland, United States, Singapore
Command economies		Equality of outcomes: heavy government intervention to redistribution wealth	Soviet Union, North Korea, pre-1980s China
Middle ground	Social democracy	Mixed: retains private property and a capitalist market, but intervenes to reduce inequality	Germany
	State-led development	Mixed: retains private property and a capitalist market, but intervenes to grow the economy	South Korea

between approximately 1500 and 1750. Today, these states—such as England, the Netherlands, and France—remain among the world's wealthiest countries, suggesting that the timing of state formation at least partly answers the question of why some countries are rich, while others remain poor. Early consolidation of sovereignty allowed European states to grow vastly more wealthy and powerful than other civilizations at that time.

The wealth these European powers accumulated came partly as a result of their colonization of most of the world between about 1500 and 1900—including all of North, Central, and South America and the Caribbean, nearly every country in Africa, and most of Asia. All of these former colonies are now independent states. However, colonization conditioned the possibilities for economic development. In some ex-colonies, Europeans brought institutions and implanted an economic system that proved beneficial over the long term. In other places, Europeans implanted political institutions and an economic system that only extracted wealth and exploited the locals, harming long-term development. Colonization does not necessarily doom a state to eternal poverty: both Ireland and China were poor just 50 years ago and both were at least partly colonized by foreign powers, but both have grown rapidly in recent decades. Even so, when one compares across all existing states, colonial legacies appear to matter a great deal, because colonization often leaves a weakened state.

China's experience is instructive: in the 1800s, European powers occupied key Chinese port cities and imposed—through superior military technology and exploitation of political divisions within China—humiliating trade policies. Japan also invaded and occupied large parts of the country in the 1930s, and after Japan's surrender in 1945, China was weakened and divided further by years of civil war. The modern Chinese state has only been consolidated since about 1950—and only in more recent decades has it combined state consolidation with market reforms to help the economy grow. For centuries, political weakness, subordination to foreign powers, and domestic chaos impeded China's growth. As China's recent experience demonstrates, countries that at one point were colonized by foreigners can overcome their weak institutional inheritance. However, many have not. In this section we discuss how late state formation and, in particular, the experience with colonization can impact states' long-term economic development.

Colonization and Long-Term Paths of Development

European colonial powers adopted different strategies and implanted different institutions when consolidating their overseas empires, and these differences are critical to understanding the present-day political and economic situation of many former colonies. These different colonial-era institutions are important because upon independence, colonies inherited these institutions and frequently found them difficult to modify.

settlement colonies
■ colonies established primarily as a place for people from Europe to settle. Examples include the United States, Canada, Australia, and New Zealand.

We can characterize colonization strategies as tending toward one of two types: "settlement" or "extractive." As the name suggests, settlement colonies were established primarily as a place for people from Europe to settle. Examples include the United States, Canada, Australia, and New Zealand. In contrast, imperial powers established extractive colonies primarily to extract abundant natural resources. Examples of extractive colonies include Bolivia, Brazil, the DRC, the Gold Coast (now Ghana), and the Ivory Coast (now known by its French name as Côte d'Ivoire); you can note the "extractive" names of the last two examples.

extractive colonies
■ colonies established primarily to exploit their abundant natural resources. Examples include Bolivia, Brazil, the DRC, the Gold Coast (now Ghana), and the Ivory Coast (Côte d'Ivoire).

Different colonization strategies led to different institutions of colonial governance. Settlement colonies—even though formally under the thumb of an imperial power—were able to establish representative assemblies, which advocated on behalf of settlers' interests, including freedom to profit by engaging in trade. Settlers also organized themselves to lobby the imperial government for treatment equal to that of citizens in the home country—or threatened to rebel, as the American colonies did. Colonial governments in settlement colonies tended to establish institutions that included limits on government expropriation of individuals' economic assets, an independent judiciary, strong property rights enforcement, and guarantees of civil liberties. These are the sorts of institutions that encourage investment in the local economy and creation of a local market.

In contrast, extractive colonies experienced minimal European settlement. Since the imperial power's primary interest was to extract and transfer wealth back to the home country, colonial administrators paid little attention to safeguarding the rights and the private property of the locals. Instead, they ruled via slave or forced labor and impeded the emergence of representative assemblies and checks on government power. Extractive colonial authorities also deliberately sought to deter the development of local trade and discouraged private sector investment in the local economy. For example, British colonial authorities in Kenya enacted policies that encouraged whites to settle, buy land, and begin farming—but in Ghana the same authorities enacted policies that discouraged settlement.[7]

When extractive and settlement colonies gained independence, they did not "wipe the institutional slate clean." Doing so would have made a bad situation worse, by replacing inadequate government institutions with complete political chaos. Instead, they began their histories as sovereign states with the institutions they inherited from their colonizers, which meant that they also inherited the colonizers' patterns of doing business and conducting government affairs. As many extractive colonies gained independence, the existing systems—which lacked checks and balances and focused on resource extraction and exploitation of labor—facilitated the establishment of non-democratic states, and in many cases permitted the newly empowered indigenous authorities to maintain the extractive political and economic system. This process simply replaced a greedy and unaccountable foreign elite with a greedy and unaccountable domestic elite, perpetuating economic inequalities and stifling economic growth.[8]

To the extent that this argument is true, it is critical to understand what originally determined a European country's colonization strategy. Why would a European government set up a settlement colony in one place and an extractive colony in another? To be sure, even in the absence of its longstanding civil conflict, the DRC would be a relatively difficult place to live due to its climate and harsh terrain, compared to say Belgium. But two centuries ago, the British authorities also considered Australia similarly inhospitable; it was precisely for that reason that they gave Australia's first "settlers"—convicted criminals—a one-way ticket!

Scholars have suggested that colonization strategy was a function of the long-term feasibility of European settlement.[9] In potential colonies where Europeans faced a high likelihood of death from disease such as malaria or yellow fever, they couldn't settle. As a result, they set up extractive states, imposing order by military force and using coerced labor provided by natives—as in the tin and silver mines in Bolivia, or the rubber plantations in the DRC—or by imported slaves, as on Caribbean and Brazilian sugar plantations.

In contrast, in places where Europeans were more likely to survive, their governments set up settlement colonies—as in North America, and eventually in New Zealand and even Australia, where convicts survived longer than predicted, so settlers gradually started arriving of their own free will. Australia and New Zealand are critical cases, because in those colonies the English authorities initially opposed the creation of institutions that would promote economic development. Such institutions did not arise naturally simply because the settlers were English and carried their cultural baggage with them; instead, the settlers had to fight for those rights.

This argument suggests the following: (1) the feasibility of Europeans settling outside Europe during the period 1500–1850 determined the sorts of political institutions that colonial authorities initially established. (2) Upon independence in the mid-to-late twentieth century, former colonies inherited these institutions and the practices associated with them; and (3) this inheritance continues to shape these countries' economic development. In short, the experience of colonization and, in particular, the institutions inherited from European colonialism, has profoundly shaped the fortunes of countries in today's world.

Nature Shapes Colonization Strategies and Long-Term Paths of Economic
HYPOTHESIS TESTING | Development

Many scholars believe that certain political institutions facilitate the process of economic development, while others slow it down. Yet, what can account for the different ways that European colonizers set up institutions—settlement colonies or extractive colonies—when they expanded their empires, centuries ago? This question is crucial for understanding the sources of growth and poverty in today's world. It is not immediately obvious why European powers would set up "settlement" colonies in one area and "extractive" colonies in others. Nor is it obvious why institutions that foster economic development emerged in some colonies but not in others. After all, European colonial powers did seek to dominate and control *all* their colonies; they did not concede liberties easily to colonists who requested them, even in "settlement" colonies. What determined whether settlement or extractive colonies eventually emerged? Let us consider the hypothesis that "nature" played an important role in determining variation on these outcomes.

To this day, even in the absence of its longstanding civil conflict, the DRC remains a relatively difficult place to live. Yet, even in the temperate regions of North America, many early European settlement efforts ended in disaster: witness the legendary story of the "lost colony" of Roanoke, North Carolina, or the famous case of Jamestown, Virginia—the first English effort to permanently colonize North America—where more than 80 percent of the initial waves of settlers perished, and the colony was for a time abandoned. At one time, nature appeared to impose barriers to settlement virtually everywhere. Still, when settlement colonies succeeded, the settlers who survived and laid down roots demanded different sorts of institutions from what European powers established in extractive colonies—institutions that these states then maintained upon independence. How does "nature" shape colonization strategy—and

thus influence whether a country can grow rich or remains poor?

GATHER EVIDENCE

Did "nature" play a key role in determining centuries-long paths of economic development? Scholars Daron Acemoglu, Simon Johnson, and James Robinson (AJR) have explored the question of whether colonization strategy—and, thus, the nature of the institutions that emerged later—was a function of the long-term feasibility of European settlement.[10] To answer that question, AJR suggest we look for evidence in the *death rates of Europeans who ventured to one of their country's colonies*. Some historians have noted that European conquerors carried germs with them, such as smallpox, which weakened or even decimated native populations and facilitated European colonization, especially in the Americas. AJR emphasize the reverse process: the germs that European settlers encountered and that killed them off to varying degrees. Different death rates of European colonists, AJR argue, in turn determined the ways in which Europeans chose to set up the institutions of government in those regions.

European colonizers were well aware that certain areas were more hospitable to settlement than others. British efforts to settle colonizers in West Africa were repeatedly dashed by high mortality rates—up to 100 percent. America's first settlers, the Pilgrims, decided to migrate to the future United States rather than to Guyana, in South America, because of the high mortality rates in the latter.[11] To get more precise information, AJR turned to historical records from European colonies in the early 1800s. Colonial powers kept very good records on the death rates of military troops, while the Vatican recorded the death rates of Catholic bishops it posted to different colonies around the world.

(Continued)

Pilgrims arriving in Massachusetts (1620), and slaves in the Congo (circa 1905). In climates where they could survive, Europeans set up settlement colonies—as in Massachusetts. Where Europeans were less likely to survive due to the harsh climate, they set up extractive colonies—as in the Congo.

(*Continued*)

ASSESS THE HYPOTHESIS

AJR assume that where large numbers of Europeans *could* settle, they eventually *would* settle, and they would then set up "high-quality" government institutions. In contrast, if the natural environment were hazardous to the health of Europeans, colonial powers would set up "extractive" colonies. Nature is not the only force at work here—but it is essential. Australia and New Zealand are critical cases, because in those colonies, the English authorities vigorously *opposed* the creation of political institutions that would promote economic development. Settlers to those colonies had to fight for those rights, just as American colonists did prior to the revolution in 1776, shouting "Give me liberty or give me death," tossing bales of tea into Boston harbor, and eventually organizing into militia forces to kick the British out. Yet, if the natural environment had remained inhospitable to European settlers in those colonies, European authorities would have set up extractive institutions when they first arrived, would not have encouraged further settlement efforts, and would have exploited the indigenous populations even more than they otherwise did.

The death rates for Europeans in their colonies serve as a way to measure the impact of "nature" on the path of economic development. After gathering their data, AJR conducted statistical analysis of the hypothesis and found a strong relationship between average European death rates and the "type" of political institutions later set up: the higher the mortality rate, the more likely was the colonial power to set up an extractive colony, minimizing the number of Europeans needed to administer the territory. In short, research confirms that nature has played an indirect role in shaping long-term paths of economic development: the feasibility of Europeans settling outside Europe during the period 1500–1850 influenced the sorts of political institutions that colonial authorities initially established. Upon independence, former colonies inherited these institutions and the practices associated with them; this inheritance continues to shape these countries' economic development. ◣

CRITICAL THINKING QUESTIONS

1. Suppose that Spain and Portugal had colonized North America, Australia, and New Zealand, while England and France had colonized Central and South America. Would the world today be very different? Why or why not?

2. Suppose no Europeans had colonized any part of Africa. Would the world today be very different? Why or why not?

Post-Colonial Status and Economic Development

The political institutions European colonizers established and then left behind perpetuated certain economic and social conditions. In terms of promoting or hindering economic development, the most important institutional inheritance from the experience of colonization includes the relative security of property rights, incentives for or against corruption, structures of the financial sector, and the capacity for investment in public infrastructure and human capital such as health and education. These are the sorts of public goods mentioned earlier; they are also the sorts of political conditions that scholars believe promote sustained economic development. Some former colonies inherited "good" institutions and became both politically stable and relatively wealthy—for example, the United States—while other inherited "bad" institutions and were burdened with instability, poverty, and inequality—for example, the DRC. These relative degrees of wealth and equality have persisted over time and continue to affect countries' development paths.

Are countries like the DRC doomed to a fate established long ago? Many believe that the argument above condemns poor countries to eternal poverty

> ### SUMMARY TABLE
>
> #### Impact of Colonial Legacies
>
> | Early forming states | Establishing sovereign authority over territory gave certain states a head start in terms of economic development, ability to exploit territories without sovereign states. Example: UK. | |
> |---|---|---|
> | Colonized states | Absence of sovereignty meant vulnerability to foreign domination and exploitation. Example: China. | Extractive colonial legacy: few constraints on government; economy designed only to export wealth; harder to overcome. Example: Congo. |
> | | | Settlement colony legacy: strong constraints on government, economy designed to promote local development; relatively easier to overcome. Example: United States. |

and political exploitation by more powerful countries. Still, the argument is not completely fatalistic. For example, Ireland and Botswana—both former British colonies—have both at least partially overcome the institutional legacy of colonization. In both countries, since about 1950, politicians have fostered political stability and helped overcome or transform its institutional inheritance and international political constraints. Despite the economic crisis since 2008, Ireland remains a fairly wealthy country; Botswana is a middle-income country with a per capita income on par with Argentina or Brazil—also former colonies—and Russia.

The "Asian Tigers" such as South Korea and contemporary China provide additional proof that poor countries are not doomed to a miserable fate. Both countries were exploited by foreign powers, and both were poor just 50 years ago. Yet both have overcome their histories. If institutional legacies were permanent, and if the world were simply full of "haves" who could permanently exploit the "have-nots," we never would have seen such amazing growth. The Asian Tigers did not become rich because they were early-forming states, or because they suddenly discovered oil, or even because they changed their cultural ways—but because they changed their political institutions and strengthened the political role of the state in the economy. Early state formation certainly offered some states a leg up on the competition, and colonization has hindered development in many states. However, colonization is not necessarily a permanent barrier to economic development.

CONCLUSION

"How do states promote economic development?" The real-world relevance of this question is important to the well-being of hundreds of millions of impoverished people around the planet. All states take actions that impact the economy; even relatively weak states engage in some political coercion to provide public goods and prevent market failures.

Although answers to this question have proven elusive, scholars have been able to show that no evidence exists of a tradeoff between democracy and development. Both democratic and non-democratic states have found recipes for economic growth. This finding offers powerful moral justification for democracy and confounds any rationalization of non-democracy, since there is no evidence that poor states will sacrifice development if they democratize.

In terms of the optimal degree of state intervention in the economy, scholars have concluded that states should be neither too weak nor too strong. This means, of course, that the idea of the "free market" can only be taken so far. States that intervene the least—because they lack any capacity to intervene, such as Somalia or the DRC—are so weak that they are failed states. They fail to generate economic growth because they cannot provide the political conditions necessary for markets to take root.

A truly weak state, one that cannot provide political stability, is clearly a bad recipe for economic growth. Yet no one knows precisely "how strong" a state must be to foster economic development. We do know that a state can be too strong and overwhelm incentives for growth. In many countries—as in North Korea—state leaders' efforts to control markets have proven highly inefficient and often counterproductive. Nevertheless, all the world's wealthy states do intervene in nearly every aspect of economic markets. The range of state intervention that promotes prosperity is wide—from relatively free-market economies like the United States, Singapore, and Ireland, to the relatively interventionist social democracies like Germany, or countries that have adopted state-led development strategies, such as South Korea. Both relatively free market and fairly interventionist states can foster economic growth.

✓•─[Study and Review the **Post-Test &** **Chapter Exam** at **mypoliscilab.com**

Finally, political scientists have suggested that colonial legacies can impact a country's long-term economic development: generally speaking, states that formed early managed to establish the political conditions to promote growth. Because they grew so powerful and successfully projected their power outside their own borders and into their imperial colonies, their success affected the subsequent trajectories of many of the world's newer states. Many of the world's politically and economically weakest states are post-colonial states. Such states, whether in Latin America, Africa, or Asia, have often struggled to establish and maintain political order and provide the necessary institutional stability to foster economic development, because the institutions they inherited were not designed for that purpose. However, the experience of such diverse countries as the United States, Ireland, South Korea, and China teaches us that historical legacies do not permanently determine a country's trajectory. So again, the answer to our question about why some countries are rich and others poor comes down to a range of factors, most importantly, the legitimacy and effectiveness of state institutions, and the timing of state formation. ▰

KEY TERMS

political economy   286
economic development   286
free-market principles   287
interventionist state   287
economic market   287

market failure   288
private goods   290
increasing returns to scale   290
monopoly   290
externality   291

REVIEW QUESTIONS

1. What—in theory—do states provide in return for taxation?
2. Why might democracy promote development better than non-democracy?
3. Why might non-democracy promote development better than democracy?
4. What are the main differences between economic liberalism and state interventionism?
5. What is the likely long-term impact of settlement colonies versus extractive colonies on long-term development?

SUGGESTED READINGS

Almond, Gabriel. "Capitalism and Democracy." *PS: Political Science* (September 1991): 467–474. Discusses the hypotheses relating free markets versus interventionist states and democracy versus non-democracy to economic development.

Easterly, William. *White Man's Burden: Why the West's Efforts to Aid the Rest Have Done So Much Ill and So Little Good.* New York: Penguin, 2006. Argues that efforts to promote economic development by organizations such as the IMF and World Bank have been counterproductive.

Hochschild, Adam. *King Leopold's Ghost: A Story of Greed, Terror and Heroism in Colonial Africa.* New York: Mariner Books, 1999. A moving historical account of the impact of Belgian colonialism on the Congo.

Polgreen, Lydia. 2008. "Congo's Riches, Looted by Renegade Troops." *New York Times* November 16, A1. Journalistic exploration of how a weak state, warfare, and greed combine to undermine development in the Democratic Republic of Congo.

Przeworski, Adam, and Fernando Limongi. "Political Regimes and Economic Growth." *Journal of Economic Perspectives* 7(1993): 51–69. An empirical comparison of the impact of democracy and non-democracy on economic development.

NOTES

1. Samuel Huntington, *Political Order in Changing Societies* (New Haven, CT: Yale University Press, 1968). Also Stephan Haggard, *Pathways from the Periphery: The Politics of Growth in Newly Industrializing Countries* (Ithaca, NY: Cornell University Press, 1990), 262.
2. See for example Mancur Olson, "Autocracy, Democracy and Prosperity," in *Strategy and Choice*, ed. Richard J. Zeckhauser (Cambridge, MA: MIT Press, 1991), 131–157.
3. See Adam Przeworski and Fernando Limongi, "Political Regimes and Economic Growth," *Journal of Economic Perspectives* 7(3)(1993): 51–69.
4. National Bureau of Statistics of China, "Communiqué on Major Data of the Second National Economic Census (No.1)" 2009), accessed July 2, 2010, http://www.stats.gov.cn/english/newsandcomingevents/t20091225_402610168.htm.
5. *Financial Times Global 500 Report,* accessed July 2, 2010, http://www.ft.com/reports/ft500-2010.
6. See for example, Alice Amsden, *Asia's Next Giant: South Korea and Late Industrialization* (Oxford: Oxford University Press, 1989); Robert Wade, *Governing the Market: Economic Theory and the Role of Government in Asian Industrialization* (Princeton,

NJ: Princeton University Press, 1990); Meredith Jung-en Woo, *The Developmental State* (Ithaca, NY: Cornell University Press, 1999).

7. Robert Bates, *Essays on the Political Economy of Rural Africa* (New York: Cambridge University Press, 1983).

8. See for example, Thomas Callaghy, *The State-Society Struggle: Zaire in Comparative Perspective* (New York: Columbia University Press, 1984).

9. See Daron Acemoglu, Simon Johnson, and James Robinson, "The Colonial Origins of Comparative Development: An Empirical Investigation," *American Economic Review* 91(5)(2001): 1369–1401.

10. See Daron Acemoglu, Simon Johnson, and James Robinson, "The Colonial Origins."

11. See Alfred Crosby. *Ecological Imperialism: The Biological Expansion of Europe 900–1900* (New York: Cambridge University Press, 1986), 143–144.

The Political Economy of Redistribution

Joe "The Plumber" Wurzelbacher queries Barack Obama about the possible impact of his tax plan, at a campaign stop near Toledo, Ohio. Obama argued that raising taxes on wealthier people would balance the government's budget without imposing an undue burden on most people. Others believed lower taxes overall and less government intervention in the economy would accomplish the same goal.

> **?** Why do some wealthy democracies engage in more economic redistribution than others?

■●⊦ Read and Listen
to **Chapter 12**
at mypoliscilab.com

✓●⊦ Study and Review
the **Pre-Test & Flashcards**
at mypoliscilab.com

A t an Ohio campaign stop during the 2008 presidential election campaign, a man named Joe Wurzelbacher asked then-Senator Barack Obama about his small-business tax policy. Wurzelbacher said he was thinking of buying a plumbing company and asked whether Obama's plan would raise taxes on small businesses that earn more than $250,000 a year. Obama replied candidly that, yes, it would. Three days later, Obama's opponent, Senator John McCain referred to Wurzelbacher as "Joe the Plumber" in a presidential debate and made Wurzelbacher's question a central point in his campaign. Joe became a media sensation as McCain tried to bolster his flagging poll numbers by painting Obama as a "tax and spend liberal," a Democrat whose tax plan would hurt average Americans like Joe—individuals chasing the American dream.

In the heat of election politics, it did not matter that fewer than 2 percent of all small-business owners declare an income of more than $250,000 a year,[1] or that Joe's actual income in 2006—about $40,000, which was about average for plumbers in Ohio at that time—would've qualified him for a tax cut under Obama's plan.[2] Taxes are a hot-button political issue in the United States, and they have been since the founding of the American republic. Advocates of "small government," like Joe the Plumber and John McCain, fervently believe that the best government is minimal government—one that intervenes in the economy as little as possible—in order to maximize individual choice. In contrast, others believe just as fervently that government intervention in the economy can be a force for good—and that such efforts cause less damage to society than do not using the government's power to intervene.

Similar debates echo around the world between advocates of economic free markets and advocates of greater government intervention. Yet, research in comparative politics suggests that there is little point to these discussions when it comes to the overall long-term growth rate of the economy. States around the world have proven that they can grow whether they embrace the free market or adopt interventionist policies. States that govern legitimately and effectively can and do vary considerably in terms of their degree of intervention in the economy.

In this chapter, we turn from questions about whether different degrees of state intervention promote economic growth and instead ask, *"why do some wealthy democracies engage in more economic redistribution than others?"* This question highlights a fundamental tension between capitalism and democracy. Capitalism tends to produce some degree of economic inequality—the extent of the wealth gap between rich and poor—even though democracy distributes political power equally (in principle, at least) by giving each person one vote. Given that the poor always outnumber the rich, philosophers and political economists have long supposed that democracy should threaten the very existence of capitalism. After all, under democracy, what stops the poor from "soaking the rich" by voting for highly interventionist "Robin Hood"–like policies that redistribute wealth to the poor? Doing so would surely dampen the incentives to invest that capitalism requires.

economic inequality ■ The extent of the wealth gap between rich and poor.

Most democracies redistribute some wealth. When a state intervenes in such a way to protect the economic and social interests of both the rich and the poor, it is called a welfare state. But what do welfare state policies look like? And how do such policies influence the economy at large? In this chapter, we will examine the different ways that states engage in redistributive spending and provide a real-world comparison of welfare state spending in the United States, Germany, and Sweden. Redistributive politics are hotly debated in wealthy as well as less-developed countries, yet to keep this chapter's discussion tractable, we then compare several explanations of the variations in levels of welfare state spending across the world's wealthy democracies.

welfare state ■ the role states play in protecting the economic and social well-being of all its citizens through redistributive taxing and spending programs.

THE WELFARE STATE

In what ways do democracies intervene to redistribute wealth? The degree of state intervention in the economy is measured as the relative size of the public sector compared to the private sector. The public sector refers to government delivery of goods and services such as Social Security in the United States, while the private sector refers to all economic activity undertaken outside the purview of the state, by individuals or private corporations. The overall size of the public sector is measured as the amount of economic activity the state undertakes through taxing and spending on government programs relative to the total amount of activity in an economy.

12.1 Why do some wealthy democracies engage in more economic redistribution than others?

What sorts of government programs are "welfare-state" programs? Not all public sector programs fall under the heading of "welfare state" spending. For example, about 35 percent of the U.S. government budget goes for national defense and veterans' affairs, interest payments on the national debt, investment in transportation and infrastructure, law enforcement and federal prisons, and general government expenditures. In this section, we first describe the sorts of policies that define the welfare state and note the extent of variation in welfare state spending in the world's wealthy democracies and then conduct a more focused comparison of welfare state spending in Sweden, Germany and the United States.

public sector ■ the government delivery of goods and services.

private sector ■ all economic activity undertaken outside the purview of the state, whether by individuals or private corporations.

Explore the Comparative "Social Welfare Systems" at mypoliscilab.com

Measuring the "Size" of the Welfare State

The sorts of government spending that fall under the rubric of the "welfare state" include programs pertaining to old age, survivors', and disability pensions; publicly provided healthcare; family support such as childcare subsidies; job training and retraining programs and unemployment compensation; public education; and housing subsidies. Table 12.1 lists the world's wealthiest democracies in descending order in terms of how much they spend on welfare state policies as a percentage of all economic activity.

All of the countries in Table 12.1 share important attributes: they are wealthy, are democratic, and have "strong" states, meaning that they all could spend a great deal on welfare state redistributive programs if they wanted. However, even though they share these characteristics, considerable variation exists in terms of the amount these states spend on social welfare programs: some spend more, and some spend less.

> **TABLE 12.1**
>
> ## Welfare State Spending in the World's Wealthiest Democracies, 2005
>
> | Country | Social Welfare Spending (Percent of GDP) |
> |---|---|
> | Sweden | 29.4 |
> | France | 29.2 |
> | Austria | 27.2 |
> | Denmark | 27.1 |
> | Germany | 26.7 |
> | Belgium | 26.4 |
> | Finland | 26.1 |
> | Italy | 25.0 |
> | Portugal | 23.1 |
> | Norway | 21.6 |
> | UK | 21.3 |
> | Spain | 21.2 |
> | Netherlands | 20.9 |
> | Greece | 20.5 |
> | Switzerland | 20.3 |
> | Japan | 18.6 |
> | New Zealand | 18.5 |
> | Australia | 17.1 |
> | Iceland | 16.9 |
> | Ireland | 16.7 |
> | Canada | 16.5 |
> | *USA* | *15.9* |
>
> Source: OECD Social Welfare Expenditure database, 1980–2005, accessed December 15, 2011, http://stats.oecd.org/Index.aspx?datasetcode=SOCX_AGG.

The government of Sweden, for example, redistributes the equivalent of about 30 cents of every dollar earned in all of Sweden, while the U.S. government redistributes about 16 cents of every dollar Americans earn. Before we attempt to explain this variation, let us learn a bit more about the nature of welfare state programs in the United States, Sweden, and Germany. Remember that the "welfare state" includes only government spending on programs such as health care, retirement pensions, unemployment insurance, and poverty relief.

Comparing Health-Care Spending

Perhaps the most noticeable difference across the United States, Sweden, and Germany is in terms of public health insurance provisions. In the United States, about two-thirds of the population has private health insurance. Two government-funded programs—Medicare and Medicaid—provide health-care support for the elderly and the poor. However, until the 2010 health care reform, about 15 percent of the population—mostly lower-income people—had no health insurance.[3] The 2010 reform insures nearly everyone—but only fully covers the cost of insurance for the very poorest people. For families that earn between the poverty line and about $88,000, the government will partially subsidize health insurance premiums.[4] The reform does not create a national government-run or -funded health care system.

In contrast, both Germany and Sweden provide "universal" health care coverage, with unlimited benefits. This means that citizens do not worry if they are eligible for coverage because everyone is eligible, and they do not worry about losing their health insurance if they lose or change their job. In both countries, individuals pay a small deductible (about $12 per visit in Germany) for doctor or hospital visits but pay no other out-of-pocket expenses. Taxes fund the system, and lower-wage workers pay a smaller health insurance tax than do higher-wage workers. In Germany, about 85 percent of the population uses the government-run healthcare system; in Sweden, this figure reaches about 97 percent. The remainder opts out of the public system and seeks private insurance, for which they must pay separately.

Differences in welfare state spending go beyond healthcare provision; let us now consider the extent to which governments subsidize childcare or provide poverty relief.

Comparing Childcare and Poverty Relief Programs

In addition to more generous health-care provisions, German and Swedish government programs also provide subsidies for families to pay for childcare and other expenses associated with raising children. All parents are eligible to receive these benefits, which amount to approximately $135 per month per child in Germany until a child is 18, and $85 per child per month in Sweden until a child is 16, regardless of the family's income. In the United States, some assistance is available through the Temporary Assistance for Needy Families program, but for only the very poorest families.

As for poverty relief programs, in the United States, benefits provided by Supplemental Security Income programs target poor, elderly, and disabled individuals who make less than approximately $6,000 per year. Needy families are also eligible for the Temporary Assistance for Needy Families program. However, as the word "Temporary" in that program's title suggests, recipients are limited to two years of aid, after which time they must find employment. In contrast, poverty relief programs in Germany and Sweden are universal and unconditional. This means that anyone is eligible, and there are no requirements to find a job after a certain period of time.

The welfare states of Germany and Sweden are clearly more generous in terms of health care and support for children and families. Our final comparison will consider how labor laws in Germany and Sweden provide relatively larger cushion for workers against potential job losses.

Comparing Labor Laws

Relative to the United States, labor laws in Sweden, Germany, and other European Union countries provide greater economic insurance to "working-class" families.

Minimum wages are on average much higher in Europe than in the United States, and labor standards and job protection laws are far more stringent, as well. For example, in Germany and Sweden, government-funded disability benefits are more generous than comparable benefits in the United States. Government programs in Germany and Sweden also provide for paid sick leave at between 70–80 percent of a person's salary. In Germany, such benefits last up to a year and a half, while in Sweden there is no time limit for sick leave. In contrast, the United States has no federal, guaranteed sick-leave policy.[5]

To illustrate variation in the nature and size of the welfare state across the world's wealthy democracies, Table 12.2 provides the total amount of government social welfare spending in the United States, Germany, and Sweden as a proportion of all economic activity and breaks spending down by the categories discussed in this section. It also provides a comparison with the average for 33 member-states of the Organization for Economic Cooperation and Development (OECD), a group of wealthy democracies. The table shows that the United States spends only about 80 percent of what other OECD members spend on social welfare programs (about 16 percent of GDP versus about 20 percent), and about half of what Sweden spends. Moreover, it reveals that the difference between the United States, Germany, and Sweden arises not because of differences in health-care spending but because Germany, and especially Sweden, spend more on child and family poverty relief and on the jobless—the latter a function of cross-national differences in labor laws. The fact that the U.S. government spends proportionally about as much as Germany and Sweden on health care—even though many Americans have private health insurance—suggests that U.S. spending is relatively inefficient.

Variation in welfare state spending can generate substantial differences in redistributive outcomes: in the United States, government welfare state policies in 1994 led to a decline in the poverty rate of 13 percent; the comparable figure for Sweden that same year was 82 percent.[6] This means that without government redistribution programs, economic inequality would have been 13 percent worse in the United

---

TABLE 12.2

The "Size" of the Welfare State as a Proportion of GDP (2005)

	Total	Of Which				
		Old Age, Survivors', and Disability Benefits	Health Care	Family Support	Unemployment Benefits and Training Programs	Other
Sweden	29.4	15.8	6.8	3.2	2.5	1.1
Germany	26.7	13.5	7.7	2.2	2.7	0.8
USA	15.9	7.4	7.0	0.6	0.4	0.6
OECD Avg.	20.6	12.8	6.2	2.0	1.5	0.8

Source: OECD Social Welfare Expenditure database, 1980–2005, accessed December 15, 2011, http://stats.oecd.org/Index.aspx?datasetcode=SOCX_AGG.

States and 82 percent worse in Sweden. In short, both the extent of taxation and redistributive spending vary widely across wealthy democracies, with diverse effects on economic equality and inequality. The United States hews to its traditions of economic liberalism, with relatively low redistributive taxing and spending in comparative perspective. In contrast, Germany and, especially, Sweden have adopted more generous approaches to welfare state spending. In the next section, we turn to the question of why all democracies engage in progressive redistribution and then endeavor to explain these cross-national differences.

WHY WELFARE STATES EXIST

Why do all democratic states redistribute some degree of wealth through progressive taxation and social insurance provision?[7] The answer lies in democratic politics: elected leaders believe that providing for the well-being of all citizens will help them keep their jobs. As Obama's campaign trail discussion with Joe the Plumber about tax rates and the contentious debate about health-care reforms in the United States illustrate, wide disagreements exist about how much governments should spend, who should benefit, who should pay relatively more in taxes, and who should pay relatively less. To understand why all states redistribute wealth to some degree, let us explore the logic behind progressive taxation and social insurance provision.

12.2 Why do all governments engage in some degree of wealth redistribution?

Progressive Taxation

Redistribution involves taking resources from some people and giving them to others. Politicians typically advertise government social welfare programs as a form of progressive redistribution—which means that such programs act like Robin Hood and take from richer folks and give to poorer folks. To support these programs, most governments use progressive taxation, which means that individuals' tax burdens go up as their incomes go up. To what extent are different countries' tax policies really progressive? As Table 12.3 reveals, in 2009, taxation of wages was progressive across all the world's wealthy democracies. Notice that the tax rate for lower-income people (shown in the middle column) is lower in every case than the rate for higher-income people (shown in the right column).

progressive redistribution ■ programs that act like Robin Hood and take from rich folks and give to poor folks.

progressive taxation ■ occurs when individuals' tax burdens go up as their incomes go up.

On average, in all wealthy democracies, a person who makes only two-thirds of the average wage—that is, someone in the lower-middle class—pays about 15 percent less in income taxes than does someone in the upper-middle class who makes about 1-and-two-thirds of the average wage. In the United States, this means that the income tax rate for an individual who makes $27,000 per year is about 21.7 percent, while the tax rate for a person who makes about $65,000 per year is about 31.7 percent. In short, people in wealthy democracies who make less money typically pay less in taxes, as a proportion of their income, than do people who make more money. Table 12.3 lists countries from most to least progressive—the larger the difference between the two tax rates, the more progressive the tax system.

Some forms of taxation may be regressive, meaning that they tend to benefit relatively wealthy people more than relatively poor people. For example, governments

regressive taxation ■ taxes that tend to benefit relatively wealthy people more than relatively poor people.

> ### TABLE 12.3
>
> ### Average Income Tax Rates in Wealthy Democracies (Percent), 2009
>
> **Tax Rate as a Percent of Wages**
>
> | Country | For Someone Making ⅔ the Average Wage | For Someone Making 1⅔ the Average Wage |
> |---|---|---|
> | Netherlands | 11.2 | 50.0 |
> | Sweden | 22.5 | 56.5 |
> | Ireland | 21.7 | 42.7 |
> | Denmark | 34.1 | 54.8 |
> | UK | 20.0 | 40.0 |
> | New Zealand | 21.0 | 38.0 |
> | Japan | 8.7 | 25.6 |
> | Germany | 29.4 | 44.3 |
> | Spain | 22.5 | 37.0 |
> | Canada | 19.6 | 33.0 |
> | Switzerland | 14.0 | 26.8 |
> | France | 18.0 | 30.1 |
> | Norway | 28.0 | 40.0 |
> | Austria | 25.6 | 37.0 |
> | Portugal | 23.5 | 34.0 |
> | **United States** | **21.7** | **31.7** |
> | Italy | 29.2 | 38.7 |
> | Greece | 21.0 | 29.4 |
> | Australia | 35.5 | 41.5 |
> | Finland | 35.5 | 40.5 |
> | Belgium | 40.8 | 45.3 |
>
> Source: OECD, "Marginal Personal Income Tax and Social Security Contribution Rates on Gross Labor Income," accessed July 4, 2010, http://www.oecd.org/document/60/0,3343 ,en_2649_34533_1942460_1_1_1_1,00.html.

often provide subsidies, investment incentives, and tax breaks to investors and corporations in efforts to promote economic development or to protect powerful interest groups. Still, Table 12.3 clearly establishes that income taxes, one of the largest sources of government revenue, are somewhat progressive across the world's wealthiest democracies.

Democracy and Redistribution   Debates about taxation and redistribution are frequently framed in moralistic terms like "progressive" and "regressive" for intuitive reasons: most people believe taking from the poor to give to the rich would be cruel and wrong. Moreover, the principles of democracy—which require political equality—frown on policies that promote economic inequality. Scholars have puzzled over the tension between capitalism and democracy: in principle, democracy distributes power equally through universal suffrage, while historically—for a variety of reasons—capitalism has tended to create economic inequalities. People disagree about whether extreme economic inequality is morally acceptable or not—but regardless, the tension between political and economic inequality implies that all democracies confront inevitable political demands for progressive taxation and income redistribution.[8]

A political reality explains why this is so: in every country in the world, poor voters outnumber rich voters. Another way of saying this is that a country's median income is always lower than mean income. Median income is the amount that divides income distribution into two equal groups: half of the country earns an income above the median, and half earns below that amount. In contrast, the "mean" income is the average or the sum of everyone's income, divided by the number of people in the population.[9] Median and mean incomes can differ substantially within a country, depending on the degree of economic inequality. For example, if a country contains a high percentage of unemployed people and a handful of billionaires like Bill Gates, then median income will be much lower than mean income, because the billionaires "bring up the average." Median income is equal to mean income only when everyone makes exactly the same amount of money. And since individuals like Bill Gates are the exception rather than the norm, median income is always lower than mean or average income.

In a democracy, economic inequality can have important political consequences. In particular, because median income is always lower than mean income, and because more than 50 percent of all voters in any given country make less than the average income, in theory most voters ought to prefer progressive taxation and redistributive public policies. By majority rule, then, the not-so-wealthy majority could vote to impose higher taxes on the wealthier minority—and they could also vote into office politicians who promise to enact social welfare programs that redistribute wealth. In short, to the extent that median income is lower than mean income, we ought to see political pressure for a progressive tax system and progressively redistributive welfare-state policies.

Why Is Redistribution Lower than "Expected"?   The fact that income tax systems in the wealthiest democracies are progressive makes sense in light of the fact that some degree of economic inequality characterizes every country in the world. However, existing rates of progressive taxation are lower than one would expect, given actual levels of economic inequality. That is, tax rates are progressive but are not as progressive as they "should" be. Voters apparently do not soak the rich as much as they could.

This finding has caused endless head scratching among economists and political scientists. If the poor always outnumber the rich, then why don't the poor vote for politicians who promise greater wealth redistribution? Why does Joe the Plumber, who made $40,000 the year before he met Barack Obama, worry about tax rates on people who make $250,000? Scholars have offered six potential answers to this question—some having to do with the power of the wealthy, and some having to do with the interests of the poor or average voter.

1. The wealthy have the means to mobilize and lobby against redistributive policies, solving their collective action problems more easily than the poor. Thus, even if the poor wanted higher taxes and more redistribution, their efforts to

median income ■ the amount that divides income distribution into two equal groups: half of the country earns an income above the median, and half earns below that amount.

mean income ■ the average or the sum of everyone's income, divided by the number of people in the population.

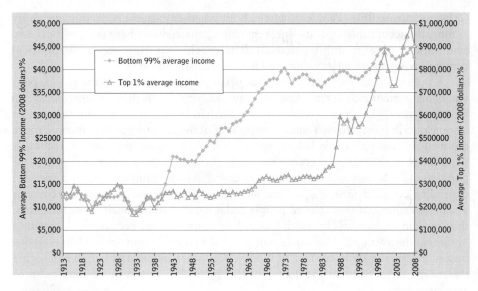

FIGURE 12.1

Average Income of the Bottom 99% and Top 1%, United States 1917–2008

The average income of the bottom 99 percent of the U.S. population (indicated in the left axis, which follows the line with diamonds) more than quadrupled from 1933 to 1973, going from about $9,000 to about $40,000 per year. Over the same period, the average income of the wealthiest 1 percent of the U.S. population (indicated by the right axis) only doubled, from about $168,000 to about $335,000. During that period, income inequality was on the decline. Yet since 1973, the average income for the bottom 99 percent has stagnated, increasing only about 8 percent through 2008, while the average income of the wealthiest has tripled to almost $1 million per year. Inequality has increased in the United States since 1973, primarily because the richest 1 percent are getting richer, while everyone else's wages remained flat.

Source: Emmanuel Saez, University of California—Berkeley, accessed March 12, 2011, http://www.econ .berkeley.edu/~saez/.

mobilize for such policies would be thwarted by the counter-mobilization efforts of the wealthy.

2. Faced with the threat of higher taxation, the wealthy can choose not to invest or even save in their home country and move their money elsewhere. The ability of holders of capital to place their money in offshore banks or to invest in countries with lower tax rates dampens political pressures for redistribution.

3. In less-established democracies, the wealthy can pressure governments to violently repress political parties or social movements that favor increased redistribution, and they can even threaten to overthrow the government.

4. The average voter mitigates his or her own demands for redistribution, believing that upward mobility is possible for themselves or their children. Therefore, individuals may not vote on what they are earning today, but rather on what they hope to earn in the future.

5. Poor voters oppose redistribution because they believe one gets what one deserves in life and should not ask for a handout.

6. Individuals mitigate their demands for redistribution because they believe they are richer than they are, in the present.

All states engage in some degree of redistribution because there are always more poor folks than rich folks—and in a democracy, majority rule implies that voters have incentives to demand more such policies. Moreover, because politicians need votes, they have incentives to appease the majority of voters. However, even given increased economic inequality in most wealthy democracies in recent decades, the poor do not soak the rich as much as scholars predict.

The arguments above help explain why redistribution is "lower than expected." For example, many people—including many poor people—believe that poverty is a result of poor individual choices or lack of effort rather than bad luck or inadequate opportunities,[10] and that laziness or foolishness should not be rewarded with redistributive social welfare policies. These sentiments weaken the political demand for progressive taxation and redistributive spending. Many relatively poor people also believe they are in a higher economic class than their actual income suggests, and as a result—like Joe the Plumber—they believe they would suffer from any tax increases rather than benefit from increased redistribution.[11] These six factors help us understand why progressive taxation and redistribution are not higher than they already are.

Nevertheless, the fact remains that taxing and spending is at least partially progressive in all democracies, and the logic of majority rule helps explain why this is so: politicians fear that they will lose their next election if they do not craft policies that appeal—at least in part—to voters with below-average incomes. However, the explanation of why all democracies engage in welfare state spending remains incomplete. To understand why all democracies engage in some amount of welfare state spending, we must again consider the political implications of market failures by exploring the concept of "social insurance."

Social Insurance Provision

Insurance offers people a way to deal with the risk of potential financial losses in the future. When you purchase insurance, you pay a monthly premium to transfer the cost of your potential future losses onto an insurance company. The insurance company determines your premium by calculating your probability for losses in the future—hoping, of course, that you will never incur such costs and it will never have to pay you for them. Private sector companies insure people for just about anything: the hands of professional pianists and the noses of professional wine tasters, or more generally, auto theft, workplace accidents, or damage to a home.

What is political about insurance provision? All over the world, governments are heavily involved in providing social insurance—forms of insurance that are available to all citizens, regardless of ability to pay. For example, the U.S. government provides Social Security, which is insurance against the possibility that you will have no pension or savings when you are old; unemployment insurance against the risk that you will lose your job; "deposit insurance" up to $100,000 through the Federal Deposit Insurance Corporation (FDIC) against the risk that your bank will collapse; health insurance for the poor and elderly through Medicaid and

social insurance ■ forms of insurance that are available to all citizens, regardless of their ability to pay.

Medicare; and financial insurance against the possibility that you will experience a drop into poverty through Supplemental Security Income and Temporary Assistance for Needy Families payments.

In many countries, public sector or "social" insurance provision is more important than is private sector insurance. Moreover, although the U.S. government funds a wide array of social insurance through tax revenue, most other wealthy democracies fund even broader forms of pension, health, family, and employment insurance. For example, some countries completely fund job training, which lowers the risk of long-term unemployment; childcare, which insures that parents can keep their jobs if they want; and some countries subsidize extensive maternal and even paternal employment leaves following the birth of a child, to replace lost income and insure that having a child does not cost new parents a loss of economic status.

Why do all democratic governments provide these kinds of insurance? And why isn't this job left to the private sector? Would the private sector provide old age pensions or health-care insurance if the government did not? Let us consider three potential answers: political identity, avoiding depopulation, and providing public goods by preventing market failures. As we shall see, the political implications of market failures provide the most satisfactory answer.

Political Identity   A feeling of solidarity might potentially justify the welfare state. That is, perhaps citizens feel they share a common fate with others in their country, based on nationalistic or patriotic feelings or on sympathies for their less-fortunate fellow citizens. Thus perhaps the relatively wealthy keep their compatriots healthy and out of poverty because they feel it is the right thing to do. Many people might not only feel sympathy but also recognize that they, too, might one day be down on their luck and need a helping hand from the government. If such sentiments were widespread, many citizens might voluntarily contribute a portion of their income to the state. However, no state has ever survived on voluntary contributions. And if people really had such strong feelings of solidarity, the government would have little reason to take action because communities would care for their own without needing the state to compel contributions. Feelings of solidarity based in shared political identity do not provide a solid explanation for insurance provision and thus welfare spending.

Avoiding Depopulation   In the 1930s, Swedish social scientists Alva and Gunnar Myrdal noted that many European governments sought to increase their country's populations for reasons of nationalism and national security—a large population meant an ability to field a big army and to gain recognition as a major player on the world stage.[12] By the 1920s, the birth rate in many countries—including Sweden—had fallen drastically, endangering economic growth. The Myrdals used this demographic trend to support an argument in favor of social welfare. They suggested that one way the Swedish government could encourage its citizens to have more babies was to guarantee that children would have access to health care, education, and job training. Avoiding a dramatic decline in population provides a second potential rationale for government insurance provision.

The U.S. government produced this poster in 1936 to advertise an expansion in the Social Security system. The poster attempts to generate support for the program by appealing to Americans' sense of solidarity, presenting the idea that Americans from all walks of life would benefit.

The Myrdals are considered the intellectual architects of Swedish welfare state policies. However, few people today suggest that welfare states exist primarily to encourage population growth. In fact, birthrates remain low around Europe, even though most European countries spend generously on social welfare programs. As with the previous argument of solidarity, avoiding depopulation provides an incomplete explanation for government insurance provision. For a more satisfactory political explanation, let us return to the concept of market failure.

Market Failures   Recall that a market failure occurs when an economic market fails to supply a product for which demand exists. Each of us confronts some risk of losing our jobs, getting sick or injured, or retiring in poverty. Of course, people face different degrees of risk: people with fewer assets, skills, or education confront relatively greater risks of unemployment or poverty. Still, even well-educated or wealthy people face some degree of risk of catastrophe. Over an entire lifetime, no one can predict with absolute certainty his or her degree of risk. For example, while a blue-collar factory worker's job might get outsourced or downsized, so might the job of the corporate vice-president of finance. And both the hourly worker and the corporate executive have equal probabilities of slipping on an unseen patch of ice and breaking an arm. Many individuals may believe they confront low risks over the long term, but this is an illusion.

The free market fails to provide insurance to cover these kinds of risks for the following reason: in order to cover its expected losses and still make a profit, private sector insurance companies charge a higher premium on higher-risk people. As a result, many high-risk individuals are unable to find insurance at any price. Insurance premiums are only affordable when scores of low-risk people purchase insurance policies. Of course, people who believe they are low-risk types are unlikely to want to purchase insurance that insures everyone, because they recognize that their premium subsidizes high-risk types. This means that private insurance companies have interests in identifying and excluding high-risk people from their pool of potential customers in order to convince more low-risk types to purchase insurance. In the end, although everyone wants insurance, the cost for many (high-risk) people remains too high, and the private sector will not provide the product.

Of course, many people cannot afford a Lexus, but that does not mean the government should give everyone a Lexus. A political rationale for government provision of social insurance—which necessarily entails coercing people to pay taxes that fund such programs as social security, unemployment insurance, Medicare, and Medicaid, for example—derives from the idea that such programs generate a critically important public good, by making society as a whole better off and minimizing everyone's exposure to an unknown future degree of risk. If insuring everyone serves a socially desirable purpose, governments should compel everyone, including both high-risk and low-risk people, to contribute.

In theory, compulsory taxation to provide universal insurance programs generates public goods. That is, in theory, forcing everyone to contribute a little makes everyone in the end a lot better off, whether directly or indirectly. The basic idea follows the notion that "an ounce of prevention is worth a pound of cure." People without health insurance are loath to visit a doctor precisely because it is expensive. Consequently, uninsured people tend to be more susceptible to illness because they don't go in for regular checkups. And when uninsured people get sick enough to be admitted to the hospital, they go to a public hospital—one funded by all taxpayers—and it costs the public much more to make them better than if they had been insured—whether by the private or the public sector—and had seen a doctor before becoming seriously ill.

The desirability, efficacy, and efficiency of social insurance is hotly debated in the United States, but the issue is more settled in other wealthy democracies. Many criticize welfare programs as wasteful and suggest that they generate incentives for people not to work and to remain dependent on government handouts. Others respond by suggesting that if they are well designed, social welfare programs can be socially efficient—that is, they can make everyone better off. For example: approximately one billion people around the world eat enough per day to survive, but not to work. A small government subsidy, which would give them money to eat a bit more, would make them economically productive members of society.[13] Such arguments provide political ammunition to those who support government welfare programs.

American citizens generally agree that some social welfare programs provide public goods and are socially efficient, even though the welfare state is less extensive in the United States than in most other wealthy democracies. For example, most Americans support the idea that free education for all children—regardless of their ability to pay—has a high rate of social return. However, support for public education in the United States ends when a child turns 18; at that point,

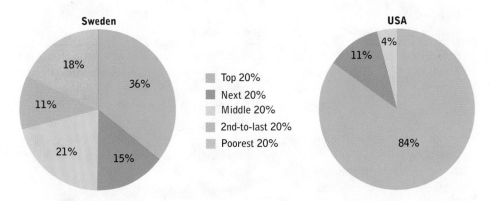

FIGURE 12.2

Relative Distribution of Wealth: Sweden versus United States

In Sweden, wealth is more equally distributed than in the United States. The top 20 percent of the population has 36 percent of the wealth in Sweden, but in the United States, the comparable figure is 84 percent (in the United States, the bottom 40 percent have so little wealth that they do not show up in the pie chart). Yet, when shown these two pie charts without the names of the two countries attached, 92 percent of Americans surveyed said they would choose to live in a country with Sweden's wealth distribution rather than a country like the United States. Americans favor reducing inequality, but oppose the policies necessary to make that happen.

Source: Michael Norton and Dan Ariely, "Building a Better America—One Wealth Quintile at a Time," *Perspectives on Psychological Science* 6(1)(2011): 9–12, 10.

even supposedly "public" colleges and universities charge tuition. In contrast, in several European democracies, such as Sweden and Germany, university education is free.

In recent years, a similar debate has raged in the United States about adopting national healthcare, a policy long in place in Canada, the UK, and many other countries. Such systems do not necessarily prohibit private healthcare insurance or provision, but they do compel everyone to pay for health insurance—just like Social Security compels everyone to save for their own retirement, whether they want to or not. One side of the debate suggests that national health insurance would save billions of dollars in health-care costs for all Americans in the long run; those on the other side argue that national health insurance would generate unforeseen economic inefficiencies.

The point here is not to resolve this debate, but to highlight how in many countries the possibility of government provision of insurance has—just like redistribution—provided politicians with ideas that enjoy broad popular appeal. This helps explain why governments provide various forms of social insurance: in many cases the market fails to do so, but politicians suspect that old-age pensions,

---

◣ SUMMARY TABLE

Why Welfare States?

Element of the Welfare State	Definition	Hypothesis
Progressive Taxation	Tax burdens that go up as income goes up. Example: income tax rates.	Democracy necessarily implies a tension between political equality and economic inequality: there are always more poor people than rich people, which gives politicians an incentive to create 'Robin Hood' like programs.
Social Insurance	Forms of insurance available to all citizens, regardless of ability to pay. Examples: unemployment insurance, old-age pensions.	■ Political identity: governments provide social insurance because the wealthy feel solidarity with the poor. Evidence for this hypothesis is weak. ■ Avoiding depopulation: governments provide social insurance to encourage people to have more children. Some support for this hypothesis exists, but it is an incomplete explanation. ■ Providing public goods by avoiding market failures: governments provide social insurance to make society as a whole better off by minimizing everyone's exposure to unforeseen risks. As with progressive taxation, politicians recognize that social insurance programs have broad electoral appeal.

public education, and public healthcare will have broad political appeal. As with redistribution, the relatively poorer majority often bears less of the cost for social insurance but gains more of the benefit. The logic of democratic politics is inescapable: majority rule generates incentives for politicians to solve market failures and engage in the provision of social insurance.

Debating the Welfare State

Politics explains why all democracies engage in some degree of welfare state spending: elected politicians have strong incentives to redistribute wealth and to solve market failures by providing insurance. Doing so enhances their legitimacy as capable leaders, which in turn enhances their chances of reelection; doing nothing can have the opposite effect. Even politicians who favor minimal government intervention in the economy often find it hard to resist supporting some redistribution and social insurance programs, because that is what their constituents—both rich and poor—usually want.

Elected officials create and support welfare state programs by claiming that their efforts will improve citizens' lives. Yet because politicians' self-interest in reelection at least partly explains these efforts, citizens the world over have good reason to cast a critical eye on such claims—and political science students have good reason to consider the ongoing debates about the relative impact of welfare state policies on outcomes such as economic growth or other public goods. The debate about health care in the United States provides an illustrative example. Proponents argue that providing universal health care generates a public good: a healthier society. Fewer sick people means more people working, studying, or supporting their family, for example—all of which strengthen society—and provide less of a drain on public coffers. Opponents argue that greater government intervention harms the public good by making the health-care system less efficient and by increasing government spending, which may impede investment in other economically productive activities.

Similar debates echo about other forms of government spending: is society made better or worse off by increasing spending on old age and disability benefits, so that people who cannot work can nonetheless live out their lives without worrying about where their next meal will come from? Should the government subsidize day care for families with young children, so that parents can hold onto their jobs? Should government provide relatively more- or relatively less-generous poverty relief and unemployment benefits for people hurt by economic misfortune, or should individuals be left to pull themselves up by their own bootstraps?

These are difficult questions to answer, partly because at root they are philosophical in nature and have to do with the nature of the individual in society. Yet, even in terms of empirical analysis, answers do not come easily. For example, will increasing government health-care spending improve health-care outcomes in the United States? Currently, the combined total of public and private sector spending on healthcare in the United States is almost double the average for other wealthy democracies, yet healthcare outcomes in the United States such as infant mortality and life expectancy are worse than in similar societies. This suggests that Americans are not getting their money's worth in a system dominated by the private sector, compared to citizens in countries where the public sector dominates.

Skeptics of government-provided health care will respond that increasing government spending sacrifices consumer choice and flexibility, and they will argue that differences in health-care outcomes do not arise because of differences in health-care spending but from other factors, such as the fact that the United States has a higher proportion of immigrants, many of whom arrive with preexisting conditions, and because Americans' dietary and other social habits lead to a higher rate of obesity—both of which may cause higher health-care spending, as well as worse health-care outcomes.

Although debate about the welfare state is more settled in Europe, many Americans remain fundamentally opposed—on principle—to government intervention in the economy, believing that the best government is the least government. Many others believe differently, that society—not just poor people—could be made much better off were government to step in and expand public services such as health care. All democracies redistribute wealth to some degree, but the United States stands out among the world's wealthy democracies for having a relatively small "welfare state." The intensity of the debate behind health care in the United States—and the intensity of political debate about taxes and spending more generally—brings us back to this chapter's main question. Having explored the reasons why all democracies engage in some degree of welfare state spending, it is now time to explain why some states redistribute more, while others redistribute less.

EXPLAINING VARIATION IN WELFARE STATE SPENDING

12.3 What explains why some democracies spend more—and others less—on social welfare?

Now that we have established what the welfare state is, and we understand that economic inequality and the occurrence of market failures give elected officials everywhere reason to engage in progressive taxation and redistributive spending, we can return to our original question: *why do some wealthy democracies engage in more economic redistribution than others?* What explains, for example, why many Americans are—like Joe the Plumber—much more reluctant to support welfare state spending than citizens of other wealthy democracies? Why does the level of taxing and spending differ so widely across countries? Five factors shape politicians' incentives to create welfare state policies; we shall consider each in turn.

✳ Explore the Comparative "Welfare States" at mypoliscilab.com

Labor Unions: Economic Interest Groups

The first factor focuses on the relative strength of organized labor compared to big business, because the strength of organized labor as an economic interest group is thought to explain variation in how much states redistribute wealth. Three elements define the strength of organized labor: its size, its cohesiveness, and the degree to which it is directly "incorporated" into the apparatus of the state. The larger, more cohesive, and more incorporated is organized labor, the more likely we are to see relatively generous welfare state policies.

Many scholars have explained the size of welfare states as a function of the growth of unions and the leftist political parties that mobilize at least partly on their behalf. If unions and leftist parties are strong and well organized, policies regarding taxation and redistribution will reflect that strength. In contrast, if big business is well organized, but labor is small and divided and without a place at the government negotiating table, policies will tilt in favor of big business.

The extent of interest group representation is particularly important. In Western Europe, labor unions' emerging strength in the early twentieth century led to their being "incorporated" directly into the apparatus of the state, where they now participate in the creation, development, and administration of social policy. This situation virtually guarantees that labor's voice will be heard alongside business. As a result, in countries with extensive labor incorporation into the apparatus of the state—such as Germany and Sweden—we generally see greater government spending on social welfare programs.

Business and labor have varying strength around the world, and this variation has political consequences for the development of welfare state policies. Generally, to the extent that labor is well organized and well represented in politics, or even directly incorporated into the state, we ought to see larger welfare states.

The Left–Right Economic Divide and Political Identities

We sometimes think that politics is dominated by "left–right" competition between liberals and conservatives. The left–right political spectrum ranges from liberal to moderate to conservative, with those on the left favoring greater government

The strength of organized labor supports welfare state spending in Germany. Here, union members stand amidst boxes labeled "austerity package" in a late 2010 Berlin protest against a proposal to increase the age at which German workers become eligible for government pensions.

intervention in the market—to promote equality of outcomes—and those on the right favoring less government intervention in the market—to promote equality of opportunity.

Although this is a conventional way of speaking about ideological differences, political competition in most countries does not fit neatly onto a left–right spectrum. This is because differences in political identity frequently dilute the salience of the left–right divide. For example, if ethnicity divides a country into two groups, the political parties that form in that country may base their campaigns on ethnic appeals rather than expanding or limiting social welfare programs for all citizens. Given this, in an ethnically divided society, a party that wants to advocate higher (or lower) government spending might find that neither ethnic group pays much attention to that appeal, because ethnicity is more politically salient. A party that wanted to focus on redistribution, for example, would have to find a way to bridge the ethnic divide before it could find a receptive audience for its proposals.

Consider the way that the linguistic divide shapes political competition in Canada, where many voters regard the difference between English- and French-speaking citizens as more important than any economic debate that pits small-government conservatives against big-government liberals. Likewise, in many Western European countries, Christian Democratic parties have historically added a religious dimension to politics, focusing on the relationship between church and state rather than economic issues.

Issues of political identity such as ethnicity, race, religion, and nationalism can dilute the importance of economic interests and the left–right dimension of politics. When political identity divides voters from each other, few care about taxation and redistribution—they tend to focus their energy instead on whether politicians advocate policies that protect the interests of only their group. The salience of political identity in many societies complicates the task of politicians who want to focus on questions of taxing and spending—especially those politicians who wish to unite people across different races or religions to increase social spending. In short, to the extent that identity-based conflicts dominate politics in a country, we tend to see less government redistribution.

The Impact of Political Institutions

The relative strength of labor unions and the importance of non-economic political identities are not the only factors that help explain cross-national variation in government intervention in the economy. A third factor is the extent to which political institutions provide opportunities for political minorities to participate in government. In particular, proportional representation (PR) electoral rules and the distinction between unitarism and federalism may be related to the extent of taxation and redistribution. Scholars have noted that countries with multiparty political systems, such as Belgium and Denmark, tend to tax and spend relatively more than do countries with two-party systems. In multiparty systems, to succeed, governments must form multiparty coalitions. Each party in the coalition wants to focus government spending on its own supporters, but this dynamic tends to increase overall pressures for spending.

In contrast, in a two-party system, each of the main parties is a diverse coalition of social groups. This tends to dilute the influence of each particular group in the government process, which limits upward pressures on spending. Multiparty systems are associated with proportional representation electoral rules, while two-party systems are associated in many cases with plurality electoral rules. The electoral system in the United States and UK—single-member district plurality—has worked against the growth of the welfare state by diluting group demands. In contrast, in most continental European states, PR electoral systems facilitate the birth and growth of socialist and labor parties alongside a far broader and more varied constellation of political parties. This fragmentation of the party system has encouraged the growth of the welfare state.[14]

Federalism also seems to be associated with smaller government, while unitarism is associated with bigger government. This is perhaps because federal systems require a second legislative chamber. Bicameral legislatures make passing any legislative proposal more difficult—simply because each proposal requires two separate and potentially nonoverlapping majorities. Under these circumstances, the passage of welfare-enhancing legislation becomes more difficult. All else equal, federal systems should see somewhat smaller states. However, because some federal systems such as that of Germany tax and spend relatively heavily, we can see that political institutions such as federalism and electoral rules provide only partial explanations for cross-country variation in levels and taxation.

The Impact of State Strength

A fourth factor helping explain variation in state intervention in the economy is the relative strength of the state. State strength focuses on legitimacy and effectiveness, while the degree of state intervention in the economy is measured in terms of the amount of taxes the state takes from citizens as a proportion of all economic activity. These two concepts are related, because the degree of state intervention is a function of state strength.

State strength refers to the capacity of the people and the institutions of the government bureaucracy to (1) efficiently collect taxes and (2) effectively implement spending programs—to avoid corruption and "get the job done." Politicians in democratic states with high legitimacy and effectiveness can intervene to tax and spend more heavily. They know that if they win an election based on a pledge to increase spending in a certain area, they will be able to both raise the funds and effectively implement the new public policy. Sweden provides an example of a highly effective state: there is little corruption, and the government bureaucracy is relatively efficient.

In contrast, the bureaucracies of weak states are unlikely to have the capacity to collect sufficient tax revenue to fund social welfare programs—and even if taxes were collected, much revenue would likely be lost to waste, corruption, or inefficiency. Moreover, in weak states, it does not matter if citizens or politicians want the government to engage in taxation and redistribution, because such policies could never be well implemented. Tax evasion might be high; corruption might be rampant; or bureaucrats might be poorly educated and trained.

States with low corruption and relatively high bureaucratic capacity tend to be relatively wealthy countries where state strength has evolved over decades, if not centuries. In contrast, low state capacity characterizes many poorer countries. In many of these countries, current-day state capacity was highly conditioned by the experience of past colonization—recall that countries established as extractive colonies are unlikely to have strong states today. In sum, weak states confront considerable tax evasion and are therefore unable to redistribute wealth, as opposed to strong states with substantial bureaucratic capacities. Not all strong states engage in considerable redistribution; state strength merely makes redistribution possible.

The Role of Globalization

The last key factor explaining levels of welfare state spending in different countries is globalization. Globalization refers to the spread of cultural, political, and economic dynamics beyond the borders of any one country and into the international realm. Economic globalization refers more specifically to the exposure of a country's financial and industrial sectors to the global network of production, trade, and consumption. In recent decades, all countries have become more integrated into global economic markets. However, countries with smaller populations and smaller domestic markets—such as Sweden—tend to be more exposed to the global economy, while larger economies—such as the United States, where companies can often remain competitive even if they focus only on the domestic market—remain relatively less exposed to globalization. For instance, the health of a giant U.S. corporation such as General Motors depends heavily on domestic auto and truck sales, even though GM's overseas vehicle sales are an important part of its business. In contrast, the health of Swedish bus and truck manufacturer Volvo cannot depend on sales within Sweden alone—the jobs of its Swedish employees depend entirely on how well the company does in "foreign" markets. (For instance, Mack Trucks, based in North Carolina, is a wholly owned subsidiary of Volvo.)

capital mobility ■ the ability of an investor to move his or her money across borders and invest where profits are highest and costs are lowest.

Globalization impacts what governments can do, regardless of what they might want to do. Many expect that the increase in capital mobility—the ability of an investor to move his or her money across borders and invest where profits are highest and costs are lowest—makes governments more dependent on market forces, and, therefore, particularly responsive to the political interests of those who hold capital: large firms, banks, investors and investment funds, and financial speculators.

Perhaps it goes without saying that industrialists, investors, and financiers favor low taxes and limited government spending on social welfare programs. Because globalization allows holders of capital to move their assets out of one country and into another, scholars have long predicted a "race to the bottom," in which globalization causes countries to compete to attract and hold onto high-value yet mobile economic assets by reducing taxes and social welfare spending. According to this logic, holders of capital are globalization's main winners, while average workers are globalization's big losers. Many assume that globalization weakens labor unions and pushes governments to eliminate worker protections and cut social welfare benefits. These negative effects of globalization would particularly harm leftist politicians and their supporters in the electorate.[15]

Globalization has the biggest effect in countries most exposed to the world market: smaller countries, such as Sweden. In larger countries such as the United States, the hypothesized effect of globalization on government redistribution and insurance provision is more limited. While some research suggests that economic globalization drives wages down and tends to increase economic inequality, extensive empirical research has found no evidence linking globalization to a shrinking welfare state—at least in advanced capitalist democracies. Instead, scholars have found that long-standing national social welfare policies, institutions, and practices tend to successfully resist the forces of globalization. Tax burdens in high-tax states such as France or Sweden have not declined as one might expect, given the forces of globalization—and as a result, welfare benefits have not declined as predicted, either.[16] Such findings imply that criticism of globalization may be overblown. However, these findings only hold for the world's wealthiest democracies; globalization has different effects in poorer countries.

Five factors—summarized in the table below—shape the extent to which the state engages in redistributive welfare state taxing and spending: the organization of societal interests, primarily capital and labor; the impact of political identity; the impact of political institutions; the relative strength of state institutions; and the impact of globalization. These factors all reflect aspects of societal or state strength. In democracies where organized labor is strong, where no other form

SUMMARY TABLE

Factors That Lead to Variation in Welfare State Spending

Factor	Key Hypothesis	Value	Example
Relative strength of business versus labor	If labor unions are large, cohesive and incorporated into the state, redistribution should be higher.	Strong labor unions	Germany
		Weak labor unions	United States
Relative salience of left–right economic divide	Non-economic political identities can dilute the salience of economics in politics, which tends to reduce redistribution.	Homogenous society	Sweden
		Diverse society	United States
Political institutions	Proportional representation allows more parties into government; each party presses to deliver resources to its supporters, increasing the chances of redistributive spending.	Yes	Sweden
		No	United States
	Federalism is associated with bicameralism, making passage of redistributive spending proposals more difficult.	Yes	United States, Germany
		No	Sweden

(Continued)

SUMMARY TABLE (CONTINUED)

Factor	Key Hypothesis	Value	Example
State strength	Higher bureaucratic capacity makes greater redistribution possible and is associated with higher spending.	Strong state	Sweden, Germany, United States
		Weak state	Congo
Globalization	The extent to which an economy is integrated into global markets causes a "race to the bottom" as states compete to prevent outsourcing and remain competitive, reducing taxes and redistributive spending.	Highly exposed	Sweden
		Not highly exposed	United States

of political identity dilutes the mobilizational appeal of working-class economic interests, where organized societal interests can turn their votes into policy output through formal political institutions, and where the state has high bureaucratic capacity, we expect to see comparatively greater government intervention in the economy. The opposite will be true where organized labor is weak, society is fragmented along multiple ethnic or religious divides, institutions weaken the ability of political minorities to influence policy outputs, and where the state is weak.

No single factor provides a complete explanation for the size of the welfare state. Moreover, as the table above suggests, sometimes a factor thought to increase or decrease social welfare spending has the opposite effect—or no clear effect at all. For example, Germany is federal, but federalism has not dampened redistributive spending there as it has in the United States. Neither the Swedish or German state is that much "stronger" than the American state, meaning that at least among these three countries, variation in state strength cannot explain variation in government redistribution and/or insurance provision. Finally, although globalization has been increasing for all wealthy democracies in recent decades, social welfare spending has also been increasing, suggesting that globalization does not have the predicted effect on government intervention in the economy. To explain why we see so much variation in welfare state spending among wealthy democracies, these five factors provide a useful starting point for careful comparison—but they also provide no easy answers.

HYPOTHESIS TESTING | Greater Ethnic Diversity Explains Low Levels of Welfare Spending: Sweden and the United States

Both the United States and Sweden are among the world's wealthiest countries, and both are strong and stable democracies. However, such similarities aside, several key differences explain why social welfare spending is much higher in Sweden than in the United States. Organized labor is stronger in Sweden, and Sweden uses proportional representation, while the United States has a single-member district electoral system; the United States is federal, while Sweden has a unitary system, and Sweden's economy is more globalized. However, the starkest difference may be in terms of ethnic diversity—and some scholars argue that this last difference rather than any other explains why social welfare spending is so much higher in Sweden. Let's puzzle through the following hypothesis: *the higher the ethnic diversity, the lower the social welfare spending.*

GATHER EVIDENCE

Sweden is—and has historically been—an ethnically homogenous society. In the last two decades, Sweden has experienced a wave of immigration, but most immigrants have tended to come from other European countries. Only in recent years has the country experienced arrivals of large numbers of non-Europeans from countries such as Iraq, Iran, and Turkey. In 1998, 98 percent of the population was either of Swedish origin or other European ethnic origin; this number had dropped to 94 percent by 2010.[17] Still, Sweden remains ethnically homogenous in comparative perspective.

In contrast, the United States is and has historically been a more ethnically diverse society, and racial divisions have been the source of great conflict. In 2010, partly as a result of recent waves of immigration from outside of Europe, and partly as a result of the history of African-American slavery, the U.S. population was estimated to have the following

characteristics: whites comprised 65 percent, Latinos about 16 percent, African-Americans about 13 percent, and Asian Americans about 5 percent. The U.S. Census Bureau estimates that whites will comprise a minority by 2050.[18]

ASSESS THE HYPOTHESIS

Could the different levels of diversity in Sweden and the United States account for differences in levels of social welfare spending? This hypothesis suggests that ethnic diversity undermines political mobilization that seeks to increase redistributive spending. Let's consider what might explain this connection. The argument begins with a general proposition: an individual's willingness to support welfare programs is stronger if the programs benefit members of that person's ethnic or racial group and weaker if the programs benefit members of different groups. Evidence of such "in-group bias"—a tendency to trust people whom you know or even people who look like you more than strangers and/or people who look different from you—comes from research from social psychology.

One way to explore this hypothesis is with survey data from the General Social Survey (GSS) and the World Values Surveys (WVS).[19] Using these surveys, scholars have found evidence connecting ethnic diversity to lower public support for social welfare spending. In the United States, support for welfare spending is higher among people who live near welfare recipients of the same race, but lower among people who live near welfare recipients of a different race. Given these findings, the more diverse a country, the lower public support for welfare spending should be. Scholars have found evidence supporting this connection: among wealthy democratic countries, the higher the ethnic/racial diversity—measured using census data—the lower the level of welfare spending.[20] The implication is that (white) Americans

(Continued)

A diverse crowd in New York, and a homogenous crowd in Stockholm, Sweden's capital. Could differences in the level of ethnic and racial diversity be connected to levels of social welfare spending?

(*Continued*)

TABLE 12.4 Swedish and American Responses to World Values Survey Questions on Redistribution

World Values Survey Question	United States	Sweden
"People who don't work turn lazy."	55%	40%
"It is humiliating to receive money without having to work for it."	43%	31%
"Hard work brings success."	31%	20%

tend to dislike welfare programs they associate with spending on ethnic or racial minorities.[21]

It is possible that the connection between diversity and variation in welfare spending is not due to racism per se, but with Americans' belief that poverty and laziness are connected. Americans tend to think that poor people are poor because they don't work hard—and as a result, they do not deserve taxpayer support. In contrast, Europeans tend to think that poor people are unfortunate, and thus deserve some compensation. Consider the comparisons in Table 12.4 of responses to questions in the 2006 World Values Surveys in Sweden and the United States. Like other Europeans, Swedes are more likely to believe that people are poor because of society, not laziness. In contrast, Americans are more likely to believe one can get out of poverty through hard work, and the poor remain poor because they refuse to put in the effort.

Race and poverty have always been linked in the United States—but not, historically, in Europe. More American blacks are poor, proportionally, than are whites, a legacy many attribute to systematic economic discrimination—a lack of equality of opportunity for education and jobs long after slavery was abolished. Such legal barriers to social mobility never existed for whites. Yet, given Americans' belief that individuals can work their way up the ladder,

many whites interpret persistent poverty among racial minorities as a sign of laziness, and so oppose welfare spending. In short, it is not simply the existence of diversity in the United States, but the connection between race and poverty that has undermined the construction of a political coalition favoring greater government social spending.

This argument continues to spark debate in academic circles as well as on talk radio and on the web. It is difficult to determine whether the comparatively low level of welfare spending in the United States is a function of Americans' sentiments about other races or Americans' equation of poor people with laziness, because it is difficult to tease out the difference between "in group ethnic/racial bias" from feelings about whether poor people "deserve" government support.

CRITICAL THINKING QUESTIONS

1. What is the hypothesized connection between ethnic/racial diversity and social welfare spending?
2. To what extent do you think racial diversity is important in explaining the comparatively low level of social welfare spending in the United States, relative to federalism, the electoral system, weak unions, and globalization?

CONCLUSION

States tax citizens so that they can spend money on all sorts of programs that encourage economic development, invest in infrastructure, and provide for national defense. In this chapter, we focused on "welfare state" spending, the extent to which states engage in income redistribution and the provision of social insurance. Welfare state spending can support many sorts of government programs, and the amount of tax revenue that governments spend on welfare programs can redistribute wealth considerably from the relatively rich to the relatively poor.

We first defined the "size" of the welfare state by considering what proportion of all national economic activity governments spend on healthcare, poverty relief, and benefits for workers. Then, in seeking to answer this chapter's main question—*why do some wealthy democracies engage in more economic redistribution than others?*—we discovered that all democratic governments confront demands for progressive taxation and income redistribution—and politicians have strong interests in meeting these demands by promising to redistribute some wealth. This is because to the extent that capitalism produces economic inequality, an inevitable tension exists between capitalism and democracy.

Capitalist market failures also help explain why politicians in the world's wealthy democracies all offer old age, health, and unemployment insurance: if insuring everyone improves everyone's welfare, then governments have good reason to compel everyone—both high- and low-risk people—to contribute. Of course, the notion of what counts as "improving everyone's welfare" remains highly contested, but the logic of market failures provides politicians with powerful arguments supporting government insurance programs.

✓●─ Study and Review the Post-Test & Chapter Exam at mypoliscilab.com

Incentives for governments to spend on social welfare exist in all democracies. To explain why some states spend more than others, we turned to five factors: the relative strength of social forces such as organized labor; the way that different forms of political identity may dilute demand for redistribution; the extent to which political institutions such as proportional representation and/or federalism provide opportunities for minorities to participate in policymaking; the legitimacy and effectiveness of state institutions; and the impact of globalization. ▴

KEY TERMS

economic inequality   316
welfare state   317
public sector   317
private sector   317
progressive redistribution   321
progressive taxation   321

regressive taxation   321
median income   323
mean income   323
social insurance   325
capital mobility   336

REVIEW QUESTIONS

1. What is the main way that scholars measure the size of the "welfare state"?
2. Why do governments in all democratic states engage in progressive taxation?
3. What are the main differences between the "welfare states" of the United States, Germany, and Sweden?
4. Why do governments in all democratic states provide some forms of social insurance?
5. What are the most important reasons why welfare state spending varies across the world's wealthy democratic states?

ADDITIONAL READINGS

Alesina, Alberto, and Edward Glaeser. *Fighting Poverty in the US and Europe: A World of Difference*. New York: Oxford University Press, 2004. A comprehensive examination of the historical reasons that most European states spend more on social welfare programs than the United States does.

Bartels, Larry. "Homer Gets a Tax Cut? Inequality and Public Policy in the American Mind." *Perspectives on Politics* 3, 1(2005): 15–31. Finds that even though most Americans are aware that inequality has increased and regard that development as bad, most still support tax cuts for the very wealthy, largely because they think that their own tax burdens are too high.

Gilens, Martin. "Inequality and Democratic Responsiveness." *Public Opinion Quarterly* 69, 5(2005): 778–796. Using public opinion surveys, finds that redistributive policy in the United States reflects the preferences of affluent voters, not poor or middle-income Americans.

Kenworthy, Lane, and Jonas Pontusson. "Rising Inequality and the Politics of Redistribution in Affluent Countries." *Perspectives on Politics*, 3, 3(2005): 449–471. Examines the relationship between rising inequality and rising redistribution in wealthy democracies.

Shorto, Russell. "Going Dutch: How I Learned to Loved the European Welfare State." *The New York Times Magazine,* April 29, 2009. An insightful first-person account of an American reporter's experiences dealing with a very different health-care system.

NOTES

1. See the report from the nonpartisan Tax Policy Center, accessed January 14, 2009, http://taxvox.taxpolicycenter.org/blog/Campaign08/_archives/2008/10/20/3938265.html.

2. Larry Vellequette and Tom Troy, "'Joe the Plumber' Isn't Licensed. Local Man Focus of Presidential Debate," *Toledo Blade,* October 10 2008, accessed January 14, 2009, www.toledoblade.com/apps/pbcs.dll/article?AID=/20081016/NEWS09/810160418.

3. US Census Bureau, "Income, Poverty, and Health Insurance Coverage in the United States: 2007," 2008, accessed December 15, 2011, http://www.census.gov/prod/2008pubs/p60-235.pdf.

4. See Peter Grier, "Health Care Reform Bill 101: Who Gets Subsidized Insurance?" *Christian Science Monitor,* March 20, 2010, accessed December 15, 2001, http://www.csmonitor.com/USA/Politics/2010/0320/Health-care-reform-bill-101-Who-gets-subsidized-insurance.

5. See Alberto Alesina, Edward Glaeser, and Bruce Sacerdote, "Why Doesn't the US Have a European-Style Welfare State?" (unpublished paper, Harvard University/National Bureau of Economic Research, 2001), 7–10. Alesina and Glaeser later expanded on this research in a book entitled *Fighting Poverty in the US and Europe*. For a reaction from a European scholar to their arguments, see Jonas Pontusson, "The American Welfare State in Comparative Perspective," *Perspectives on Politics* 4(2)(2006): 315–326.

6. See Torben Iversen, "Capitalism and Democracy," In *The Oxford Handbook of Political Economy*, ed. Barry Weingast and Donald Wittman (New York: Oxford University Press, 2006), 601–623.

7. The discussion in this section owes a great deal to Adam Przeworski, *States and Markets: A Primer in Political Economy* (New York: Cambridge University Press, 1991).

8. This section is derived from Allan Meltzer and Scott Richard, "A Rational Theory of the Siz of Government," *Journal of Political Economy* 89(51)(1981): 914–927.

9. For example, in the set [1,1,2,4,5,6,7,24,40], the mean is 10, since there are nine numbers and they add up to 90, but the median is 5, since there are four numbers smaller than 5 in the series and four numbers larger than 5.

10. See for example, Larry Bartels, "Homer Gets a Tax Cut? Inequality and Public Policy in the American Mind," *Perspectives on Politics* 3(1)(2005): 15–31.

11. See for example, Larry Bartels, *Unequal Democracy: The Political Economy of the New Gilded Age* ((Princeton, NJ: Princeton University Press, 2008).

12. Their book on the subject was called *Crisis and the Population Question*.

13. Nobel prize–winning economist Amartya Sen has been a major proponent of this view. See his books *Poverty and Famines* (Oxford: Oxford University Press, 1983); and *Development as Freedom* (New York: Anchor Press, 1999).

14. See Torsten Persson and Guido Tabellini, *The Economic Effects of Constitutions* (Cambridge, MA: MIT Press, 2005).

15. See for example, Layna Mosley, "Room to Move: International Financial Markets and National Welfare States," *International Organization* 54 (4)(2000): 737–773; or Duane Swank, "Funding the Welfare State: Globalization and the Taxation of Business in Advanced Market Economies," *Political Studies* 46 (4)(1998): 671–692.

16. See for example, Dani Rodrik, "Sense and Nonsense in the Globalization Debate," *Foreign Policy* 107(1997): 19–36.

17. See Statistics Sweden website, http://www.scb.se/default____2154.aspx, December 9, 2010.

18. "Projections of the Population by Sex, Race, and Hispanic Origin for the United States: 2010 to 2050," accessed December 9, 2010, http://www.census.gov/population/www/projections/files/nation/summary/np2008-t4.xls.

19. GSS: http://www.norc.uchicago.edu/GSS+Website/, WVS: http://www.worldvaluessurvey.org/.

20. See Alberto Alesina and Glaeser, *Fighting Poverty in the US and Europe: A World of Difference* (Oxford: Oxford University Press, 2004).

21. See Martin Gilens, *Why Americans Hate Welfare: Race, Media and the Politics of Antipoverty Policy* (Chicago: University of Chicago Press, 1999).

Globalization

French and German farmers blockade Strasbourg with their tractors in December 2005, in protest against an upcoming WTO conference that threatened European Union price supports for their products.

> **?** How has globalization shaped politics in the world's states?

📖 Read and Listen
to **Chapter 13**
at **mypoliscilab.com**

✓ Study and Review
the **Pre-Test & Flashcards**
at **mypoliscilab.com**

In November 1999, government representatives from around the world gathered in Seattle for a planning meeting of the World Trade Organization (WTO) to discuss technical issues pertaining to international trade barriers. Conferences on arcane international policy issues typically attract little attention from the media. However, more than 40,000 anti-globalization protesters had assembled, and they managed to shut down traffic, force the cancellation of the conference's opening ceremonies, and impede delegates from attending meetings. A few rowdier protesters caused property damage that attracted a heavy police response and intense media scrutiny—of the protesters and of the WTO and its aims—precisely what the protesters sought to accomplish.

Protests against the WTO continue to flare around the world. In 2005, thousands of French and German farmers clambered aboard their tractors and drove into downtown Strasbourg, France—a city near the German border that hosts the European Union's (EU) legislature—to protest a WTO meeting to be held later that month in Hong Kong. The farmers sought to "defend European agriculture" against what they perceived to be unfair competition from producers in the United States, Canada, Brazil, and elsewhere. Without EU subsidies, many farmers across the continent would be uncompetitive—and as such they fear the WTO's efforts to promote free trade in agricultural commodities.

The issue of free trade in agriculture is but one issue the WTO discusses—and it is but one element in debates surrounding globalization. Why has this issue become so contentious, debated in classrooms, corporate boardrooms, and legislatures all over the world? *How does globalization impact politics in the world's states?* How do political institutions, identities, and interests in the world's states respond to foreign influences? In the next section, we clarify the meaning of the word "globalization," and in the remainder of the chapter we explore its political, economic, and cultural consequences.

DEFINING GLOBALIZATION

13.1
What is globalization?

globalization ■ the spread of political, economic, and cultural dynamics among governments, groups, and individuals beyond the borders of any one particular country.

✴ Explore the Comparative "Economic Policy" at **mypoliscilab.com**

What do we mean when we refer to "globalization" and politics? Globalization works at the intersection of comparative politics and international relations: it refers to the increase in the scope and extent of political, economic, and cultural connections between governments, organizations, and individuals across state borders. Such connections are hardly new—people have come into contact with other cultures to exchange goods and ideas for thousands of years. However, the reason globalization has become such a buzzword in recent years is because the scope and extent of such interactions have expanded and deepened so dramatically.

By the *scope* of global connections, we mean that in the contemporary world an ever-increasing number of issues are transnational—their causes and effects cannot be confined to the borders of any single sovereign state. Such issues—which include terrorism, environmental degradation, human rights violations, international migration, drug and human trafficking, and trade disputes—cannot be considered simply a matter of domestic politics. No single state can resolve any of these problems—whether for itself or for all other states. Transnational problems require transnational solutions—and the responses to such issues have spawned new forms of cross-border interaction between individuals and groups. Transnational networks of citizens and governments—including both the WTO and antiglobalization activists, for example—are now an integral part of both domestic and international politics. In today's world, the issues and efforts to address them are transnational in scope and cannot be thought of as taking place merely within the borders of this or that sovereign state.

We can also define globalization by the *extent* or the "amount" of transnational connections between people and governments. Recent decades have seen dramatic increases in the amount of information, goods, and people flowing across borders, through trade, tourism, migration, and the media. Advances in technology—from the launching of communications satellites in the 1970s to the invention of the Internet in the 1980s—have dramatically reduced costs and facilitated an astounding leap in communication and capital flows. Innovations in transportation—particularly the spread of cheap jet travel and the invention of massive container ships—have also made long-distance travel and trade in goods easier and cheaper. Quite simply, recent years have witnessed a dramatic expansion of economic, political, and sociocultural integration, so that people, goods, and information can travel faster and further.

Scholars have confirmed that such changes have accelerated in recent decades, by measuring the growth of international trade and information flows, transnational personal contacts, and the spread of a single global culture. Figure 13.1

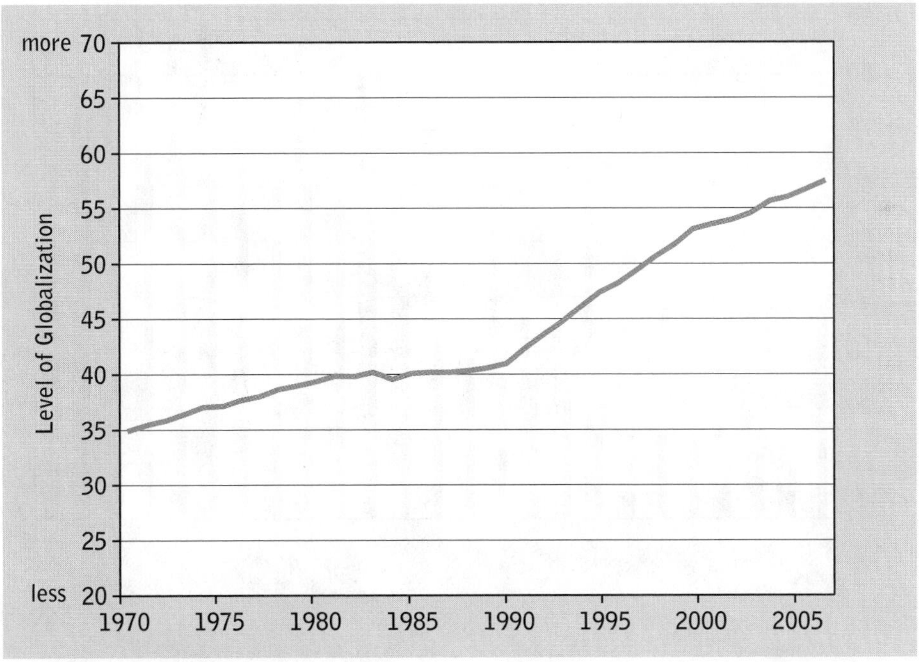

transnational ■
issues with causes and effects that extend beyond the borders of any single sovereign state and that cannot be considered simply a matter of domestic politics.

FIGURE 13.1

Average Level of Globalization, 1970–2010

The average "level" of globalization has increased for all countries in the world since 1970. This "Index of Globalization" ranges from 0–100, and integrates a series of measures, including countries' openness to foreign trade and investment; extent of tourism; number of Internet users; and the number of McDonald's and Ikea stores per capita.

Source: Calculated from the KOF Swiss Federal Institute of Technology "Index of Globalization," accessed June 5, 2011, http://globalization.kof.ethz.ch.

provides the average "level" of globalization since 1970 for all countries in the world. The scale ranges from 0–100 and integrates a series of measures, including countries' openness to foreign trade and investment; extent of international tourism; number of internet users; participation in international organizations, and even the number of McDonald's and Ikea stores per capita—a rough indicator of lifestyle similarities across countries.[1] Higher numbers indicate that the world's states are more globalized on average.

On this measure, the average country has opened up to the world significantly, especially after 1990. Figure 13.2 uses the same source of information from Figure 13.1, but compares the extent of globalization in 1970 and 2010 for just a few countries, including some of the least- and most-globalized.

All countries have opened up and become more integrated with others over the last 40 years. Some—notably India and China—have globalized a great deal, especially considering their relative political, economic, and cultural isolation in 1970. The United States is relatively globalized, but several other Western

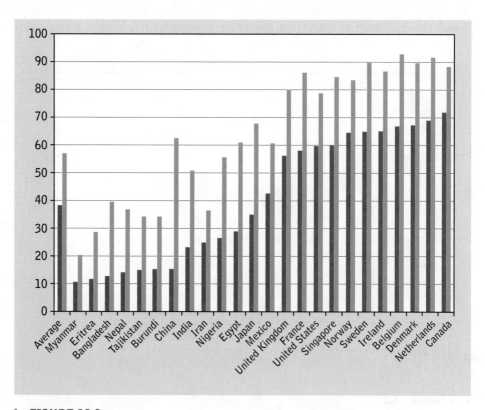

FIGURE 13.2

Globalization (Selected Countries), 1970 and 2010

This graph shows the different levels of globalization for selected countries in 1970 (in green) and 2010 (in red). Some countries opened up more than others.

Source: Calculated from the KOF Swiss Federal Institute of Technology "Index of Globalization," accessed June 5, 2011, http://globalization.kof.ethz.ch.

European democracies are even more open to foreign economic, political, and cultural flows. Overall, since 1970, the scope and extent of international communication and exchange has increased dramatically. Globalization represents a profound increase in the nature and extent of human interconnectedness. This intensification of cross-border linkages and activity tends to break down the distinction between domestic and international politics, as forces outside any state's borders increasingly impact politics within each and every state. This means that to explain comparative politics, we must consider how globalization impacts the world's states.[2] In the next section, we focus on the political impact of these transnational forces.

POLITICAL GLOBALIZATION

Sovereign states first emerged centuries ago, but it was not until the final collapse of European empires in the 1960s that nearly every populated territory in the world gained status as an independent state. Ironically, very soon after states covered the world's territory, observers began to wonder whether globalization would make the concept of sovereignty irrelevant.

Political globalization involves the growth in the number and scope of transnational political and economic issues, and the increasingly transnational responses to such issues. In the contemporary world, states increasingly cannot solve the problems that affect their territory or citizens on their own. In response, two kinds of transnational political institutions have gained importance. Both the rise of transnational issues and the nature of the reaction to those issues may weaken state sovereignty.

The first kind of transnational political institutions that have arisen as globalization has advanced are called international governmental organizations (IGOs). IGOs are political institutions made up of member-states that have a transnational presence and that take on governmental roles. They are not technically governments and do not have sovereignty, but they play increasingly important roles in managing transnational political and economic problems. Well-known IGOs include the United Nations (UN) (which is committed to promoting world peace), the World Trade Organization (WTO) (which regulates commerce between countries), the European Union (EU) (which governs finance and other policies across borders in Europe), and the Organization of Petroleum Exporting Countries (OPEC) (which seeks to regulate the supply and price of oil).

The second kind of transnational political institutions that have gained prominence recently are international non-governmental organizations (INGOs). INGOs are voluntary associations that form independently of any state's authority, made up of citizens from several states who engage in political activism within or outside their own states' borders. Thousands of INGOs have been formed in recent decades around the world.[3] No one knows how many exist, and their numbers are constantly growing. Prominent examples include Amnesty International, the International Red Cross, and Greenpeace. Many are religious in nature, such as Caritas (backed by the Catholic Church), the International Islamic Relief Organization (which has operations in more than 100 countries), and World Vision (an evangelical Christian organization). INGOs can also include criminal organizations and terrorist groups such as al-Qaeda.

13.2 What are the consequences of political globalization for sovereignty and democracy?

political globalization ■ the growth in the number and scope of transnational political and economic issues, and the increasingly transnational responses to such issues.

international governmental organizations (IGOs) ■ political institutions made up of member-states that have a transnational presence and that take on governmental roles.

international non-governmental organizations (INGOs) ■ voluntary organizations that form independently of any state's authority, made up of citizens of several states engaged in political activism within or outside their own states' borders.

◉ **Watch** the **Video** "State Sovereignty and the 'Responsibility to Protect'" at **mypoliscilab.com**

What are the political consequences of the growing importance of transnational issues and the IGOs and INGOS that have emerge in response? Debate about the political consequences of globalization centers on two questions: (1) whether IGOs and INGOS undermine states' sovereignty; and (2) more specifically, whether they weaken *democratic* states' sovereignty.

Consequences for State Sovereignty

Sovereignty—maintaining authority over borders and the conduct of internal affairs—is each state's core function. Do the growing importance of transnational issues and the emergence of IGOs and INGOS challenge states' ability to maintain sovereignty? Some believe that the answer to this question is yes, while others remain skeptical. Let us consider the arguments in turn.

Globalization Weakens Sovereignty   Some suggest that IGOs and INGOS are increasingly replacing states' political functions, limiting their autonomy to control their own territory and people. The rise of IGOs and INGOS does not mean we are seeing the rise of global government—a system in which states relinquish sovereignty and acknowledge their subordination to a single global authority. Instead, globalization has brought about global governance, a situation in which states, IGOs, and INGOS must increasingly act in concert to address specific transnational challenges. Yet, to the extent that states willingly or unwillingly become enmeshed in networks of IGOs and INGOS, they may no longer be making "sovereign" decisions about those issues within their own territory.

Limits on state sovereignty might follow from the growing influence of IGOs, because membership in such organizations binds states' hands to the interests and influence of other states. Although states set up IGOs in their own interests—usually to help address complicated transnational policy issues—they may later come to find that membership comes with strings attached that cannot be cut. The European Union offers a good example. A few European states—notably France and Germany—were integral to the EU's formation in the 1950s. They believed that facilitating the flow of goods and people would bind Europe's states to each other, helping to prevent a third World War. In 1985, all member-states agreed to allow anyone to travel anywhere within the entire union without a passport. (People from outside Europe still typically need a passport to enter the EU zone.) Yet recently, citizens in some European countries have had second thoughts about this policy, believing it facilitates drug and human trafficking and illegal immigration. However, individual EU member-states cannot reimpose border controls on their own without violating union regulations and risking penalties.[4]

The EU's authority has grown in many ways—some intended, and some not—since its founding. Today, member-states have largely relinquished autonomous control over economic policy. For example, to stave off economic collapse, in 2011, Greece had to agree to deep budget cuts other EU governments demanded, even though many Greek citizens took to the streets to protest what they felt were unfair impositions. Many Greeks now believe that membership in the EU has involved capitulation to forces beyond their country's control. Clearly, membership

global government ■ a system in which states relinquish power and acknowledge their subordination to a single global authority.

global governance ■ a situation in which states, IGOs, and INGOS must increasingly act in concert to address transnational challenges.

in IGOs such as the EU can involve tradeoffs, some of which may involve significant sacrifices of political autonomy.

Globalization Does Not Weaken Sovereignty   Despite the growing importance of transnational issues, IGOs, and INGOs, many do not accept that globalization truly limits state sovereignty. For one, IGOs always represent, at a basic level, the interests of member-states. While it is true that EU members lack full autonomy over economic policy, membership does bring considerable benefits. For example, although Greece has been asked to make deep budget cuts, it—along with every other EU member—benefits from billions of dollars in agricultural subsidies. The EU distributes about $70 billion a year to its members—about 40 percent of its entire budget, and about four times what the United States provides to its farmers.[5] Such subsidies keep European farmers in business in the face of competition from countries that can cheaply export food, such as the United States, Russia, and Brazil. Membership in the EU does not eliminate sovereignty—it serves member-states' interests by providing benefits they would not obtain were they to remain outside the EU system.

A second reason IGOs and INGOs may not threaten state sovereignty is that they do not possess the resources to solve many difficult transnational issues. For example, although terrorists and criminals pose transnational threats, only sovereign states possess military and police forces to fight them. So, although the EU may be the most powerful IGO on the planet, it lacks an army—the one thing essential to establish sovereignty over territory. (Each EU member maintains military forces.) In fact, EU member-states frequently divide on questions of national security or foreign policy. For example, the UK and Spain initially supported the U.S. decision to invade Iraq in 2003, while France and Germany did not. In this crucial case, no "European" foreign policy existed—only the diverse policies of sovereign states.

Third, many states continue to ignore the advice of IGOs, such as the International Monetary Fund (IMF) and WTO, which advocate free-market economic policies. For example, countries such as Russia, Venezuela, Saudi Arabia, Brazil, South Africa, and India continue to maintain at least partial government ownership of key industries such as petroleum, mining, and telecommunications, despite pressure to sell off government assets. One observer has recently suggested that the future will see increasing competition between the U.S. model of limited government intervention in the economy versus the Chinese model of heavy state intervention.[6] If China continues to grow while the United States stagnates, more countries may come to emulate China's policies, further confounding the notion that states have lost control over economic policymaking in this globalized era.

Finally, it is worth noting that in contrast to EU efforts to eliminate frontier controls, many states in recent years have *strengthened* their national borders, in reaction to perceived threats from terrorism, drug trafficking, and immigration.[7] American efforts to bolster border security is just one example of "rebordering" occurring even as globalization advances. In short, although the traditional boundaries between domestic and international politics are weakening, one should not exaggerate globalization's political consequences. The evidence does not suggest that increased international cooperation means the end of state sovereignty, but rather that states must increasingly work with other states, IGOs, and INGOs to address political and economic challenges.

Consequences for Democracy

Perhaps globalization does not mean the end of sovereignty for all states—but only for some. Does political, economic, and cultural integration strengthen or weaken democratic states in particular? On the one hand, pessimists suggest that globalization delegitimizes democracy by transferring accountability for policy to unelected and distant foreign bureaucrats. On the other hand, optimists believe that IGOs and INGOs strengthen democracy because they limit states' power to coerce their own citizens, and they force states to respect emerging global norms of bureaucratic transparency, freedom of speech, human rights, and free and fair elections. If the optimists are right, globalization is *good* for democracy: the more influential that IGOs and INGOs become, the less that states can ignore democratic norms and rules. Let us weigh both sides of this question.

Globalization Weakens Democracy   Pessimists suggest that globalization could undermine democracy by weakening the already tenuous relationship between citizens and government officials as IGOs and INGOs accumulate increasing influence and authority over policy. To the extent this is true, globalization short-circuits a core feature of democracy: the possibility that citizens can hold rulers accountable for their actions.

Pessimists fear the growing power of IGOs, which are run by unelected bureaucrats who have little incentive to respond to public opinion. Citizens in IGO member-states cannot hold IGO leaders accountable as they do their elected leaders, because no one votes for leaders of the UN, WTO, or IMF, for example. This means that unelected IGO bureaucrats can make or change policy without fear of being tossed from office if citizens object.

The EU offers a pointed example of this problem. Europeans can regularly vote for representatives to the European Parliament (EP), but these campaigns generate little interest and low turnout. Such disaffection results from a widespread belief that a small group of unelected EU bureaucrats controls policy, not EP legislators. Indeed, in contrast to national parliaments, the EP lacks the ability to select and hold accountable the EU's executive branch. Given this, many believe there is little point to voting.[8] The union's success in binding states to each other offers a cautionary tale: as IGOs' power grows, citizens may grow less interested in participating in politics, believing that their words and deeds will not influence outcomes.

Democratic accountability can also be weakened because INGOs do not answer to the public or the government of any state. Instead, they are only accountable to their members or financial backers. INGOs operate across borders, lobbying for policy changes. Americans or Europeans might reasonably object if influential Brazilian, Chinese, or Nigerian citizens pushed for change in U.S. policies, just as citizens of those countries might not appreciate meddling by European or American activists. In short, according to pessimists, IGOs and INGOs are bad for democracy primarily because they short-circuit the possibility of accountability.

Globalization Strengthens Democracy   The growing influence of INGOs—particularly those that focus on human rights and civil conflict such as Amnesty International or Human Rights Watch (HRW)—could also support a different conclusion—that political globalization can strengthen democracy. The rise of such groups makes it more difficult for rulers to hide their actions from outsiders and from their citizens. For example, governments sometimes ratify international treaties believing they will face little pressure to comply. However, research has shown that ratification generates greater protections against human rights abuses, because both domestic and international NGOs work to hold abusers to accounts.[9]

Several IGOs are also designed specifically to defend democratic principles. For example, the International Criminal Court (ICC)—created in 2002 by an act of the United Nations and based in The Hague, Netherlands—claims legal jurisdiction over sovereign states to prosecute genocide and human rights violations. Any

International Criminal Court (ICC)
■ an IGO created in 2002 and based in The Hague, Netherlands, which claims jurisdiction to prosecute genocide and human rights violations worldwide.

Executive Director Kenneth Roth presents Human Rights Watch's annual report to the press in January 2011. HRW has its headquarters in New York but operates in more than 90 countries. It focuses on researching, documenting, and drawing media attention to cases of systematic human rights violations around the world and on lobbying for policy change.

member-state concedes ICC jurisdiction over its territory; joining the ICC thus makes it harder for future leaders to violate human rights without fear of being held to accounts for their crimes. (The United States is not currently a member.) As with the spread of INGOs, examples like the ICC suggest that the spread of IGOs can also foster the conditions for greater democratic accountability.

Several states have also developed new forms of international law to protect democratic rights around the world. Belgium and Spain, for example, have advocated the concept of universal jurisdiction, which holds that states can prosecute crimes that occurred outside their borders, based on the notion that crimes against humanity know no boundaries. For example, in 2003, a Spanish judge indicted a former member of an Argentine military junta who was then living in Mexico, alleging gross human rights violations. This marked the first time that one country had extradited someone to another country to stand trial for crimes allegedly committed in a third country.[10] Opponents regard the principle of universal jurisdiction as an affront to national sovereignty.[11]

In short, pessimists believe that globalization undermines democracy by short-circuiting the possibility that voters can hold elected leaders to accounts. In contrast, optimists believe that IGO and INGO human rights advocacy serves to protect average people everywhere against government abuses of authority. Those who hold to this view want even *more* global political integration, believing that globalization tends to threaten non-democratic regimes far more than it undermines democracy.[12]

In the end, the political consequences of globalization remain unclear. The table below summarizes the key lines of debate we've covered in this section. The rise of new transnational issues and of IGOs and INGOs surely complicates states' ability to exercise sovereignty, but greater global political integration has hardly *eliminated* such authority. The consequences for democracy are similarly unclear: on the one hand, the rise of IGOs and INGOs makes it harder for states to hide violations of democratic rights. Yet on the other hand, IGOs and INGOs are themselves unaccountable organizations.

universal jurisdiction ■ holds that states can claim legal jurisdiction over people who committed crimes outside the borders of that state, based on the notion that crimes against humanity know no boundaries.

SUMMARY TABLE

Potential Consequences of Political Globalization

	Weakens	Does Not Weaken
For State Sovereignty	Globalization weakens state sovereignty because of the growing importance of both transnational issues and the IGOs and INGOs that have arisen to address those issues.	Globalization does not weaken state sovereignty because IGOs tend to represent state interests; because only states possess the resources to solve transnational challenges; and because many states have recently intervened in their economies and enhanced border controls.

(Continued)

	Weakens	**Does Not Weaken**
SUMMARY TABLE (CONTINUED)		
For Democracy	The rise of IGOs and INGOs transfers democratic authority beyond the borders of the state, weakening accountability between citizens and rulers. IGOs and INGOs are unelected and unaccountable, and tend to delegitimize democracy.	The rise of IGOs and INGOs and of human-rights treaties protects individual rights by making it harder for state rulers to commit or hide non-democratic behavior. The more globalized the world, the more democratic the world.

ECONOMIC GLOBALIZATION

If the consequences of political globalization are unclear, are the consequences of *economic* globalization, as well? In this section, we measure the growth of global economic integration, and then explain why this process has advanced so rapidly. Finally, we consider two potential consequences of economic globalization: its impact on economic development in poor countries, and its impact on overall economic inequality around the world.

When people think about globalization, what often comes to mind are international trade and financial flows—the kinds of things that the WTO tries to regulate—both of which have expanded rapidly in recent decades. Figure 13.3 shows that international trade in goods accounted for one in every five dollars of global economic activity in 1970 but for over half of all global economic activity by the late 2000s.[13]

13.3 What is economic globalization and what are its consequences?

👁 Watch the Video "IMF Conditionality and the Irish Bailout" at **mypoliscilab.com**

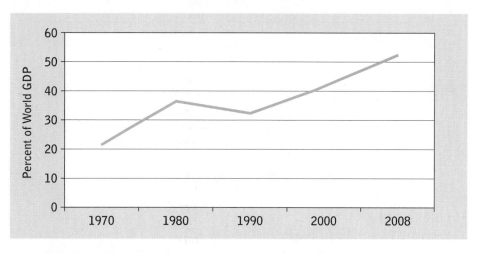

FIGURE 13.3

International Merchandise Trade as a Percent of World GDP

The key component of economic globalization—international trade—has grown nearly continuously since the 1970s.

Source: The World Bank Databank online resource, http://data.worldbank.org, accessed June 5, 2011.

Foreign Direct Investment (FDI) ■ the purchase or creation of assets in one country by an individual, firm, or government based in a different country.

multinational corporations (MNCs) ■ firms with headquarters in one country but with operations and employees in many countries.

International financial flows have also skyrocketed. Foreign Direct Investment (FDI) is the purchase or creation of assets in one country by an individual, firm, or government based in another country. For example, the Japanese car company Toyota spent approximately $800 million recently to build a factory in Blue Springs, Mississippi, where it expects to eventually employ 2,000 people.[14] As Figure 13.4 reveals, total global FDI increased from about $55 billion in 1970 to a peak of almost $2.2 trillion in 2007. FDI declined after the attacks of 9/11 and again during the global recession in 2008, but the global volume of FDI in 2009 was still more than three times as great as it was 20 years earlier.[15]

Expanding global trade and investment has been accompanied by the growth of multinational corporations (MNCs)—firms that are headquartered in one country but that have operations and employees in many others. McDonald's is perhaps the most ubiquitous MNC—it has more than 31,000 restaurants in 119 countries.[16] AB InBev is another—it makes Budweiser, Bud Lite, and Michelob; controls 25 percent of the global beer market; and employs more than 116,000 people in 23 countries. This MNC resulted from the merger of Brazilian, Belgian, and American brewers; it is headquartered in Belgium today, which technically makes those popular brands "foreign" beers!

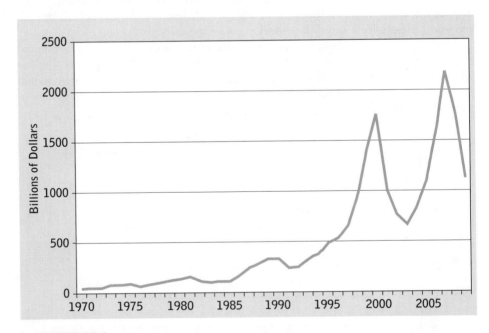

FIGURE 13.4

Volume of Foreign Direct Investment Over Time

Despite dips after 9/11 and the global recession of 2008, another component of economic globalization—Foreign Direct Investment—remains three times as great as it was in 1988.

Source: The World Bank Databank online resource, accessed June 5, 2011, http://data.worldbank.org

Explaining Economic Globalization

Three reasons explain why economic globalization deepened so fast. First, the growth of MNCs favors globalization. As Toyota's investment in Mississippi illustrates, MNCs have interests in integrating global markets. Corporations want to lower costs and increase profits, and expanding globally creates advantages over smaller, less-nimble firms. To expand, MNCs seek political influence. For example, corporations can use the threat to offshore jobs—move them to another country—when negotiating with unions for lower salaries or with governments about tax rates or labor or environmental regulations. MNCs also lobby against protectionism and for free trade—the elimination of tariffs, quotas, and other measures that make foreign imports more expensive than domestically produced goods—because they may be based in one country, have a factory in another country, but want to export to other countries.

offshore jobs ■ the movement of jobs outside a corporation's home country.

free trade ■ the elimination of tariffs, quotas, and other measures that make imports more expensive than domestically produced goods.

Many MNCs have grown so big that their annual revenues dwarf some countries' economies. For example, the world's largest MNC—Royal Dutch Shell, an oil company based in the Netherlands—had global sales of over $458 billion in 2008, about the same as all economic activity in Belgium, the world's twentieth-largest economy.[17] Given their global growth, MNCs have become so politically influential that critics allege they can dictate policies to governments on everything from taxes to labor laws to environmental protection.

The second factor driving economic globalization is technological change. Rapid advances in communications and computing have changed the way corporations and consumers interact. For example, the Internet creates cheap and instantaneous global links, integrates MNCs' global business operations, gives even small businesses in one country the opportunity to market to consumers in any other, and allows consumers to interact directly with corporations anywhere in the globe. Technological change reduces costs—which makes the global business environment more competitive.

Innovations in transportation have also lowered costs, making international trade possible for an ever-wider number of products. For example, Americans have grown accustomed to seeing supermarkets stocked with apples and blueberries in January, even though the fruit must be shipped thousands of miles from Chile or New Zealand. These advances—much like the invention of the railroad or the telephone in earlier generations—have transformed the way that goods and services are bought, sold, and marketed. Independently of MNCs' influence, technological change has promoted economic globalization.

IGOs are the final force promoting economic globalization. In the wake of World War II, American and European leaders concluded that protectionist trade barriers enacted in the 1930s had exacerbated the Great Depression and pushed the world towards war. To prevent another conflict, they created the IMF and the World Bank in 1944 to maintain stable international currency markets and promote economic development. To promote free trade, in 1947, they then encouraged the UN to establish the General Agreement on Tariffs and Trade (GATT), which in 1995 became the WTO.

neoliberal economic policies ■ policies which seek to limit governments' role in setting economic policy.

Washington Consensus ■ neoliberal economic agreement between MNCs, the main IGOs, and the U.S. government regarding how to promote economic stability and growth in poorer countries.

Today, the IMF, World Bank, and WTO are the main IGOs shaping the rules of international trade and finance. Along with MNCs, they promote neoliberal economic policies, which seek to limit governments' role in setting economic policy. In the 1980s, these policies came to be known as the Washington Consensus—an agreement between MNCs, the main IGOs, and the U.S. government about how to promote economic stability and growth in poorer countries. The policy recommendations included balanced budgets; promotion of free trade and reduction of barriers to foreign investment; privatization of government-owned enterprises; and deregulation—all of which worked to promote economic globalization.[18]

The Washington Consensus embodied free-market capitalism, with few government restrictions on international trade and finance. Critics argue that MNCs, IGOs, and the U.S. government promoted these policies to maintain leverage over poor countries, and that such policies hypocritically forced poorer countries to adopt austerity budgets even as social welfare spending continued to increase in the wealthy countries. It is certainly the case that MNCs, technology, and IGOs proved a powerful mix of forces; let us now consider how they have impacted global economic growth and inequality.

Globalization and Poverty

The most important question about economic globalization focuses on whether it increases or reduces prosperity—particularly for the world's poorest. Our point of comparison is whether a less-economically integrated world would be richer or poorer. If globalization stopped tomorrow, would more people be lifted out of poverty? Let us consider the potential answers to this question.

Does Economic Globalization Increase Global Poverty? Protesters in Seattle, Strasbourg, and elsewhere believe that economic globalization generates only negative consequences, working to keep poor countries on the periphery of the world economy, for example. This argument suggests that increased foreign direct investment strengthens MNCs and puts developing countries at a disadvantage: to the extent that openness makes it easier to move money, jobs, and factories around the world, globalization helps MNCs find the weakest regulations, the cheapest labor, and the lowest tax rates, hurting workers and weakening governments' tax base. Pessimists conclude that globalization enhances corporate power over workers and governments. A more open world means greater poverty and inequality.

Optimists derive a different conclusion. Most economists, for example, believe that eliminating trade barriers generates opportunities for new industries to emerge, creating jobs and lowering prices, thereby enhancing consumer purchasing power. In this view, free exchange generates prosperity and lowers inequality. Optimists point out that economic openness has pulled hundreds of millions of people out of poverty, particularly in Asian countries that have benefited from growth of export industries. They acknowledge that globalization has not created *enough* prosperity or equality, because hundreds of millions of people remain mired in poverty around the world. However, they argue that an open markets lead to a wealthier world. Who is right?

Assess the Evidence   Recent research has concluded that *the more globalized a country, the more it grows and reduces poverty.*[19] To derive this conclusion, economists compare changes over time on the KOF Index of Globalization (see Figure 13.1) to changes over time in countries' growth and poverty rates.[20] The reason is that open economies have industries that are better situated to profit when new markets open up, because openness makes them more efficient and agile. In contrast, industries in closed economies have been protected from competition, making them far less innovative and efficient.

A good example of this dynamic is the Indian automotive industry. Prior to 1991, not a single car was produced in India, even though the country has more than 1 billion people. After the government lowered trade barriers and opened up to foreign investment, India's auto industry took root and rapidly grew. Today, both domestic and multinational corporations produce hundreds of thousands of vehicles a year in India, employing millions of people.[21] An Indian MNC named Tata Motors has even emerged as a global powerhouse, buying up large South Korean and Spanish bus manufacturers and building assembly plants in Argentina, Russia, South Africa, and Thailand. Tata even bought the storied British auto brands Jaguar and Land Rover, all part of its effort to become globally competitive.

A single example from India does not prove the case that globalization has benefited the world's poor. Does economic integration help the world's poorest? In India, the population living at the absolute poverty level—measured by the World Bank as the proportion of a country's population that earns $1.25 a day or less—declined from 66 percent in 1976 to 42 percent in 2004. China has made even greater strides: In 1981, 835 million people, or 84 percent of the total population, lived in absolute poverty—more than three times the total population of the United States at the time! However, by 2005, only 16 percent of China's total population of 1.3 billion remained mired in absolute poverty.[22] Millions of people remain poor in India, China, and elsewhere—but hundreds of millions are no longer destitute.

absolute poverty level ■ measured as the proportion of a country's population that earns $1.25 a day or less.

How have countries like India and China reduced absolute poverty? By opening up to the world market, which helps grow their economies. The news is filled with stories of China's fantastic economic boom in recent decades, and in fact since 1980 China's economy has grown faster than the United States' economy in every year. This growth has created millions of new jobs, which helps reduce poverty. China and India have combined economic openness, growth, and declining poverty. Because together they hold such a large proportion of the world's overall population, economic growth in just those two countries has reduced total global poverty. However, globalization has had uneven effects across the world, as Figure 13.5 reveals.

Since 1980, absolute poverty has declined most in South Asia (where India's economy dominates) and East Asia (where China's economy dominates), but not much in Latin America or sub-Saharan Africa. Today, most of the world's poorest live in Africa—a change from 30 years ago, when misery was concentrated in Asia. Poverty remains widespread in Africa because economies there did not grow—partly because they did not open up to globalization as much as did China or India, for example.

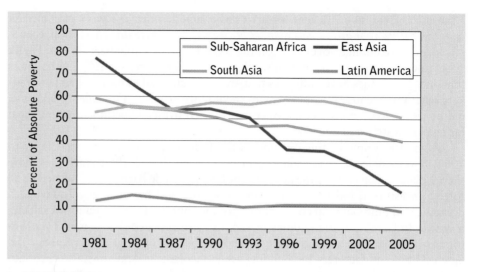

FIGURE 13.5

Absolute Poverty Levels by World Region

Countries in Latin America and sub-Saharan Africa have not globalized as successfully as China and India. As a result, their levels of absolute poverty have not diminished as drastically as they have in East Asia and South Asia.

Source: The World Bank, "PovcalNet Online Poverty Analysis Tool," accessed December 15, 2011, http://web.worldbank.org.

In 1980, China was the world's most populous country but its economy was the world's eleventh largest, smaller than Mexico's. Thirty years later, China still had the most people, but its economy had become the world's second largest, behind only the United States.[23] China's astonishing growth rate—along with recent sustained economic growth in such countries as India, Brazil, and Indonesia—means that it makes little sense to argue that globalization is a plot by rich countries to exploit the poor. Today, the media in the United States sometimes portrays China as a global "bad guy" because overseas branches of Chinese MNCs exploit local workers![24]

Has economic integration helped or hurt the world's poorest? On the one hand, globalization does bring rapid change, which means social disruption and economic instability—the kinds of things that bring protesters to the streets against the WTO or IMF. Some critics suggest that the rapid pace of change has not allowed countries to adapt on their own terms. On the other hand, the evidence is clear that greater and more open trade and financial flows have benefited hundreds of millions of poor people in countries such China and India. In short, globalization increases opportunities for growth but also increases economic risks and uncertainties.

Globalization and Social Welfare

A second issue is whether economic globalization has forced states to cut social welfare benefits such as public pensions, health care, or unemployment insurance. The logic behind this intuition derives from the fact that governments depend on tax revenue from economic production, but wealthy investors can shift assets from one country to another. This creates a dilemma: governments need taxes to pay for the social welfare programs, but they can't raise tax rates too high or investors will take their money somewhere else—somewhere with a lower tax rate.

Economic globalization—by making the movement of goods and finance easier—may intensify this dilemma by putting greater downward pressure on governments to adopt business-friendly policies—particularly lower tax rates—in order to keep jobs and attract investment. If governments try to ignore this imperative of the globalized economy, so the argument goes, investments will dry up, jobs will go to other countries, and tax revenue will decline. In theory, this generates a race to the bottom, in which all countries lower tax rates and eliminate government social welfare programs in order to stay competitive.[25]

race to the bottom ■ a situation in which all countries lower tax rates as much as possible and eliminate government social welfare programs in order to balance their budgets.

The logic of economic globalization appears to privilege the political and economic interests of holders of capital—financiers, bankers, and investors. The enhanced power of capital conflicts with other political interests, especially those of workers, consumers, and retirees, who may demand pensions, health care, unemployment insurance, or government spending on education, infrastructure, the environment, or other public goods. Wealthy financiers are only a minority of voters, but governments must consider interests of the majority of the population. This means that increased economic integration generates tension between the demands of capital for market liberalization and the demands of workers and consumers for protection from the destruction of jobs due to technological change or recessions. Does globalization cause a race to the bottom?

The Race to the Bottom in Wealthy Countries   If the "race to the bottom" hypothesis were true, we should see a relationship between trade or financial openness and declining social welfare spending in the world's wealthy economies. However, this is not the case: in the world's wealthy countries both economic globalization *and* social welfare spending have increased rapidly in recent decades.

To explain the puzzle of rising social spending in wealthy democracies, some scholars have turned the "race to the bottom" hypothesis on its head, suggesting that more trade does not mean *less* government—more trade means *more* government. Because globalization brings greater economic uncertainty, citizens demand more protection—and politicians respond by increasing social welfare spending, in order to win elections.[26] Most scholarship finds little support for the "race to the bottom" hypothesis: government social welfare spending remains high, and tax rates have not declined precipitously.

Of course, wealthy countries do face challenges to their social welfare programs. The most important is demographic: the aging of the population. Many European democracies, such as Greece, Denmark, and Italy, are facing huge public pension system deficits because the number of workers paying into the system is declining relative to the number of retirees receiving benefits, due to a long-term decline in birthrates.[27]

Another challenge comes from technological change. Wealthy countries have experienced a long-term shift away from manufacturing and agriculture as the main sources of jobs, and an expansion of the service sector, which includes medicine, law, transportation, retail sales, tourism, and entertainment. For example, the manufacturing sector in the United States accounted for 28.3 percent of GDP in 1953, but only 11.0 percent by 2009.[28] The shift is driven by technological change—which improves productivity and reduces prices for consumers, but which also destroys jobs in industries that become inefficient and generates a constant demand for unemployment insurance, education, and job retraining programs. However, like declining birthrates, technological change is unrelated to globalization.

service sector ■ jobs outside of manufacturing and agriculture that include medicine, law, transportation, retail sales, tourism, and entertainment.

The Race to the Bottom in Developing Countries

Globalization has not caused a race to the bottom in the world's wealthiest states. However, developing countries tend to have relatively weaker state capacity—and, as a result, they may be less able than wealthier states to maintain or even increase social welfare spending as pressure to open up their economies mounts. That is, perhaps globalization causes a "race to the bottom" only in developing countries.

The poor in any country are extremely vulnerable to downturns in social spending. However, developing countries have historically spent relatively little on the poor to begin with.[29] Instead, government spending on social security pensions and secondary or higher education, for example, has typically benefited the middle or upper classes. Obviously, globalization cannot eliminate welfare programs for the poor if they never existed in the first place. In fact, in developing countries, the poor may benefit most from economic opening, because free trade tends to lower consumer prices and generate job opportunities.

Leaders of developing countries also appear able to address the needs of the poor through social welfare spending, if they so desire.[30] For example, in the early 1990s, Brazil's government began a conditional cash transfer program—which gives poor families a small amount of money based on certain conditions—called *Bolsa Familia* (Family Grant). *Bolsa Familia* provides families up to $120 per month, on the condition that their children stay in school rather than work. *Bolsa Familia* now covers more than 12.4 million families—almost 50 million people and about 25 percent of Brazil's population, and it is currently the largest program of its kind in the world.

conditional cash transfer program ■ welfare programs that give people a small amount of money based on certain required conditions.

Brazil has long had one of the highest levels of economic inequality in the world, and a great need to address poverty, malnutrition, and lack of education. Brazil's leaders implemented *Bolsa Familia after* they liberalized the country's economy—and the program has helped reduce inequality and the number of people living in absolute poverty.[31] *Bolsa Familia* is such an obvious success that other

SUMMARY TABLE

Potential Consequences of Economic Globalization

	Pessimist	Optimist	Evidence
On Poverty and Inequality	Globalization worsens inequality and poverty because it facilitates moving money, jobs, and factories around the world, giving corporations greater advantages over governments and citizens, particularly those in developing countries.	Globalization opens up opportunities for new industries to emerge, creating jobs and lowering prices, especially for the world's poorest.	Globalization causes greater economic instability and puts downward pressure on wages in uncompetitive industries in wealthy countries. However, poor countries that globalize have experienced growth and declining inequality.
On Social Welfare Spending	Globalization forces states to lower taxes to keep jobs and attract investment, creating a "race to the bottom" which forces them to cut social-welfare spending.	Globalization generates greater demand for protection from economic instability and change, enhancing demand for government social-welfare spending.	Globalization does not obviously cause a race to the bottom in either wealthy or poor countries. Governments can create policies that respond to the instability and enhanced competition globalization brings.

countries have begun to copy it.[32] To be sure, *Bolsa Familia* is only one example of increased social welfare spending in an increasingly globalized world, but its success suggests that governments of developing countries can implement pro-poor policies even as globalization advances.

The table above summarizes the pessimists' and optimists' views of the effects of economic globalization. The impact on poverty and social welfare spending has been exaggerated, both in wealthy and developing economies. Globalization does put increased pressure on jobs and social safety nets, yet as India and China reveal, economic openness can help poor countries reduce poverty. Moreover, thus far, economic integration appears to be compatible with high social welfare spending.

HYPOTHESIS TESTING | Poor People in Developing Countries Oppose Economic Globalization: The Case of Bolivia

Conventional wisdom supposes that economic globalization hurts the world's poor. Like protesters at the "Battle in Seattle" in 1999, masses of angry citizens in many poor countries lend support to this view by taking to the streets to oppose free trade agreements and privatization of government-owned enterprises, believing that the social and economic costs of such changes dramatically exceed the promised benefits. Is economic globalization really such a bad thing? How would you go about confirming or refuting the hypothesis that *"Poor people in developing countries have strong incentives to oppose globalization"*?

GATHER EVIDENCE

One example that appears to confirm the connection between poverty and opposition to globalization comes from Bolivia. In 1999, the World Bank threatened to withhold millions of dollars in debt relief if Bolivia did not privatize the publicly owned water distribution company in Cochabamba, a city of about one million people. The company provided residents with subsidized drinking water—meaning they paid less than it cost to filter and distribute. The bank argued that ridding Bolivia of such inefficiency would improve its economy and suggested that Bolivia sell the water company to a consortium that included Bechtel, an American multinational corporation. After the sale, the new owners raised the monthly household fee for water delivery by 35 percent, to about $20 a month.[33] This made clean water unaffordable for many of Cochabamba's residents—the average Bolivian earns only about $1,000 per year.

In response to the price hikes, thousands of poor Cochabamba residents took to the streets and blocked access to the city for days. The government sent in the army, and violent clashes erupted, resulting in dozens of injuries. Bolivians in other cities joined the protests, blockading major highways, and causing widespread economic disruption. The president then suspended constitutional liberties such as freedom

of assembly and freedom of the press, but this did nothing to stop the protesters, who began to demand government action on a range of other issues, such as unemployment, racial discrimination, and inflation.

Because of the violent protests, the multinational's executives fled the country. This allowed the government to declare that the corporation had "abandoned" the water company, meaning the privatization could be rescinded. Jubilant Bolivians celebrated, and leaders of the protests became prominent in Bolivian national politics—including Evo Morales, who would leverage his role in the protests to win Bolivia's 2005 presidential election.

A man with "Die, Aguas Tunari!"—the foreign water distribution company—written on his chest holds a sign saying, "What is ours is ours and cannot be taken away" during a protest against water rate hikes in Cochabamba, a city of about one million in southeastern Bolivia in April 2000.

(*Continued*)

In this case poor Bolivians mobilized because globalization—the privatization of a local public utility and its sale to a MNC—directly harmed their economic interests. Can this case be generalized more widely? Somewhat surprisingly, research on popular attitudes towards globalization in Latin America suggests that the answer is both yes *and* no.

ASSESS THE HYPOTHESIS

Poor people around the world oppose globalization— *when it has obvious negative consequences.* On the one hand, about 75 percent of Latin Americans oppose selling off government-owned assets such as water, electricity, or oil companies in the name of global efficiency. Like the Bolivian government in 2000, governments across the region that have privatized public utilities have often paid a heavy electoral price, because the poor know by checking their wallets that privatization harms their economic interests.

However, globalization can also bring benefits— something the poor know very well. For example, about 75 percent of Latin Americans *favor* free trade

and direct foreign investment, other core globalization policies.[34] Surveys even repeatedly find that about 75 percent of Latin Americans support the U.S.-sponsored "Free Trade Agreement for the Americas," and majorities ranging between 60 percent and 80 percent agree with statements that, "large foreign companies are good [for our country]."[35]

These attitudes hold no matter what the respondent's income—that is, both poor and rich Latin Americans understand that privatization and free trade impact their interests very differently. People across income levels welcome foreign trade and investment, while opposing privatization of public utilities. The explanation for these diverging attitudes lies with citizens' positions as consumers: consumers want quality products at low prices—and globalization of trade and foreign investment has brought wider availability of cheaper but better-quality goods. In contrast, privatization of public utilities is unpopular because it typically leads to leads to huge increases in prices of crucial services such as water, sanitation, electricity, and telecommunications.

A man loads his trunk with goods purchased at a WalMart store in Mexico City. Many Latin Americans have benefited from lower prices and greater availability of consumer goods due to economic globalization.

(Continued)

For example, in Brazil, huge rate spikes followed in the wake of electric and telephone company privatization in the 1990s. However, prices of TVs, washing machines, and clothing fell by more than 50 percent in real terms between 1989 and 2006—a period in which Brazil reduced trade barriers and opened up to FDI.[36] Wal-Mart—appreciated by consumers but feared by competitors because of its cutthroat approach to competitive pricing—opened its first store in Brazil in 1995 and had 450 stores just 15 years later.[37] The poor can see the positive effects of globalization in their purses and wallets—greater affordability, availability, and quality of consumer goods such as processed foods, computers, refrigerators, and cell phones. Moreover, they can distinguish the positive from the negative effects brought about by privatization.

In Latin America—and by extension elsewhere—globalization does not have uniform effects. Globalization brings pressure to reduce barriers to foreign trade and investment and to reduce the size and scope of government by selling off government assets. The poor see the positive impact of some aspects of globalization but also recognize the negative effects of other aspects. The hypothesis that the poor have strong incentives to oppose globalization is only half-correct. ◣

CRITICAL THINKING QUESTIONS

1. Why do poor people in developing countries tend to oppose privatization?
2. Why do the poor in developing countries tend to favor free trade?

CULTURAL GLOBALIZATION

13.4 How has cultural globalization shaped politics in the world's states?

◉ Watch the **Video** **"Anti-Globalization Protests"** at **mypoliscilab.com**

Antiglobalization activists are not just preoccupied with the economic or political consequences of global integration. They also believe globalization replaces local, regional, or even national identities with a homogenous cosmopolitan global culture—a bland Americanization of the world that is disconnected from local traditions and history. Skeptics of this view respond that the backlash against globalization has reenergized established forms of political identity and even generated new cultural practices. That is, as the world becomes more integrated politically and economically, people adopt aspects of other cultures they find appealing and cast off elements of their own culture that they disdain. Does globalization homogenize the world, or does it create opportunities for even greater global cultural diversity?

Globalization Homogenizes World Culture

About 200 years ago, the rise of nationalism and the sovereign state weakened local forms of identity based on family, clan, tribe, village, or religion. Nationalism tended to broaden the horizons of people who lived in isolation from other communities, linking local cultural attachments into a larger community. Many believe that globalization exacerbates cultural assimilation, extending this process beyond national and state boundaries so that eventually indigenous local and national cultures will disappear. The increased volume and speed of global trade and finance; the rise of MNCs, IGOs, and INGOs; the spread of communication technology; and the yearly flow of hundreds of millions of people via tourism and migration all contribute to this process.

The sources of globalization's homogenizing impact on culture are commercial and technological. Open markets undermine efforts at cultural and political isolation and erode existing forms of cultural identity. This is because in a global marketplace, cultural particularities get in the way of making a profit. For example, the existence of a single, integrated global market increasingly requires a single global language—English. The more that people need to speak English to succeed in life, the less they will value local languages and dialects. The imperatives of producing for the global marketplace—where only the quick, clever, and flexible can survive—may imply that local, regional, or national cultures will remain important only insofar as they can be marketed to tourists as quaint museum pieces, relics of the past.

Technological change also draws isolated communities into a homogenized global culture. Large multinational media corporations want to market music, TV shows, video games, and movies to the largest audiences possible at the lowest possible cost. The Internet has also lowered the cost, ease, and speed of global communications—once connected to the web, people in isolated communities gain instant access to images, video, and information from and about the entire world.

There are positive aspects to the advance of communications technology: media and the Internet facilitate the spread of new ideas and information, which allows people with shared interests and ideas to form friendships, business partnerships, and activist networks. Technological globalization might support democratic activism—but non-democratic governments also understand technology's potential impact on politics and often seek to control access to the web. China's government, for example, has created the so-called Great Firewall to block websites it deems subversive such as Amnesty International, the *New York Times,* or websites advocating Tibetan independence. The Chinese government also employs "Internet police" to search for antigovernment content,[38] and has arrested activists who post information critical of the government.[39]

Despite its potential benefits, critics have focused on globalization's negative cultural consequences. Benjamin Barber has argued that economic and technological integration tend to destroy what makes cultures unique in order to find what is most easily marketable to the largest potential pool of consumers. He calls this trend McWorld,[40] the idea that globalization homogenizes and Americanizes different cultures. The image of a McDonalds in every town in the world evokes cultural integration and uniformity—the elimination of local, regional, and national political identities and the emergence of a culture of trashy convenience and superficiality.

McWorld ∎ the idea that globalization homogenizes and Americanizes different cultures.

The impact of American culture on the rest of the world is obvious. Commerce and technology come together in the influence of American media and entertainment, which have reshaped even the most isolated and xenophobic communities. Hip-hop culture, for example, can be seen and heard in the slums of Havana or Rio de Janeiro, as well as in swanky nightclubs in Berlin or Seoul; the Big Mac, fries, and a Coke are so ubiquitous that by 2002 half of Chinese children under the age of 12 thought that McDonalds' was a *Chinese* restaurant chain, not an American MNC.[41] Hundreds of millions of people around the world appreciate different aspects of American culture—and they may also welcome the way that cultural globalization undermines repressive, misogynist, or anti-democratic local traditions.

Yet. even where we see this effect, many decry the influence of American culture because they believe it erodes valued local, regional, or national traditions, such as religion, language, cuisine, or music. A famous example of such anti-globalization and anti-American sentiment occurred in France in 1999, when farmer/activist José Bové led a protest against perceived threats to French agriculture and cuisine by spearheading the ransacking of a McDonald's restaurant construction site. Bové knew that McDonald's symbolizes more than just a quick and cheap meal option—the opposite of France's vaunted classical cuisine. As Barber notes, "McDonald's in Moscow and Coke in China do more to create a global culture than military colonization ever could. It is less the goods themselves than the brand names that do the work, because they convey lifestyle images that alter perceptions and challenge behavior."[37]

To what extent do we see evidence that antiglobalization activists' worst fears have come true? Has globalization created a new cosmopolitan culture that has destroyed indigenous local, regional, and national identities? If so, Europe—where the EU has opened borders and tied the region's countries tightly to each other— serves as the best case study. EU political elites have actively sought to *promote* a European identity, believing that nationalism is behind international war. If globalization has the effect many predict, we should see a decline in national identity and an increase in identification with Europe as a whole, or even an increase in identification with a cosmopolitan or "global" political identity.

French farmer. Jose Bové eats food that symbolically epitomizes France's local traditions and his opposition to economic globalization— a baguette, bleu cheese, and wine—immediately after his release from three weeks in prison for vandalism. Bové's group views McDonald's as a threat to France's economy and traditional culture.

TABLE 13.1

World Values Survey Question, 14 European Countries: "Which Geographic Group Do You Belong To First?"

	1980	2000
Locality	48.4%	49.3%
Region	13.4%	14.9%
Country	29.0%	26.0%
Continent	2.9%	3.5%
The World	6.4%	6.2%

Source: World Values Survey—Online Data Analysis, accessed June 5, 2011, http://www.wvsevsdb.com/wvs/WVSAnalize.jsp

Evidence from the World Values Surveys dispels this hypothesis. As Tables 13.1 and 13.2 reveal, there was virtually no decline in nationalist sentiment across 14 European countries for which data exist in surveys taken in 1980 and again in 2000. Europeans remain proud of their national identity as well as tightly bound to their local roots—to a city, village, or region within a country such as Wales in the UK or Catalonia in Spain. Despite the ever-expanding web of regional political, social, and economic ties that the EU has created, the proportion of Europeans with a continent-wide or "global" identity remains minuscule. In short, even where globalization has advanced the most, nationalism remains a potent political force.

Evidence from other countries confirms the findings from Europe: local, regional, and even national identities are not giving way to a global cosmopolitan culture or to American culture. This is not to say that American culture is not influential, and one can hardly deny the fact that certain cultural traits have become global. Still, evidence suggests that local, regional, and national political identities remain powerful. In fact, while some believe globalization weakens local or national political identities, others believe it creates new identities and reinvigorates old ones—creating new borders and boundaries between groups.

TABLE 13.2

World Values Survey Question, 14 European Countries: "How Proud Are You of Your Nationality?"

	1980	2000
Very proud	44.4%	42.7%
Quite proud	37.8%	44.0%
Not very proud	12.7%	10.1%
Not at all proud	5.1%	3.2%

Source: World Values Survey—Online Data Analysis, accessed June 5, 2011, http://www.wvsevsdb.com/wvs/WVSAnalize.jsp

Globalization Allows Cultures to Flourish

Perhaps globalization does not homogenize global culture but instead paradoxically strengthens local, regional, and national cultures because it increases the perception that local forms of culture are under siege. On the one hand, economic and political integration—accompanied by dramatic rapid changes in communications technology—do expose even the most isolated communities to outside influences. Yet, on the other hand, technology also helps people gather information about how to successfully counteract such threats and to mobilize in their community's defense. In this way, the presence of foreign companies and influences may generate a backlash—one that reinvigorates local, regional, and national cultures.

Globalization can simultaneously cause both cultural homogenization and an escalation of cultural conflict. It can bring about "retribalization," a defense of group distinctiveness and autonomy against the forces that promote similarity everywhere. That is, the forces that encourage homogeneity also spread the seeds of resistance against such forces, generating popular sentiment against global homogenization as groups seek to protect what they hold dear. For example, as China has opened up to the world and accepted aspects of Western capitalism and culture, its government and population have also become more nationalistic.[43]

In particular, Barber and others have pointed to the rise of new nationalist and religious movements that seek cultural autonomy and political self-determination. Since the end of the Cold War, we have seen movements for "national autonomy" emerge among Kurds in Iraq and Turkey, Timorese in Indonesia, Catalans in Spain, and Scots in the UK, for example—groups who believe their people constitutes a nation but who do not possess a state they can call their own. The rise of such movements indicates that globalization does not homogenize world culture but rather creates opportunities for groups to reassert their cultural distinctiveness. In some of these cases—as in Catalonia—we see peaceful mobilization; in others—as in East Timor—we see bloody conflict. In either case, existing states are weakened—but the *concept* of the sovereign state is not, because autonomist groups typically seek their own state!

In the contemporary world, technology helps groups gather information about successful mobilization practices. If we were heading toward "McWorld," cultures would have little reason to fight each other for recognition, whether in legislative committees, in the streets, or on the battlefield. However, globalization does not weaken cultural groups' desire for their own sovereign state. People mobilize to preserve and defend their communities. Such forms of mobilization tend to be culturally exclusionary, strengthening the boundaries of their group against perceived threats from outsiders.

Around the world, many worry about globalization's political and economic consequences and also fear the homogenizing impact of McWorld—the spread and preeminence of American culture and the disappearance of dozens or even hundreds of local, regional, and national forms of cultural identity. However, evidence does not confirm critics' worst fears. The table on the following page sums up the arguments: on the one hand, cultural globalization is obviously real. However, such homogenizing imperatives have not eroded individual or group attachments to local or regional identities. Indeed, globalization simultaneously encourages greater similarity across world cultures and permits rapid reaction *against* homogeniza-

SUMMARY TABLE

Potential Consequences of Cultural Globalization

	Hypothesis	Evidence
Globalization homogenizes world cultures.	Globalization of commerce and technology undermine efforts at cultural and political isolation and erode existing forms of cultural identity.	On the one hand, American culture (McWorld) is widespread. On the other hand, local and national cultures have not disappeared.
Globalization allows cultures to flourish.	Globalization simultaneously causes both cultural homogenization and a backlash in defense of cultural distinctiveness and autonomy.	Nationalist and other movements for autonomy have flourished along with the rise of political and economic globalization.

tion. Given the number and strength of movements demanding cultural autonomy around the world, it seems as if the reactions against globalization are stronger than its homogenizing imperatives.

CONCLUSION

What impact does globalization have on politics, economics, and culture? Protesters in Seattle, Strasbourg, Cochabamba, and elsewhere see the growth of worldwide connections between governments, businesses, and individuals very differently from executives on Wall Street or bureaucrats in Washington, DC. Yet, globalization is neither purely good nor bad; proponents tend to overlook its negative consequences, while opponents tend to ignore its benefits.

For example, in terms of its political consequences, although the growing importance of transnational issues and of IGOs and INGOs can complicate states' ability to *exercise* sovereignty, globalization has not *eliminated* state sovereignty. Globalization certainly has enhanced the influence of unaccountable IGOs and INGOs, but it has also helped spread democratic norms of government around the world.

Economically, globalization has increased job market volatility and the pace of change in industry and agriculture in both developed and developing countries. These transformations generate fear that governments will lose the ability to protect citizens from impoverishment. Economic damage due to globalization also tends to draw media attention—as well as the sorts of protests that we have seen against the WTO. However, evidence suggests that poverty declines most in those countries that have embraced economic globalization, and there is little evidence that economic globalization has eviscerated the welfare state, despite critics' fears.

The cultural consequences of globalization also appear similarly exaggerated. It is certainly true that the rapid spread of consumer culture and information technology work to expose culturally isolated communities, which sometimes undermines local cultures. McWorld is a reality—yet so is the reaction against globalization's homogenizing impulses. In the end, neither local nor national cultures have simply disappeared, and new forms of identity have gained strength just as political and economic globalization have advanced.

✓—Study and Review
the Post-Test &
Chapter Exam
at mypoliscilab.com

Globalization can cause harm, but it can also bring tremendous benefits—particularly for those countries willing and able to embrace it on their own terms. We have good reasons to be skeptical of the most pessimistic claims that globalization erodes sovereignty, increases poverty and inequality, and destroys indigenous cultures. Still, no government today can manage the increasing number of transnational issues—from human rights violations to the consequences of technological change to economic instability on its own. Instead, addressing contemporary challenges means working within a growing network of governments and IGOs, in which MNCs and INGOs also play increasingly influential roles. ◣

KEY TERMS

globalization   346
transnational   347
political globalization   349
international governmental organizations
    (IGOs)   349
international non-governmental
    organizations (INGOs)   349
global government   350
global governance   350
International Criminal Court (ICC)   353
universal jurisdiction   353

Foreign Direct Investment (FDI)   354
multinational corporations (MNCs)   354
offshore jobs   354
free trade   354
neoliberal economic policies   357
Washington Consensus   357
absolute poverty level   359
race to the bottom   361
service sector   362
conditional cash transfer program   362
McWorld   367

REVIEW QUESTIONS

1. What are the key elements of globalization?
2. Has globalization led to a "race to the bottom"? Why or why not?
3. Why has globalization not completely eroded state sovereignty?
4. Explain how globalization tends to homogenize world culture—but then explain why it also offers opportunities for local cultures to flourish.
5. What are the likely consequences for democracy around the world if globalization's pace increases?

SUGGESTED READINGS

Barber, Benjamin. "Jihad versus McWorld." *The Atlantic* online, accessed December 15, 2011, http://www.theatlantic.com/magazine/archive/1992/03/jihad-vs-mcworld/3882/. A classic statement of the potentially negative effects of cultural globalization in the post–Cold War era.

Erlanger, Steven. "Europeans Fear Crisis Threatens Liberal Benefits." *New York Times*, May 22, 2010. An in-depth examination of how the recent global economic crisis has brought increased budgetary pressures on the generous social welfare benefits in Europe, with an emphasis on the potential impact of globalization.

Friedman, Thomas. *The World Is Flat: A Brief History of the 21st Century* (New York: Farrar, Straus, and Giroux, 2005). A best-selling description of key factors said to be "leveling the playing field" in terms of global economics and politics. A good read, and useful for engaging classroom debates.

Naim, Moses. "Think Again: Globalization." *Foreign Policy* (2009) , accessed December 15, 2011, http://www.moisesnaim.com/writings/think-again-globalization.. A useful review of pro- and antiglobalization arguments, applied to the global economic crisis that began in 2008.

Rodrik, Dani. "Sense and Nonsense in the Globalization Debate." *Foreign Policy* 107 (1997): 19–37. A readable exploration of the issues surrounding debates about economic globalization. Stands up to the test of time.

NOTES

1. These figures are based on data from the "KOF Index of Globalization," available at http://globalization.kof.ethz.ch.

2. For space reasons, we do not consider the reverse and similarly important question, "How do states shape the nature and extent of globalization?"

3. See for example, John Boli and George Thomas, eds, *Constructing World Culture: International Nongovernmental Organizations since 1875* (Stanford, CA: Stanford University Press, 1999).

4. See for example, Michael Steininger, "Denmark Imposes New Border Checks to Keep out Immigrants, 'Criminals,'" *Christian Science Monitor,* July 5, 2011, accessed July 15, 2011, http://www.csmonitor.com/World/Europe/2011/0705/Denmark-imposes-new-border-checks-to-keep-out-immigrants-criminals.

5. *New York Times, "Europe's Vast Farm Subsidies Face Challenges."* Stephen Castle and Dorreen Carvajal, December 30, 2009, B4.

6. See Ian Bremmer, *The End of the Free Market: Who Wins the War Between States and Corporations?* (New York: Portfolio, 2010).

7. See for example, Peter Andreas, "Redrawing the Line: Borders and Security in the 21st Century," *International Security* 28(2)(2003): 78–112.

8. See for example, Andreas Follesdal and Simon Hix, "Why There is a Democratic Deficit in the EU: A Response to Majone and Moravcsik," *Journal of Common Market Studies* 44(3)(2006): 533–562.

9. See for example, Beth Simmons, *Mobilizing for Human Rights: International Law in Domestic Politics* (New York: Cambridge University Press, 2009).

10. Daniel Schweimler, "Cavallo Case Sets Precedent," BBC news online, June 29, 2003, accessed August 27, 2010, http://news.bbc.co.uk/2/hi/americas/3030030.stm.

11. Shashank Bengali, "Detainee Torture Cases Proceed Overseas as U.S. Stonewalls," August 22, 2010, accessed August 27, 2010, http://www.kansascity.com/2010/08/22/2166252/detainee-torture-cases-proceed.html.

12. See for example, David Held, *Democracy and the Global Order: From the Modern State to Cosmopolitan Governance* (Stanford, CA; Stanford University Press, 1995).

13. The World Bank Databank online resource, http://data.worldbank.org.

14. Brittany Stack, "Toyota Plant to Resume Construction," June 21, 2010, accessed August 23, 2010. http://www.thedmonline.com/article/toyota-plant-resume-construction.

15. United Nations Council on Trade and Development, "World Investment Report," http://www.unctad.org.

16. McDonald's, "About Us," accessed August 23, 2010, http://www.mcdonalds.ca/en/aboutus/faq.aspx.

17. CNN Money, "Global 500," accessed August 23, 2010, http://money.cnn.com/magazines/fortune/global500/2009/full_list/.

18. Center for International Development at Harvard University, "Washington Consensus," accessed August 23, 2010, http://www.cid.harvard.edu/cidtrade/issues/washington.html.

19. See for example, Xavier Sala-i-Martin, "The World Distribution of Income: Falling Poverty and . . . Convergence, Period," *Quarterly Journal of Economics* 121(2)(2006): 351–397.

20. Axel Dreher, "Does Globalization Affect Growth? Evidence from a New Index of Globalization," Research Paper Series #6, Thurgauer Wirtschaftinstitut, University of Konstanz, Switzerland (2005), accessed August 25, 2010, http://kops.ub.uni-konstanz.de/volltexte/2005/1655/pdf/TWI_res06.pdf.

21. Jorn Madslien, "India Eyes 25 Million Automotive Jobs," BBC News Online 2007, accessed August 25, 2010, http://news.bbc.co.uk/2/hi/business/6583203.stm.

22. The World Bank, "PovcalNet Online Poverty Analysis Tool," accessed June 12, 2011, http://web.worldbank.org.

23. See International Monetary Fund, World Economic Outlook 2011, accessed June 5, 2011, http://www.imf.org/external/pubs/ft/weo/2011/01/index.htm.

24. See for example, Simon Romero, "Tensions over Chinese Mining Venture in Peru," *New York Times,* August 15, 2010, accessed August 25, 2010, http://www.nytimes.com/2010/08/15/world/americas/15chinaperu.html?pagewanted=1&_r=1&sq=china%20peru%20&st=cse&scp=1.

25. The concept of a "race to the bottom" also refers to a range of regulatory policies, particularly in the area of wages, labor rights, and workplace safety, and in environmental protections.

26. See for example, Dani Rodrik, "Sense and Nonsense in the Globalization Debate," *Foreign Policy* 107(1997): 19–37.

27. Steven Erlanger, "Europeans Fear Crisis Threatens Liberal Benefits," *New York Times,* May 22, 2010, accessed August 26, 2010, http://www.nytimes.com/2010/05/23/world/europe/23europe.html?_r=1&sq=europeans%20fear%20deficit%20crisis%20imperils%20welfare%20state&st=cse&adxnnl=1&scp=1&adxnnlx=1282834964-LMz+asWF5nO/3qCCT/44Hw.

28. *New York Times,* "A White House Campaign for Factories," Lousi Uchitelle, September 10, 2010, B7.

29. Nita Rudra, *Globalization and the Race to the Bottom in Developing Countries: Who Really Gets Hurt?* (New York: Cambridge University Press, 2008).

30. See for example, Robert Kaufman and Sergio Segura-Ubiergo, "Globalization, Domestic Politics, and Social Spending in Latin America: A Time-Series Cross-Section Analysis, 1973–97," *World Politics* 53(4)(2001): 553–587.

31. *Economist,* "How to Get Children out of Jobs and into School," July 29, 2010, accessed August 26, 2010, http://www.economist.com/node/16690887.

32. *Economist,* "An Anti-Poverty Scheme Invented in Latin America Is Winning Converts Worldwide," February 7, 2008, accessed December 15, 2011, http://www.economist.com/node/10650663.

33. Lewis Dolinsky, "Cochabamba's Water Rebellion—And Beyond," *San Francisco Chronicle,* February 11, 2001, accessed December 15, 2011, http://www.sfgate.com/cgi-bin/article.cgi?file=/chronicle/archive/2001/02/11/SC197565.DTL.

34. See Andy Baker, *The Market and the Masses: Policy Reform and Consumption in Liberalizing Economies* (New York: Cambridge University Press, 2009), 11.

35. Baker, 95–97.
36. Baker, 176, 182–183.
37. Wal-Mart Brasil, accessed December 2, 2010, http://www.walmartbrasil.com.br/institucional/nobrasil.aspx?expandable=0
38. "Behind the Scenes: Internet Police out in Force for the Olympics," CNN Online, accessed September 17, 2010, http://articles.cnn.com/2008-08-07/world/olympics.press.freedom.florcruz_1_great-firewall-internet-access-chinese-government?_s=PM:WORLD.
39. "China Quake School Critic Receives One-Year Sentence." Reuters online, accessed September 17, 2010, http://www.reuters.com/article/idUSPEK105816.
40. Benjamin Barber, "Jihad versus McWorld," *Atlantic* online, accessed September 17, 2010, http://www.theatlantic.com/magazine/archive/1992/03/jihad-vs-mcworld/3882/.
41. Elisabeth Rosenthal, "Buicks, Starbucks and Fried Chicken. Still China?" *New York Times,* February 25, 2002, accessed December 15, 2011, http://www.nytimes.com/2002/02/25/international/asia/25CHIN.html.
42. Barber, "Jihad versus McWorld."
43. See for example, Suisheng Zhao, *A Nation-State by Construction: Dynamics of Modern Chinese Nationalism* (Stanford, CA: Stanford University Press, 2004), chapters 6–7.

GLOSSARY

absolute poverty level measured as the proportion of a country's population that earns $1.25 a day or less.

accountability a political mechanism that offers citizens regular and realistic opportunities to remove the rulers from office through peaceful and constitutional means.

Arab an ethnic group defined by language and geographic location, in countries in North Africa and the Middle East.

bourgeoisie an economic class of wealthy capitalists that emerged during the Industrial Revolution.

capital mobility the ability of an investor to move his or her money across borders and invest where profits are highest and costs are lowest.

capitalism an economic system in which individuals hold and invest property.

causation a process or event that produces an observable effect.

civic culture a key aspect of a county's cultural identity defined by three characteristics: high civic engagement, political equality, and solidarity.

civic engagement the degree of citizens' active participation in public affairs, such as by voting or participating in social movements, interest groups, or political parties.

civil law code a set of laws that covers issues pertaining to private property rights and family law.

civil war armed combat within the boundaries of a sovereign state between parties that are subject to common authority at the start of hostilities.

class-consciousness individuals' self-awareness of the political implications of being a member of a particular economic class.

coalition government a government comprising several parties that hold at least one cabinet portfolio. These are frequent in multiparty systems.

coercive recruitment where individuals are forced to take up arms to sustain an insurgent army in a civil war.

Cold War a period of international conflict lasting from 1945 to 1990, which opposed democratic capitalist countries against non-democratic communist countries.

collective action problem a situation wherein each individual has private incentives not to participate in an action that benefits all members of the group.

command economy an economy in which the central government controls and coordinates virtually all economic activity.

communism holds that under capitalist economic systems, the wealthy exploit the workers and the poor. Communists believe that efforts should be made to redistribute economic wealth as much as possible, and that a single political party should direct the government and control the state.

comparative method a way to examine patterns of facts or events to narrow down what is important in terms of building a convincing comparative politics argument.

comparative politics the systematic search for answers to political questions about how people around the world make and contest authoritative public choices.

conditional cash transfer program welfare programs that give people a small amount of money, based on certain required conditions.

constitution a set of key laws and principles that structure the extent and distribution of government authority and individual rights, by setting up the rules of the political game.

constitutional monarchy a system in which the constitution sets formal limits on the monarch's powers.

constructivism an approach to understanding identity that assumes that political identities are malleable, even if they often appear to be primordial, and suggests that we think of identity as an evolving political process rather than as a fixed set of identity categories.

corporatism pattern of interest group mobilization in which the state plays an active role in organizing groups and mediating between them.

correlation a measure of observed association between two variables.

corruption the illicit use of public authority to achieve private gain.

cultural polarization intergroup hatred fostered by cultural exclusion or repression.

democracy a political system in which the rulers are accountable to the ruled.

democratization a shift from a non-democratic to a democratic regime.

divided government occurs in presidential systems when the president comes from one party but a different party controls the legislative branch.

dual executive in hybrid democratic regimes, an executive branch of government characterized by a division of authority and responsibility between a president and a prime minister.

economic development sustained increase in the standard of living of a country's population, resulting from changes and improvements in education, infrastructure, and technology.

economic inequality the extent of the wealth gap between rich and poor.

economic liberalism an ideology that favors minimal state involvement in the economy as the best recipe for growth.

economic market mechanism of choice as to how firms produce goods and how consumers consume goods.

electoral system the political rules that translate citizens' votes into legislative seats and/or control of a directly elected executive.

electorate a group of citizens eligible to participate in the election of government leaders.

elite party a political party dominated by leaders who hold office in government rather than the party in the electorate or the party organization.

ethnicity a group of people who share an understanding of a common heritage based on religion, language, territory, or family ties.

externality an action that affects the welfare of others, whether or not on purpose.

extractive colonies colonies established primarily to exploit their abundant natural resources. Examples include Bolivia, Brazil, the Congo, the Gold Coast (now Ghana), and the Ivory Coast (Côte d'Ivoire).

failed state a state where sovereignty over claimed territory has collapsed, or was never effectively established at all.

falsifiable the possibility that a hypothesized relationship can be shown to be incorrect.

family law code a set of laws governing marriage, divorce, inheritance of family property, responsibility for children, and other related matters.

fascism a totalitarian ideology based in racist principles that glorified militarism, violence, nationalism, and the state over individual interests and identities, usually led by charismatic individual political leaders.

federalism the constitution grants two or more governments overlapping political authority over the same group of people and same piece of territory.

feudalism a form of political organization in which no single political entity or ruler held unambiguous territorial sovereignty and in which political rule involved multiple, and often overlapping, lines of authority.

foreign direct investment (FDI) the purchase or creation of assets in one country by an individual, firm, or government based in a different country.

free market principles an economic system in which individuals and firms—rather than the government—have rights to make all decisions about buying and selling private property such as land, stock, commodities, or productive industries, and they undertake all their own investment for the future.

free ride to reap the benefits that collective action provides after other people have put in the time, energy, or money to generate collective mobilization.

free trade the elimination of tariffs, quotas, and other measures that make imports more expensive than domestically produced goods.

gender a concept used to distinguish the social and cultural characteristics associated with femininity and masculinity from the biological features associated with sex, such as male or female reproductive organs.

gender as a category a form of socially constructed political identity that considers variation in the social meaning of masculinity and femininity around the world.

gender as a political process individual involvement in political institutions to either preserve or change gender relations, or ways that existing social context and political institutions shape one's relative ability to preserve and/or change gender relations.

gender quota laws   rules that require that a certain proportion of candidates for office or legislative seats be reserved for women.

genocide   a coordinated plan seeking to eliminate all members of particular ethnic, religious, or national groups through mass murder.

global governance   a situation in which states, IGOs, and INGOs must increasingly act in concert to address transnational challenges.

global government   a system in which states relinquish power and acknowledge their subordination to a single global authority.

globalization   the spread of political, economic, and cultural dynamics among governments, groups, and individuals beyond the borders of any one particular country.

government   the organization that has the authority to act on behalf of a state and the right to make decisions that affect everyone in a state.

gross domestic product (GDP)   a measure of a country's total economic output.

guerilla wars   conflicts in which small groups of insurgents use irregular military tactics, such as sabotage and ambushes, to engage the state's military forces.

hypothesis   an argument linking cause to effect.

ideology   a set of political beliefs or ideas that structures and gives meaning to political interests and that motivates people to act politically in particular ways.

illiberal democracies   regimes that combine elements of democracy, such as voting and elections, with non-democratic elements, such as restrictions on political contestation and individual rights.

increasing returns to scale   an economic principle that states that when a firm produces a product, the average cost of producing each unit of the product decreases as the scale of production increases. Can result in monopoly.

interest groups   organized groups of citizens who seek to ensure that the state enacts particular policies.

International Criminal Court (ICC)   an IGO created in 2002 and based in The Hague, the Netherlands, which claims jurisdiction to prosecute genocide and human rights violations worldwide.

international governmental organizations (IGOs) political institutions made up of member-states that have a transnational presence and that take on governmental roles.

international non-governmental organizations (INGOs)   voluntary organizations that form independently of any state's authority, made up of citizens of several states engaged in political activism within or outside their own states' borders.

interstate warfare   the use of violence by states against other states to achieve political goals.

interventionist state   an economic system in which the central government allocates resources, makes investment decisions, and owns most of the country's productive industries and/or resources.

judicial review   the ability of a country's high court to invalidate laws the legislature has enacted, by declaring them unconstitutional.

junta   the group of leaders of a military regime.

kinship bonds   a connection to others formed by blood, marriage, or other family relations.

legitimacy   the degree to which citizens willingly accept the state's sovereign authority to use power.

majority rule   requires that candidates obtain a majority of 50 percent +1 of the votes in the district to win.

Marbury v. Madison   U.S. Supreme Court case, which established that the judicial branch had the authority to undertake judicial review of laws passed by Congress and signed by the president.

market failure   the failure of an economic market to produce or distribute needed or wanted goods or services.

mass party   a political party in which the party in the electorate and the party organization are relatively important, playing an active role in deciding the party's policy commitments or ideological profile.

McWorld   the idea that globalization homogenizes and Americanizes different cultures.

median income   the amount that divides income distribution into two equal groups: half of the country earns an income above the median, and half earns below that amount.

mean income   the average or the sum of everyone's income, divided by the number of people in the population.

mestizo   in Latin America, a person of mixed white and native ancestry.

method of agreement   compares and contrasts cases with different attributes but shared outcomes, seeking the one attribute these cases share in common to attribute causality.

method of difference   compares and contrasts cases with the same attributes but different outcomes, and determines causality by finding an attribute that is present when an outcome occurs but that is absent in similar cases when the outcome does not occur.

military coup   when elements in a country's armed forces overthrow a democratically elected civilian government.

military regime   a non-democratic regime in which the selectorate is typically limited to the highest ranks of the military officer corps.

mixed electoral rules   combine a plurality or majority electoral rule to elect some members of the national legislature with a PR electoral rule to elect the remainder.

mixed methods research   uses both quantitative and qualitative techniques, in an effort to build convincing claims about the relationships between attributes and outcomes.

modern gender gap   a situation in a country in which women are more likely to be more liberal and vote for more liberal parties than are men.

modernization theory   suggests that democracy is not simply a function of economic growth, but rather that it is a function of the cultural changes that accompany economic growth.

monarchy   non-democratic systems in which rulers assume power via birthright and are removed from power when they die.

monopoly   a situation in which a single firm controls the production, distribution, or sale of a particular good, forcing all others out of business and preventing new competitors from emerging.

multinational corporations (MNCs)   firms with headquarters in one country but with operations and employees in many countries.

nation   a cultural grouping of individuals who associate with each other based on collectively held political identity.

nationalism   a subjective feeling of membership in a nation.

neighborhood effect   when countries in a particular geographic region follow their neighbors in terms of adopting a regime type.

neoliberal economic policies   policies that seek to limit governments' role in setting economic policy.

no-confidence vote   a parliamentary vote which, if successful, terminates the prime minister's appointment.

offshore jobs   the movement of jobs outside a corporation's home country.

oligarchy   a non-democratic regime in which the selectorate consists of a small social, economic, or political elite, which selects a leader to represent their interests.

parliamentary supremacy   a principle according to which judges' decisions remain subordinate to decisions of the legislative majority.

parliamentary system   a constitutional format in which the executive and legislative branches have neither separation of origin nor separation of survival.

partition   the creation of two separate sovereign states out of a territory that initially comprised only one state, in order to separate antagonistic groups.

party in the electorate   comprised of a party's supporters in the electorate—its "card-carrying" members and its local- or regional-level party organizations, but not its national-level organization.

party organization   a party's central office or national headquarters, and the party's professional staff.

party in public office   made up of (1) party members who voters elected to the executive or legislative branches of government or (2) party members appointed to high-level bureaucratic posts, for example, in the cabinet.

party system   the typical pattern of political competition and cooperation between parties within a state.

peasants   poor rural farmers who typically rent land from wealthy landowners.

personalistic regime   a system built around the glorification and empowerment of a single individual.

pluralism   a pattern of interest group mobilization in which societal interests organize freely in an unregulated fashion.

plurality rule   the candidate who receives the largest share of the votes in the district wins, even if that share is less than a majority of 50 percent +1 of the votes.

political cleavage   a deep and lasting salient dimension of political conflict and competition within a given society, such as religion, ethnicity, ideology, or other forms of identity.

political economy   the study of the relationship between economics and politics.

political equality   citizenship offers both equal rights and equal obligations.

political globalization   the growth in the number and scope of transnational political and economic issues, and the increasingly transnational responses to such issues.

political identity   the ways that individuals categorize themselves and others and how they understand the power relationships of domination and oppression that exist between groups.

political opportunity structure   the way a country's political system shapes, promotes, checks, or absorbs the challenges it confronts from organized civil society.

political party   a group of people who have organized to attain and hold political power.

political violence   the use of force by states or non-state actors to achieve political goals.

politics   the making of authoritative public choices from private preferences.

presidential system   a constitutional format in which the executive and legislative branches enjoy both separation of origin and survival.

prime minister   the chief executive in a parliamentary system.

primordialism   an approach to understanding identity that assumes that identity is something people are born with or that emerges through deep psychological processes in early childhood, given one's family and community context.

private goods   goods that only one person or a few people can consume.

private sector   all economic activity undertaken outside the purview of the state, whether by individuals or private corporations.

progressive redistribution   programs that act like Robin Hood and take from rich folks and give to poor folks.

progressive taxation   occurs when individuals' tax burdens go up as their incomes go up.

proletariat   an economic class of wage laborers who work in factories that emerged during the Industrial Revolution.

proportional representation   an electoral system that distributes seats proportionally to the vote each party receives.

Protestant Reformation   a sixteenth-century division within Christianity that resulted in the formation of various Protestant Christian religious sects, which split off from the Catholic Church.

public goods   goods that everyone can consume, whether they helped produce them or not.

public sector   the government delivery of goods and services.

quantitative research   relies on statistical data to assess relationships between attributes and outcomes, analyzing those data using computers.

qualitative research   focuses on an in-depth understanding of attributes and outcomes. Privileges depth over breadth.

race   categories of humans into large populations supposedly based on hereditable physical characteristics, such as skin color, facial features, and hair texture.

race to the bottom   a situation in which all countries lower tax rates as much as possible and eliminate government social welfare programs in order to balance their budgets.

reciprocal accountability   the selectorate chooses and removes the leadership, but the leadership also selects and removes the members of the selectorate.

regime   the basic form of a state's government.

regressive taxation   taxes that tend to benefit relatively wealthy people more than relatively poor people.

religious pluralism   a diversity of forms of worship.

resource curse   hypothesizes that any country whose economic growth relies on one valuable natural resource is unlikely to result in an equitable distribution of wealth, which, in turn, generates problematic political consequences.

revolution   armed conflict within a sovereign state between insurgents and the state, in which both the insurgents and the state claim the allegiance of a significant proportion of the population; authority over the state is forcibly transferred from the state to the insurgents; and the insurgents subsequently bring about wholesale political change.

Second Vatican Council   1965 meeting of Catholic authorities from around the world that reformulated longstanding Church doctrines.

secular–rational values   people who value secular–rational political authorities such as independent judges, nonpartisan bureaucrats, or elected officials tend to not be religious; are skeptical of authority figures in general; and are reluctant to affirm a simple difference between good and evil.

secularization   a gradual decline in the societal importance of religion.

selectorate in non-democratic regimes, a subset of the population that chooses and removes the leader.

semi-presidential hybrid a constitutional format in which the president and parliament enjoy separation of origin, but only the president enjoys separation of survival.

separation of origin voters directly elect the members of the legislature and also cast a separate ballot directly electing the chief executive, the president.

separation of survival members of both the executive and legislative branches serve for fixed terms of office.

service sector jobs outside of manufacturing and agriculture that include medicine, law, transportation, retail sales, tourism, and entertainment.

settlement colonies colonies established primarily as a place for people from Europe to settle. Examples include the United States, Canada, Australia, and New Zealand.

Sharia the body of Islamic religious law that governs individuals' public and private lives.

single-party regime in which a single political party dominates all government institutions and restricts political competition to maintain itself in power.

social contract a theoretical political agreement in which everyone agrees to limit their ability to do as they please in order to achieve some collective benefit.

social Darwinism the idea that certain races are inherently superior to others and that the superior races would inevitably conquer the weaker ones.

social democracy a political ideology practiced widely across contemporary European states that tries to balance capitalist markets and private property with some degree of state intervention in the economy to ameliorate problems of economic inequality.

social insurance forms of insurance that are available to all citizens, regardless of their ability to pay.

social movements organized, sustained, and collective efforts that make claims on behalf of members of a group; challenge the power of government authorities or other groups in civil society; contest the legitimacy of established ideas or practices; or advance new ideas or practices.

society a term for all organized groups, social movements, interest groups, and individuals who attempt to remain autonomous from the influence and authority of the state.

solidarity the feature of a civic culture related to a general trust and respect among citizens, and a willingness to lend a helping hand, even when they might disagree on matters of public policy.

sovereignty defined as ultimate responsibility for and legal authority over the conduct of internal affairs—including a claim to a monopoly on the legitimate use of physical force—within territory defined by geographic borders.

spillover effect when violence in one state spills over into neighboring states, because the latter are weak and cannot control their own borders.

state a political-legal unit with sovereignty over a particular geographic territory and the population that resides in that territory.

state-led development a strategy to promote economic growth that includes such policies as government coordination of private sector investment, forced savings, and preferential treatment to certain industries regarded as essential for national economic development.

state of nature term coined by Thomas Hobbes to describe an imaginary time before human beings organized into governments or states for the collective good.

suicide terrorism involves acts of violence perpetrated against either combatants or noncombatants by individuals who are aware that they are unlikely to survive.

terrorism threatened or actual use of violence for political purposes by non-state actors, direct particularly against civilian targets.

theocracy a non-democratic regime in which leaders who claim divine guidance hold the authority to rule.

totalitarian regime a type of non-democratic government that attempts to shape the interests and identities of its citizens through the use of ideology, coercive mobilization, and severe repression.

traditional gender gap a situation in a country in which women are more likely to be conservative and vote for conservative political parties than are men.

traditional values people who value traditional forms of political authority such as kings, tribal chiefs, and religious leaders tend to be more religious and nationalistic, express respect for hierarchical authority relations, and express a belief in a clear difference between good and evil.

transnational   issues with causes and effects that extend beyond the borders of any single sovereign state and that cannot be considered simply a matter of domestic politics.

unitarism   the constitution grants the central government exclusive and final authority over policymaking across the entire national territory.

universal jurisdiction   holds that states can claim legal jurisdiction over people who committed crimes outside the borders of that state, based on the notion that crimes against humanity know no boundaries.

universal suffrage   all adult citizens have the right to participate in the electoral process that selects and removes government leaders.

value emphasis on personal survival   people who value personal survival emphasize the importance of nuclear family, childrearing, and hard work; worry a great deal about having enough money; and wish for greater government involvement in the economy.

value emphasis on personal well-being   people who focus on personal well-being place higher value on individual freedom, leisure time, and being happy; work as a source of personal satisfaction; and value freedom of expression and the ability to participate in politics.

Washington Consensus   neoliberal economic agreement between MNCs, the main IGOs, and the U.S. government regarding how to promote economic stability and growth in poorer countries.

wage gap   the difference between what a man and a woman earn for doing the same job.

welfare state   The term used to describe the role states play in protecting the economic and social well-being of all its citizens through redistributive taxing and spending programs.

CREDITS

SUBJECT INDEX

References to figures and tables are in *italic* text.

NAME INDEX

A

Abdullah II (king), 105
Acemoglu, Daron, 308
Akihito (emperor), 35
Allende, Salvador, 122, 124
Aristotle, 6

B

Barber, Benjamin, 367–368, 370
Berlusconi, Silvio, 247, 249
Bokassa, Jean-Bedel, 111, 113
Bové, José, 368
Brown, Gordon, 75
Bush, George H.W., 136
Bush, George W., 298

C

Cage, Nicolas, 265
Cameron, David, 39, 75–76
Carter, Jimmy, 274
Chávez, Hugo, 142, 228–229
Chinchilla, Laura, 134
Chirac, Jacques, 77
Clegg, Nick, 75
Columbus, Christopher, 158

D

Debret, Jean-Baptiste, 167
DiCaprio, Leonardo, 265

E

Engels, Friedrich, 100
Erdogan, Recep, 12

F

Fillon, Francois, 77
Franco, Gen. Francisco, 140
Franklin, Benjamin, 167

G

Gandhi, Mahatma, 233
Gates, Bill, 323
Gorbachev, Mikhail, 137
Gregory XVI (pope), 181

H

Hitler, Adolf, 99–100, 102–103, 107,
    124, 127, 133, 180, 233, *234*
Hobbes, Thomas, 6, 8, 31–35, 38, 52,
    55, 288
Huntington, Samuel, 156–157, 176,
    184, 187
Hussein, Saddam, 104
Hussein bin Talal (king), 105

I

Isabel, Princess, 164

J

Jesus Christ, 178, 185
John Paul II (pope), 137, 182, 183
Johnson, Simon, 308
Jospin, Lionel, 77

K

Kabila, Laurent, 261, 265
Kagame, Paul, 213
Kennedy, John F., 166
Khomeini, Ruhollah, 233, *234*, 274
Kim Il-Sung, 92, 110, 113, 140
Kim Jong-Il, 91–92, 110, 113
King, Martin Luther, Jr., 233, *234*

L

Lasswell, Harold, 4
Lenin, Vladimir, 101
Locke, John, 6, 8
Luther, Martin, 179

M

Madison, James, 66–67, 79
Maliki, Nouri al-, 176, 200
Mandela, Nelson, 215, 233, *234*
Marx, Karl, 7, 100–101, 151,
    152–155, 160, 171
McCain, John, 316
Mobutu, Sese Seko, 260–261, 265
Montesquieu, Charles de Secondat,
    Baron de, 6, 20–21
Morales, Evo, 239, 364
Mubarak, Hosni, 58–59, 274
Mugabe, Robert, 50
Muhammad, 105, 109, 185
Mussolini, Benito, 102
Myrdal, Alva, 326, 328
Myrdal, Gunnar, 326, 328

O

Obama, Barack, 74, 160, 229, 231,
    315–316, 321, 323
Orwell, George, 99

P

Pahlavi, Mohammad Reza, 274–275
Paul VI (pope), 182
Pedro I (emperor), 164, 167
Pedro II (emperor), 164
Pinochet, Augusto, 121–122
Pius IX (pope), 181

Q

Qaddafi, Muammar, 131

R

Reagan, Ronald, 136
Revere, Paul, 167
Robin Hood, 321, *330*
Robinson, James, 308